Shojo Beat

FUSHIGI YÛGI
GENBU KAIDEN

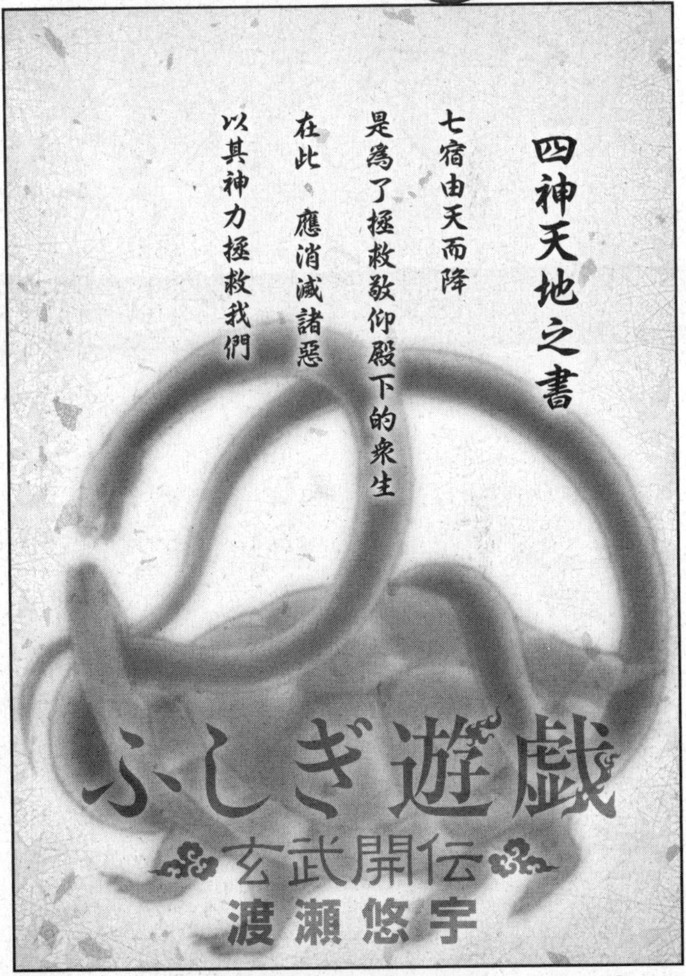
四神天地之書
七宿由天而降
是為了拯救敬仰殿下的衆生
在此、應消滅諸惡
以其神力拯救我們
ふしぎ遊戯
玄武開伝
渡瀬悠宇

story and art by **YUU WATASE**

Vol. 11

CONTENTS

TRANSLATION OF "THE UNIVERSE OF THE FOUR GODS"

We ask that you descend from the seven constellations to the earth to protect us and destroy all evil with your divine powers for the sake of the people who worship you.

Cast of Characters

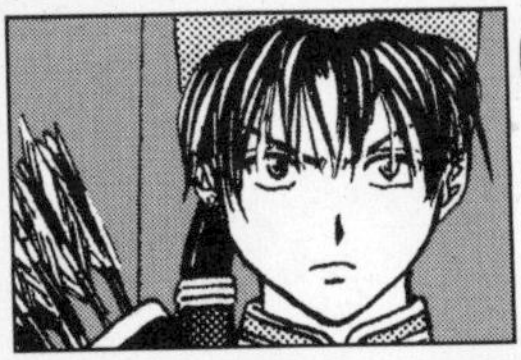

Tomite

A mischievous Celestial Warrior traveling with Takiko.

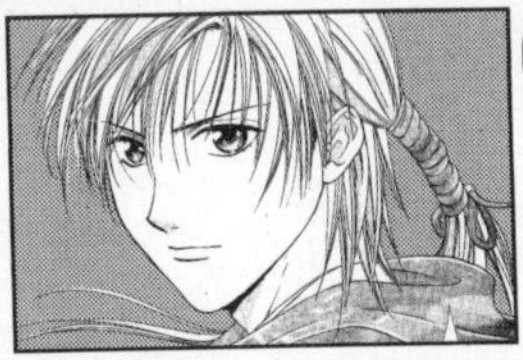

Limdo

"Uruki," a Celestial Warrior. He has the ability to take both male and female form.

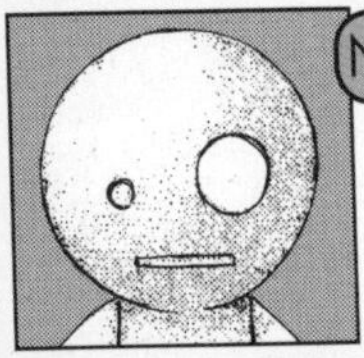

Namame

A spirit of rock made from the Star Life Stone.

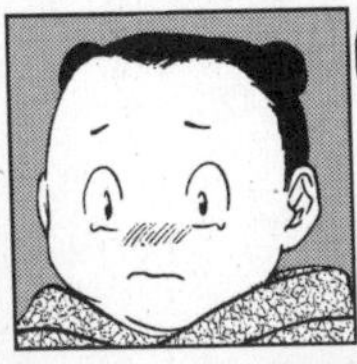

Hatsui

A Celestial Warrior, and a little timid.

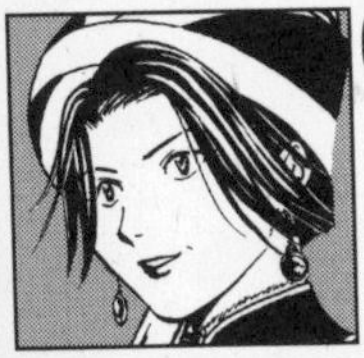

Inami

A Celestial Warrior with elastic, prehensile hair.

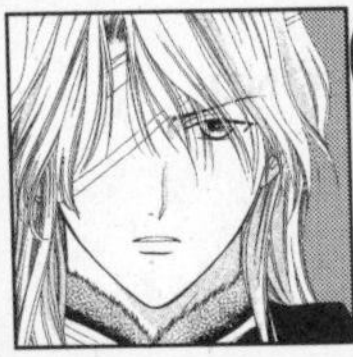

Hikitsu

A Celestial Warrior who cares deeply about his sister Ayla.

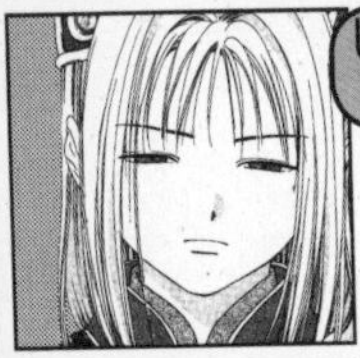

Urumiya (Teg)

A Celestial Warrior held captive in the city of Tèwulán.

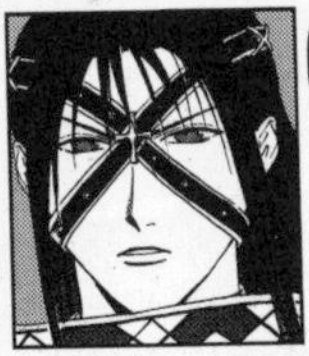

Urumiya (Hagus)

A Celestial Warrior who shares his mark with his imprisoned twin brother.

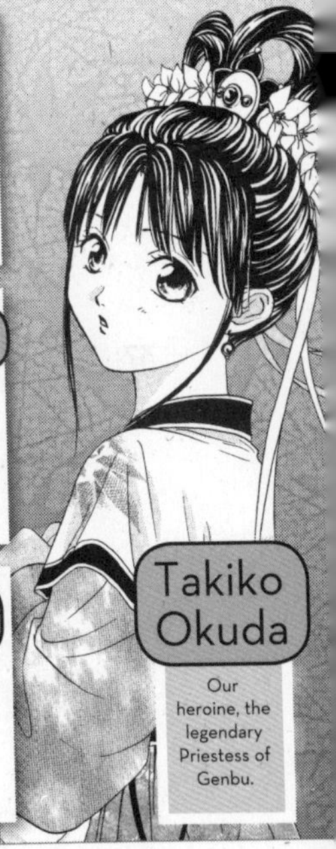

Takiko Okuda

Our heroine, the legendary Priestess of Genbu.

The Story Thus Far

The year is 1923. Takiko is drawn into the pages of *The Universe of the Four Gods*, a book her father has translated from Chinese. There, she is told that she is the legendary Priestess of Genbu, destined to save the country of Bêi-jîa. She must find the seven Celestial Warriors who will help her on her quest.

Takiko has gathered all the Celestial Warriors except Hagus and Teg, the twin brothers who represent the constellation Urumiya. She embarks on an undercover mission into the imperial palace to confront Emperor Tegil, who knows where Teg is imprisoned. Through Hikitsu's ability to see the past, she learns how Tegil betrayed his brother and seized the throne...

FUSHIGI YÛGI: GENBU KAIDEN

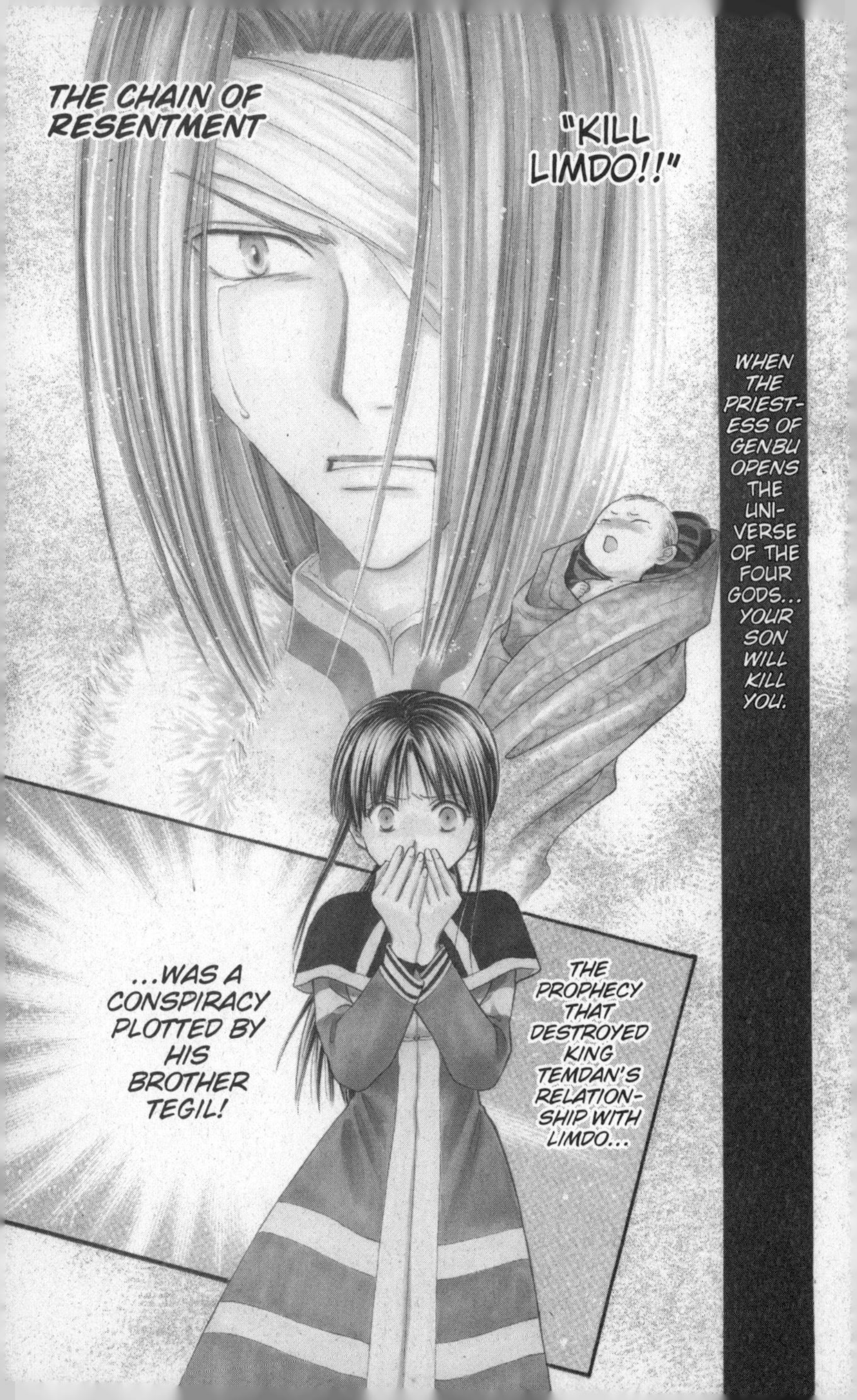
WHEN THE PRIESTESS OF GENBU OPENS THE UNIVERSE OF THE FOUR GODS... YOUR SON WILL KILL YOU.
"KILL LIMDO!!"
THE CHAIN OF RESENTMENT
THE PROPHECY THAT DESTROYED KING TEMDAN'S RELATIONSHIP WITH LIMDO...
...WAS A CONSPIRACY PLOTTED BY HIS BROTHER TEGIL!

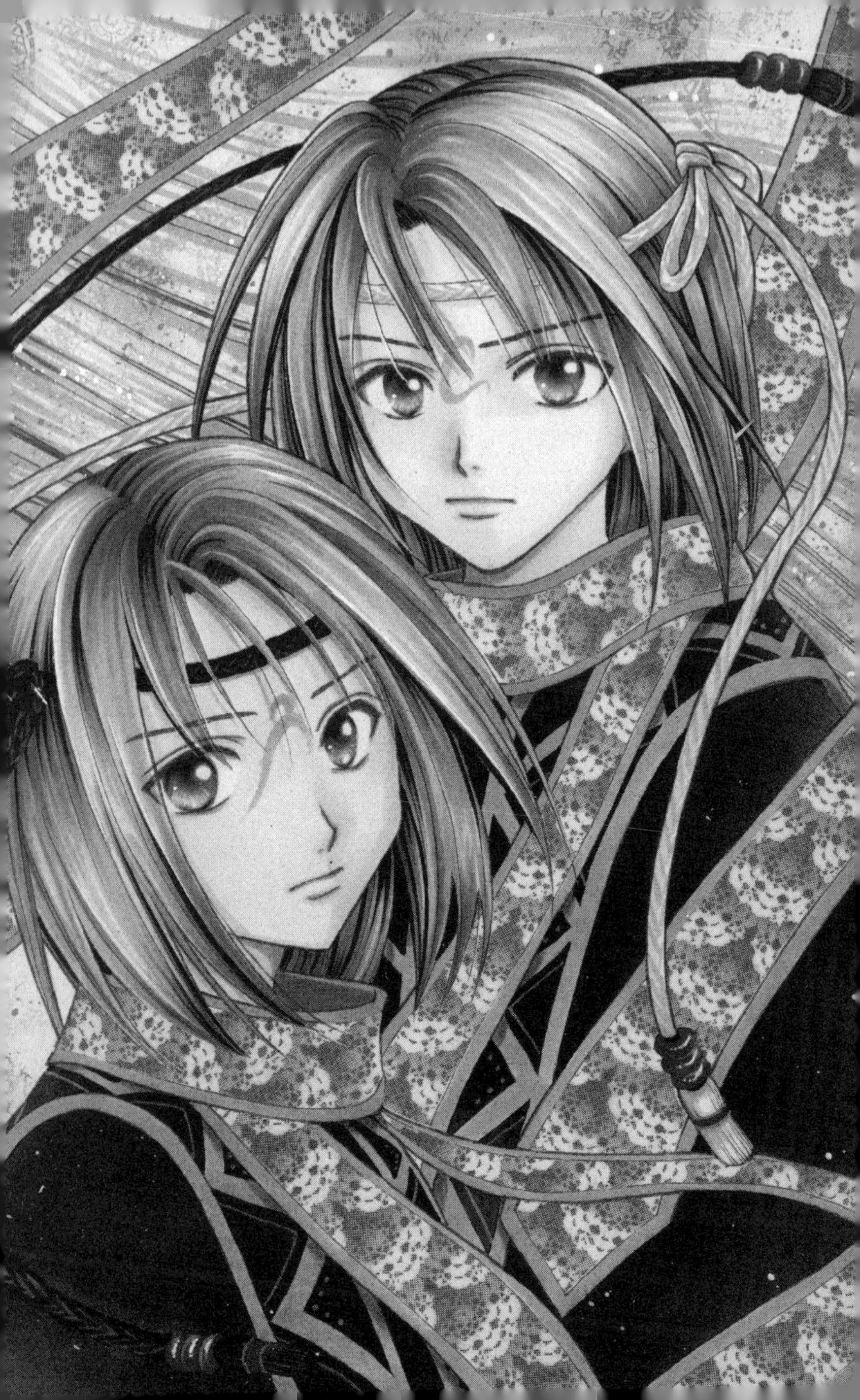

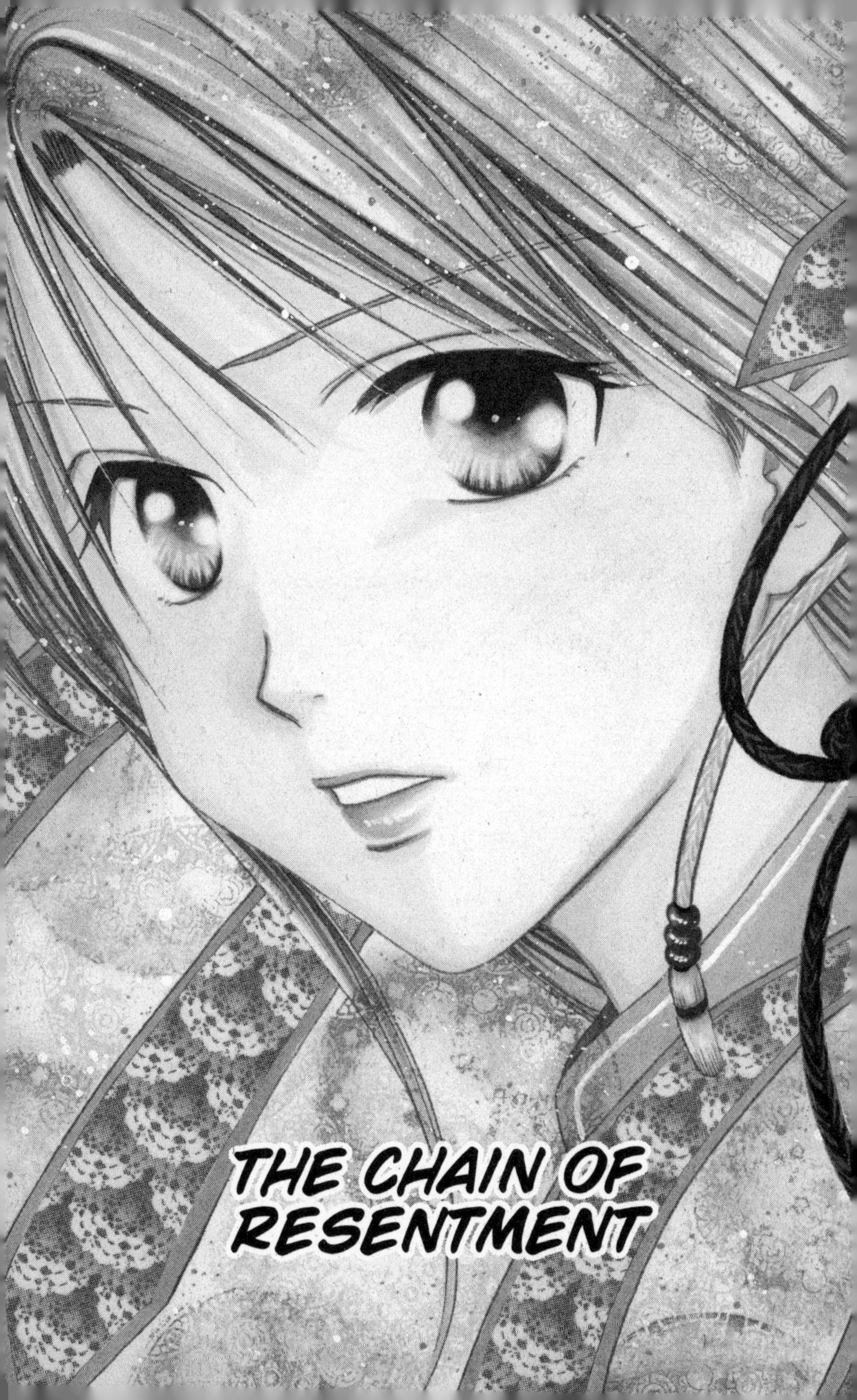
THE CHAIN OF RESENTMENT

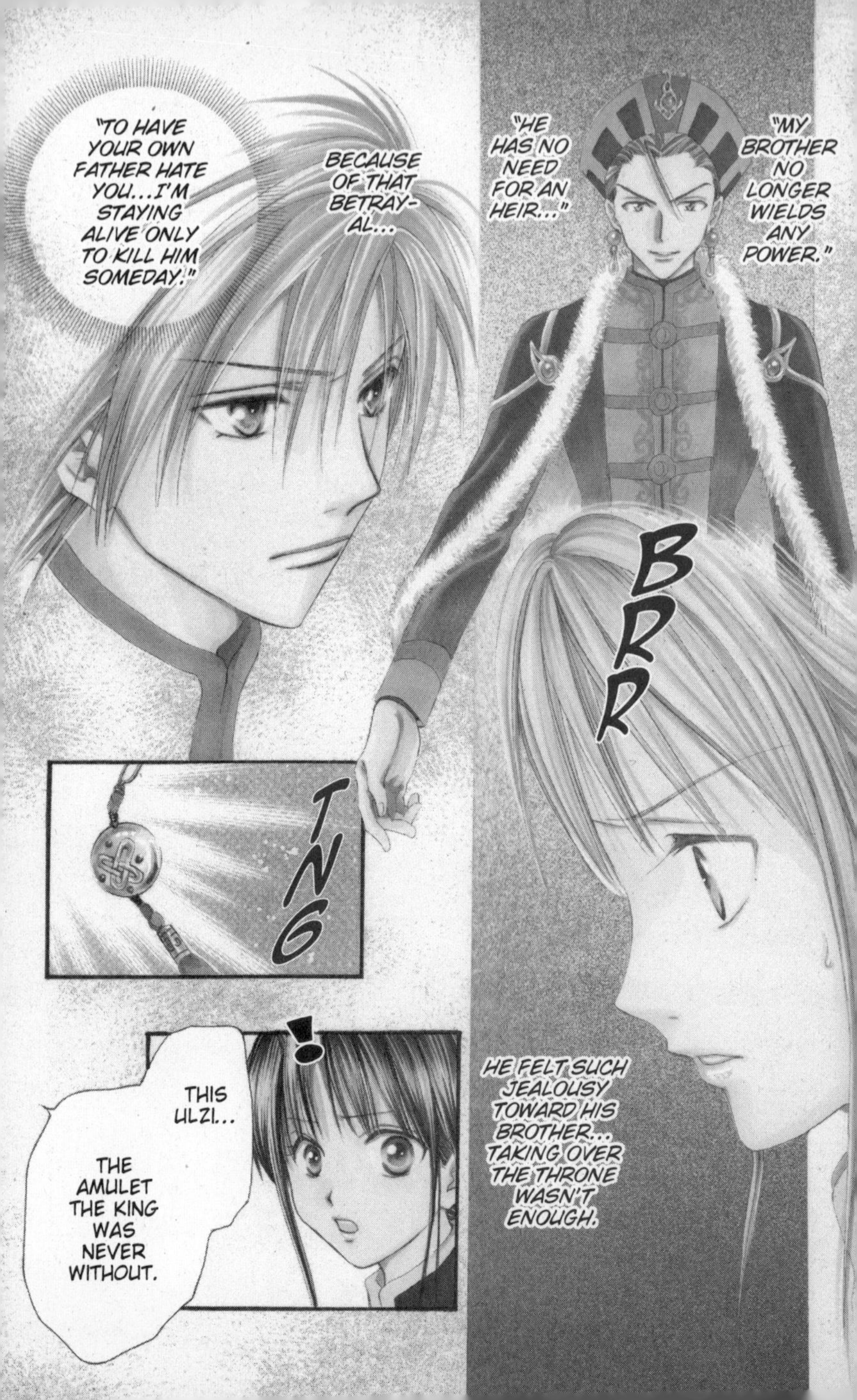
"MY BROTHER NO LONGER WIELDS ANY POWER."
"HE HAS NO NEED FOR AN HEIR..."
BECAUSE OF THAT BETRAY-AL...
"TO HAVE YOUR OWN FATHER HATE YOU...I'M STAYING ALIVE ONLY TO KILL HIM SOMEDAY."
BRR
TNG
HE FELT SUCH JEALOUSY TOWARD HIS BROTHER... TAKING OVER THE THRONE WASN'T ENOUGH.
!
THIS ULZI...
THE AMULET THE KING WAS NEVER WITHOUT.

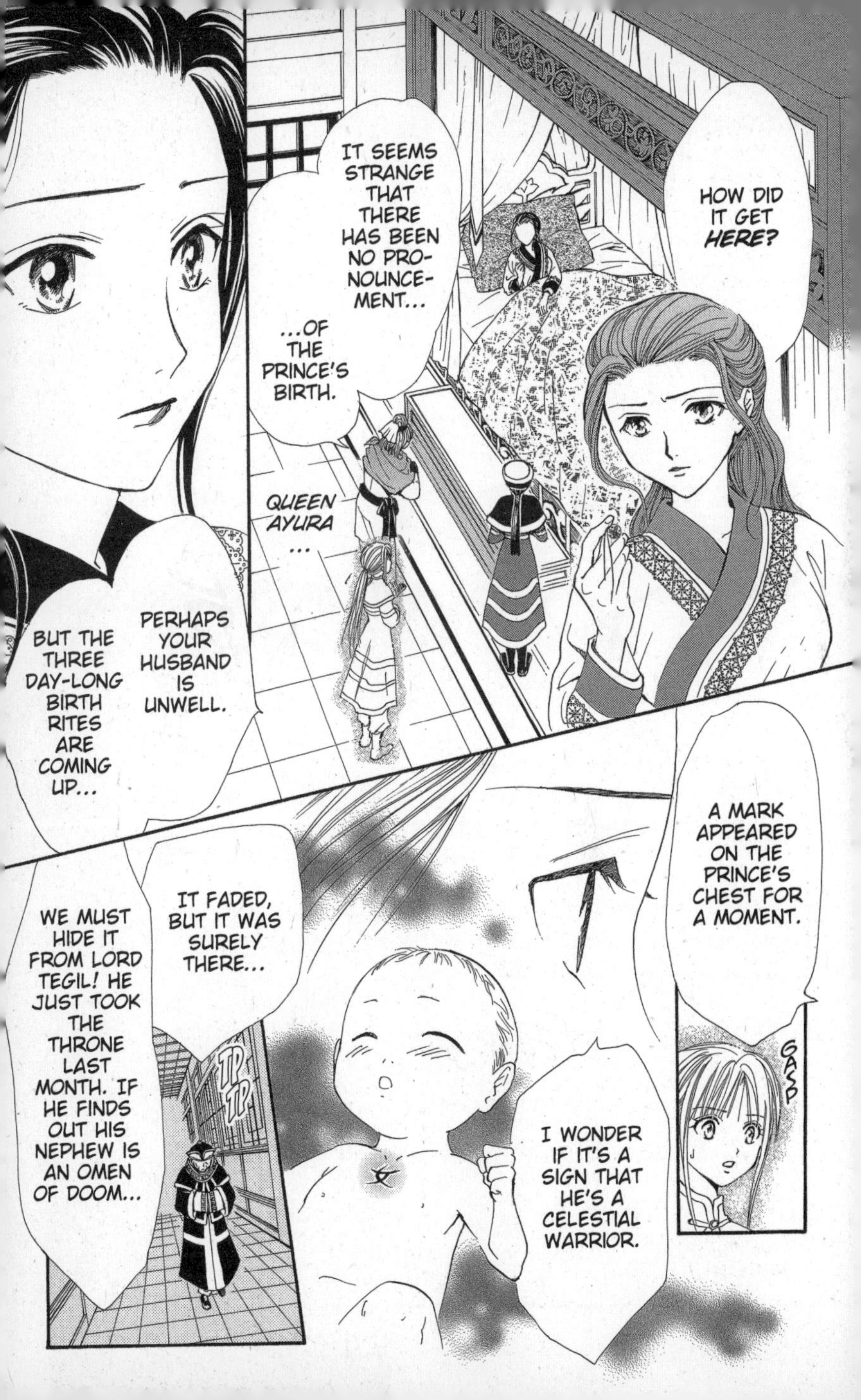
HOW DID IT GET HERE?
IT SEEMS STRANGE THAT THERE HAS BEEN NO PRONOUNCEMENT...
...OF THE PRINCE'S BIRTH.
QUEEN AYURA...
PERHAPS YOUR HUSBAND IS UNWELL.
BUT THE THREE DAY-LONG BIRTH RITES ARE COMING UP...
A MARK APPEARED ON THE PRINCE'S CHEST FOR A MOMENT.
GASP
I WONDER IF IT'S A SIGN THAT HE'S A CELESTIAL WARRIOR.
IT FADED, BUT IT WAS SURELY THERE...
WE MUST HIDE IT FROM LORD TEGIL! HE JUST TOOK THE THRONE LAST MONTH. IF HE FINDS OUT HIS NEPHEW IS AN OMEN OF DOOM...
TIP TIP

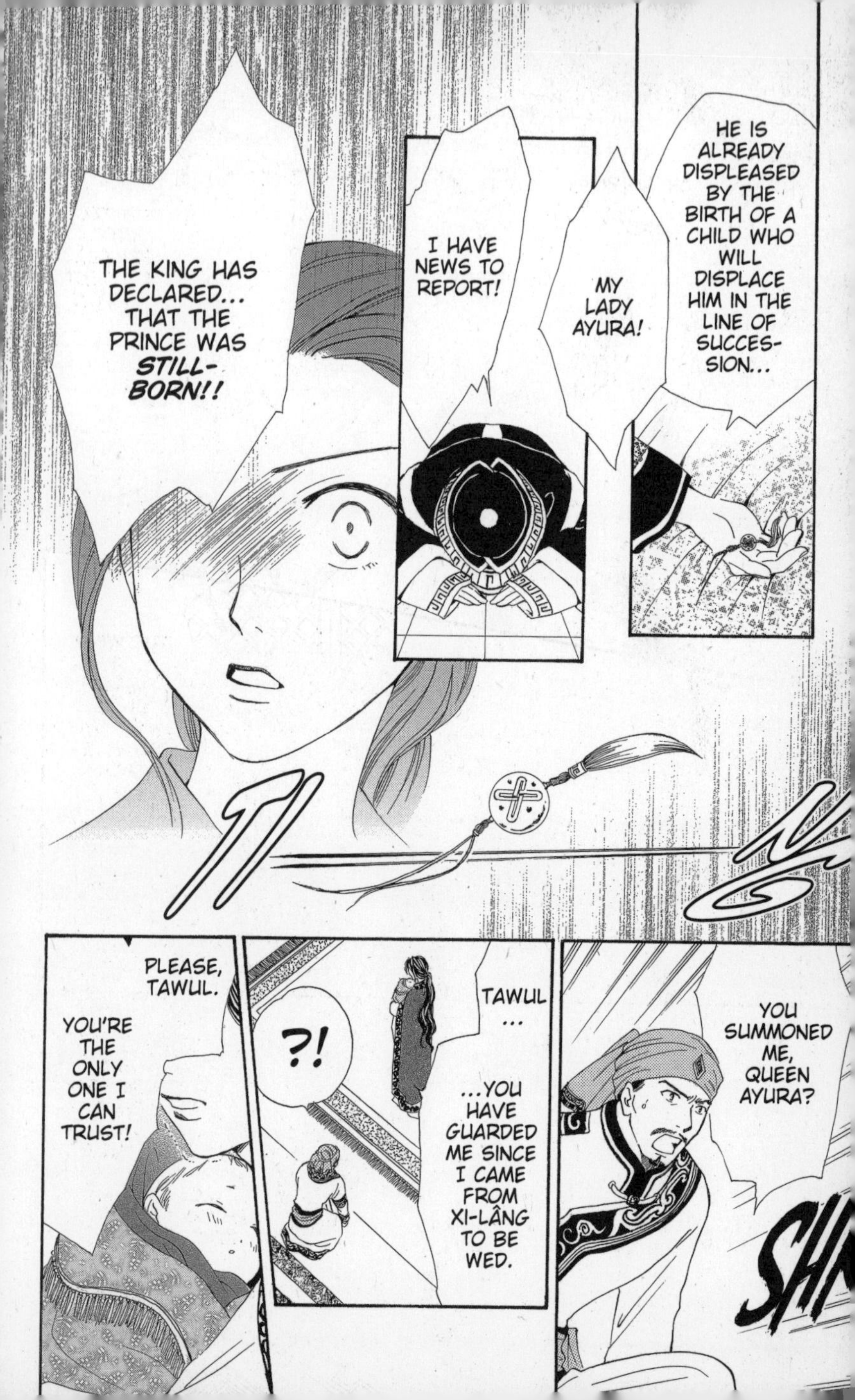
HE IS ALREADY DISPLEASED BY THE BIRTH OF A CHILD WHO WILL DISPLACE HIM IN THE LINE OF SUCCESSION...
MY LADY AYURA!
I HAVE NEWS TO REPORT!
THE KING HAS DECLARED... THAT THE PRINCE WAS **STILLBORN!!**
YOU SUMMONED ME, QUEEN AYURA?
TAWUL...
...YOU HAVE GUARDED ME SINCE I CAME FROM XI-LÂNG TO BE WED.
?!
PLEASE, TAWUL.
YOU'RE THE ONLY ONE I CAN TRUST!

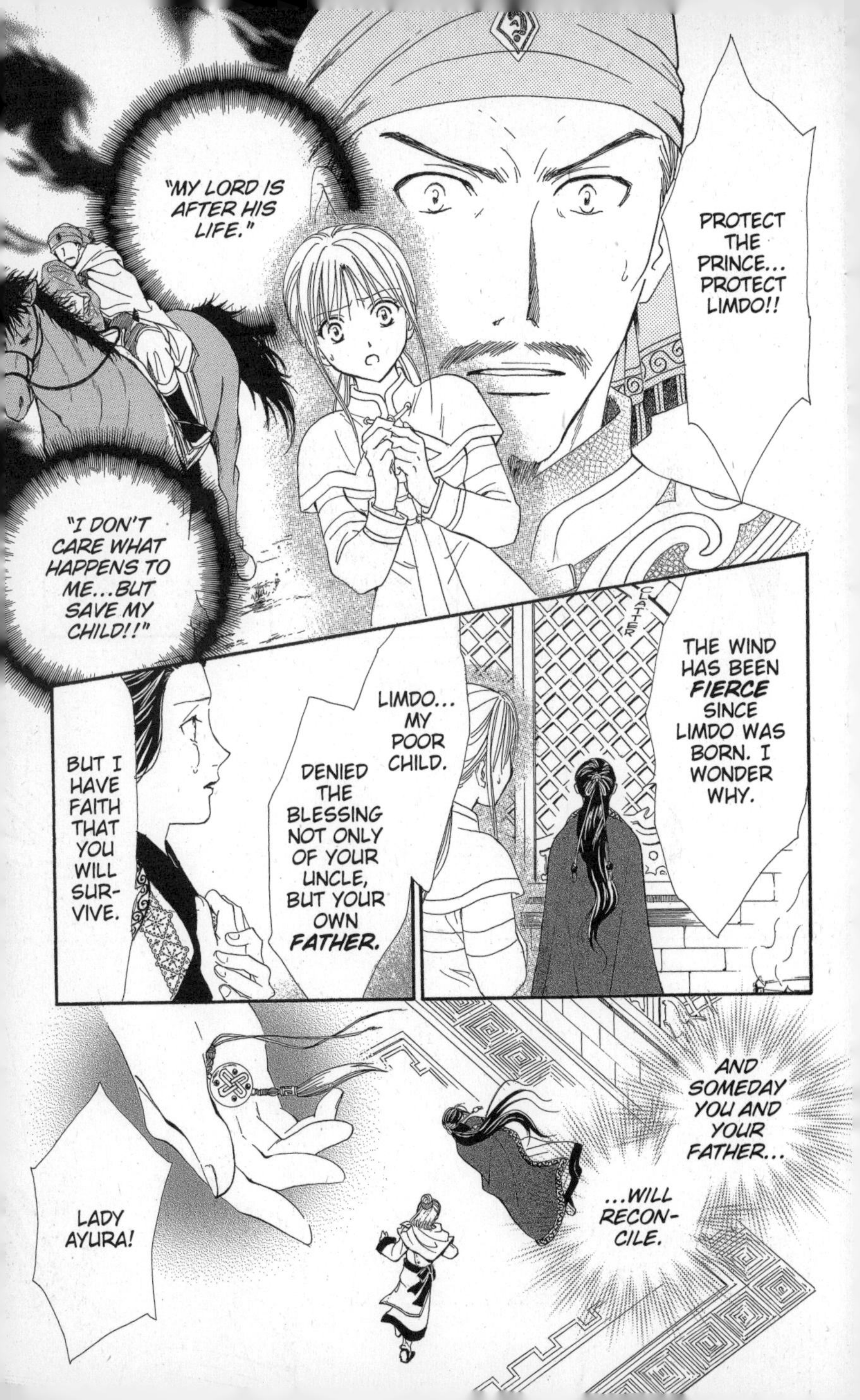
PROTECT THE PRINCE... PROTECT LIMDO!!
"MY LORD IS AFTER HIS LIFE."
"I DON'T CARE WHAT HAPPENS TO ME...BUT SAVE MY CHILD!!"
CLATTER
THE WIND HAS BEEN FIERCE SINCE LIMDO WAS BORN. I WONDER WHY.
LIMDO... MY POOR CHILD.
DENIED THE BLESSING NOT ONLY OF YOUR UNCLE, BUT YOUR OWN FATHER.
BUT I HAVE FAITH THAT YOU WILL SURVIVE.
AND SOMEDAY YOU AND YOUR FATHER...
...WILL RECONCILE.
LADY AYURA!

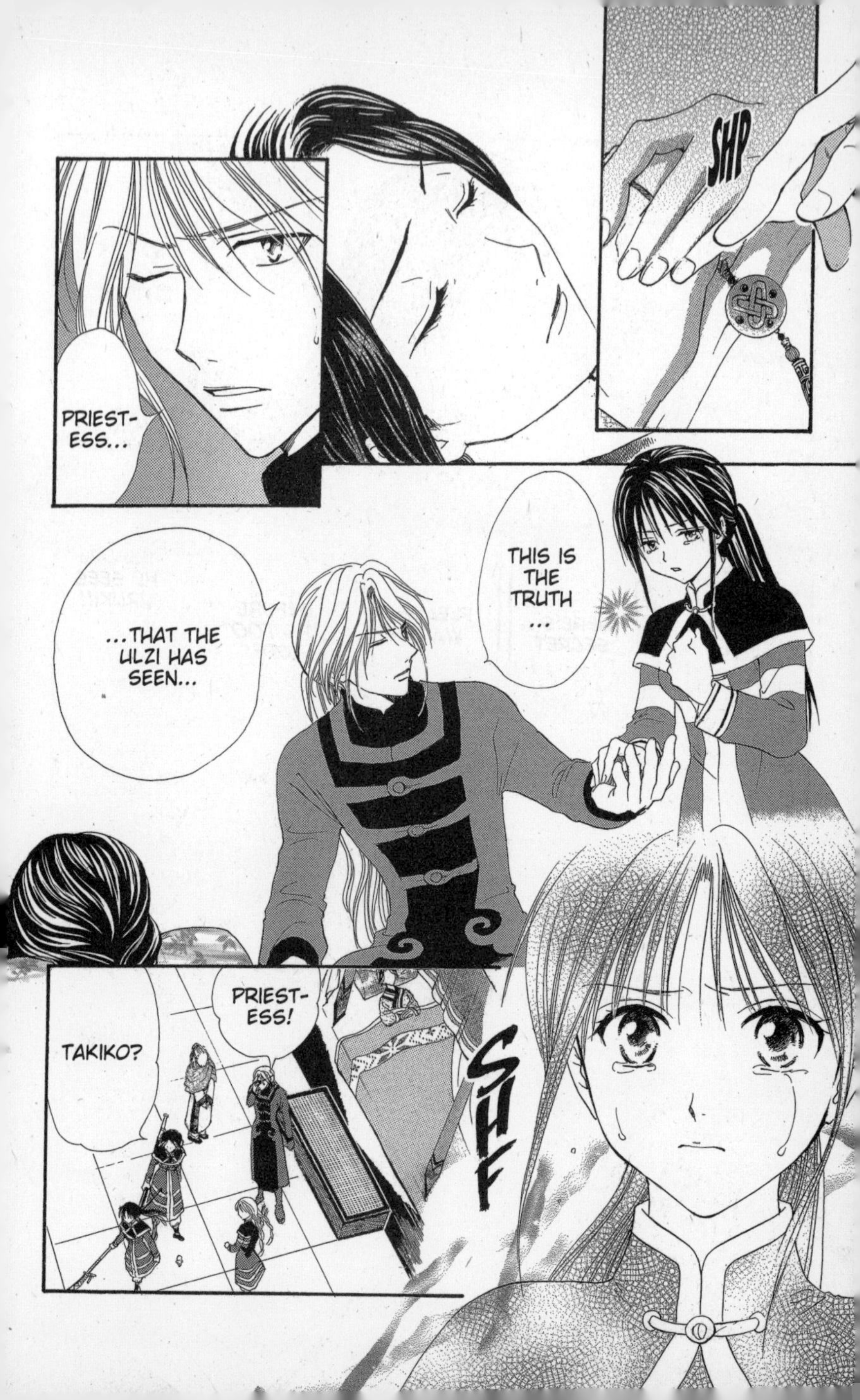
SHP
PRIEST-
ESS...
THIS IS THE TRUTH...
...THAT THE ULZI HAS SEEN...
SHF
PRIEST-
ESS!
TAKIKO?

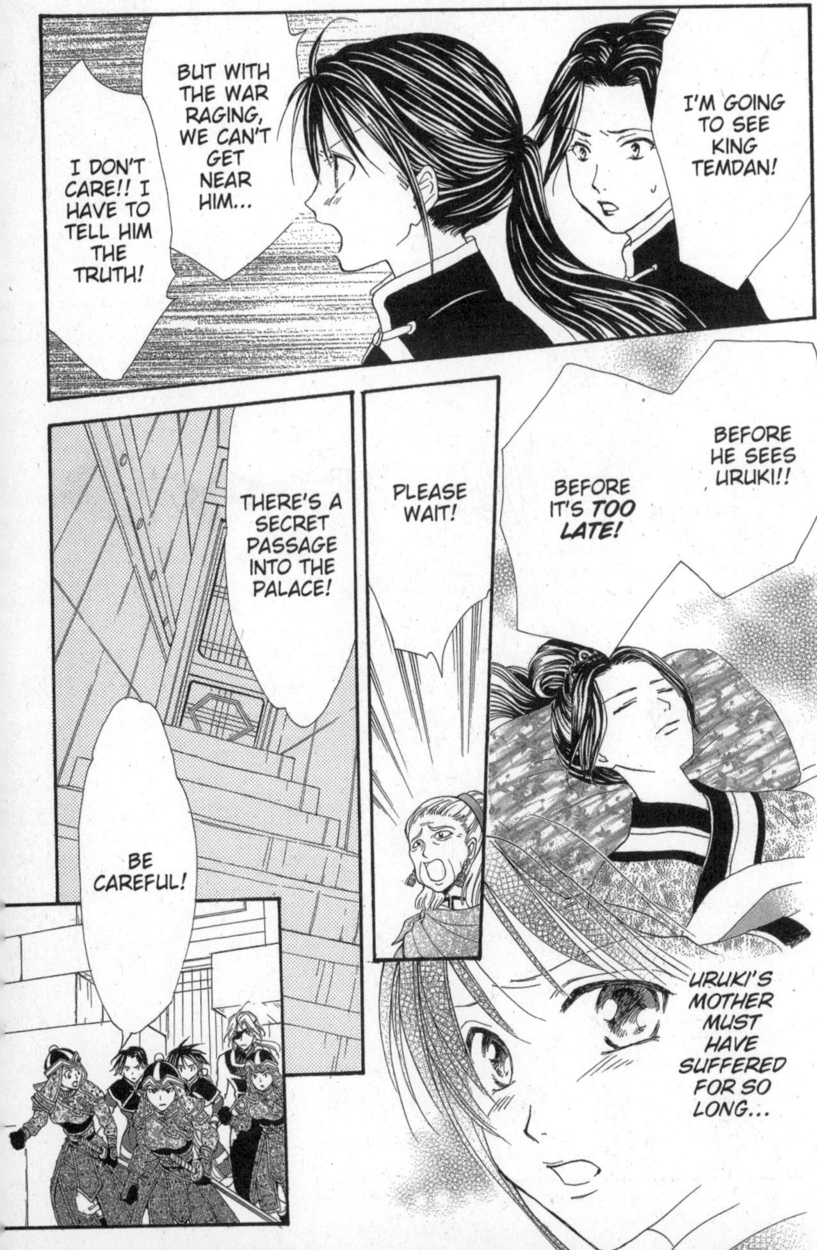
I'M GOING TO SEE KING TEMDAN!
BUT WITH THE WAR RAGING, WE CAN'T GET NEAR HIM...
I DON'T CARE!! I HAVE TO TELL HIM THE TRUTH!
BEFORE HE SEES URUKI!!
BEFORE IT'S *TOO LATE!*
URUKI'S MOTHER MUST HAVE SUFFERED FOR SO LONG...
PLEASE WAIT!
THERE'S A SECRET PASSAGE INTO THE PALACE!
BE CAREFUL!

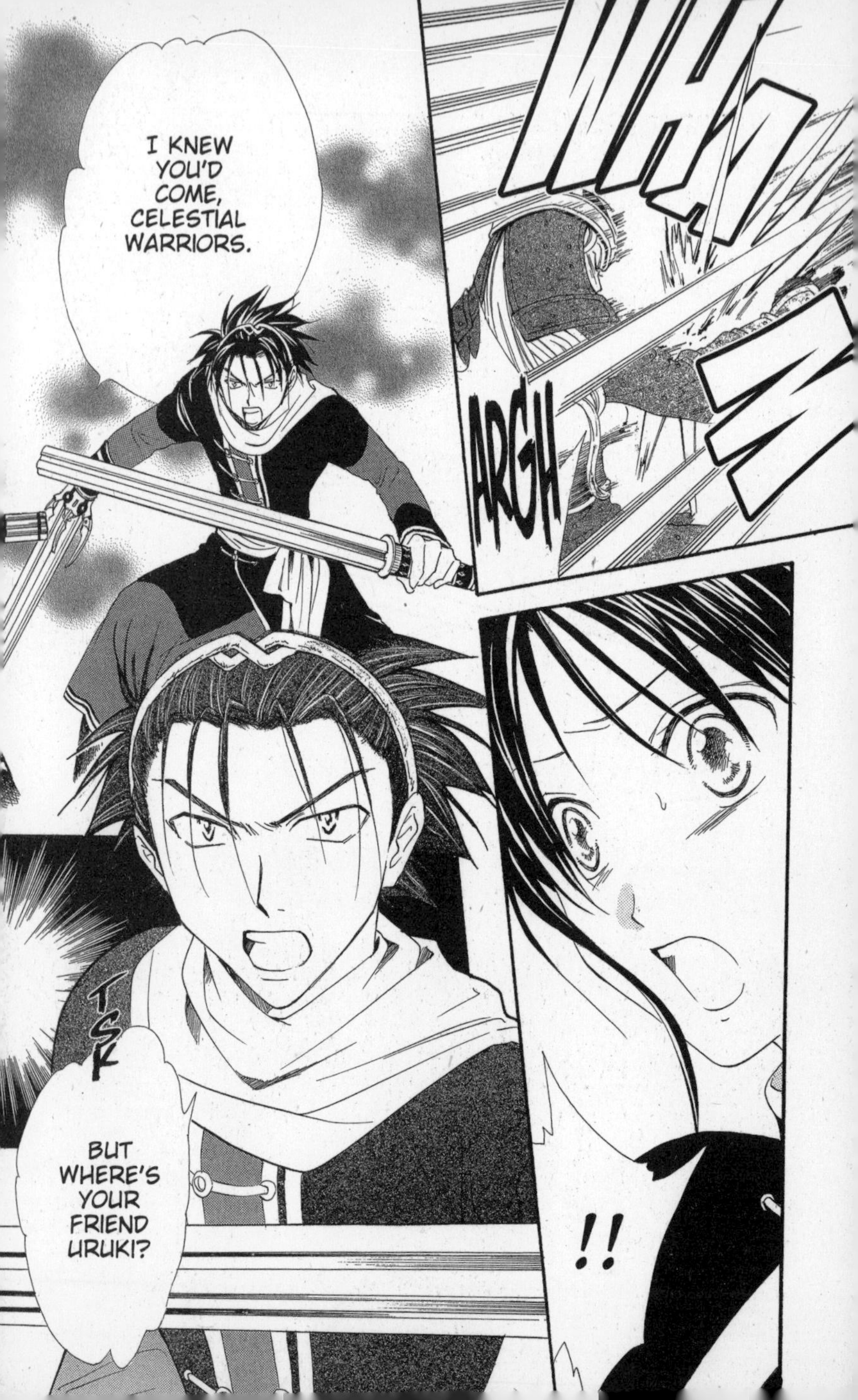
WHAM
ARGH
!!
I KNEW YOU'D COME, CELESTIAL WARRIORS.
TSK
BUT WHERE'S YOUR FRIEND URUKI?

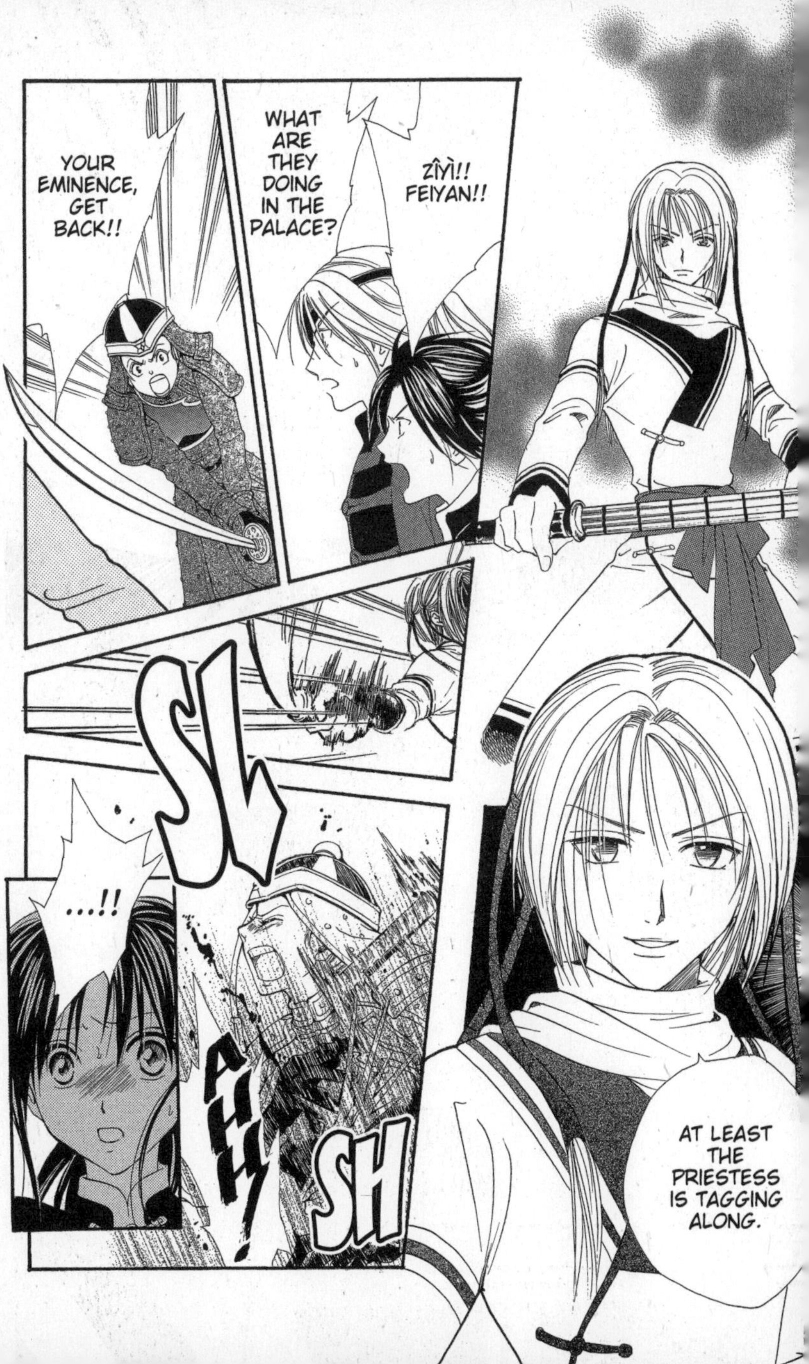
ZÎYÌ!! FEIYAN!!
WHAT ARE THEY DOING IN THE PALACE?
YOUR EMINENCE, GET BACK!!
SL
AT LEAST THE PRIESTESS IS TAGGING ALONG.
SH
AHH
...!!

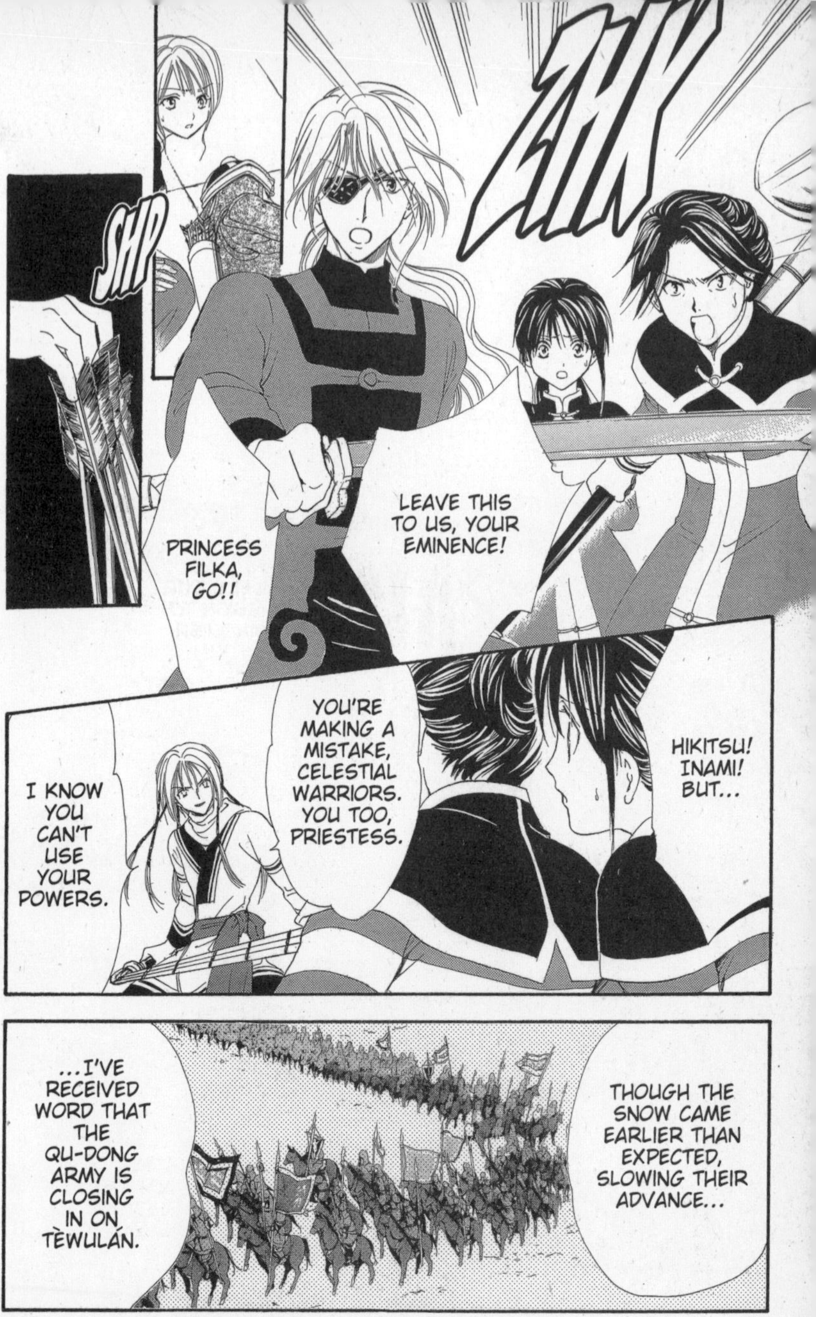
ZAK
LEAVE THIS TO US, YOUR EMINENCE!
PRINCESS FILKA, GO!!
SHP
HIKITSU! INAMI! BUT...
YOU'RE MAKING A MISTAKE, CELESTIAL WARRIORS. YOU TOO, PRIESTESS.
I KNOW YOU CAN'T USE YOUR POWERS.
THOUGH THE SNOW CAME EARLIER THAN EXPECTED, SLOWING THEIR ADVANCE...
...I'VE RECEIVED WORD THAT THE QU-DONG ARMY IS CLOSING IN ON TÈWULÁN.

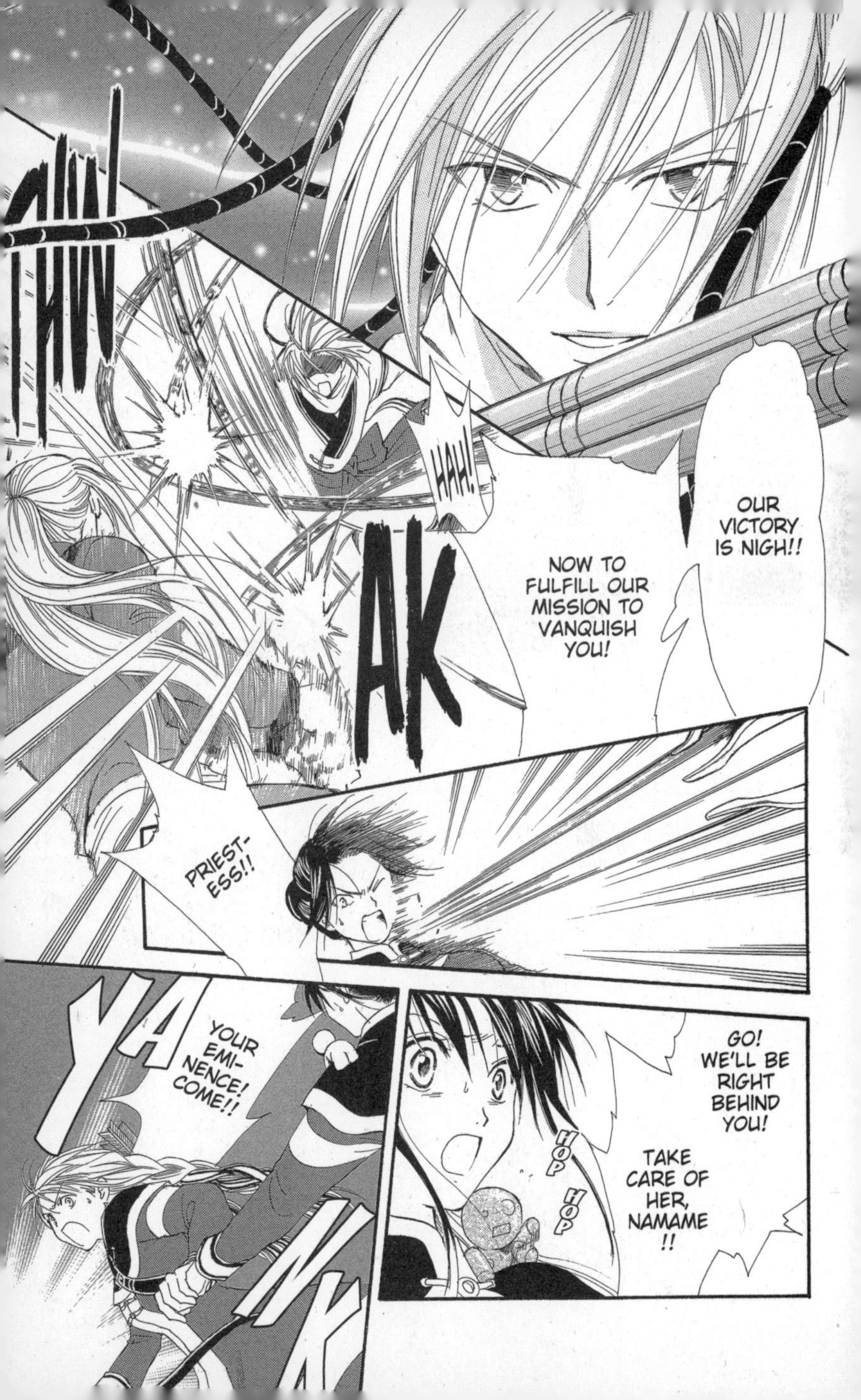
OUR VICTORY IS NIGH!!
NOW TO FULFILL OUR MISSION TO VANQUISH YOU!
HAH!
THW
AK
PRIEST-ESS!!
GO! WE'LL BE RIGHT BEHIND YOU!
TAKE CARE OF HER, NAMAME!!
HOP HOP
YOUR EMI-NENCE! COME!!
YA
NK

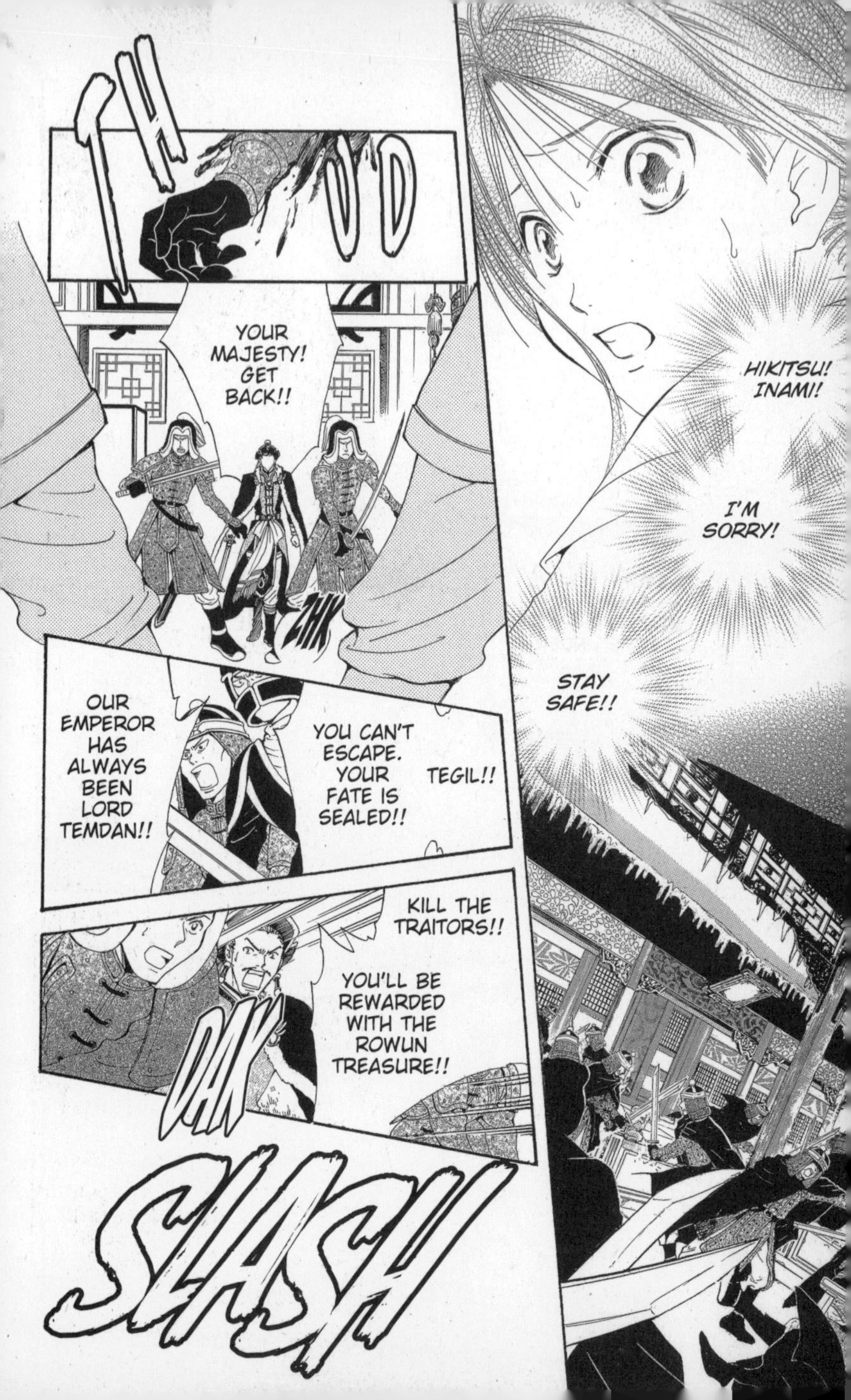
HIKITSU! INAMI!
I'M SORRY!
STAY SAFE!!
THUD
YOUR MAJESTY! GET BACK!!
ZHK
TEGIL!!
YOU CAN'T ESCAPE. YOUR FATE IS SEALED!!
OUR EMPEROR HAS ALWAYS BEEN LORD TEMDAN!!
KILL THE TRAITORS!!
YOU'LL BE REWARDED WITH THE ROWUN TREASURE!!
SLASH

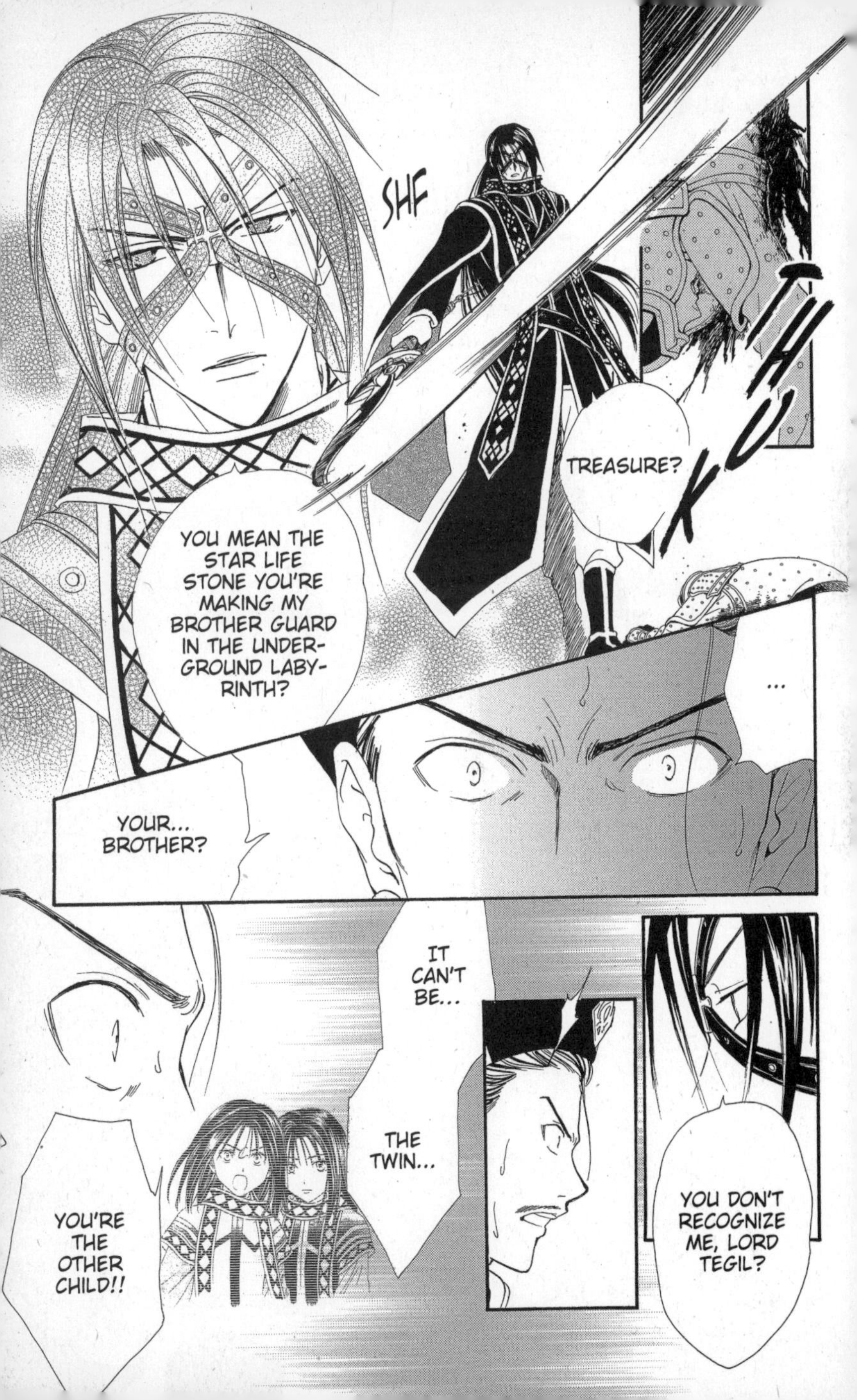
THUNK
TREASURE?
SHF
YOU MEAN THE STAR LIFE STONE YOU'RE MAKING MY BROTHER GUARD IN THE UNDER-GROUND LABY-RINTH?
...
YOUR... BROTHER?
YOU DON'T RECOGNIZE ME, LORD TEGIL?
IT CAN'T BE...
THE TWIN...
YOU'RE THE OTHER CHILD!!

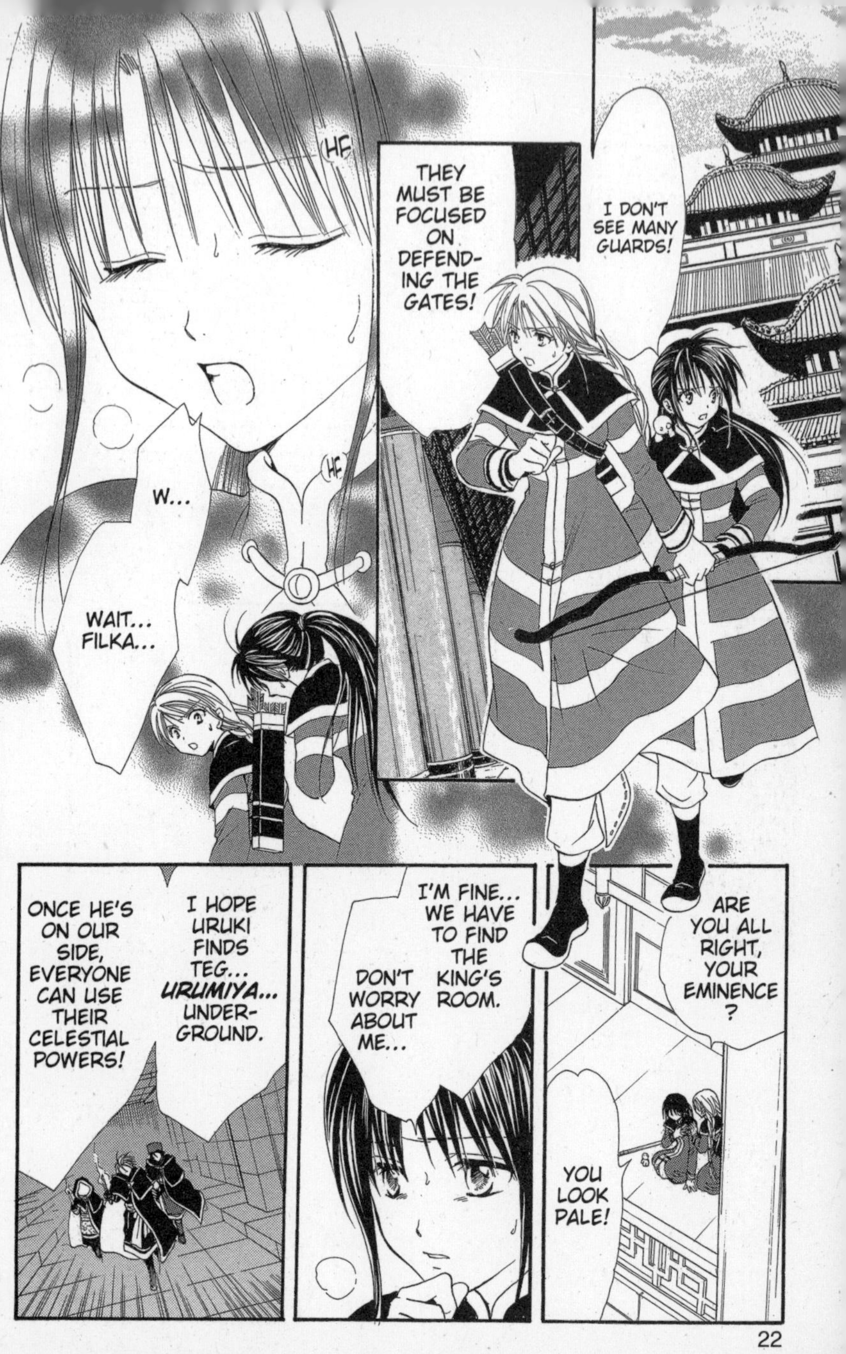
I DON'T SEE MANY GUARDS!
THEY MUST BE FOCUSED ON DEFENDING THE GATES!
HF
HF
W...
WAIT... FILKA...
ARE YOU ALL RIGHT, YOUR EMINENCE?
YOU LOOK PALE!
I'M FINE... WE HAVE TO FIND THE KING'S ROOM.
DON'T WORRY ABOUT ME...
I HOPE URUKI FINDS TEG... *URUMIYA...* UNDERGROUND.
ONCE HE'S ON OUR SIDE, EVERYONE CAN USE THEIR CELESTIAL POWERS!

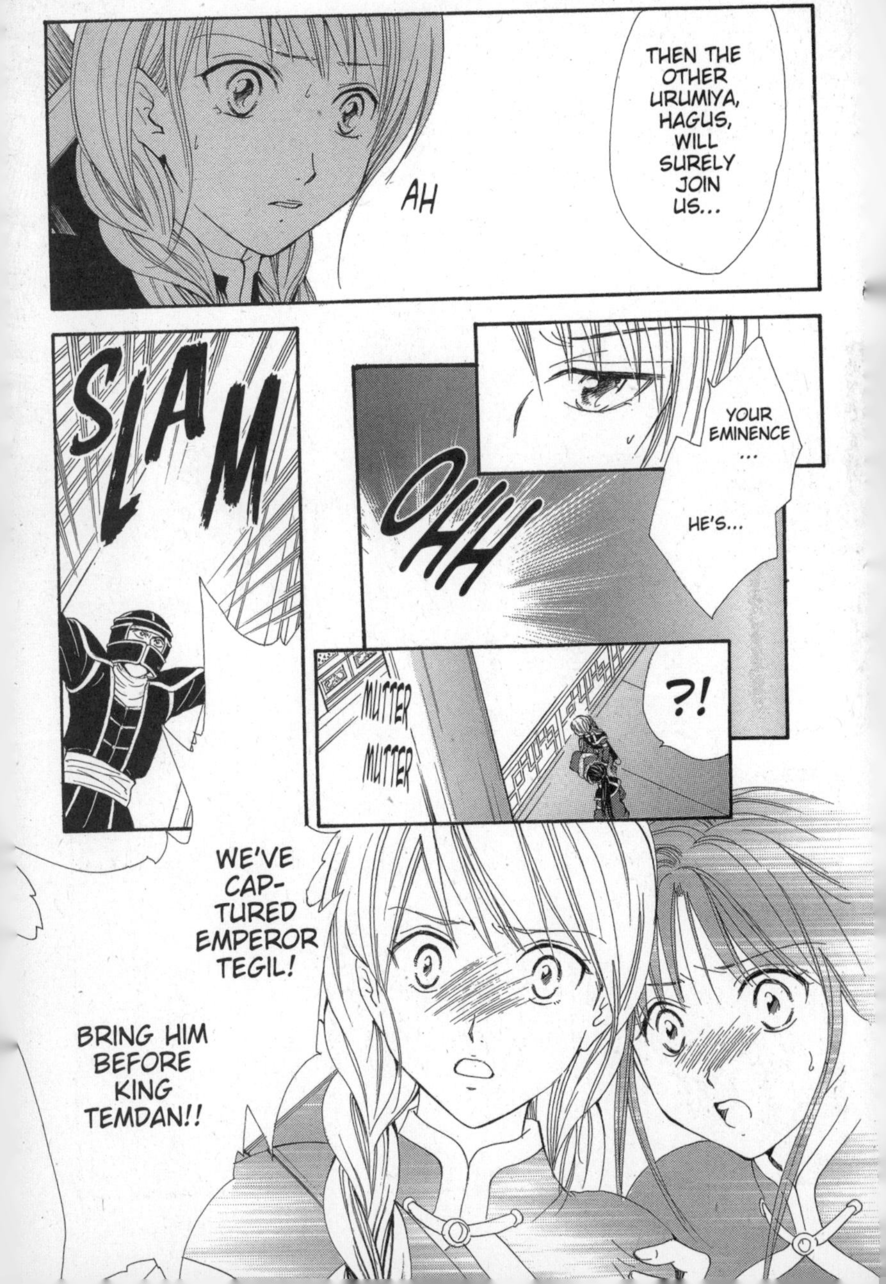
THEN THE OTHER URUMIYA, HAGUS, WILL SURELY JOIN US...
AH
YOUR EMINENCE...
HE'S...
OHH
?!
MUTTER MUTTER
SLAM
WE'VE CAPTURED EMPEROR TEGIL!
BRING HIM BEFORE KING TEMDAN!!

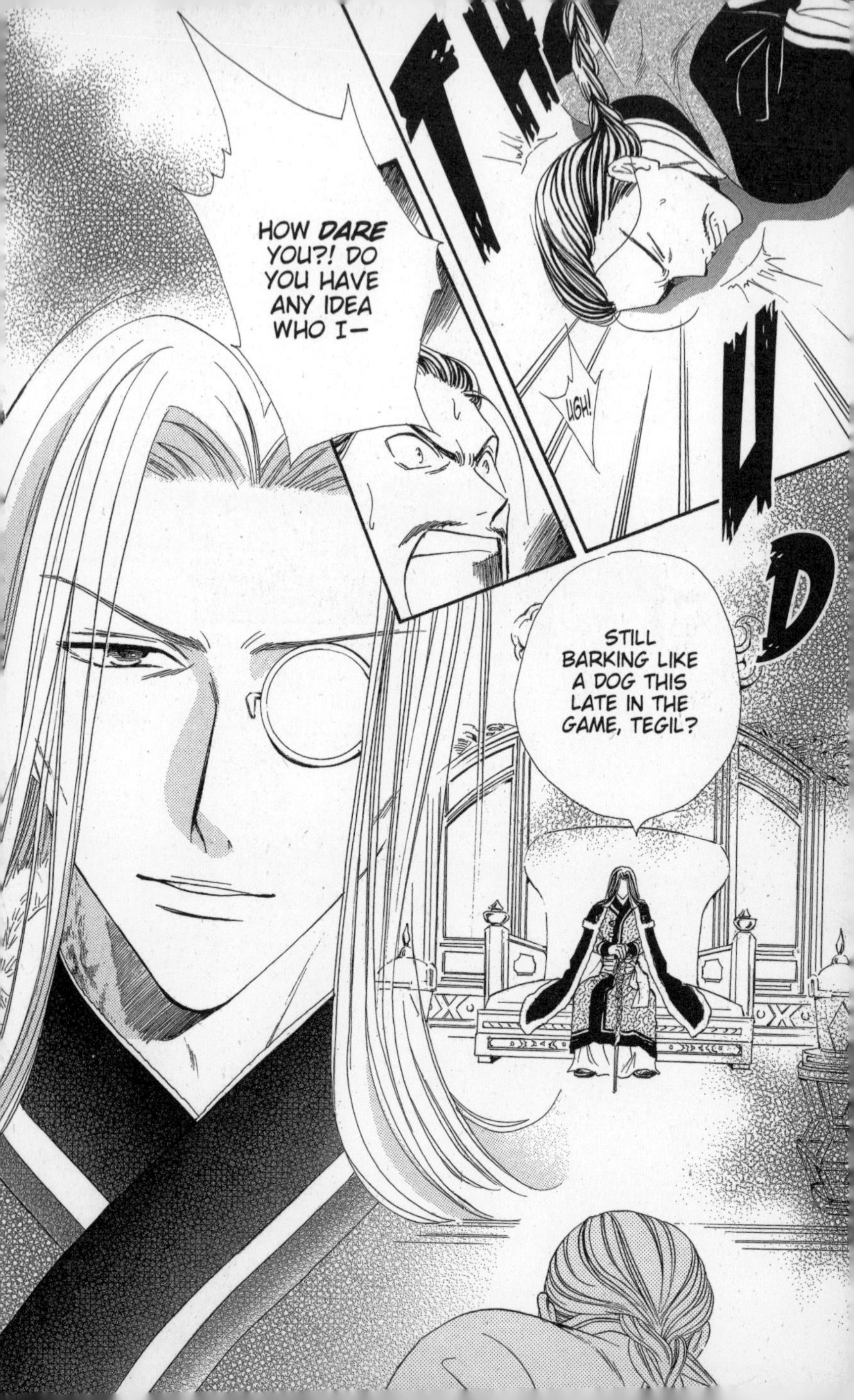
THUD
UGH!
HOW DARE YOU?! DO YOU HAVE ANY IDEA WHO I—
STILL BARKING LIKE A DOG THIS LATE IN THE GAME, TEGIL?

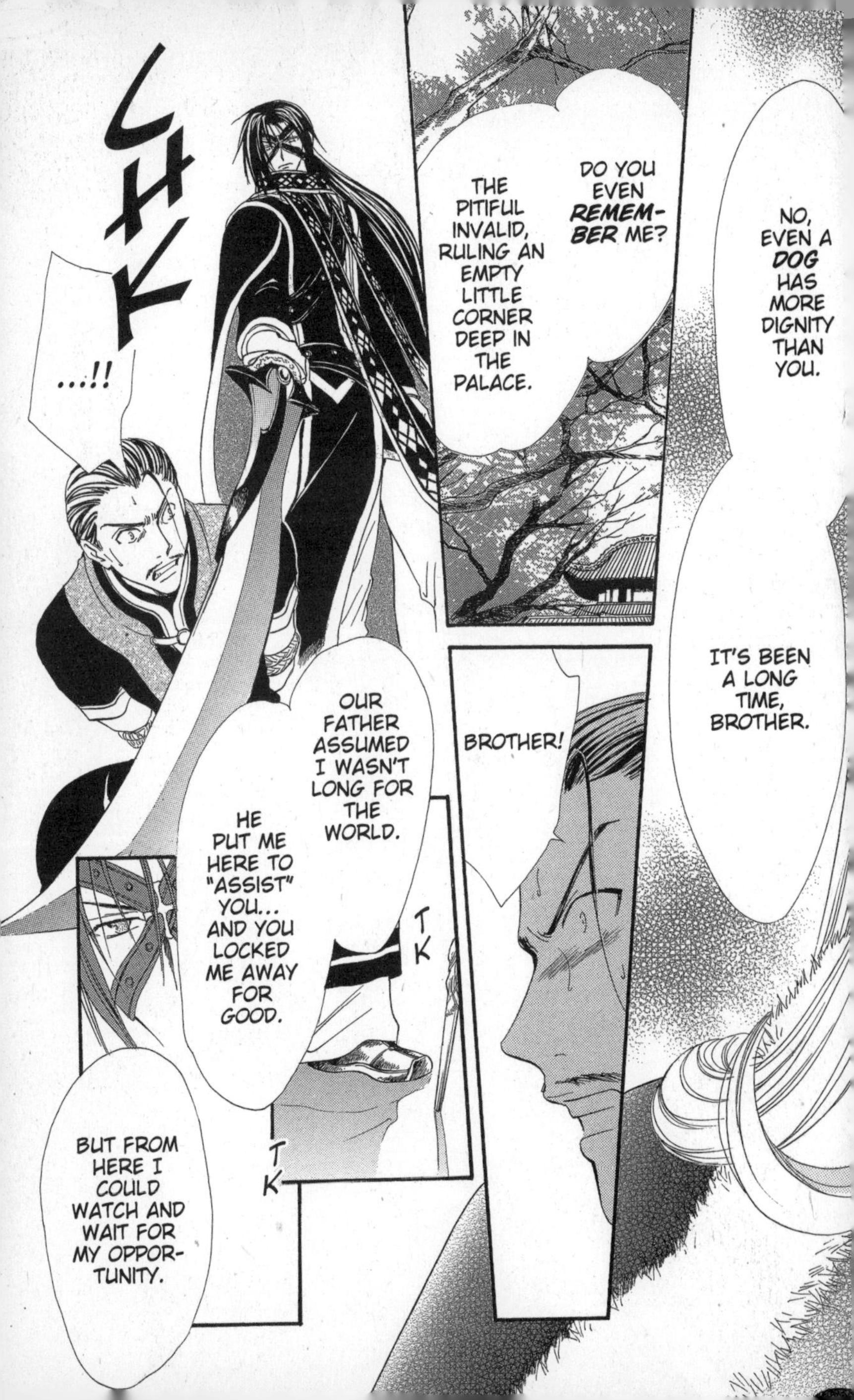
DO YOU EVEN *REMEMBER* ME?
THE PITIFUL INVALID, RULING AN EMPTY LITTLE CORNER DEEP IN THE PALACE.
NO, EVEN A *DOG* HAS MORE DIGNITY THAN YOU.
SHKK
...!!
IT'S BEEN A LONG TIME, BROTHER.
BROTHER!
OUR FATHER ASSUMED I WASN'T LONG FOR THE WORLD.
HE PUT ME HERE TO "ASSIST" YOU... AND YOU LOCKED ME AWAY FOR GOOD.
TK
TK
BUT FROM HERE I COULD WATCH AND WAIT FOR MY OPPORTUNITY.

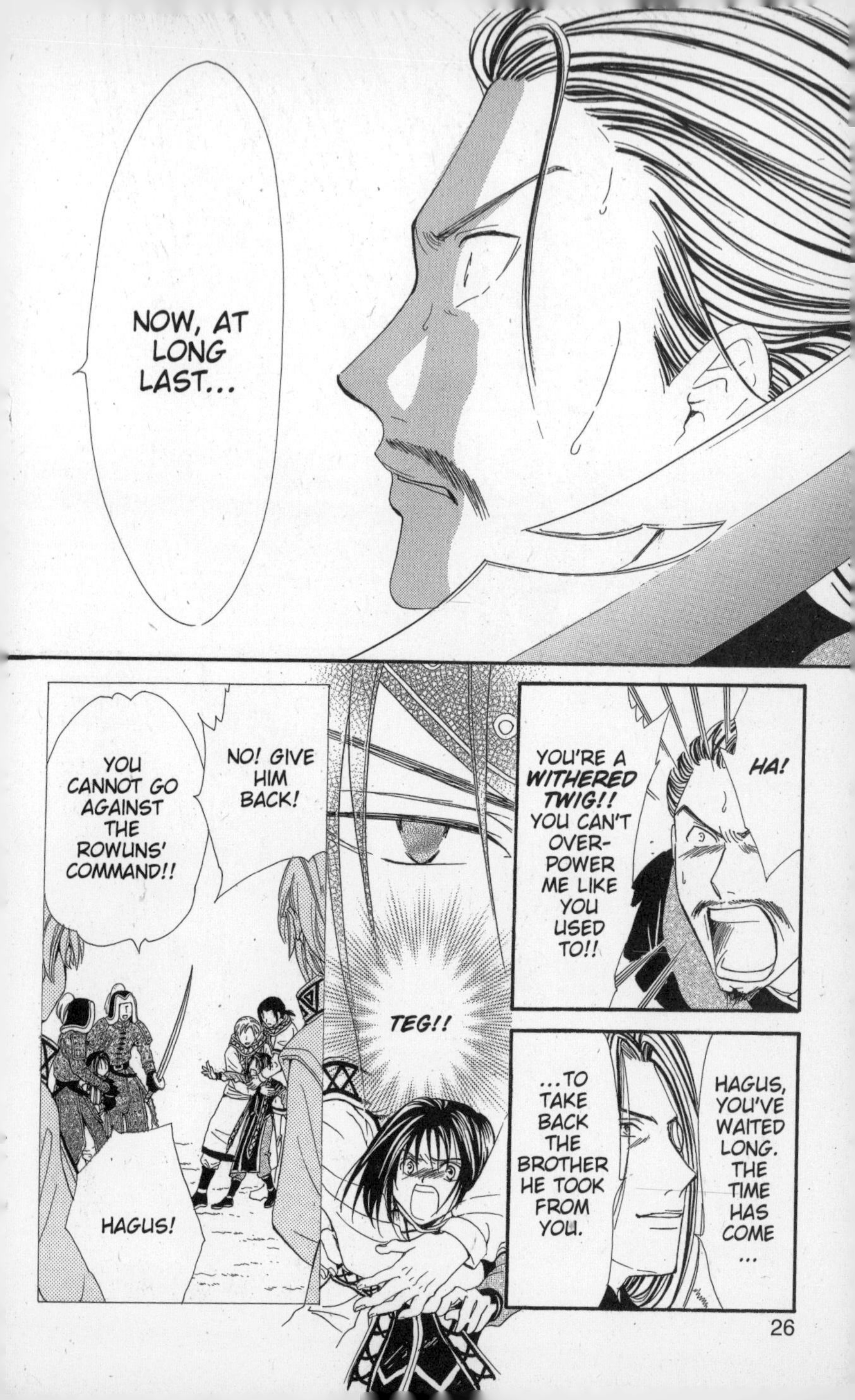
NOW, AT LONG LAST...
HA!
YOU'RE A WITHERED TWIG!! YOU CAN'T OVER-POWER ME LIKE YOU USED TO!!
HAGUS, YOU'VE WAITED LONG. THE TIME HAS COME...
...TO TAKE BACK THE BROTHER HE TOOK FROM YOU.
TEG!!
NO! GIVE HIM BACK!
YOU CANNOT GO AGAINST THE ROWUNS' COMMAND!!
HAGUS!

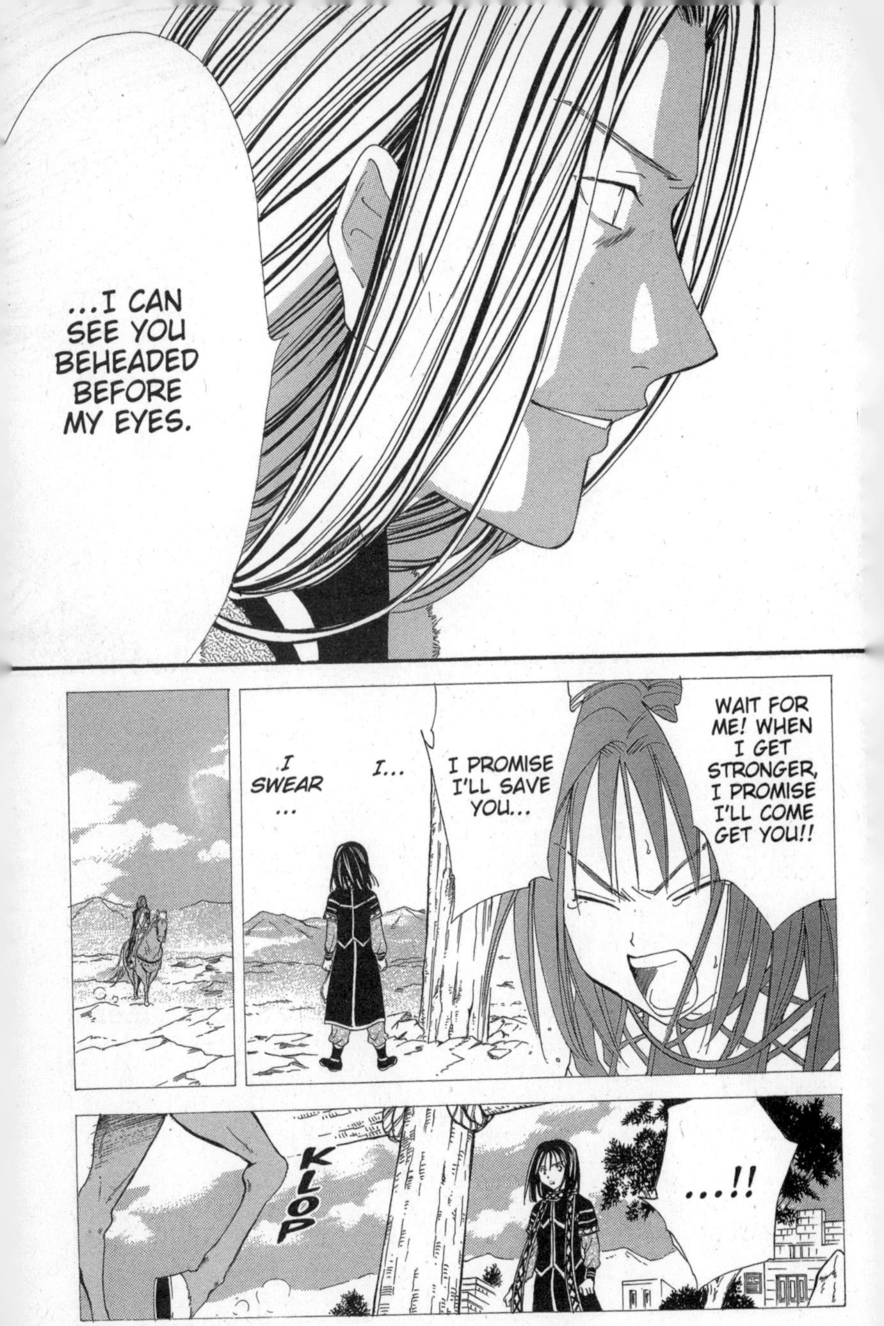
...I CAN SEE YOU BEHEADED BEFORE MY EYES.
WAIT FOR ME! WHEN I GET STRONGER, I PROMISE I'LL COME GET YOU!!
I PROMISE I'LL SAVE YOU...
I...
I SWEAR ...
...!!
KLOP

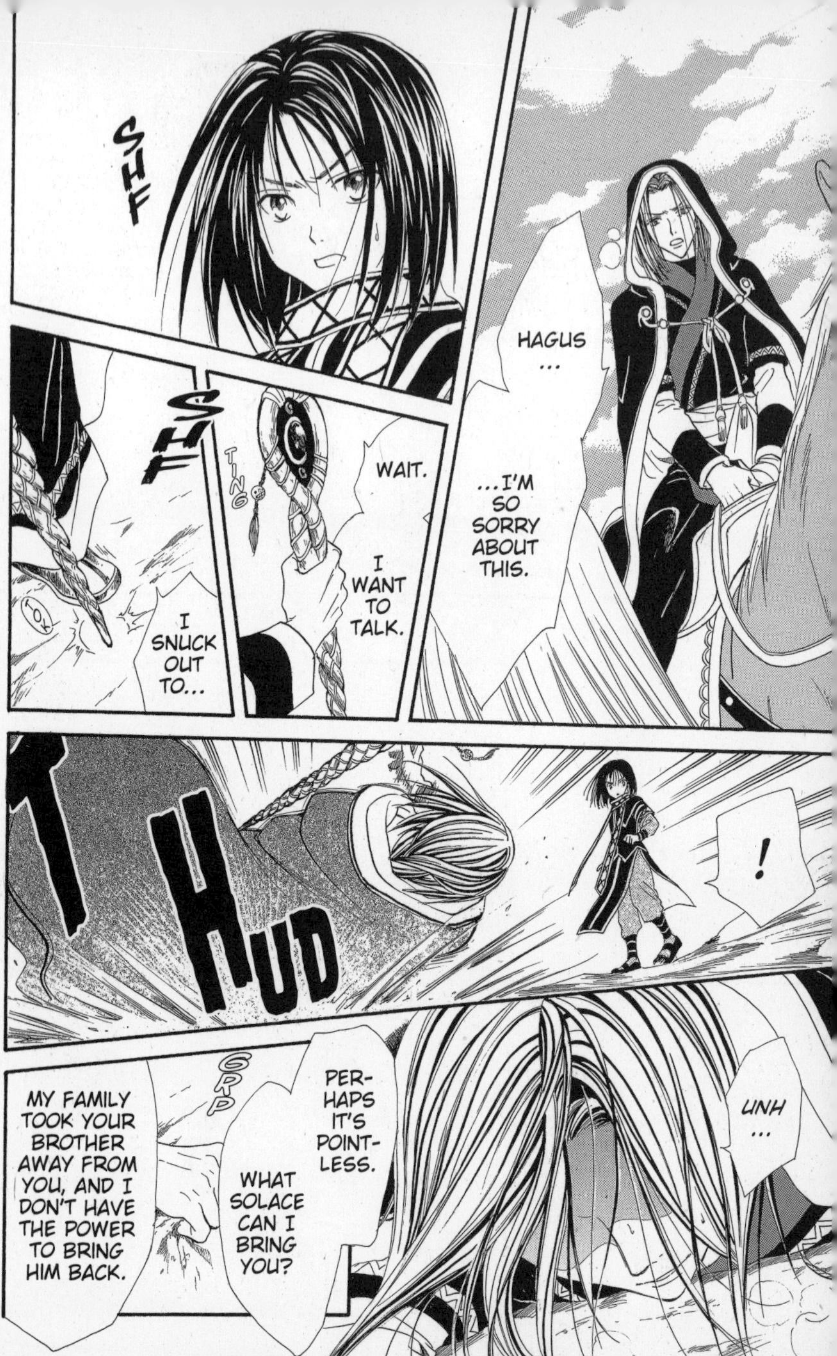
HAGUS ...
...I'M SO SORRY ABOUT THIS.
SHF
TING
WAIT.
I WANT TO TALK.
SHF
I SNUCK OUT TO...
TOK
!
THUD
UNH ...
PER-HAPS IT'S POINT-LESS.
WHAT SOLACE CAN I BRING YOU?
GRP
MY FAMILY TOOK YOUR BROTHER AWAY FROM YOU, AND I DON'T HAVE THE POWER TO BRING HIM BACK.

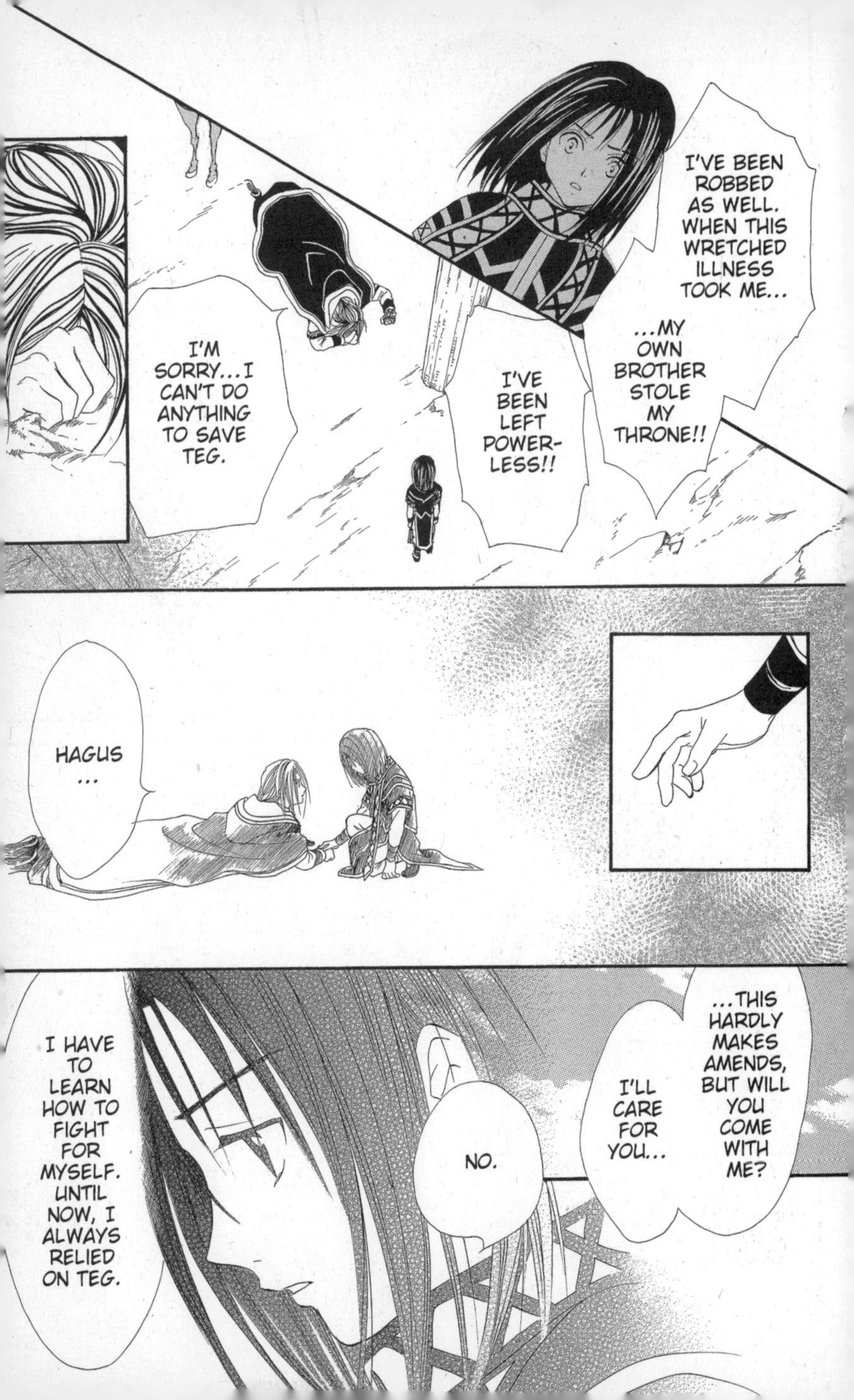
I'VE BEEN ROBBED AS WELL. WHEN THIS WRETCHED ILLNESS TOOK ME...
...MY OWN BROTHER STOLE MY THRONE!!
I'VE BEEN LEFT POWER-LESS!!
I'M SORRY...I CAN'T DO ANYTHING TO SAVE TEG.
HAGUS ...
...THIS HARDLY MAKES AMENDS, BUT WILL YOU COME WITH ME?
I'LL CARE FOR YOU...
NO.
I HAVE TO LEARN HOW TO FIGHT FOR MYSELF. UNTIL NOW, I ALWAYS RELIED ON TEG.

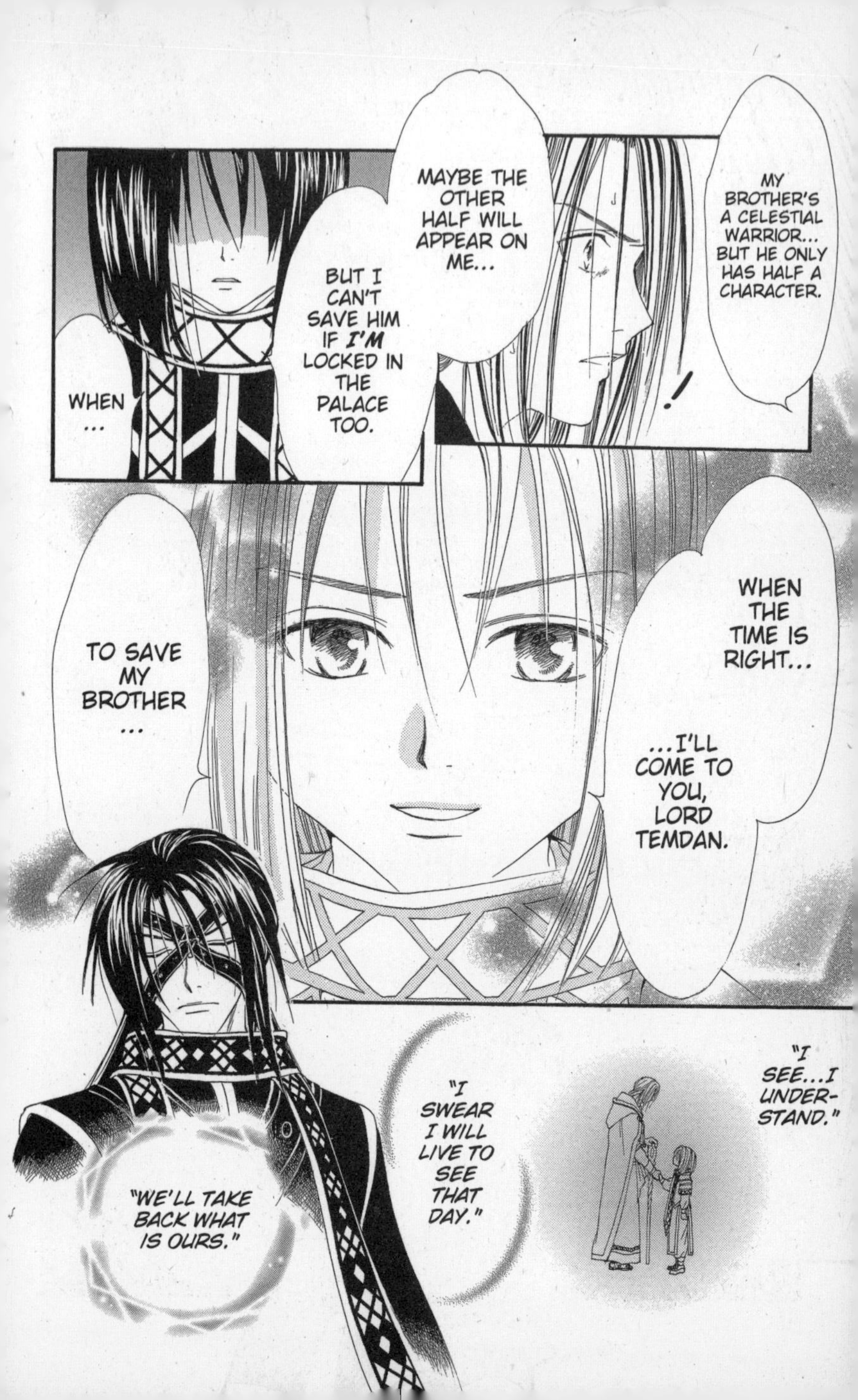
MY BROTHER'S A CELESTIAL WARRIOR... BUT HE ONLY HAS HALF A CHARACTER.
!
MAYBE THE OTHER HALF WILL APPEAR ON ME...
BUT I CAN'T SAVE HIM IF *I'M* LOCKED IN THE PALACE TOO.
WHEN ...
WHEN THE TIME IS RIGHT...
...I'LL COME TO YOU, LORD TEMDAN.
TO SAVE MY BROTHER ...
"I SEE...I UNDERSTAND."
"I SWEAR I WILL LIVE TO SEE THAT DAY."
"WE'LL TAKE BACK WHAT IS OURS."

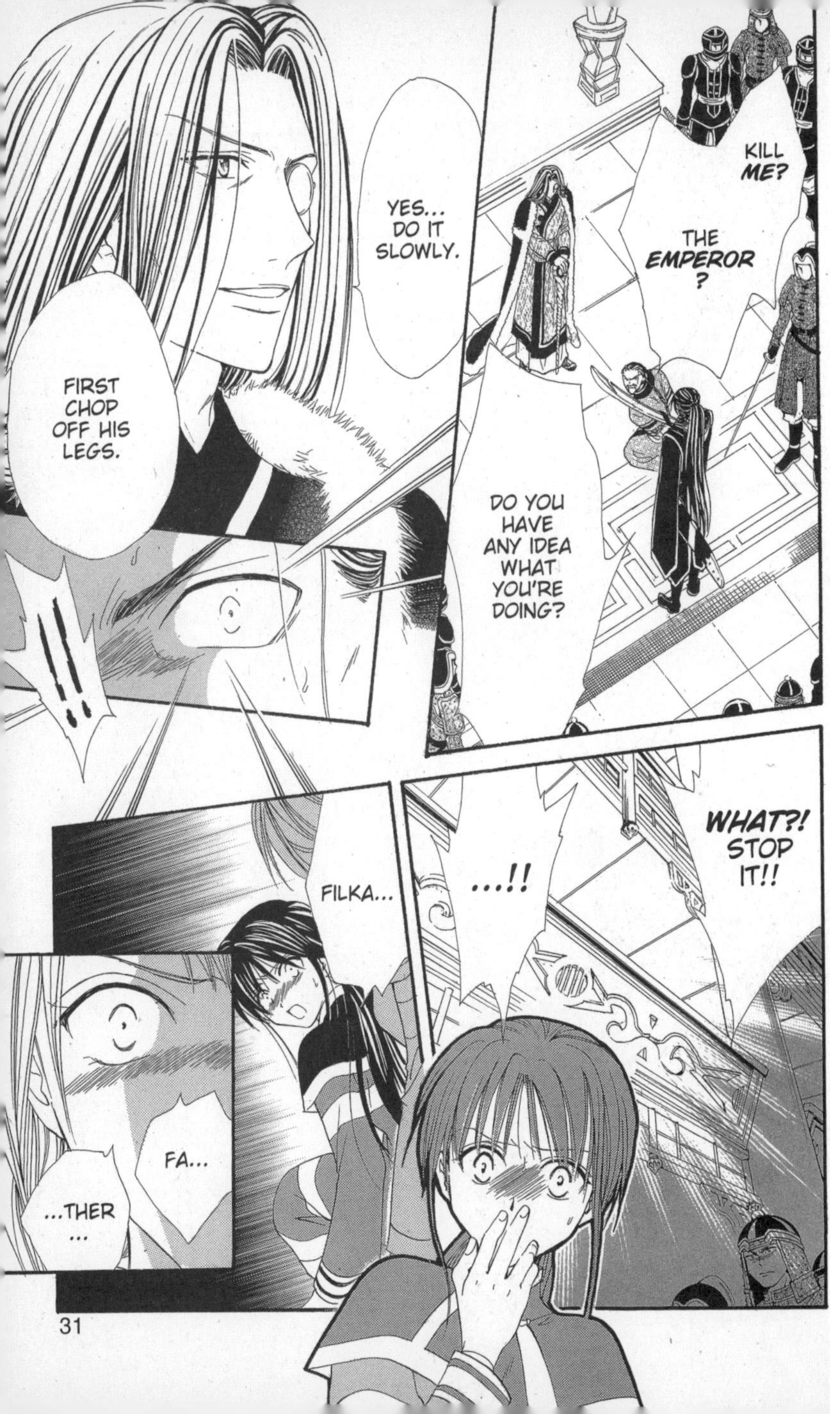
KILL ME?
THE EMPEROR ?
DO YOU HAVE ANY IDEA WHAT YOU'RE DOING?
YES... DO IT SLOWLY.
FIRST CHOP OFF HIS LEGS.
WHAT?! STOP IT!!
...!!
FILKA...
FA...
...THER ...

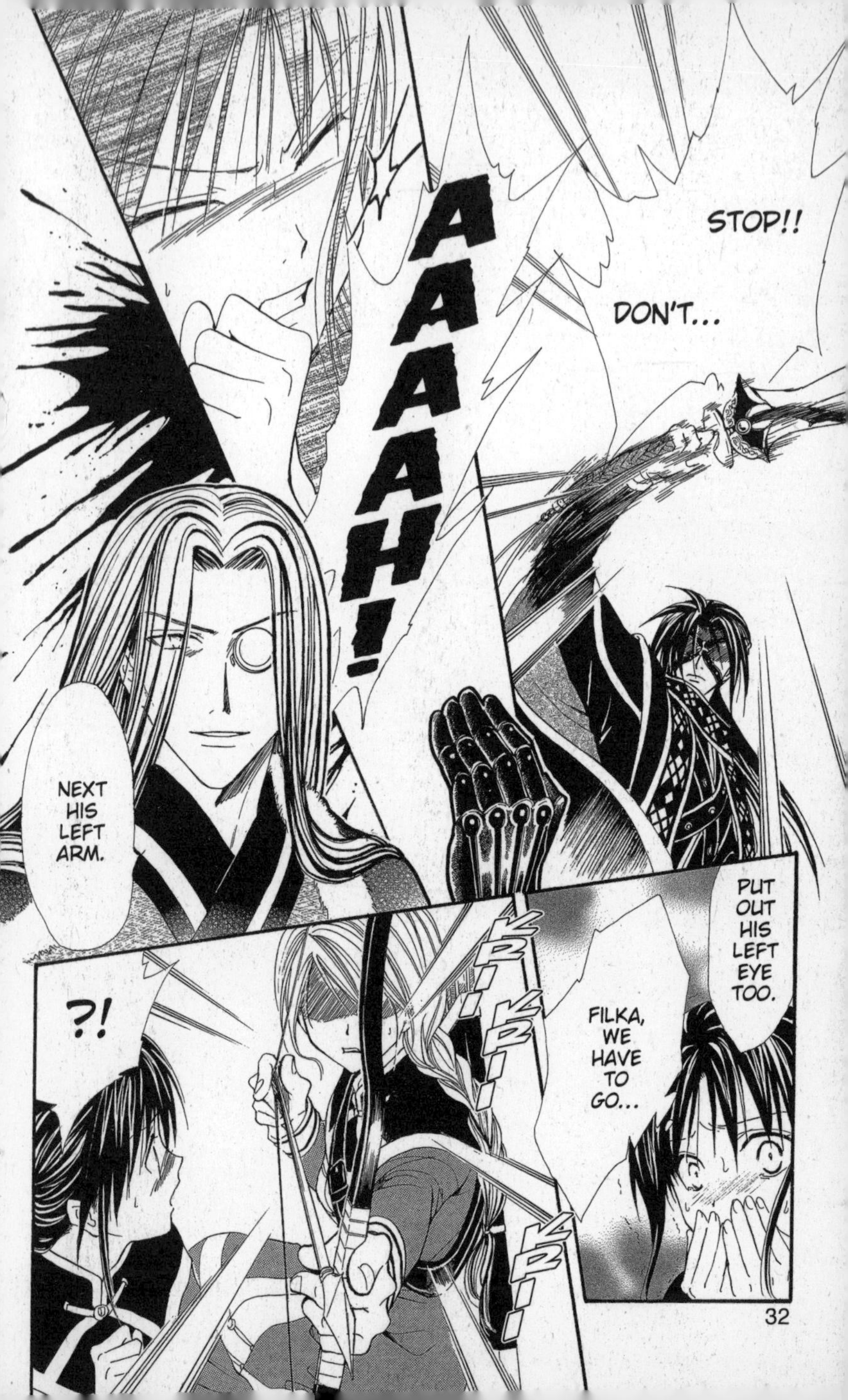

STOP!!
DON'T...
AAAAH!!
NEXT HIS LEFT ARM.
PUT OUT HIS LEFT EYE TOO.
FILKA, WE HAVE TO GO...
?!
KRI KRI KRI

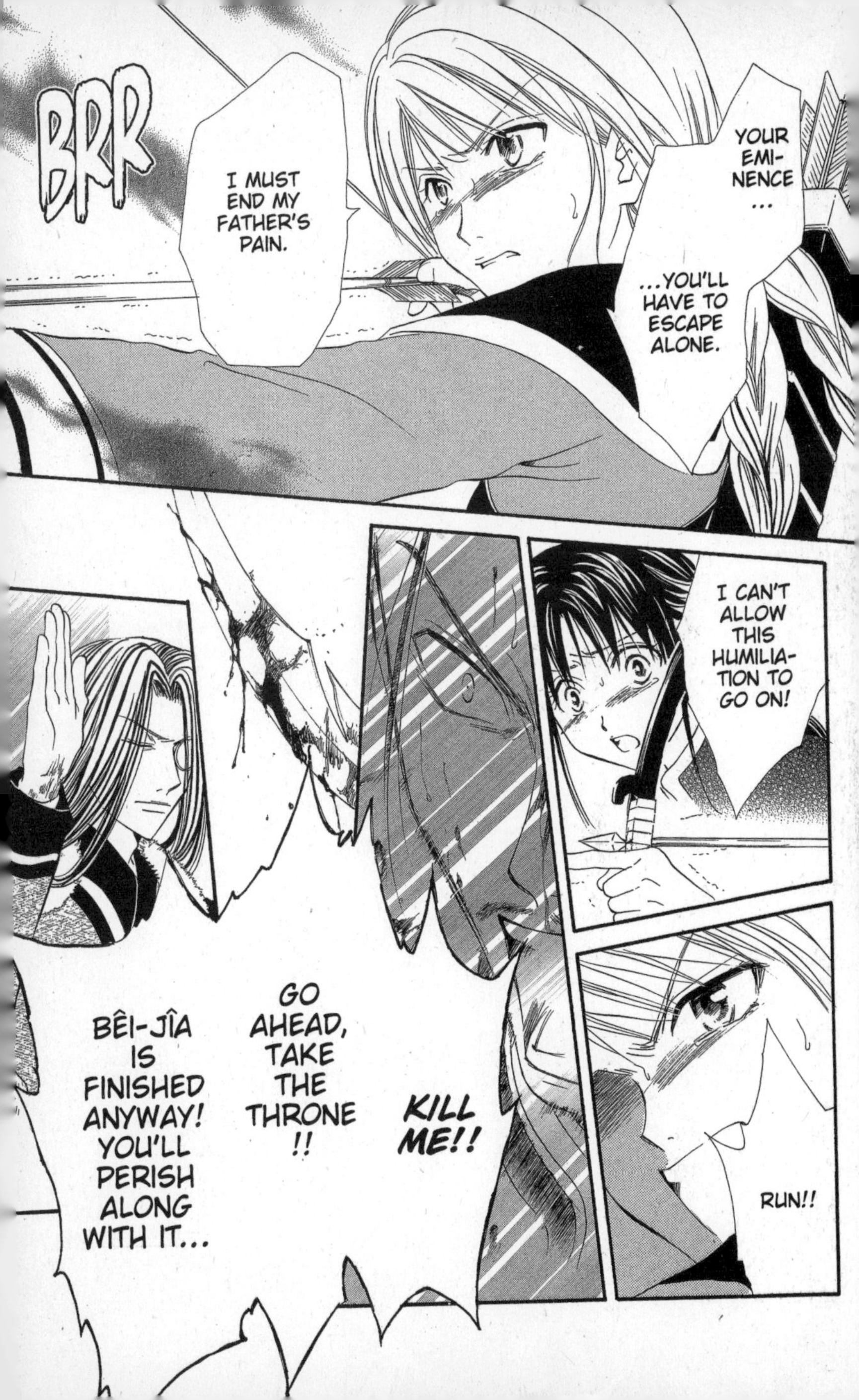
YOUR EMINENCE...
...YOU'LL HAVE TO ESCAPE ALONE.
I MUST END MY FATHER'S PAIN.
BRR
I CAN'T ALLOW THIS HUMILIATION TO GO ON!
RUN!!
KILL ME!!
GO AHEAD, TAKE THE THRONE!!
BÊI-JÎA IS FINISHED ANYWAY! YOU'LL PERISH ALONG WITH IT...

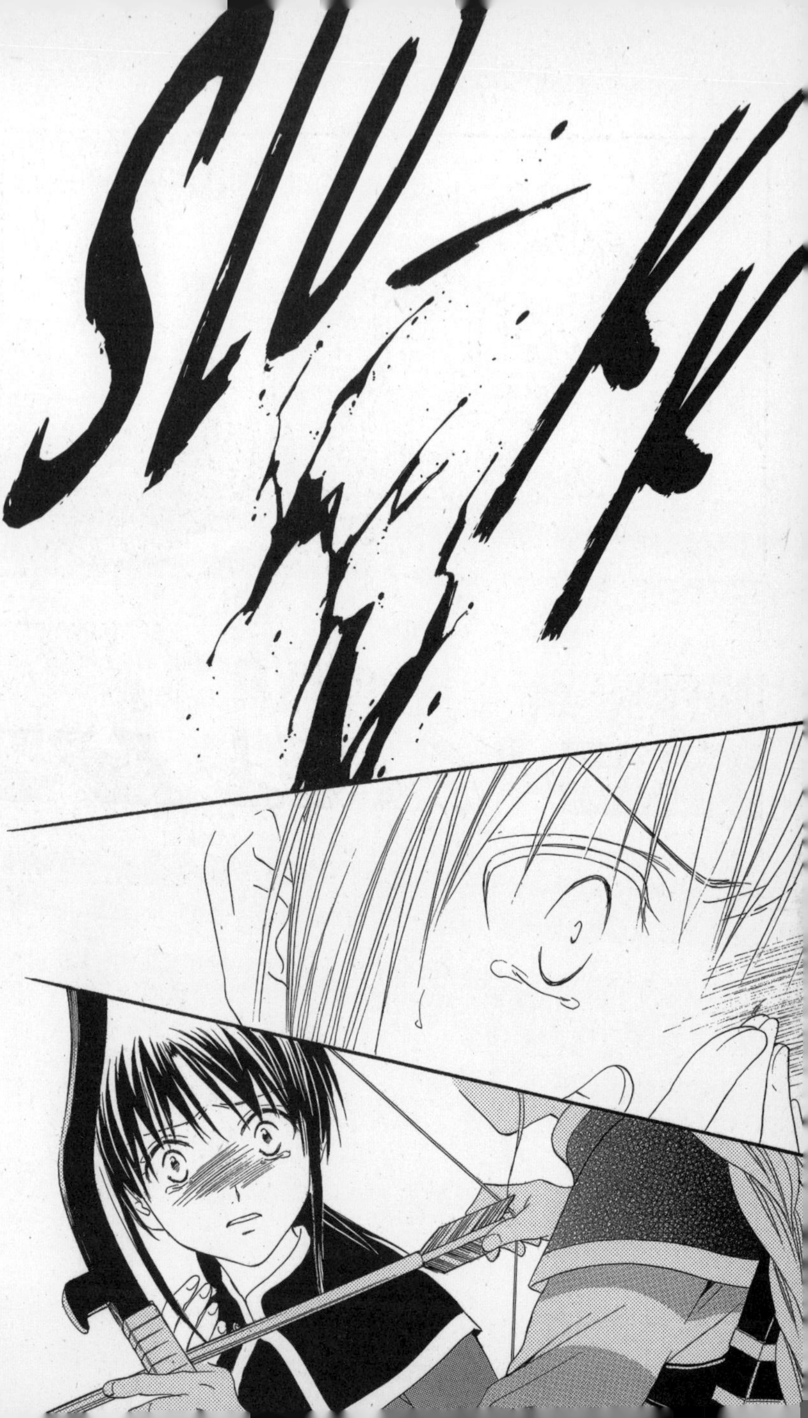

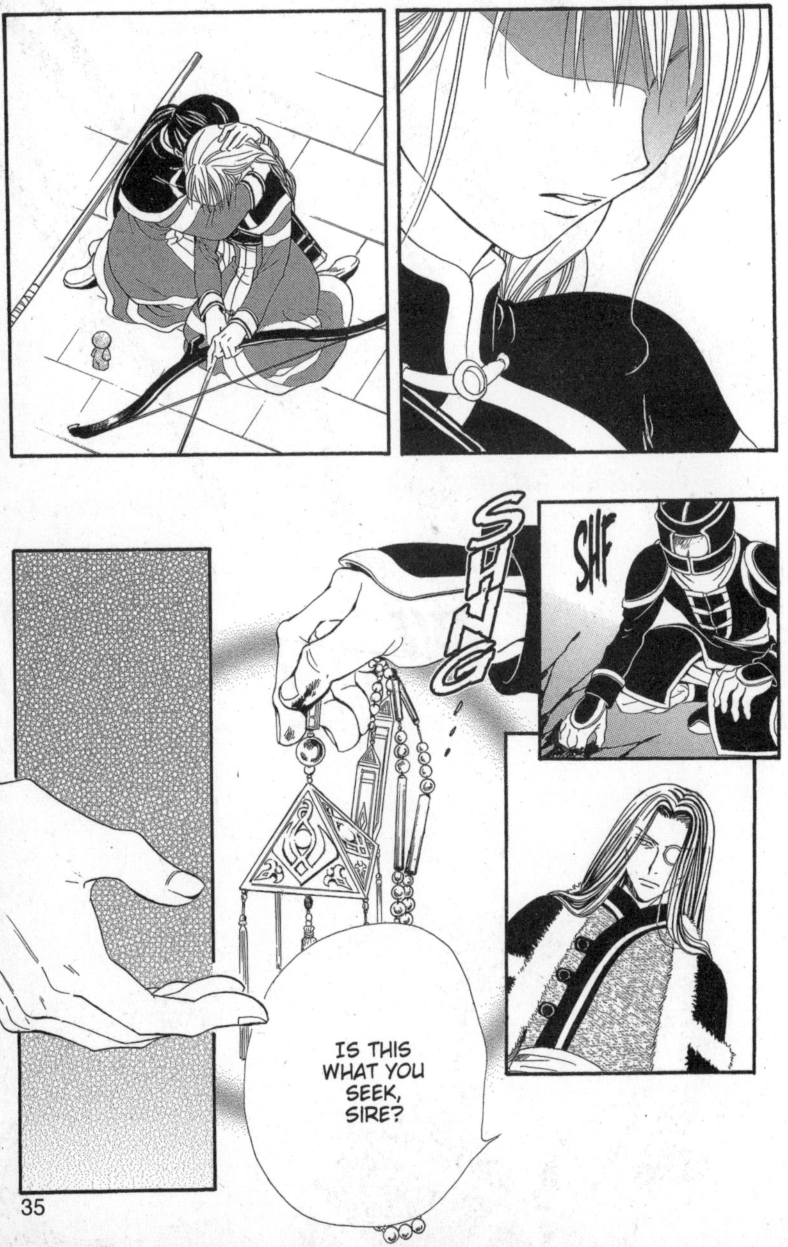
SHING
SHF
IS THIS WHAT YOU SEEK, SIRE?

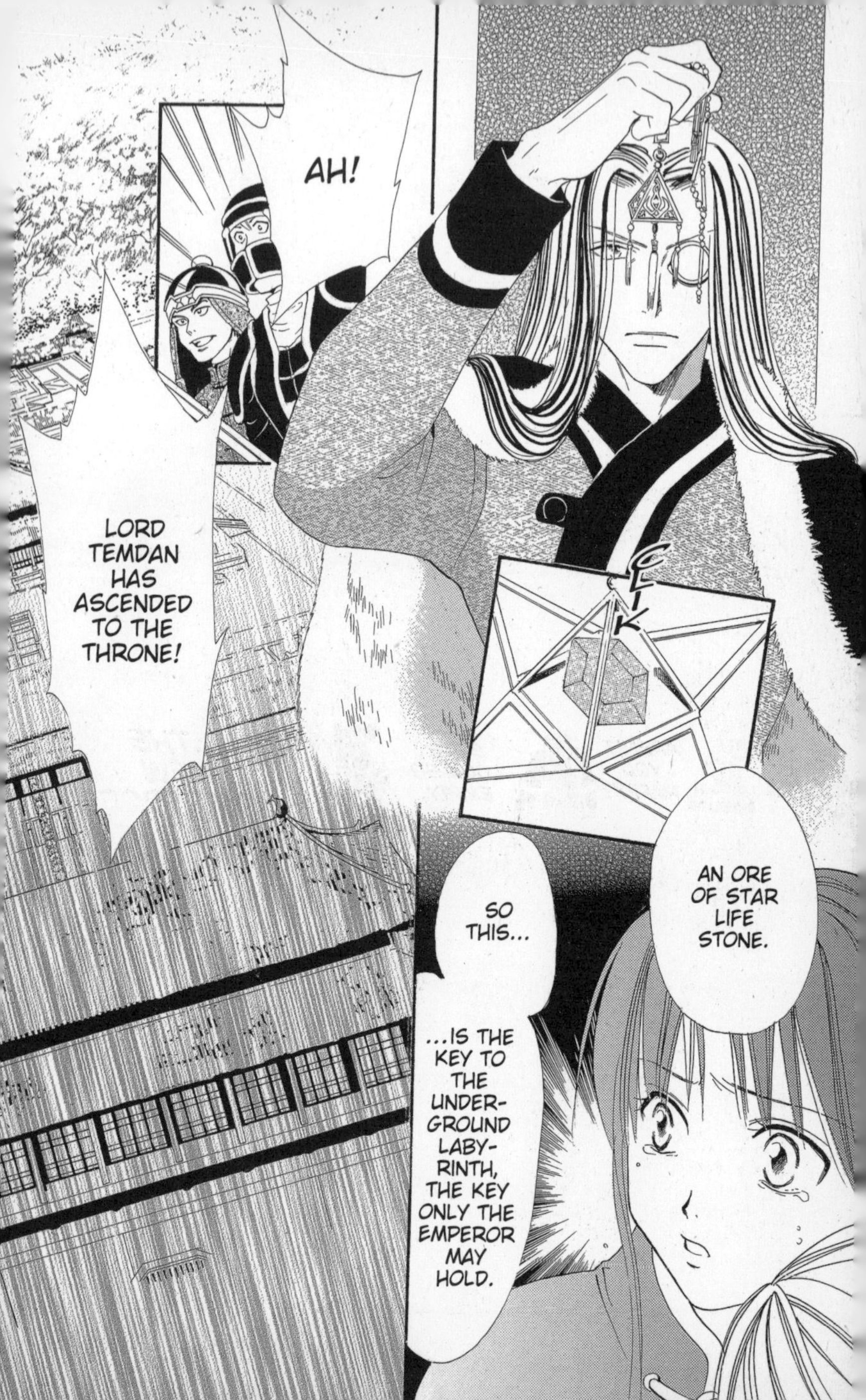
AN ORE OF STAR LIFE STONE.
SO THIS...
...IS THE KEY TO THE UNDER-GROUND LABY-RINTH, THE KEY ONLY THE EMPEROR MAY HOLD.
AH!
LORD TEMDAN HAS ASCENDED TO THE THRONE!

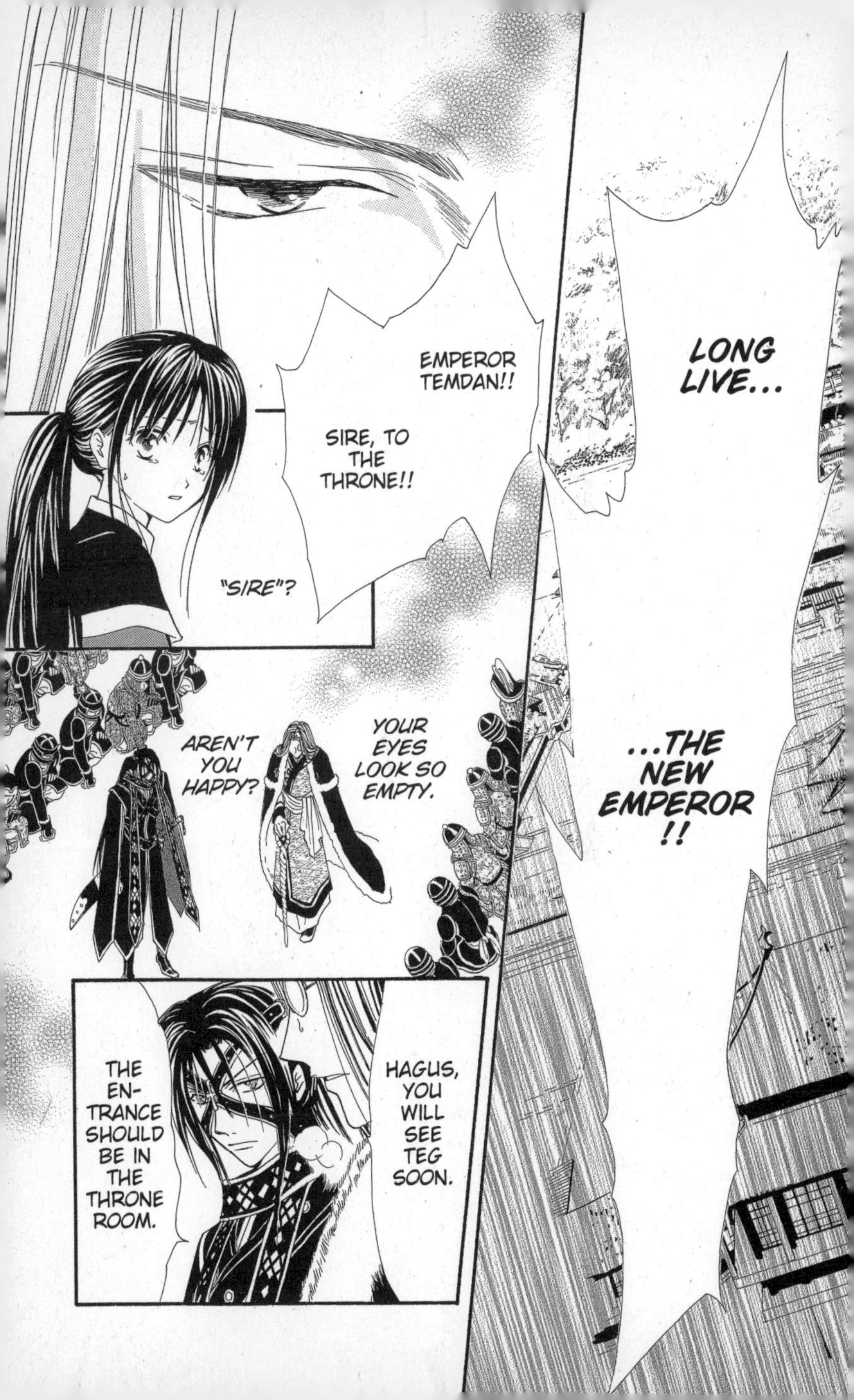
LONG LIVE...
...THE NEW EMPEROR!!
EMPEROR TEMDAN!!
SIRE, TO THE THRONE!!
"SIRE"?
YOUR EYES LOOK SO EMPTY.
AREN'T YOU HAPPY?
HAGUS, YOU WILL SEE TEG SOON.
THE EN-TRANCE SHOULD BE IN THE THRONE ROOM.

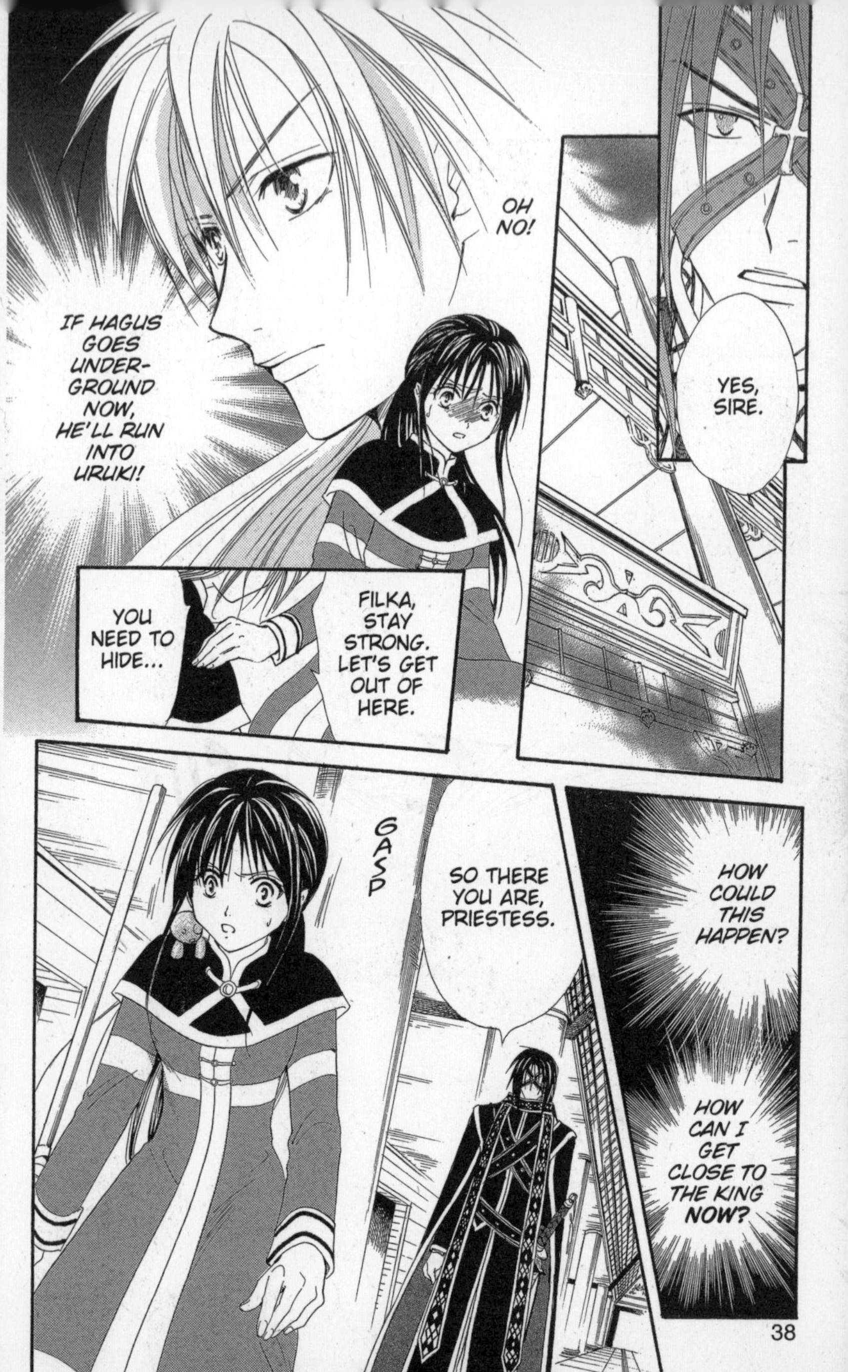
YES, SIRE.
OH NO!
IF HAGUS GOES UNDER-GROUND NOW, HE'LL RUN INTO URUKI!
FILKA, STAY STRONG. LET'S GET OUT OF HERE.
YOU NEED TO HIDE...
HOW COULD THIS HAPPEN?
HOW CAN I GET CLOSE TO THE KING NOW?
SO THERE YOU ARE, PRIESTESS.
GASP

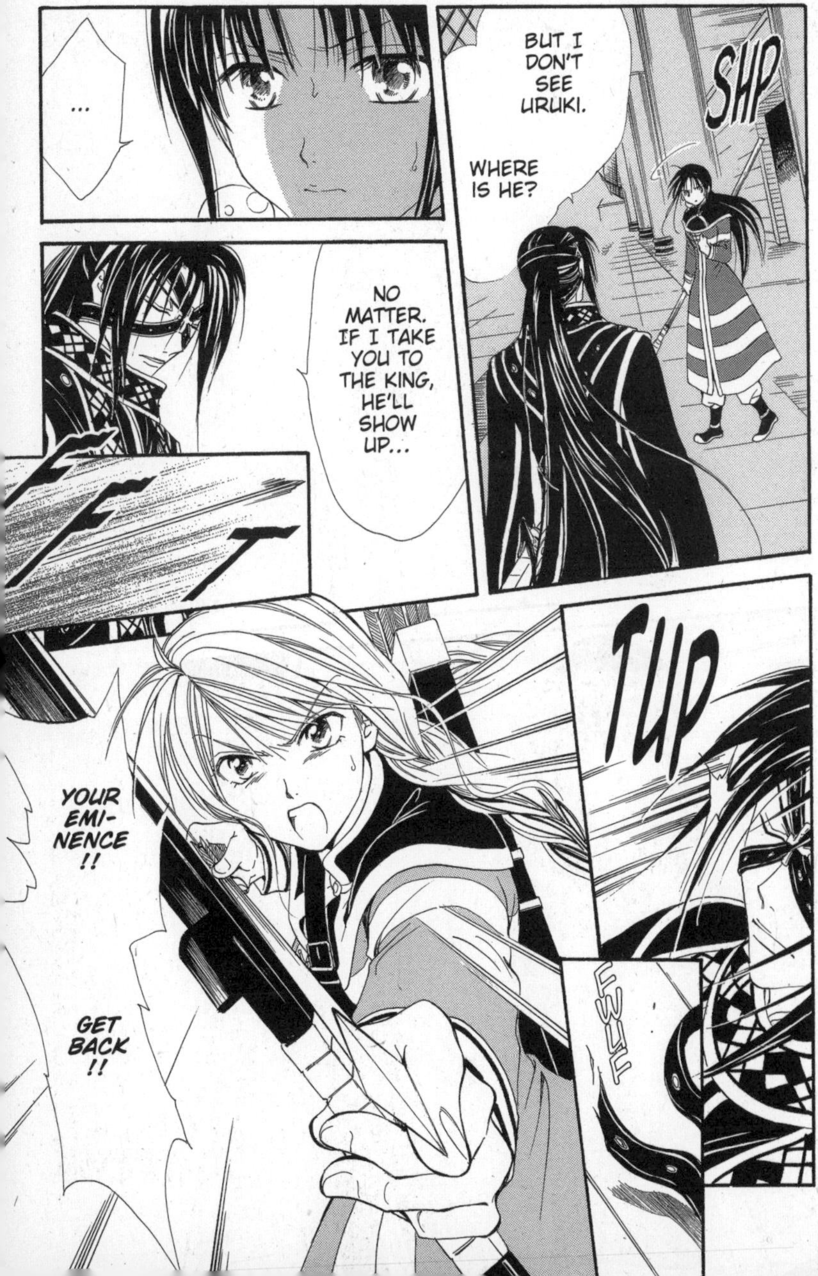

BUT I DON'T SEE URUKI.
WHERE IS HE?
SHP
...
NO MATTER. IF I TAKE YOU TO THE KING, HE'LL SHOW UP...
TUP
YOUR EMI-NENCE !!
GET BACK !!

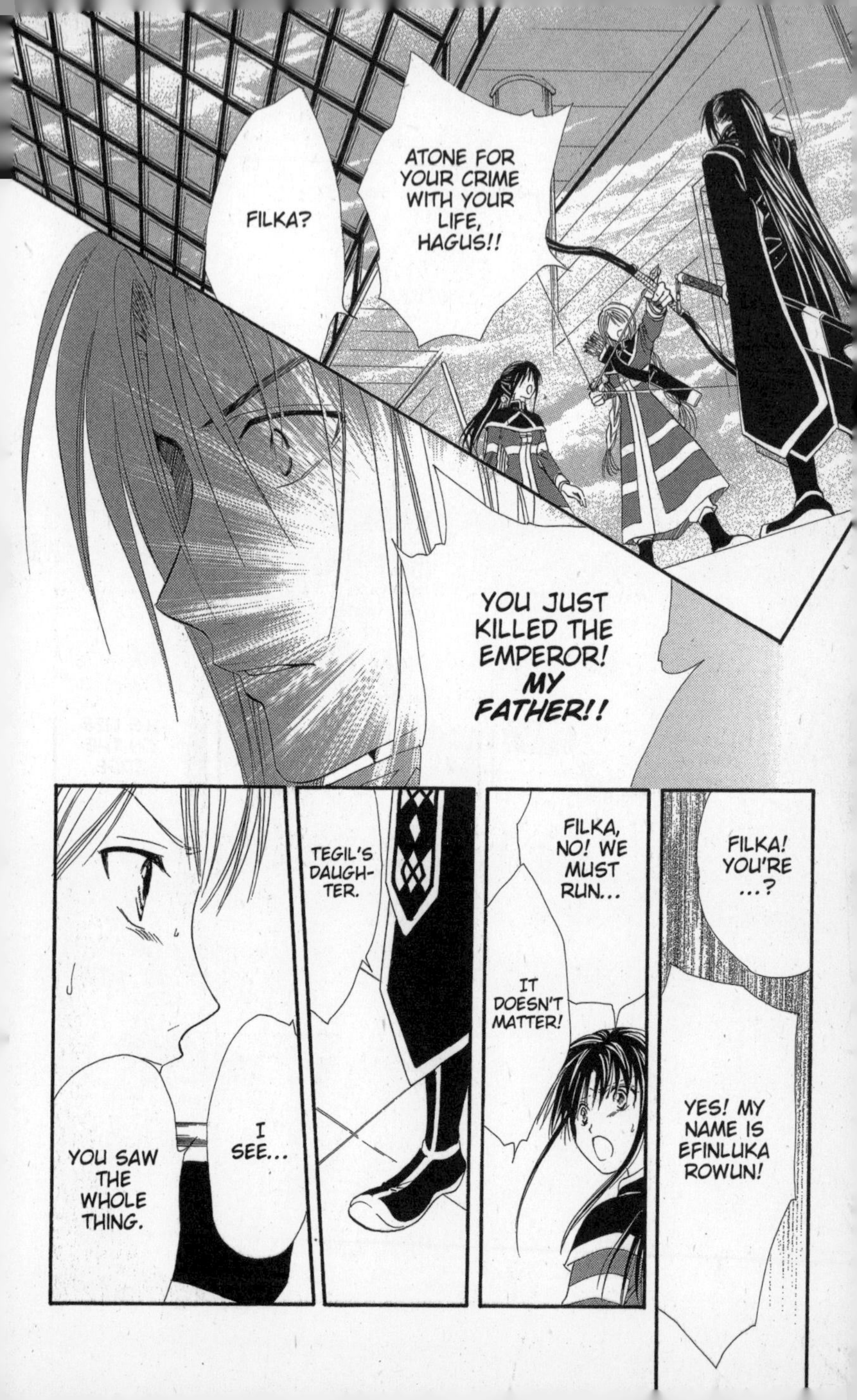
ATONE FOR YOUR CRIME WITH YOUR LIFE, HAGUS!!
FILKA?
YOU JUST KILLED THE EMPEROR! *MY FATHER!!*
FILKA! YOU'RE ...?
YES! MY NAME IS EFINLUKA ROWUN!
FILKA, NO! WE MUST RUN...
IT DOESN'T MATTER!
TEGIL'S DAUGHTER.
I SEE...
YOU SAW THE WHOLE THING.

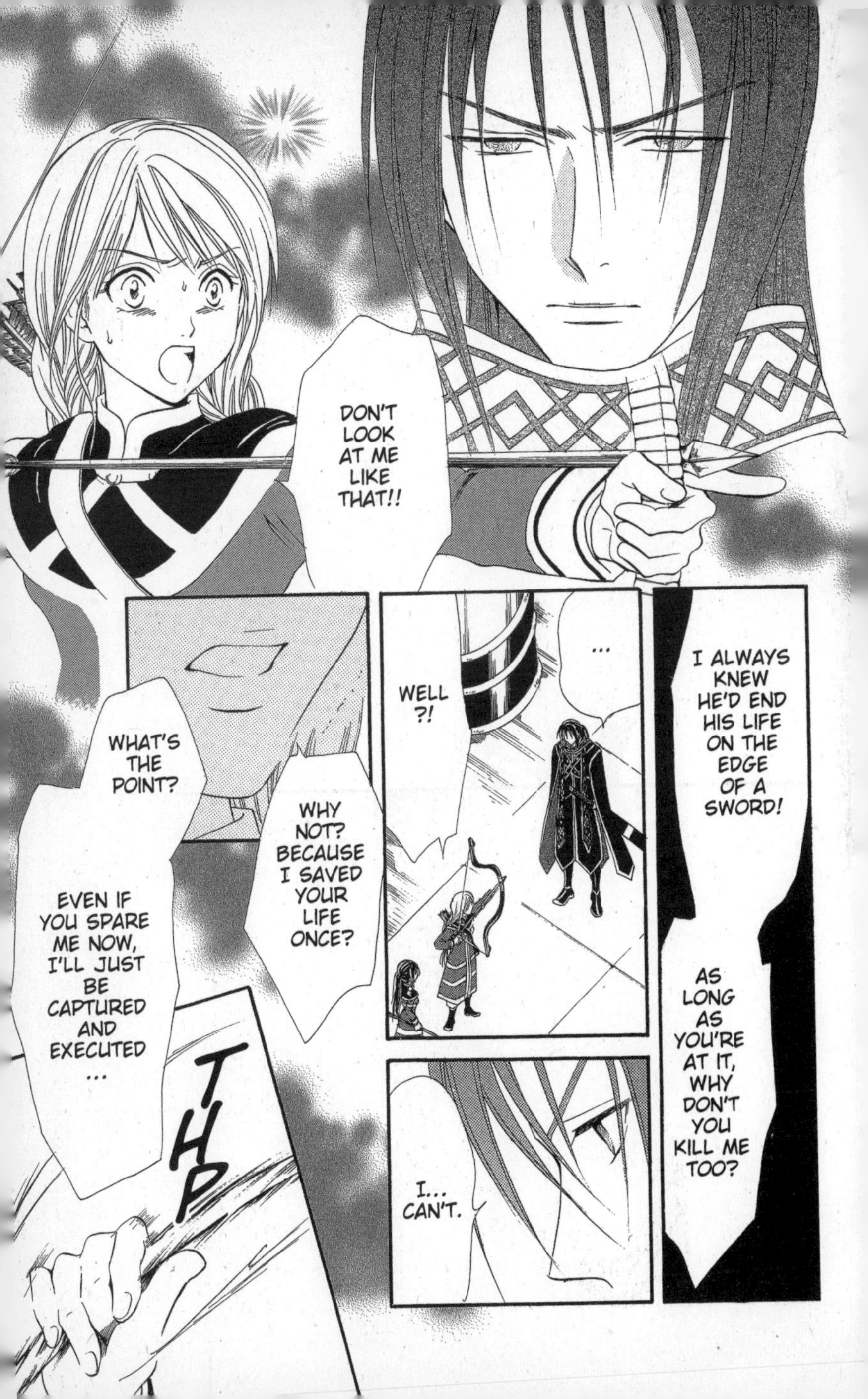
DON'T LOOK AT ME LIKE THAT!!
I ALWAYS KNEW HE'D END HIS LIFE ON THE EDGE OF A SWORD!
AS LONG AS YOU'RE AT IT, WHY DON'T YOU KILL ME TOO?
...
WELL ?!
WHY NOT? BECAUSE I SAVED YOUR LIFE ONCE?
I... CAN'T.
WHAT'S THE POINT?
EVEN IF YOU SPARE ME NOW, I'LL JUST BE CAPTURED AND EXECUTED ...
THP

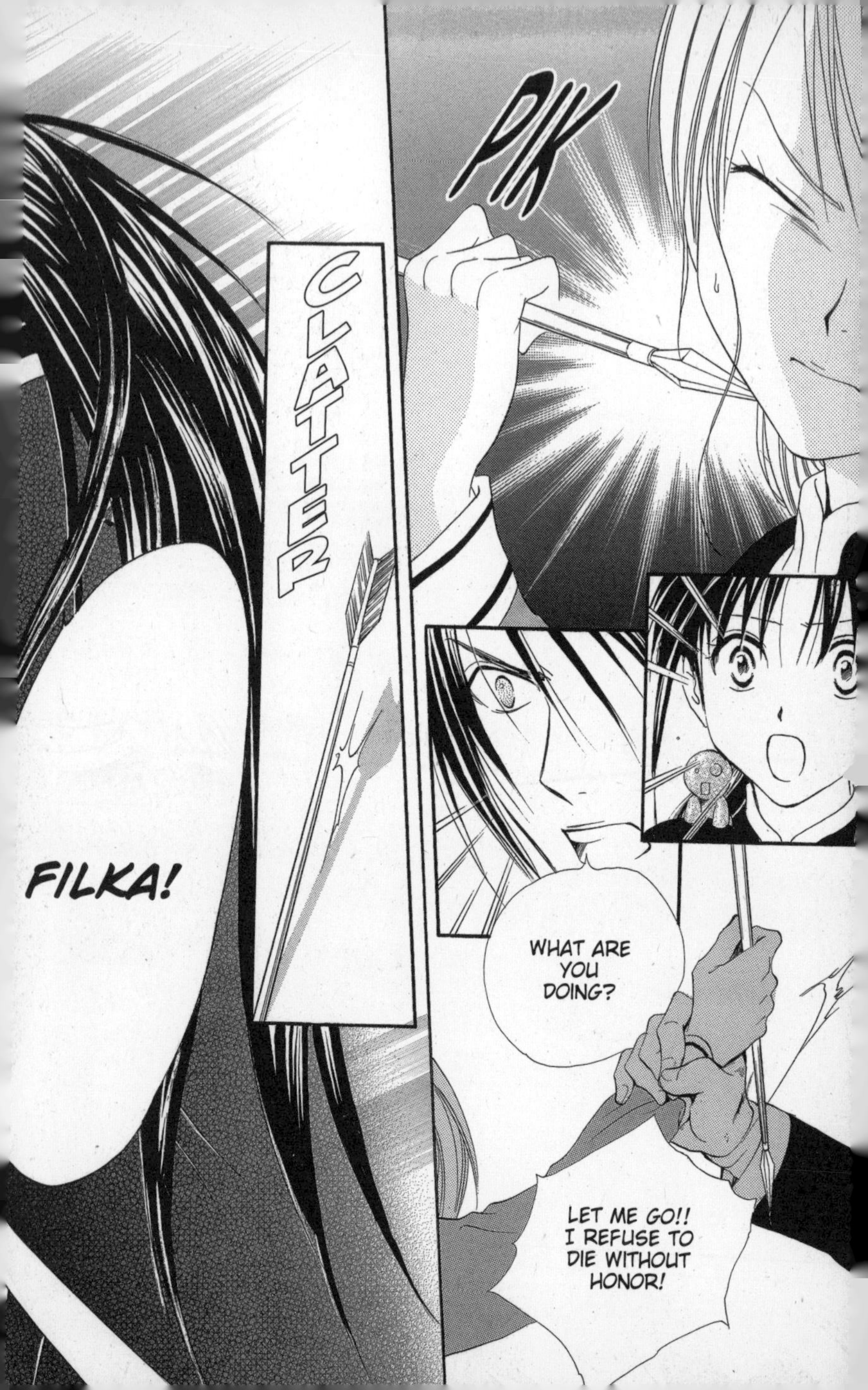
PIK
CLATTER
WHAT ARE YOU DOING?
LET ME GO!! I REFUSE TO DIE WITHOUT HONOR!
FILKA!

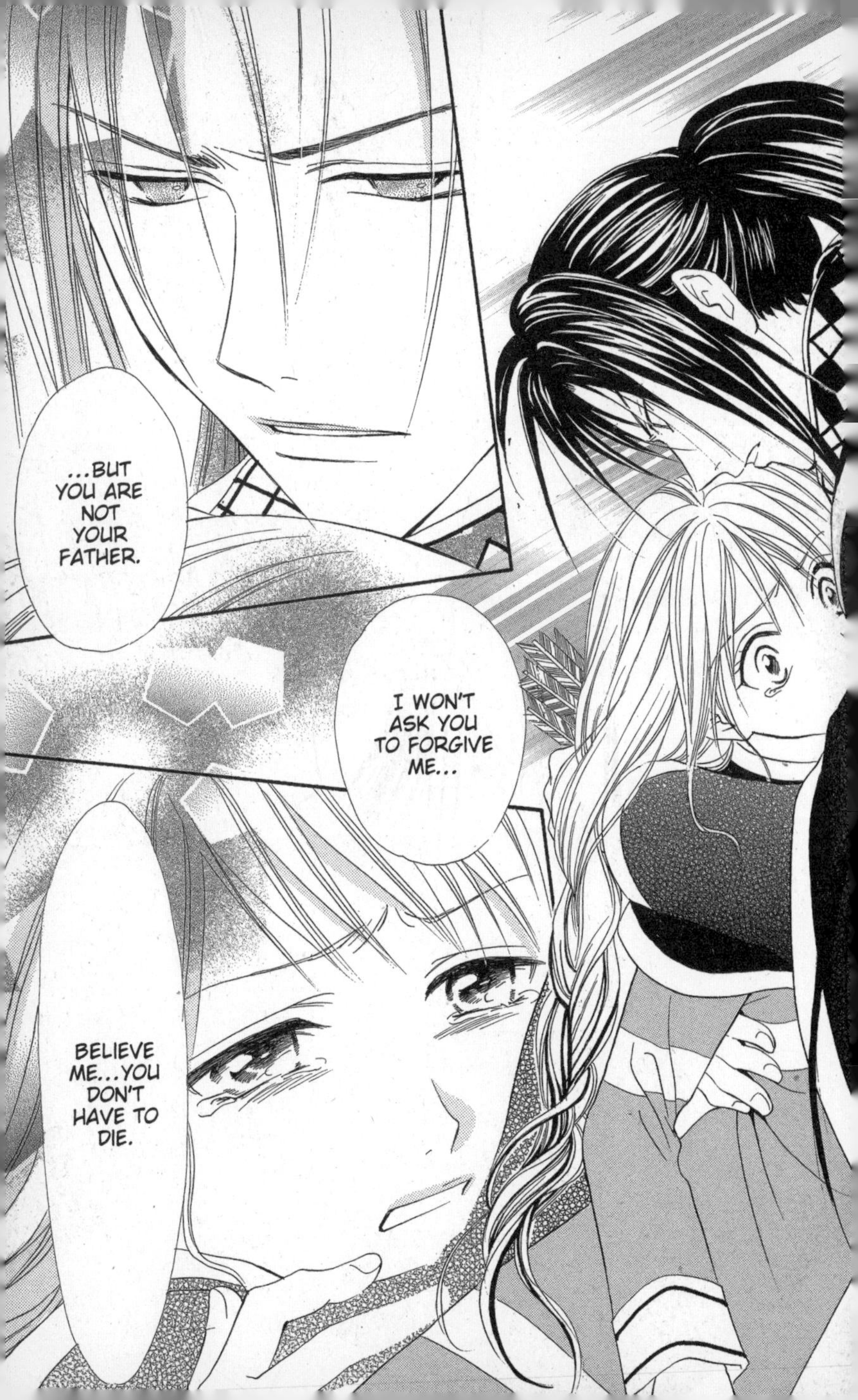
...BUT YOU ARE NOT YOUR FATHER.
I WON'T ASK YOU TO FORGIVE ME...
BELIEVE ME...YOU DON'T HAVE TO DIE.

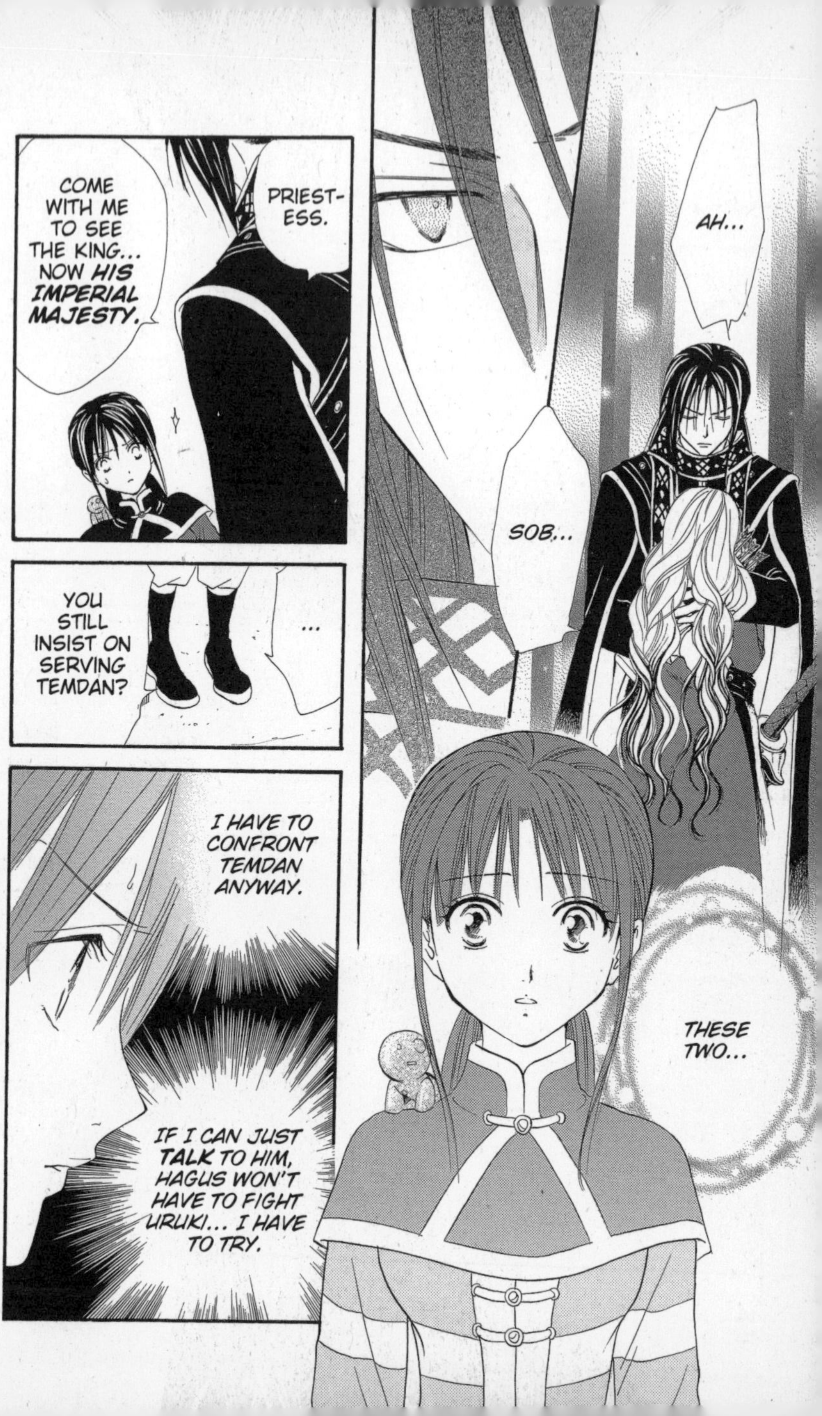
AH...
SOB...
THESE TWO...
PRIEST-ESS.
COME WITH ME TO SEE THE KING... NOW *HIS IMPERIAL MAJESTY.*
YOU STILL INSIST ON SERVING TEMDAN?
...
I HAVE TO CONFRONT TEMDAN ANYWAY.
*IF I CAN JUST **TALK** TO HIM, HAGUS WON'T HAVE TO FIGHT URUKI... I HAVE TO TRY.*

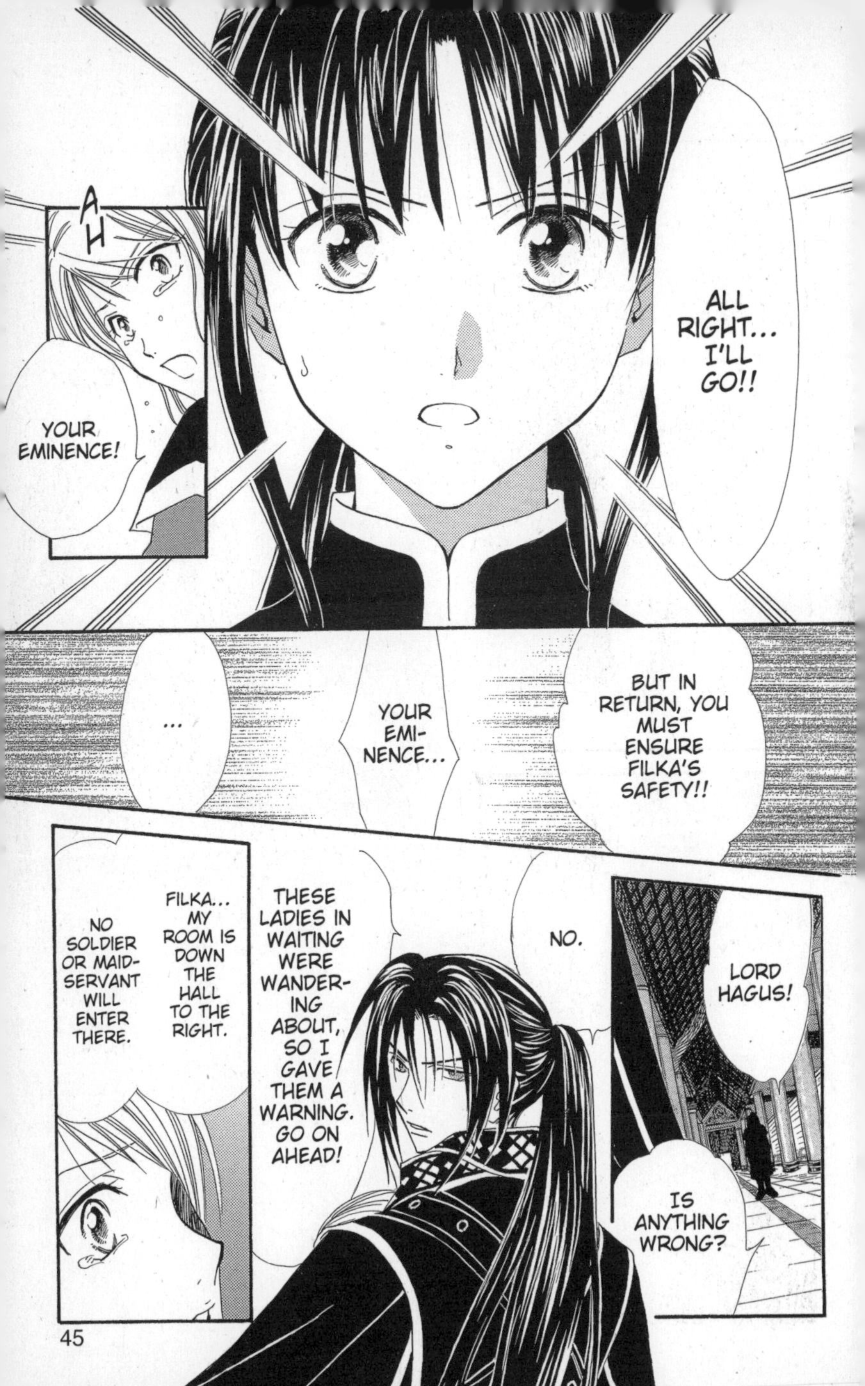
ALL RIGHT... I'LL GO!!
AH
YOUR EMINENCE!
BUT IN RETURN, YOU MUST ENSURE FILKA'S SAFETY!!
YOUR EMI-NENCE...
...
LORD HAGUS!
IS ANYTHING WRONG?
NO.
THESE LADIES IN WAITING WERE WANDER-ING ABOUT, SO I GAVE THEM A WARNING. GO ON AHEAD!
FILKA... MY ROOM IS DOWN THE HALL TO THE RIGHT.
NO SOLDIER OR MAID-SERVANT WILL ENTER THERE.

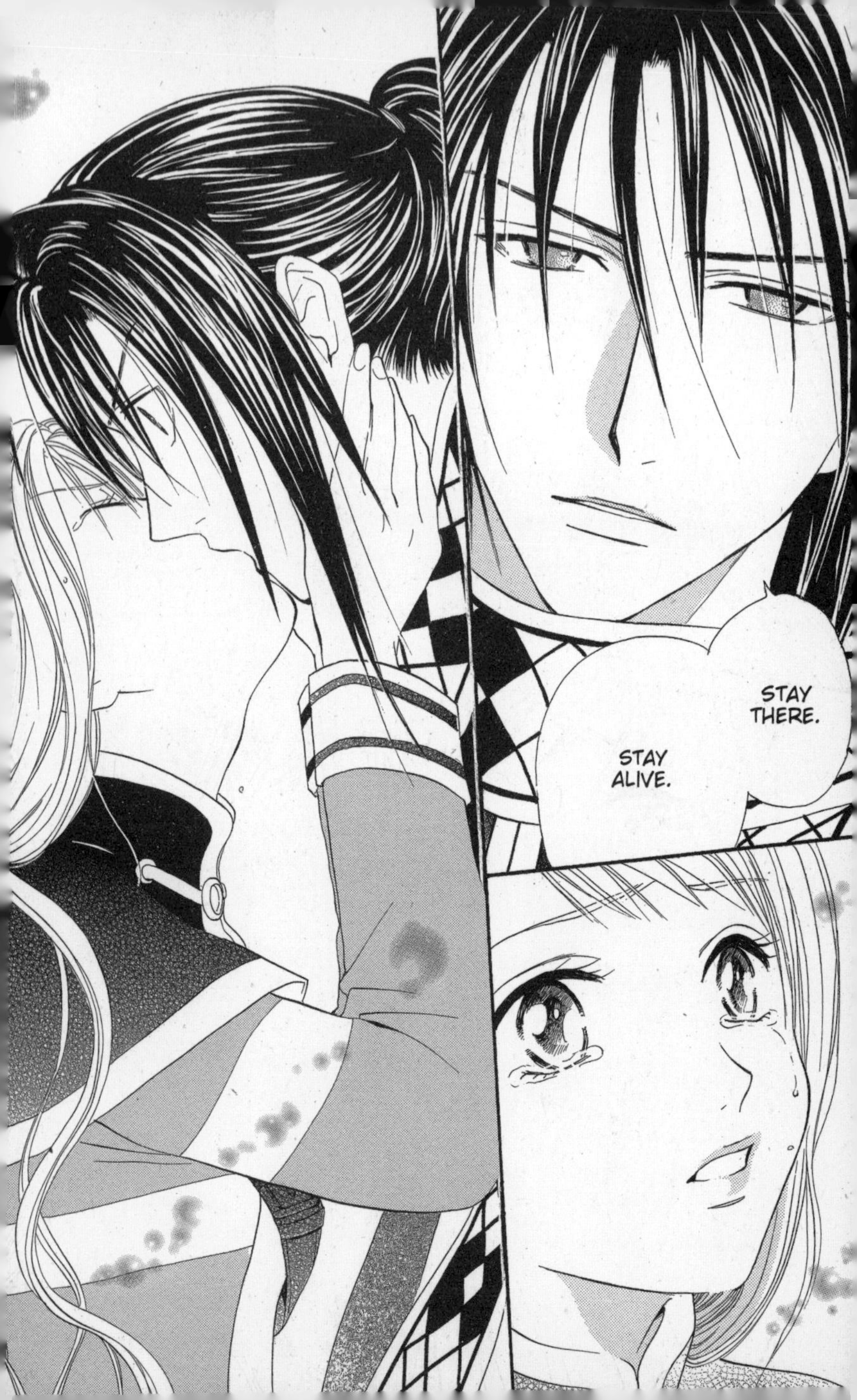
STAY THERE.
STAY ALIVE.

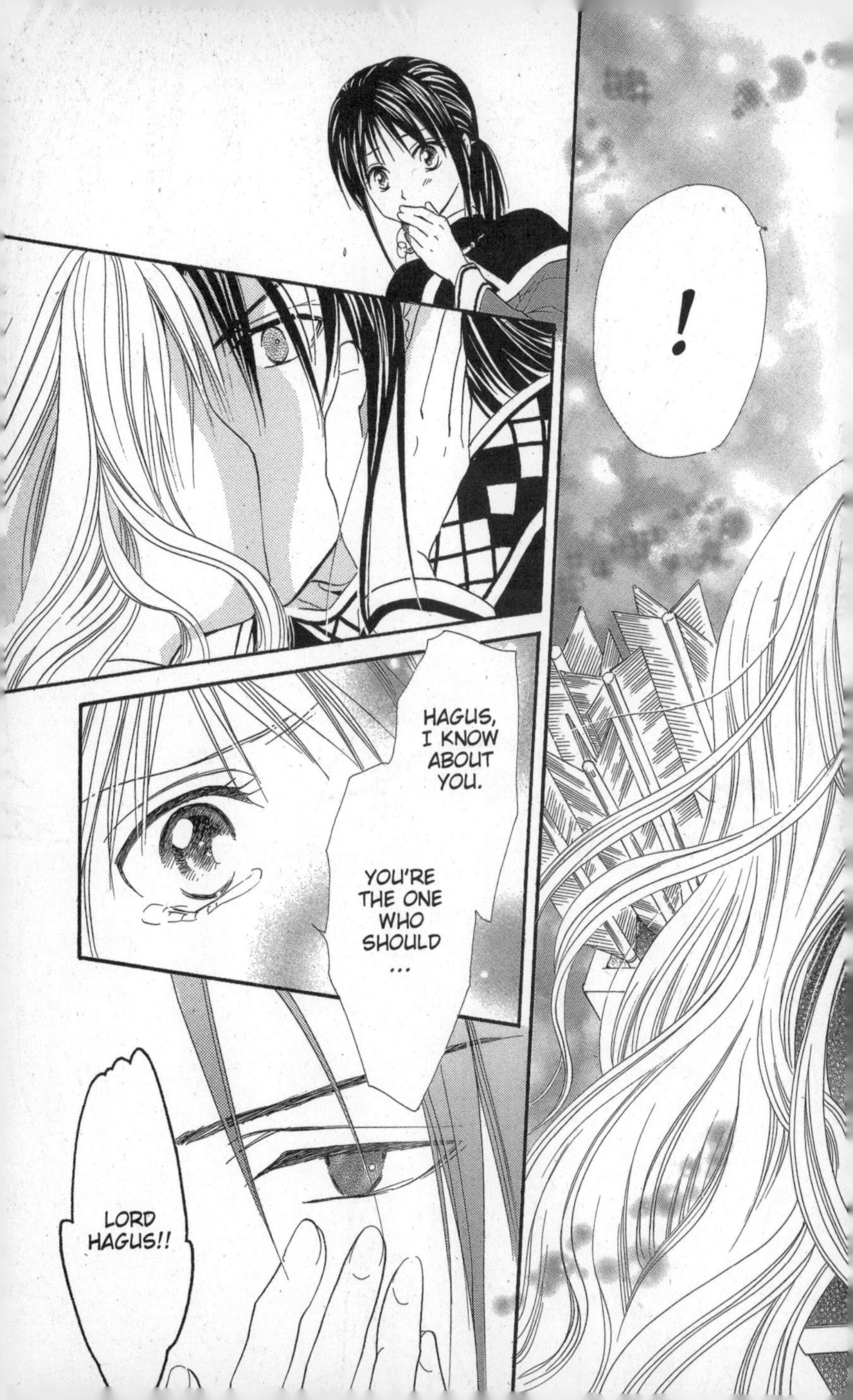
!
HAGUS, I KNOW ABOUT YOU.
YOU'RE THE ONE WHO SHOULD ...
LORD HAGUS!!

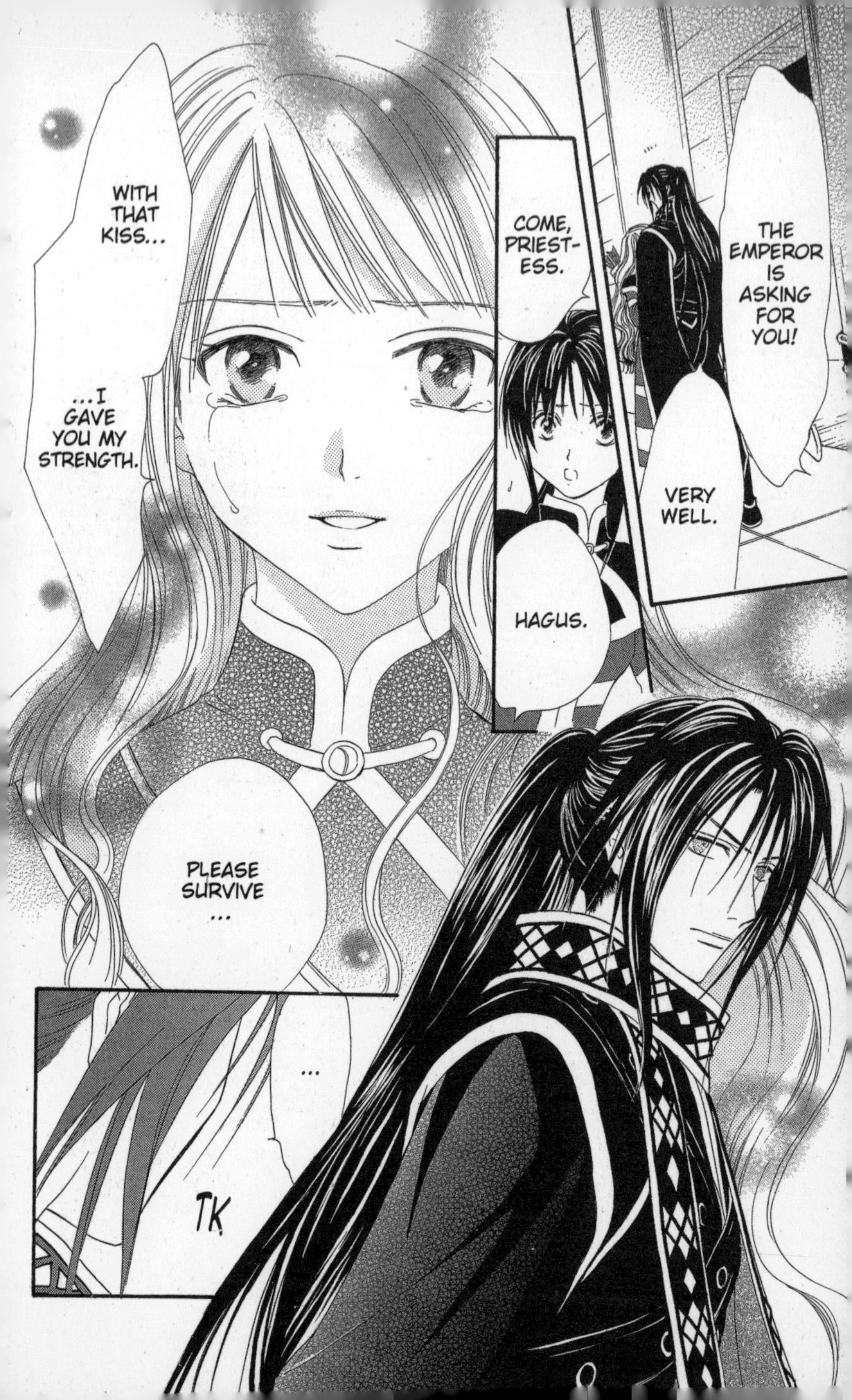
THE EMPEROR IS ASKING FOR YOU!
VERY WELL.
COME, PRIEST-ESS.
HAGUS.
WITH THAT KISS...
...I GAVE YOU MY STRENGTH.
PLEASE SURVIVE ...
...
TK

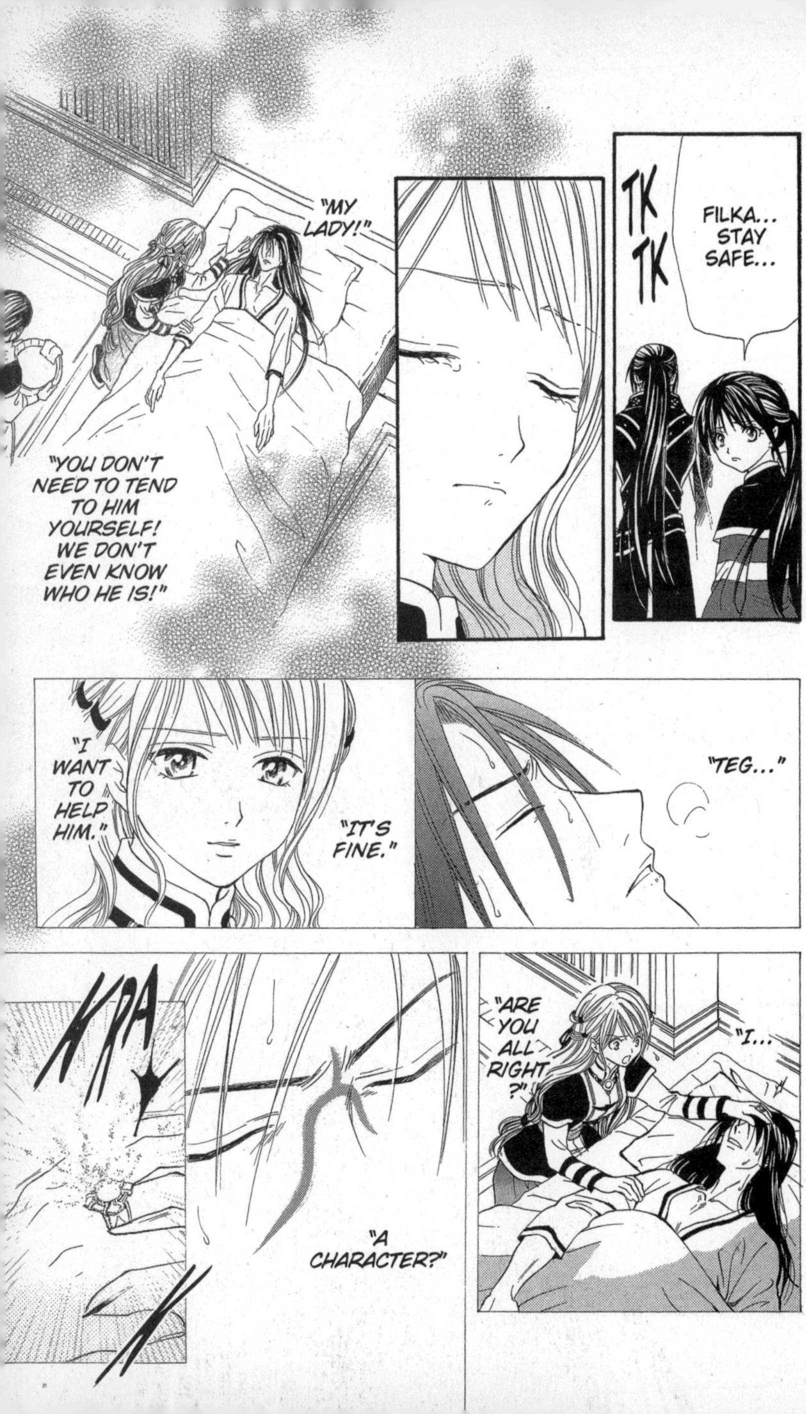
TK
TK
FILKA... STAY SAFE...
"MY LADY!"
"YOU DON'T NEED TO TEND TO HIM YOURSELF! WE DON'T EVEN KNOW WHO HE IS!"
"TEG..."
"IT'S FINE."
"I WANT TO HELP HIM."
"I...
"ARE YOU ALL RIGHT?"
KRA
K
"A CHARACTER?"

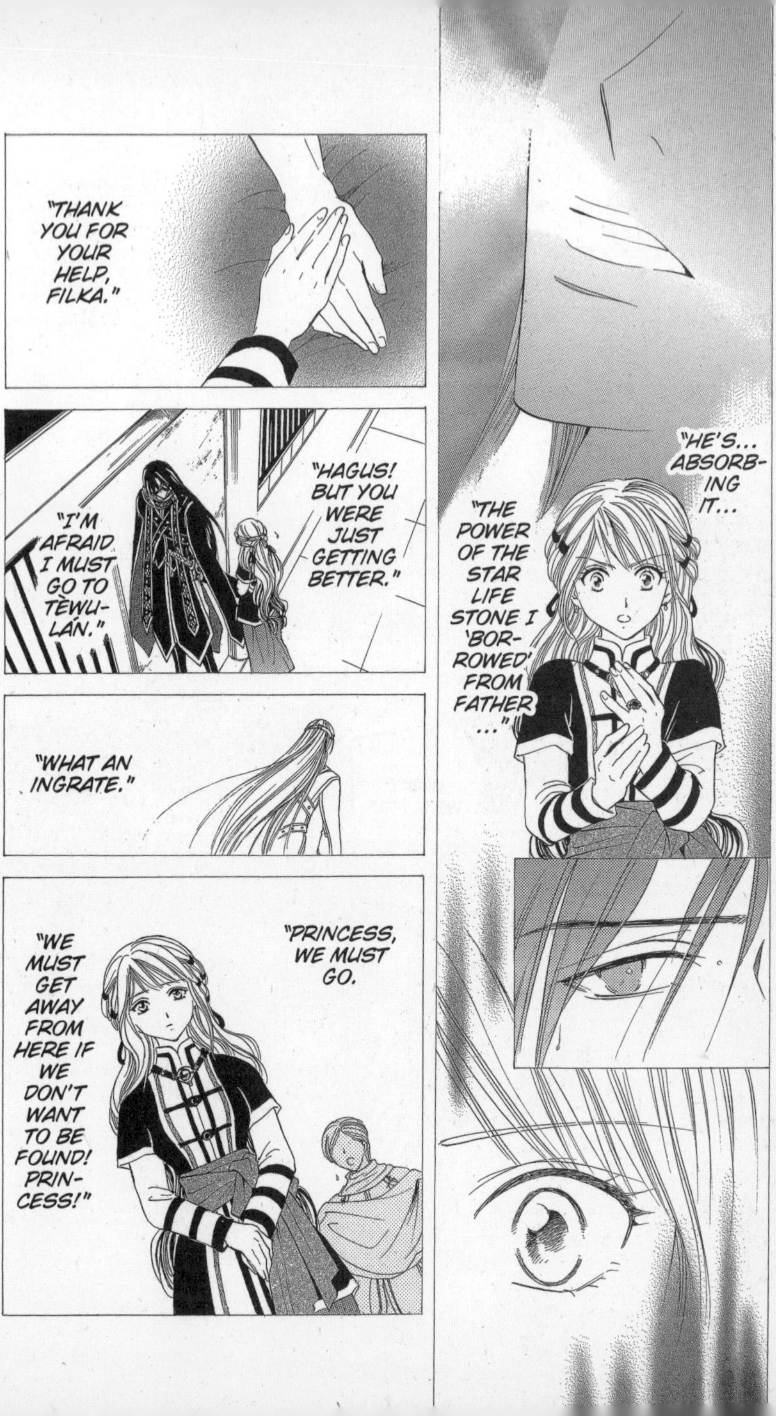
"HE'S... ABSORBING IT...
"THE POWER OF THE STAR LIFE STONE I 'BORROWED' FROM FATHER..."
"THANK YOU FOR YOUR HELP, FILKA."
"HAGUS! BUT YOU WERE JUST GETTING BETTER."
"I'M AFRAID I MUST GO TO TÈWULÁN."
"WHAT AN INGRATE."
"PRINCESS, WE MUST GO.
"WE MUST GET AWAY FROM HERE IF WE DON'T WANT TO BE FOUND! PRINCESS!"

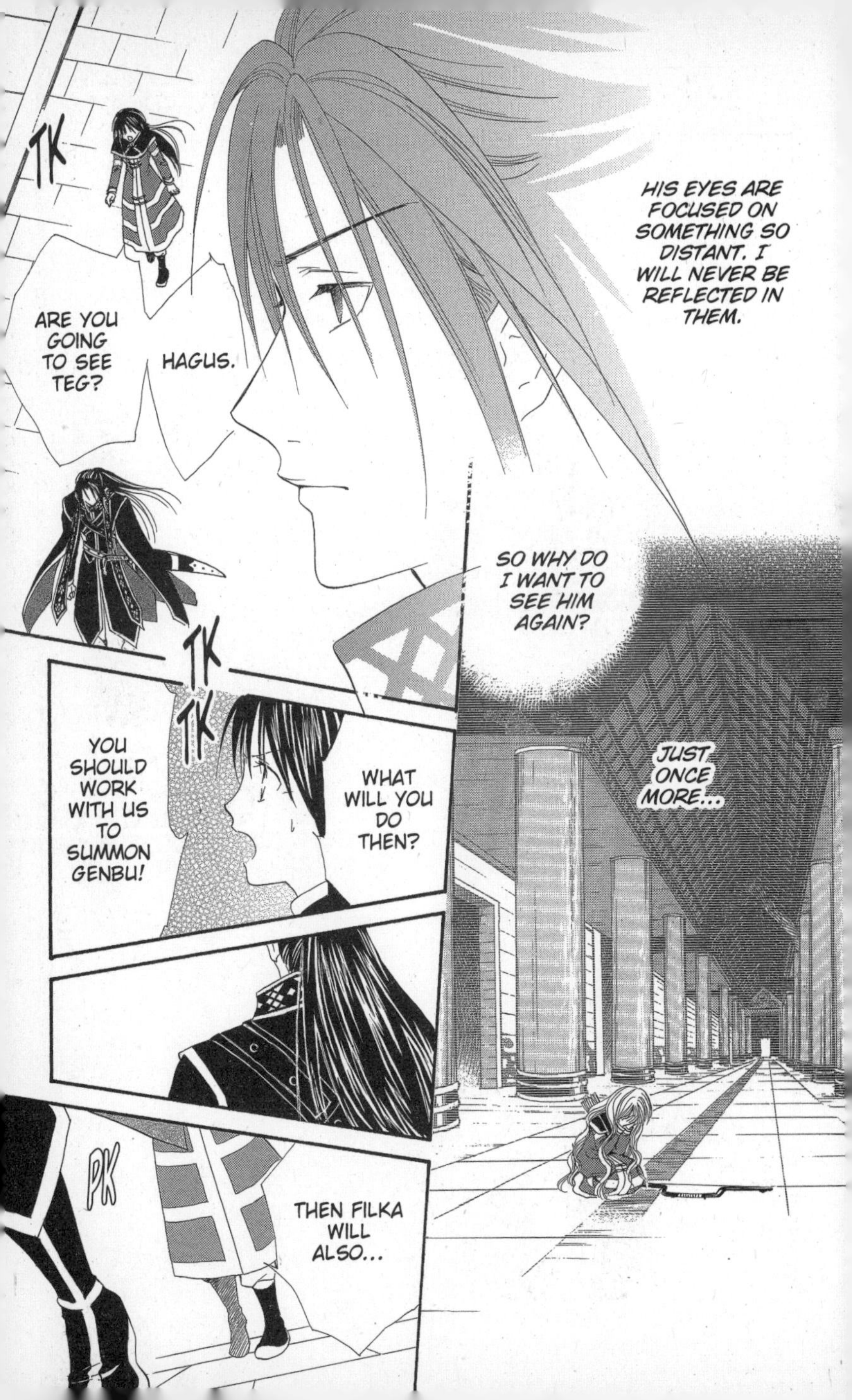
HIS EYES ARE FOCUSED ON SOMETHING SO DISTANT. I WILL NEVER BE REFLECTED IN THEM.
HAGUS.
ARE YOU GOING TO SEE TEG?
TK
SO WHY DO I WANT TO SEE HIM AGAIN?
JUST ONCE MORE...
TK
TK
WHAT WILL YOU DO THEN?
YOU SHOULD WORK WITH US TO SUMMON GENBU!
PK
THEN FILKA WILL ALSO...

KOFF
KOFF

EVEN IF THAT'S TRUE, WHAT DOES IT MATTER NOW?

YOU SHOULD BE MORE CONCERNED ABOUT YOUR *LOVER.*

YOU THINK HE AND URUKI WILL JUST KISS AND MAKE UP?

HAGUS...

THAT'S...

...THE PROPHECY GIVEN TO THE KING WAS A LIE!!

YOU'RE...

TEGIL TOOK ADVANTAGE OF THE KING'S WEAKNESS...

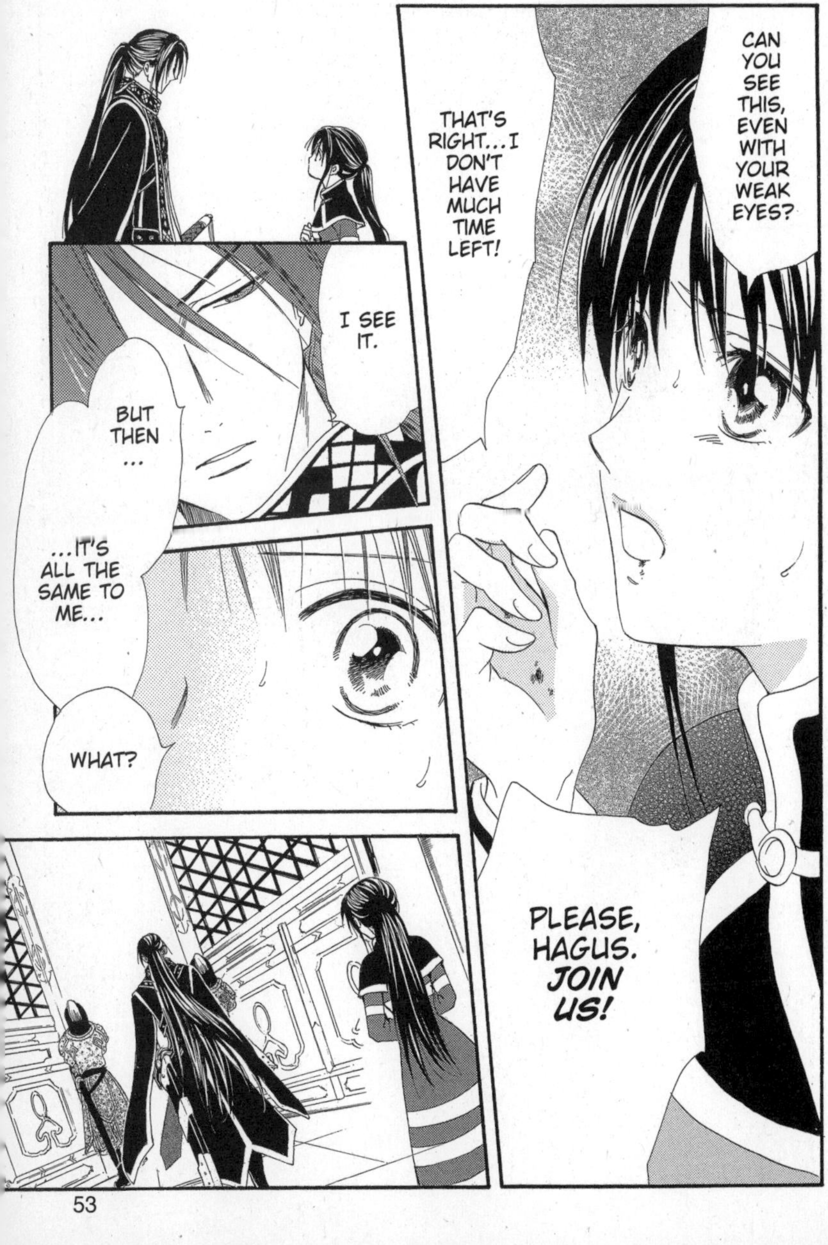
CAN YOU SEE THIS, EVEN WITH YOUR WEAK EYES?
THAT'S RIGHT...I DON'T HAVE MUCH TIME LEFT!
PLEASE, HAGUS. JOIN US!
I SEE IT.
BUT THEN...
...IT'S ALL THE SAME TO ME...
WHAT?

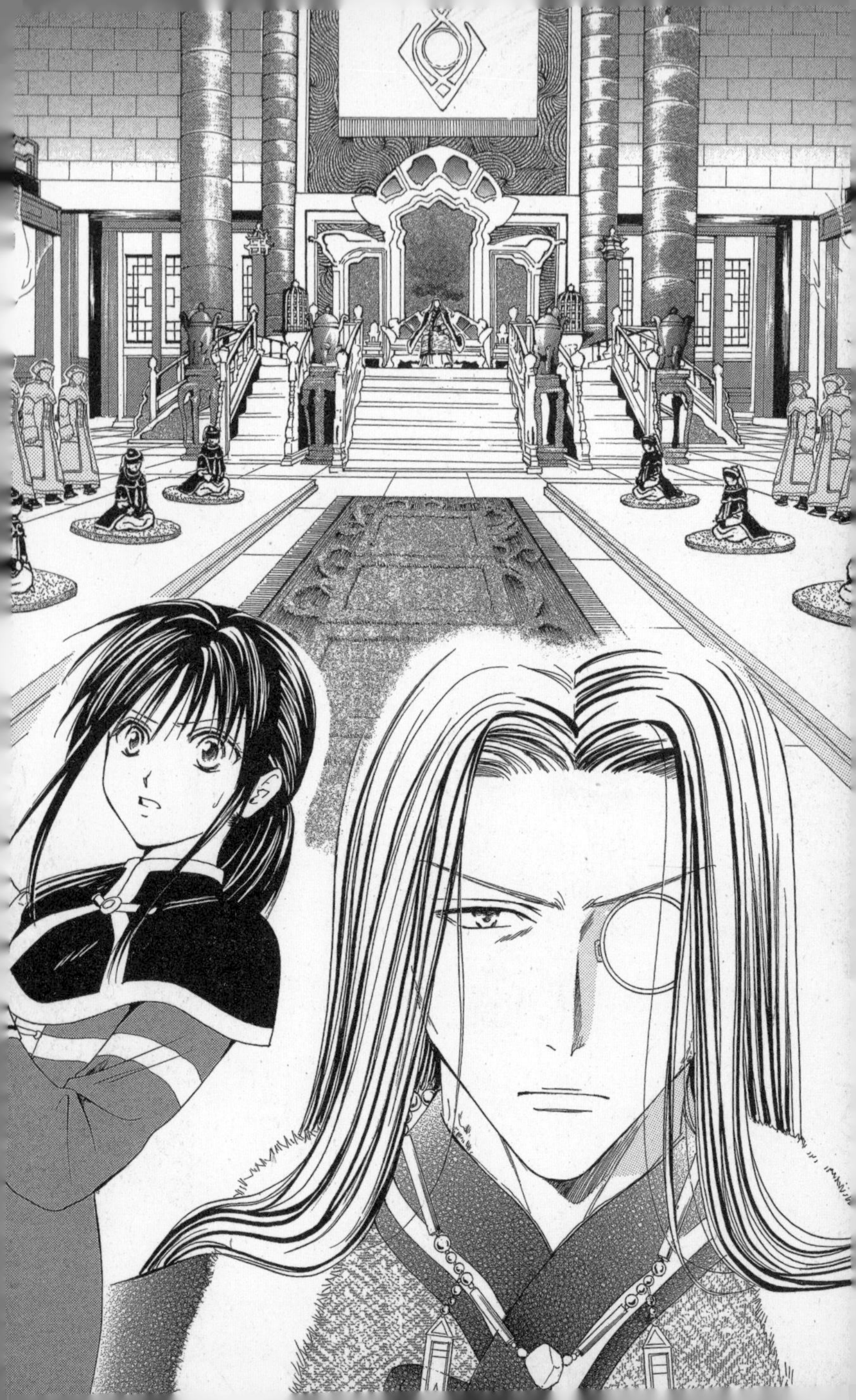

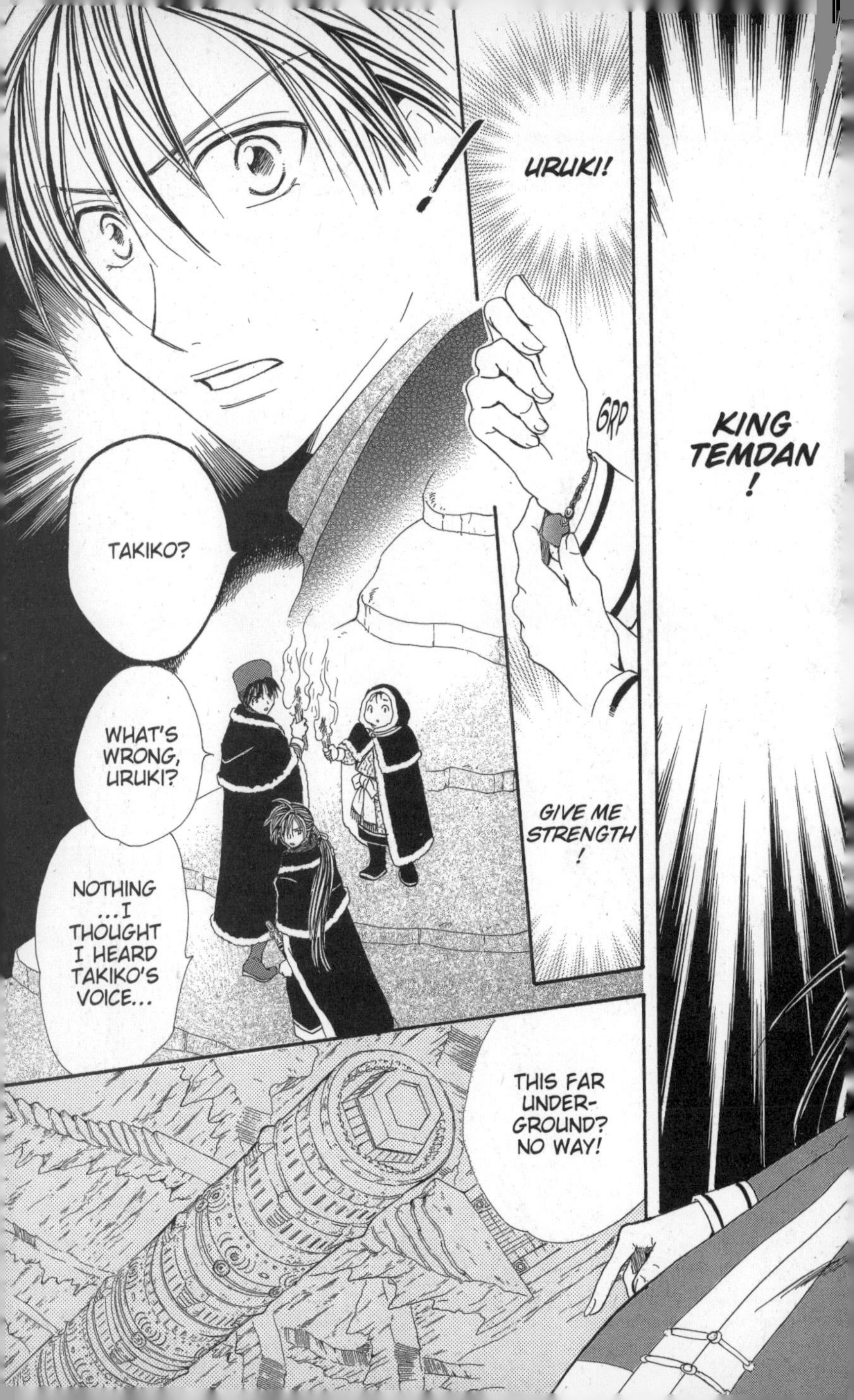
KING TEMDAN!
URUKI!
GRP
GIVE ME STRENGTH!
TAKIKO?
WHAT'S WRONG, URUKI?
NOTHING ...I THOUGHT I HEARD TAKIKO'S VOICE...
THIS FAR UNDER-GROUND? NO WAY!

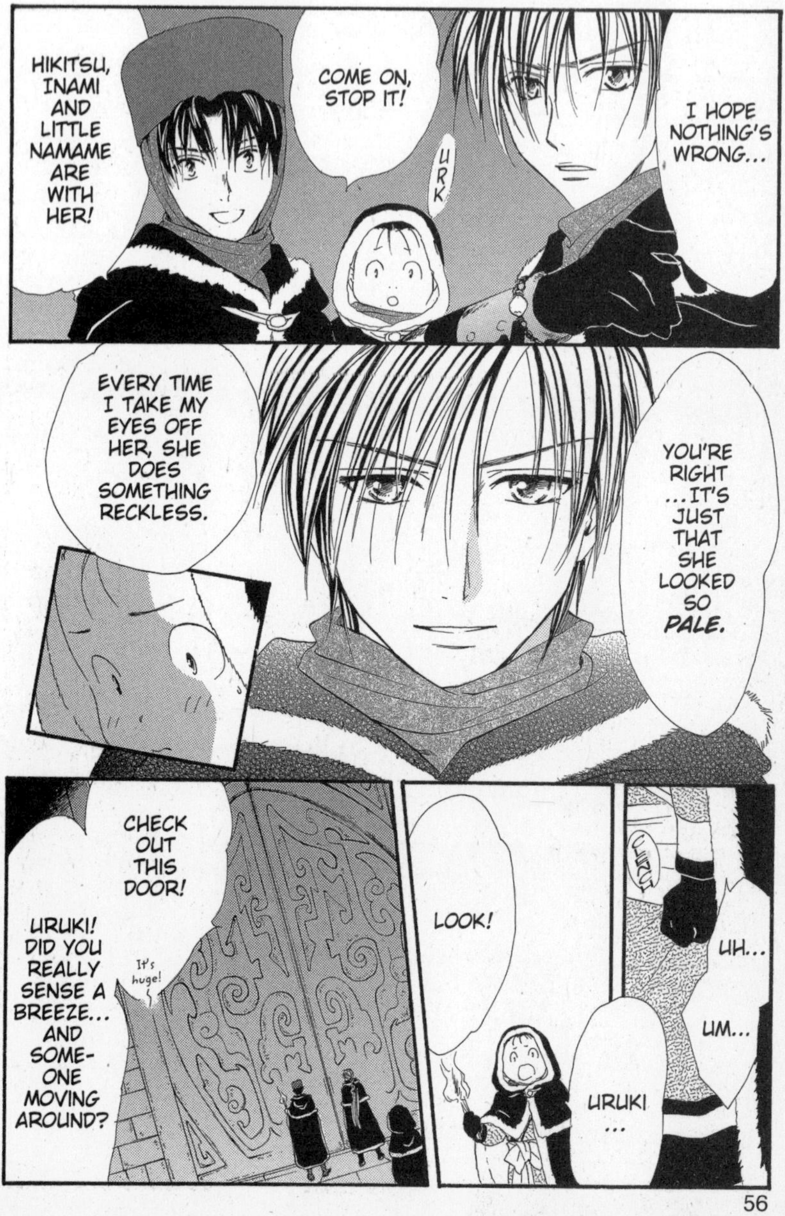
I HOPE NOTHING'S WRONG...
COME ON, STOP IT!
URK
HIKITSU, INAMI AND LITTLE NAMAME ARE WITH HER!
YOU'RE RIGHT ...IT'S JUST THAT SHE LOOKED SO PALE.
EVERY TIME I TAKE MY EYES OFF HER, SHE DOES SOMETHING RECKLESS.
CLENCH
UH...
UM...
URUKI ...
LOOK!
CHECK OUT THIS DOOR!
URUKI! DID YOU REALLY SENSE A BREEZE... AND SOMEONE MOVING AROUND?
It's huge!

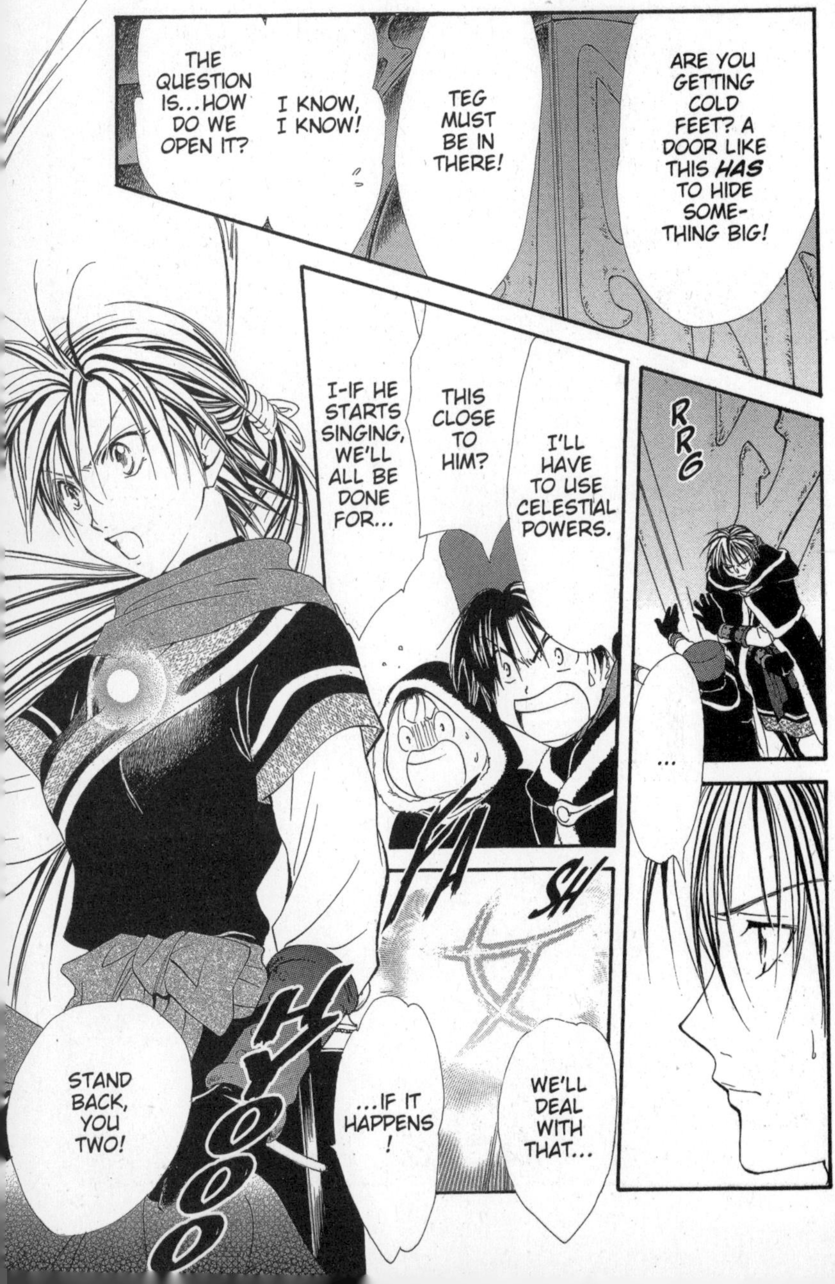
ARE YOU GETTING COLD FEET? A DOOR LIKE THIS HAS TO HIDE SOME-THING BIG!
TEG MUST BE IN THERE!
I KNOW, I KNOW!
THE QUESTION IS...HOW DO WE OPEN IT?
RRG
...
I'LL HAVE TO USE CELESTIAL POWERS.
THIS CLOSE TO HIM?
I-IF HE STARTS SINGING, WE'LL ALL BE DONE FOR...
WE'LL DEAL WITH THAT...
...IF IT HAPPENS!
SH
HA
STAND BACK, YOU TWO!
HYOOOO

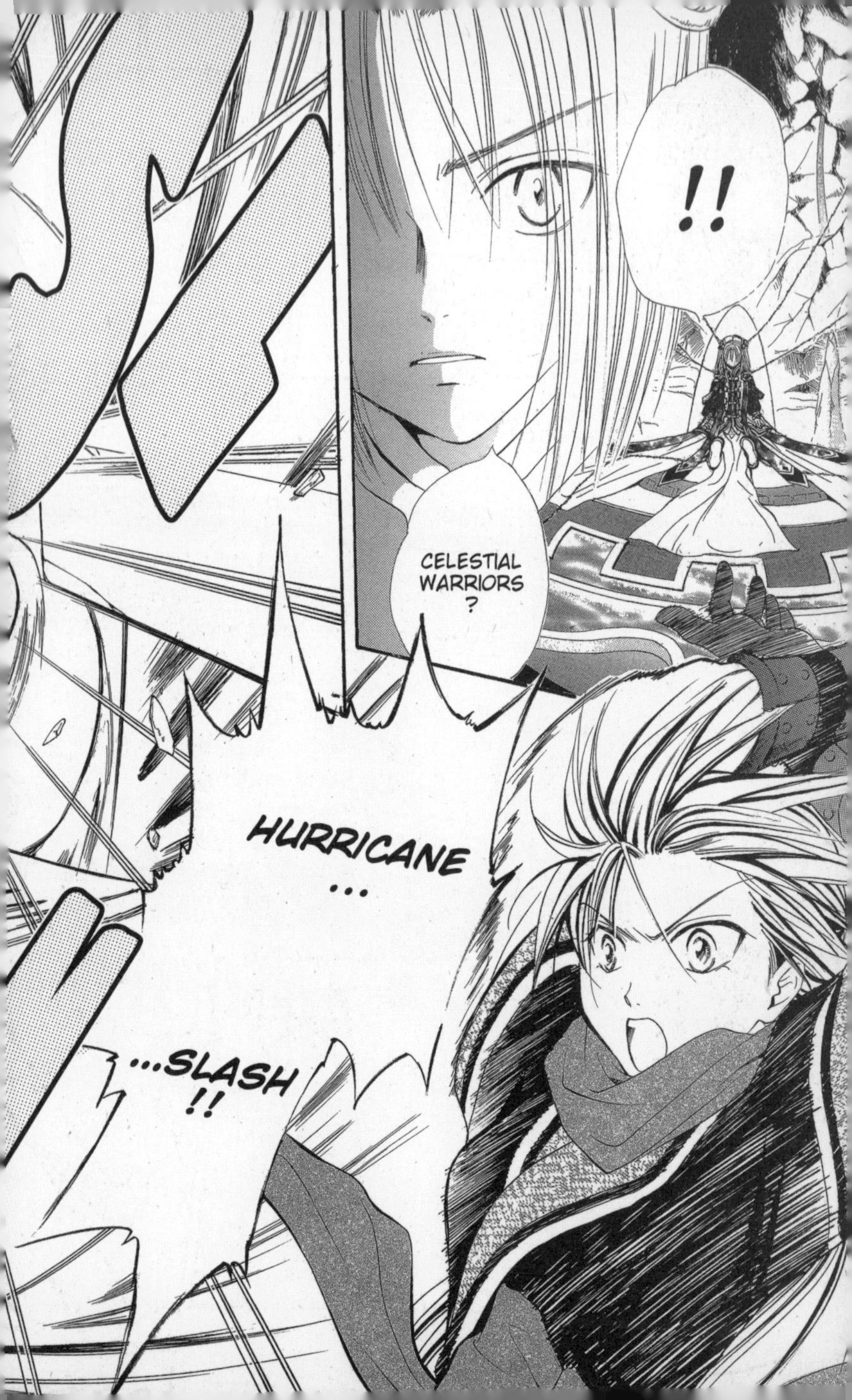
!!
CELESTIAL WARRIORS ?
HURRICANE ...
...SLASH !!

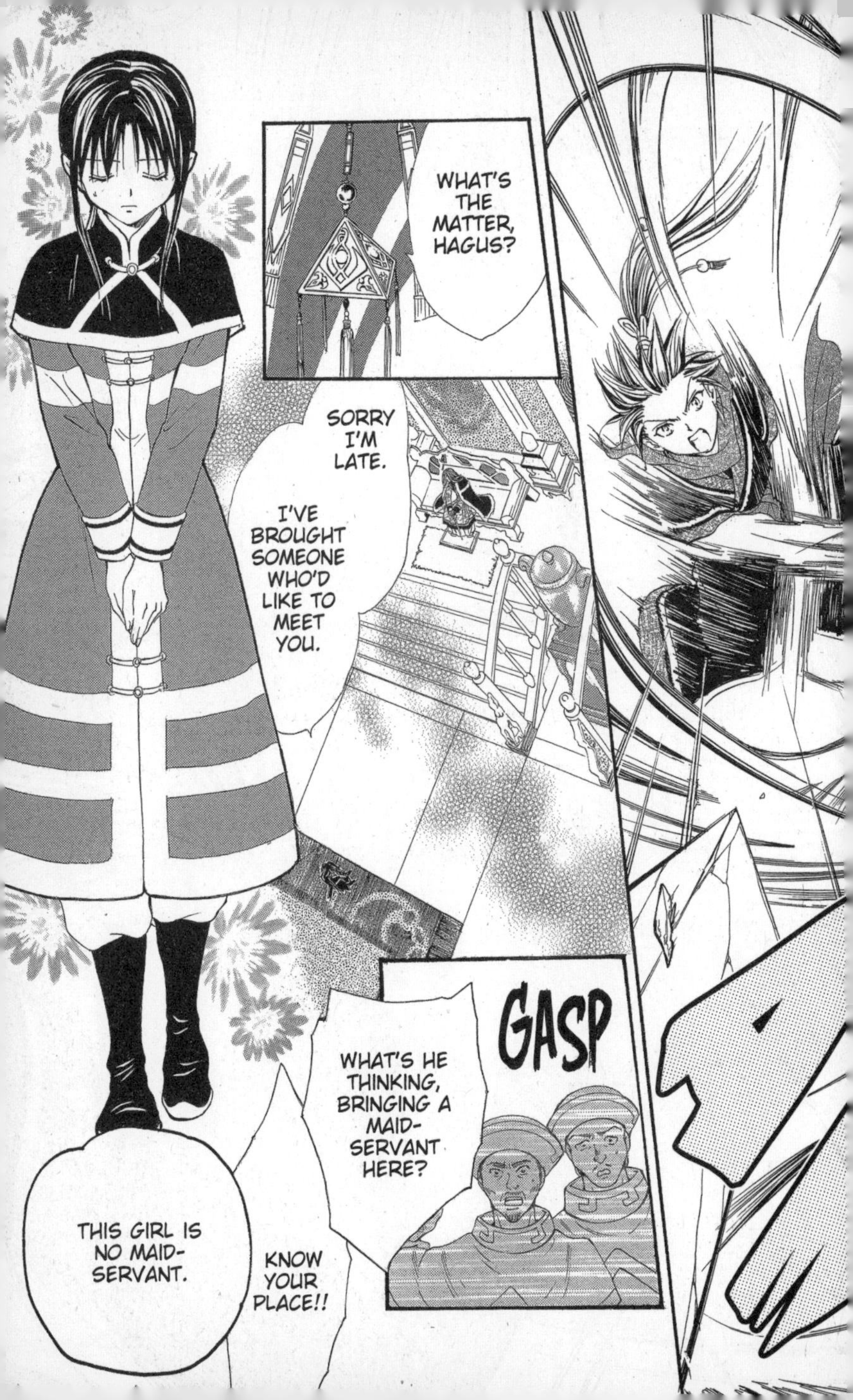
WHAT'S THE MATTER, HAGUS?
SORRY I'M LATE.
I'VE BROUGHT SOMEONE WHO'D LIKE TO MEET YOU.
GASP
WHAT'S HE THINKING, BRINGING A MAID-SERVANT HERE?
KNOW YOUR PLACE!!
THIS GIRL IS NO MAID-SERVANT.

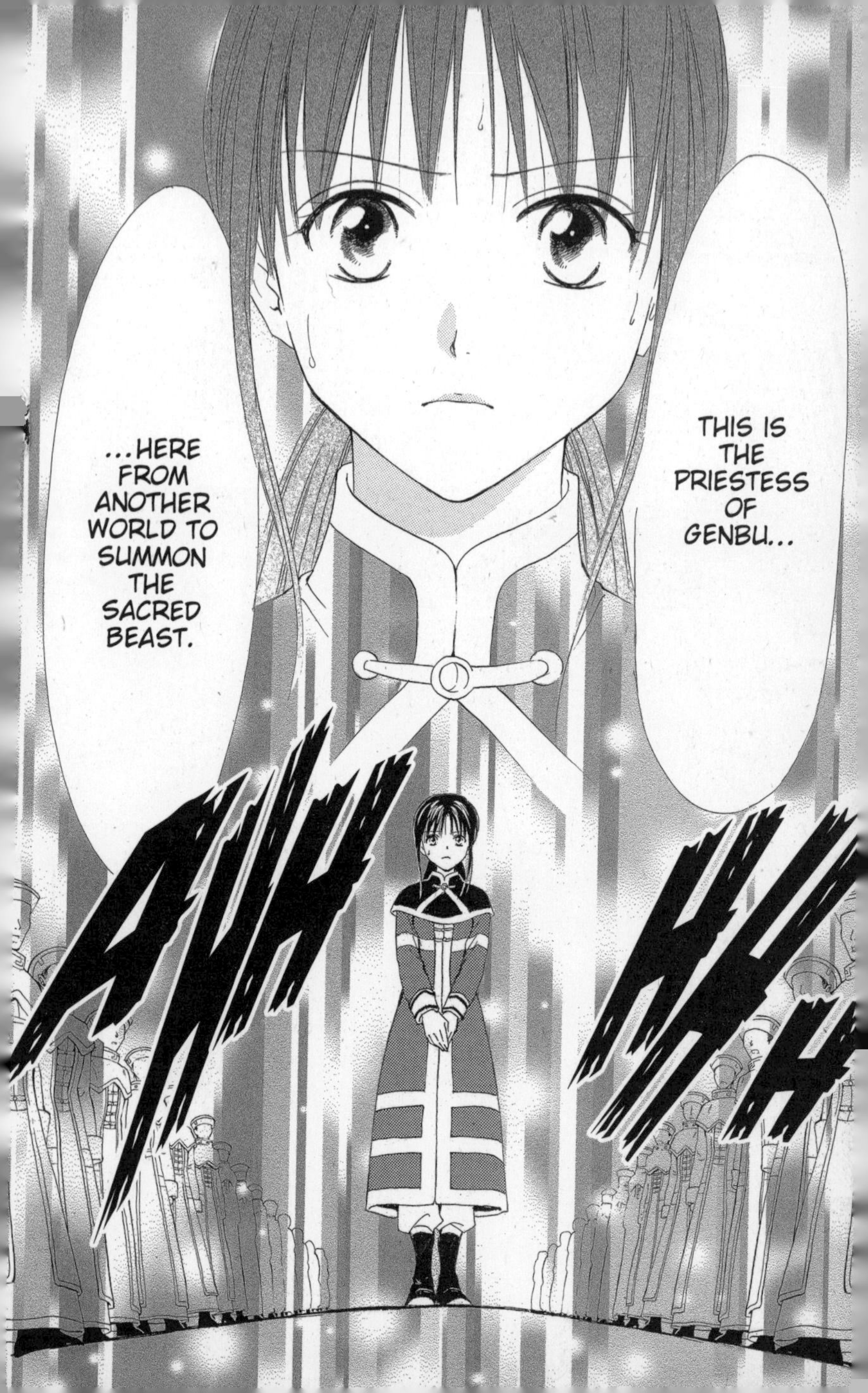
THIS IS THE PRIESTESS OF GENBU...
...HERE FROM ANOTHER WORLD TO SUMMON THE SACRED BEAST.

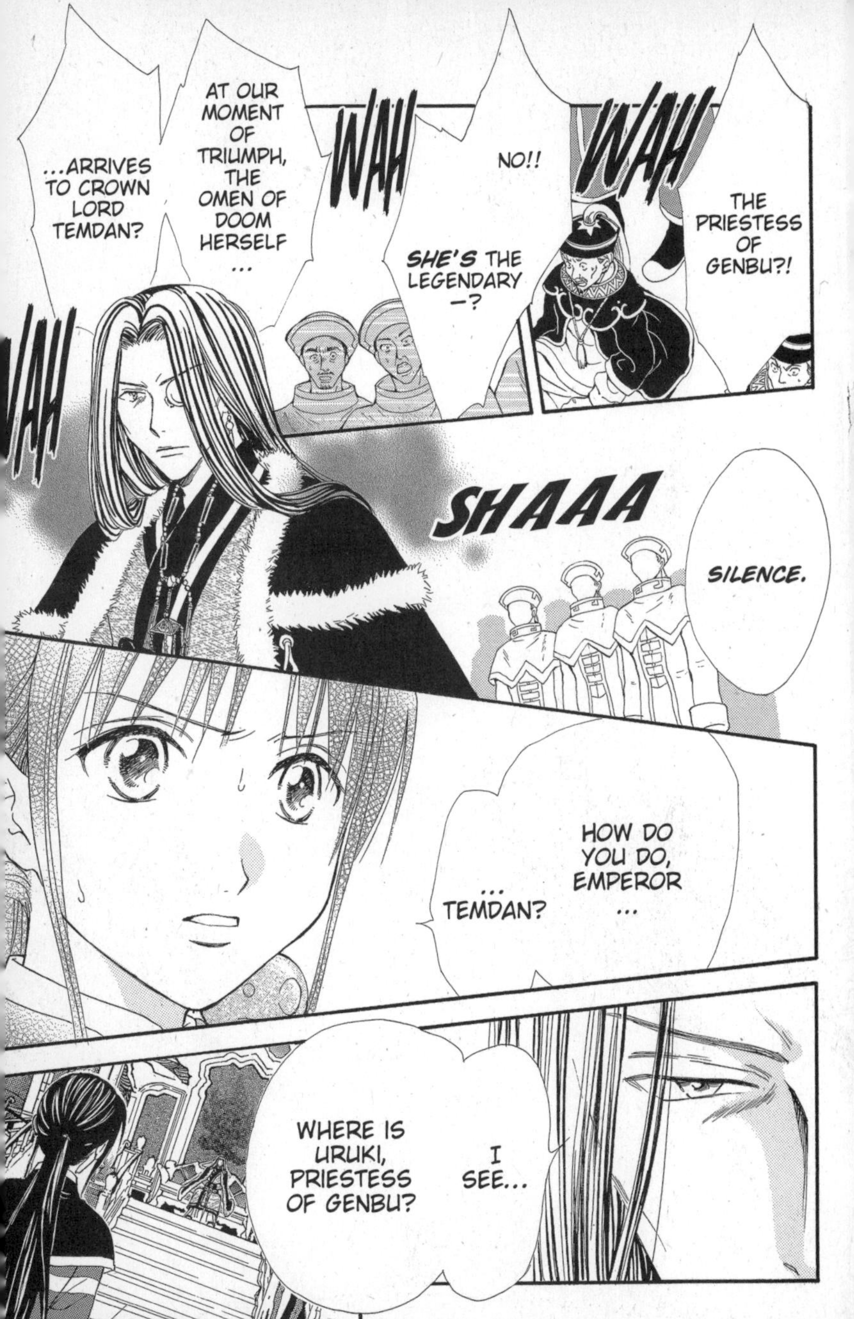
WAH
THE PRIESTESS OF GENBU?!
NO!!
SHE'S THE LEGENDARY—?
WAH
AT OUR MOMENT OF TRIUMPH, THE OMEN OF DOOM HERSELF...
...ARRIVES TO CROWN LORD TEMDAN?
WAH
SHAAA
SILENCE.
HOW DO YOU DO, EMPEROR...
...TEMDAN?
I SEE...
WHERE IS URUKI, PRIESTESS OF GENBU?

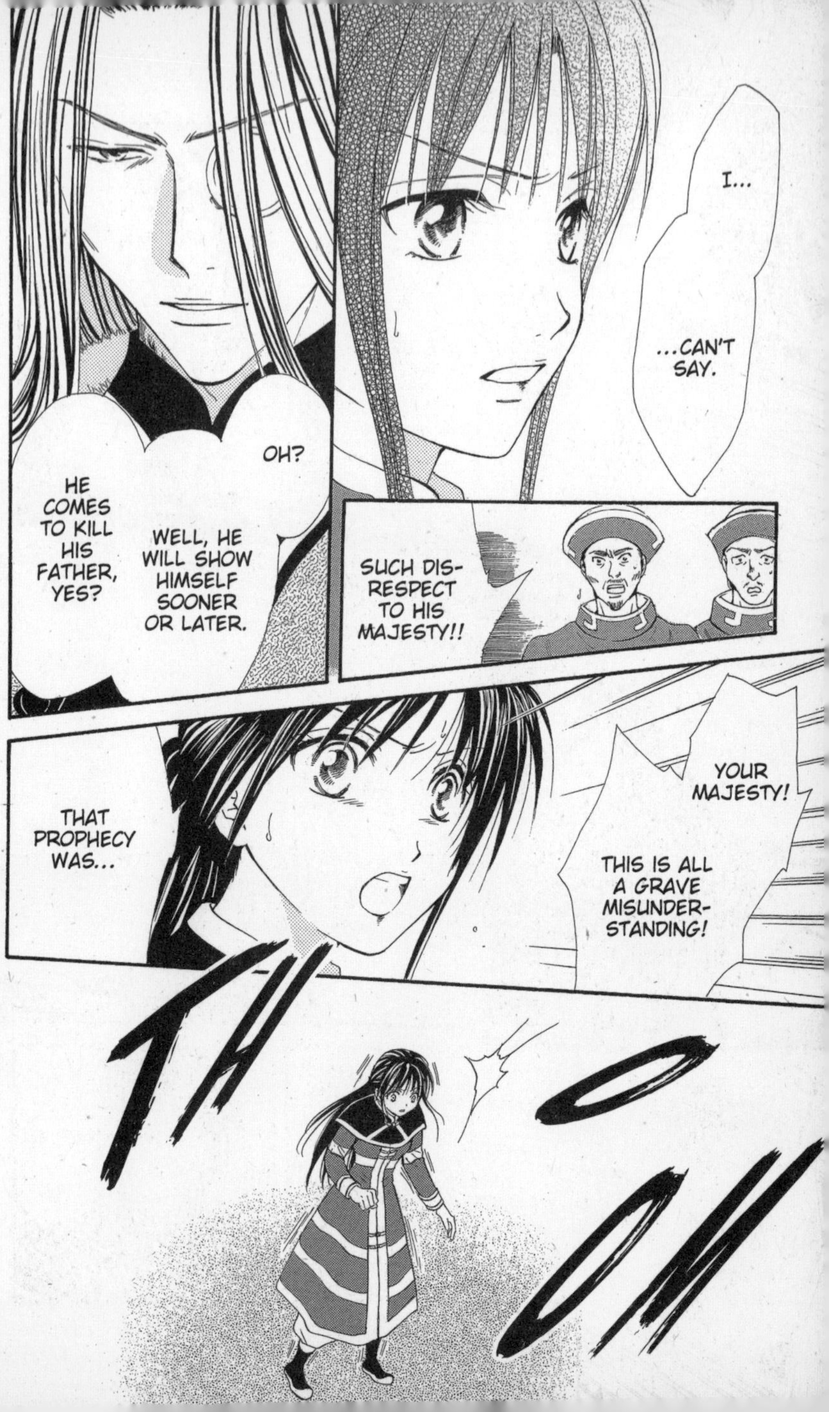
I...
...CAN'T SAY.
SUCH DIS-RESPECT TO HIS MAJESTY!!
OH?
WELL, HE WILL SHOW HIMSELF SOONER OR LATER.
HE COMES TO KILL HIS FATHER, YES?
YOUR MAJESTY!
THIS IS ALL A GRAVE MISUNDER-STANDING!
THAT PROPHECY WAS...

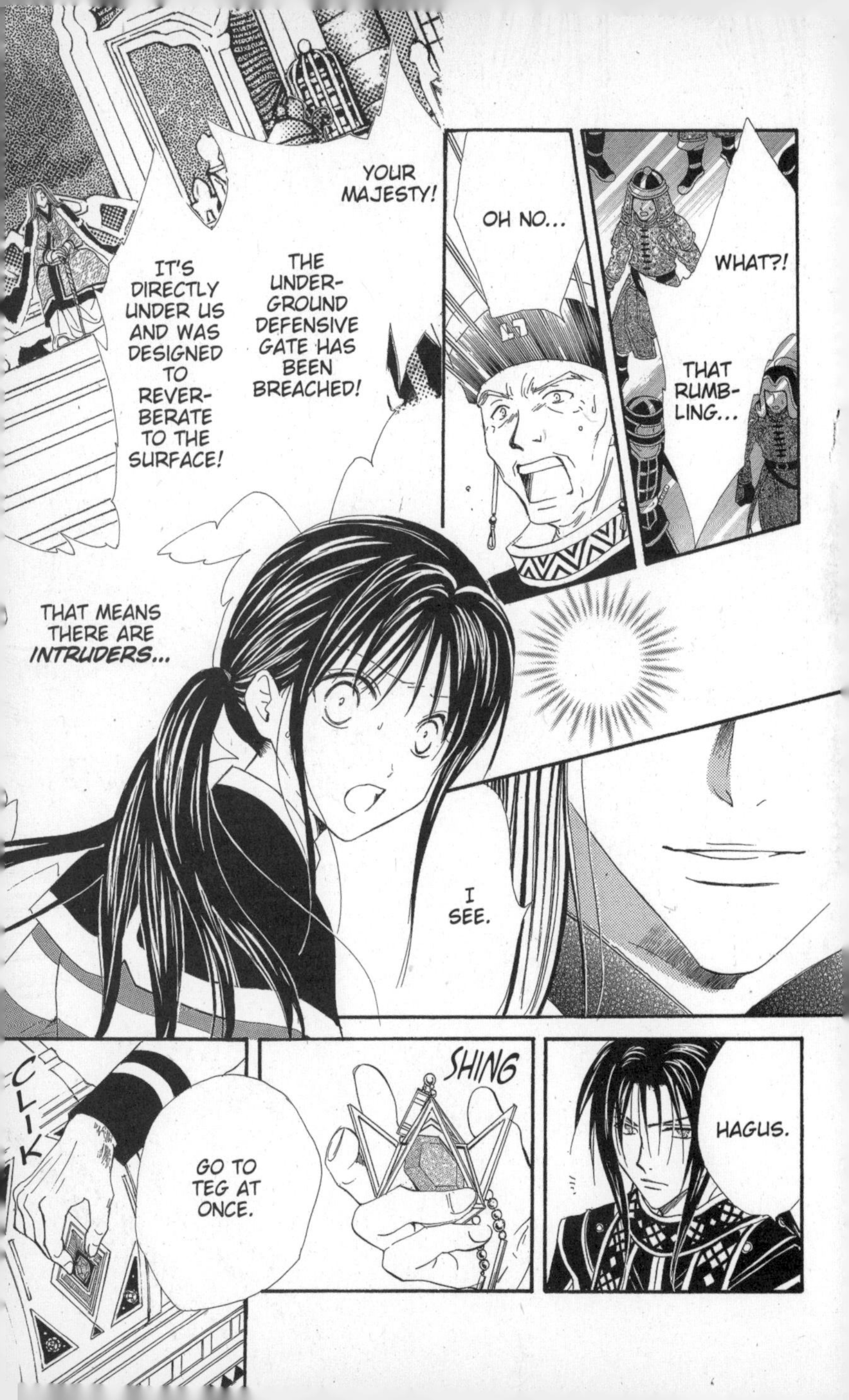
WHAT?!
THAT RUMBLING...
OH NO...
YOUR MAJESTY!
THE UNDERGROUND DEFENSIVE GATE HAS BEEN BREACHED!
IT'S DIRECTLY UNDER US AND WAS DESIGNED TO REVERBERATE TO THE SURFACE!
I SEE.
THAT MEANS THERE ARE *INTRUDERS*...
HAGUS.
SHING
GO TO TEG AT ONCE.
CLIK

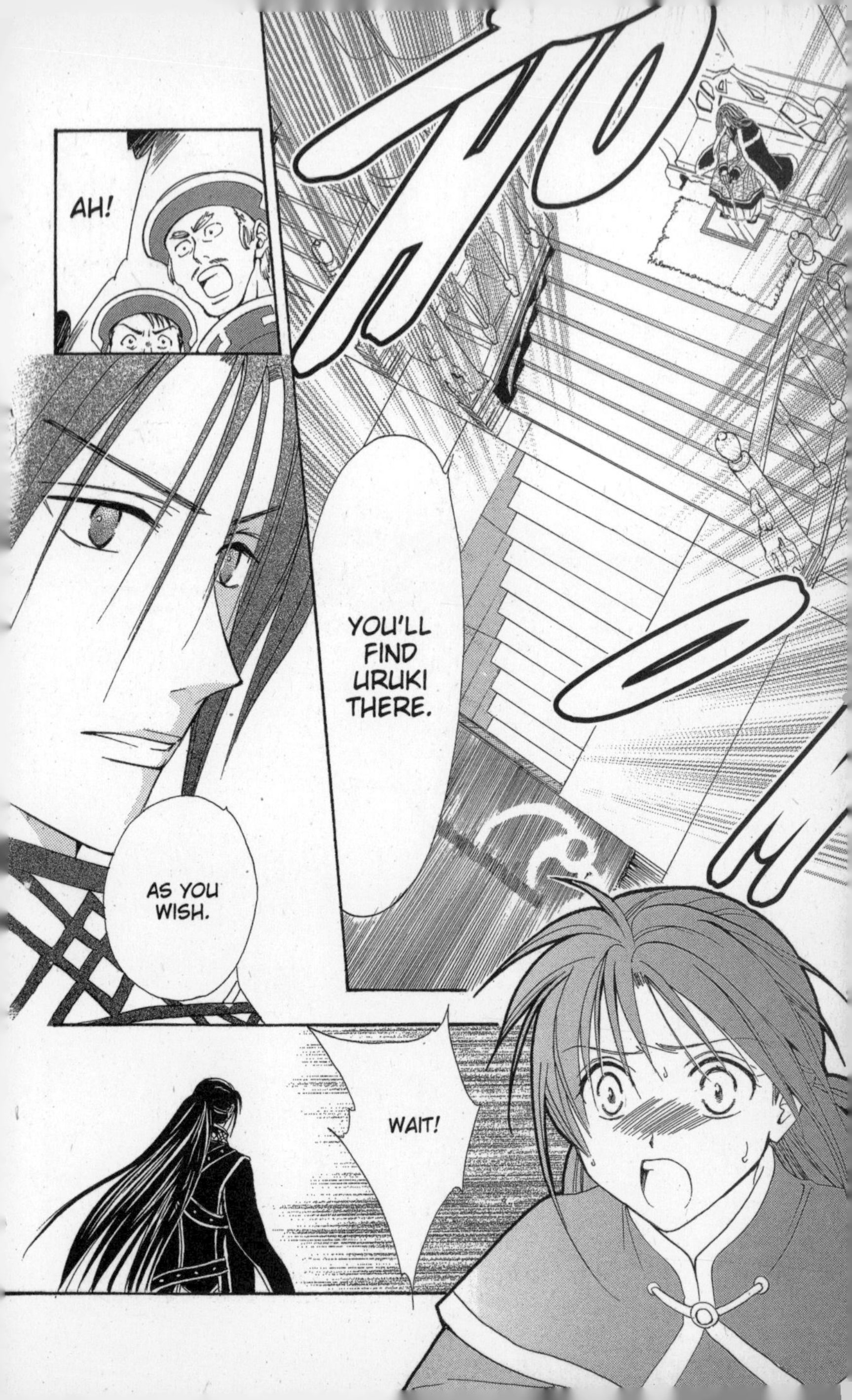
ZOOM
AH!
YOU'LL FIND URUKI THERE.
AS YOU WISH.
WAIT!

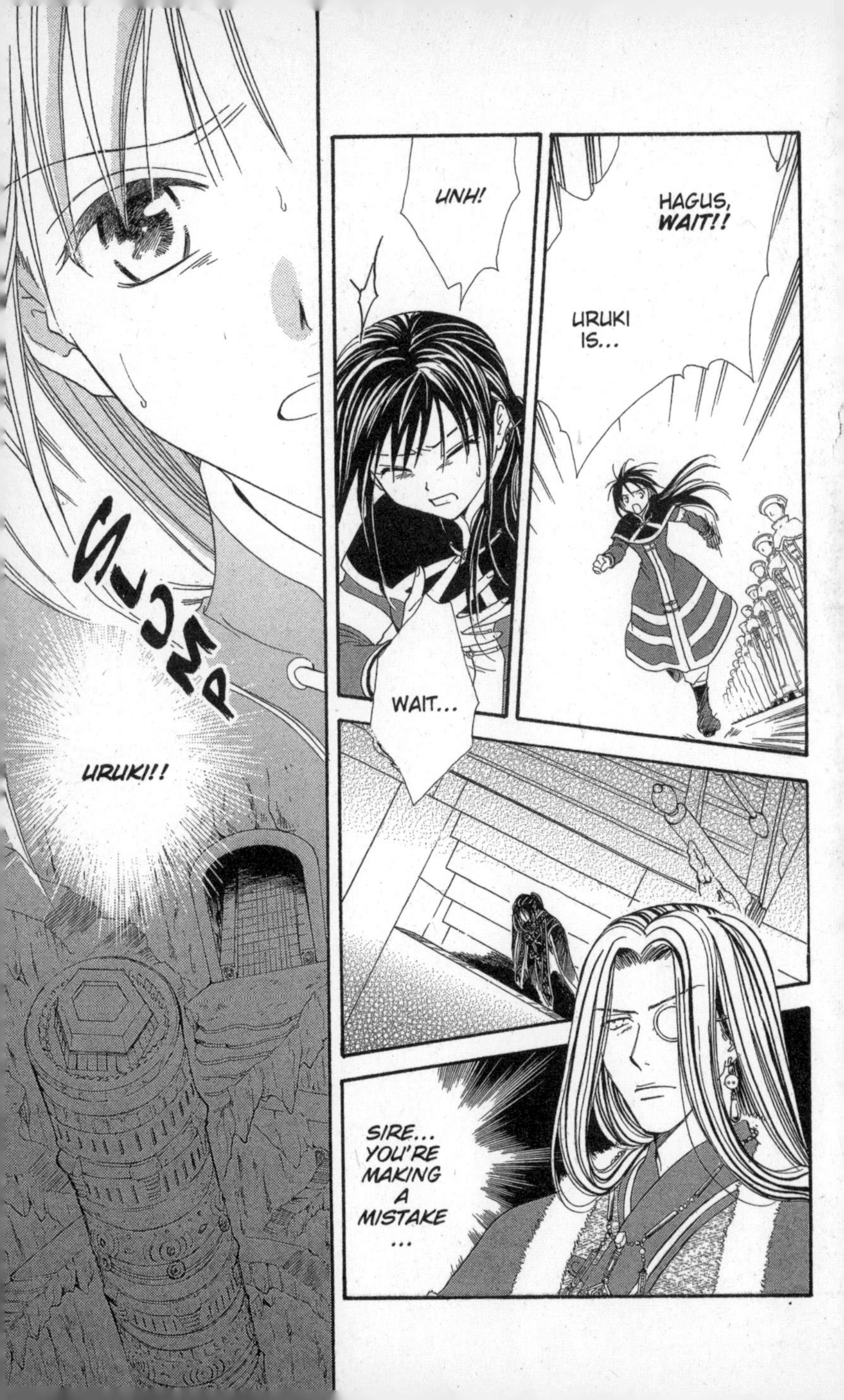
HAGUS, WAIT!!
URUKI IS...
UNH!
WAIT...
SIRE... YOU'RE MAKING A MISTAKE ...
SLUMP
URUKI!!

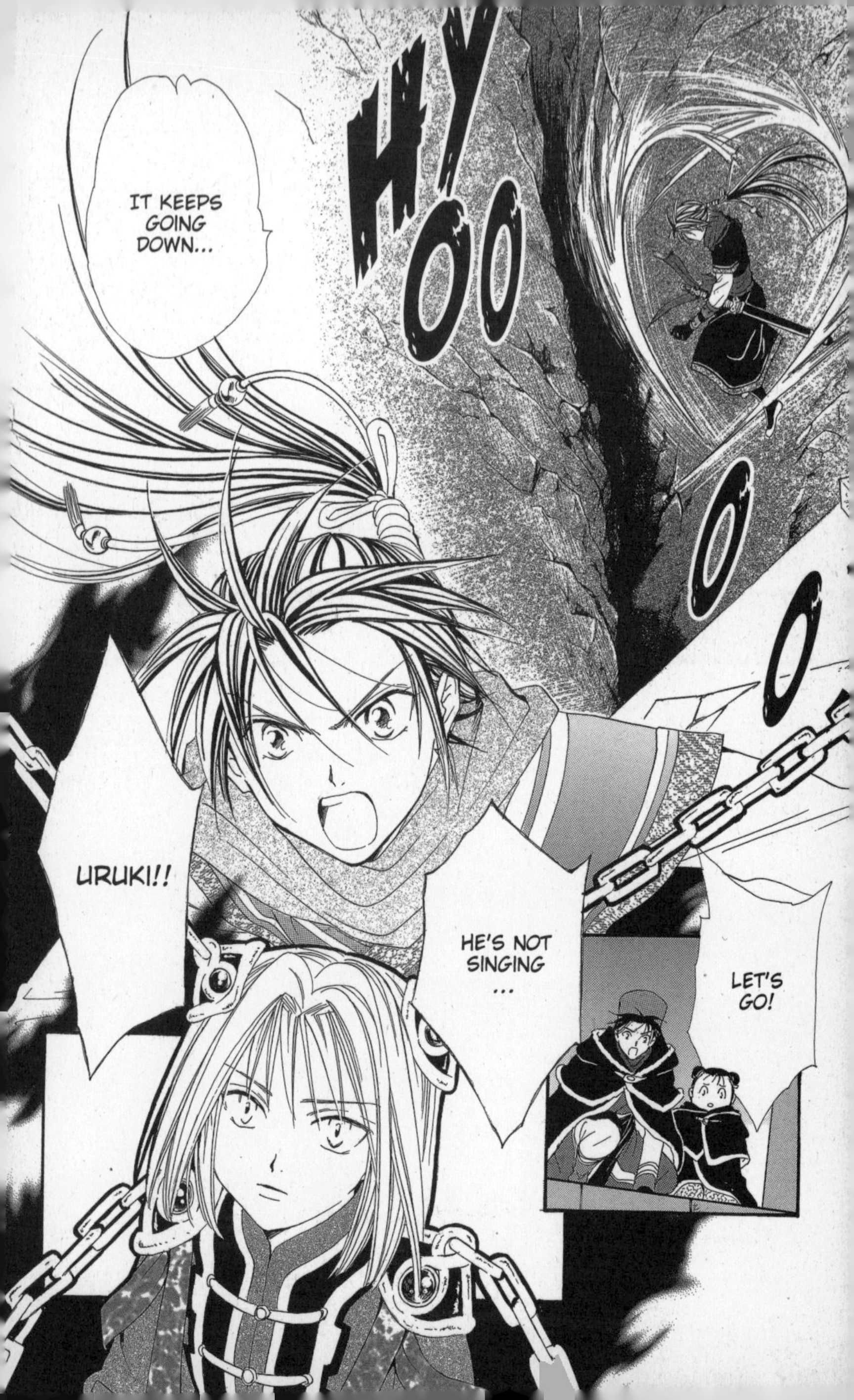
HYOOOOO
IT KEEPS GOING DOWN...
URUKI!!
HE'S NOT SINGING ...
LET'S GO!

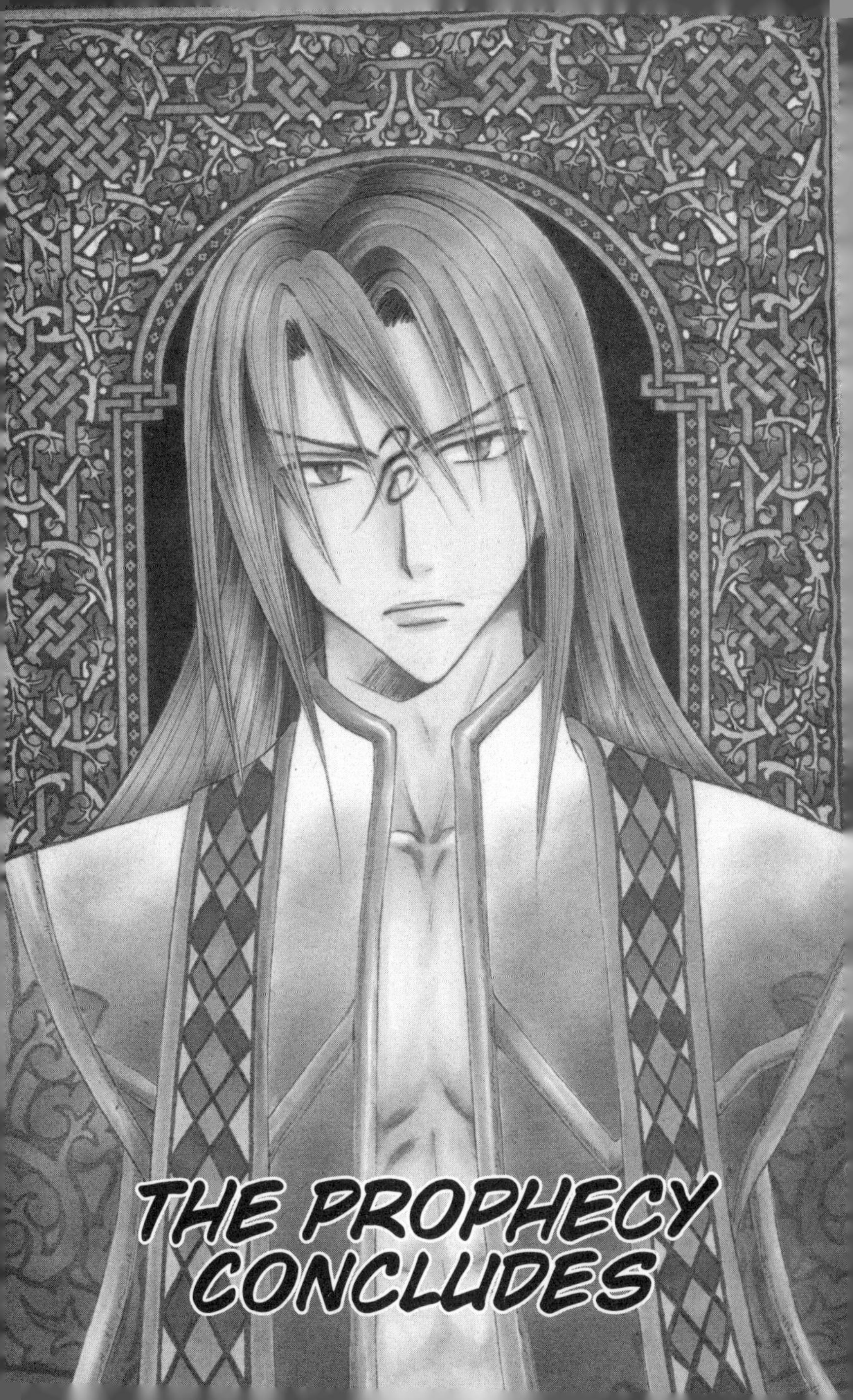
THE PROPHECY
CONCLUDES

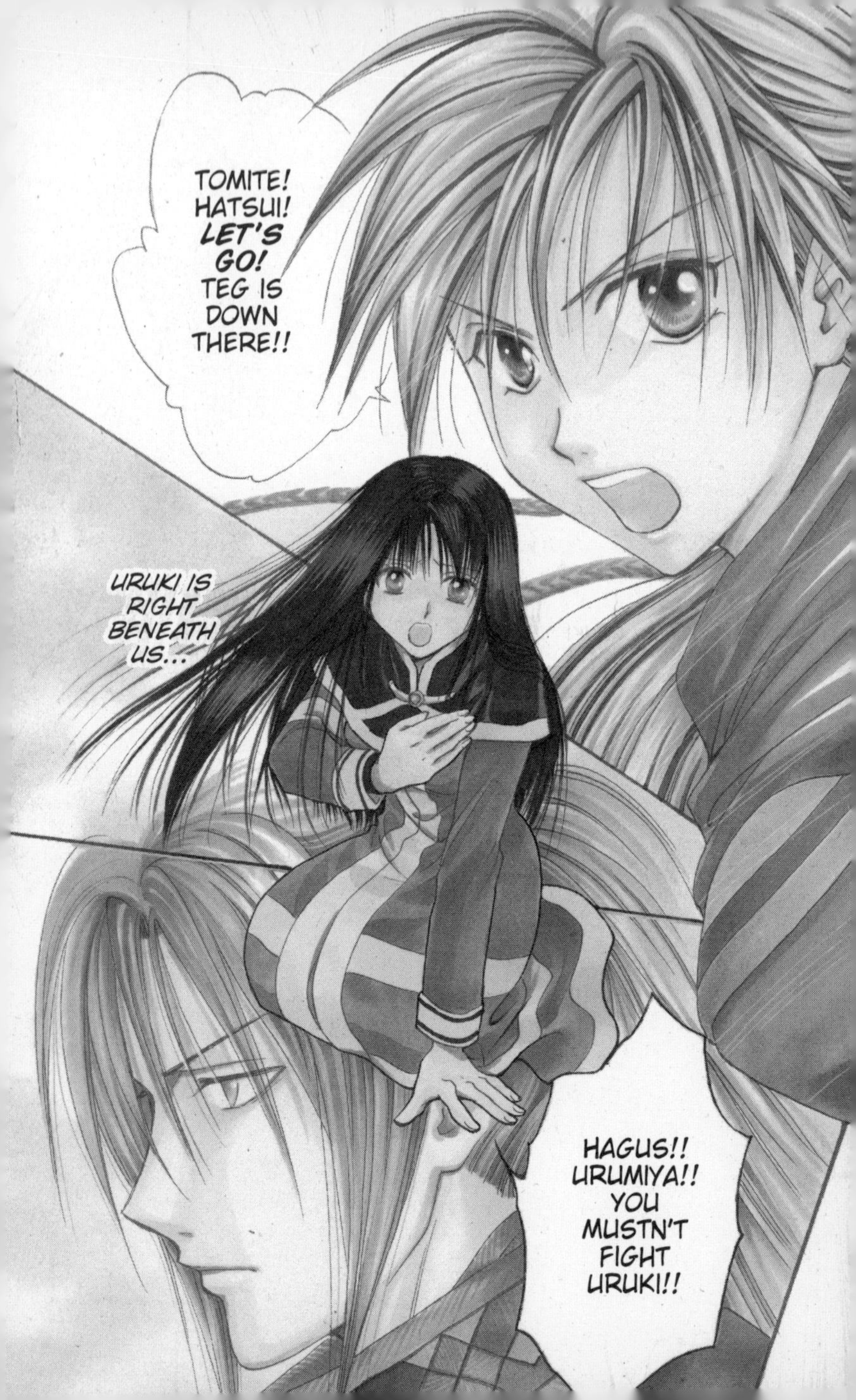
TOMITE! HATSUI! LET'S GO! TEG IS DOWN THERE!!
URUKI IS RIGHT BENEATH US...
HAGUS!! URUMIYA!! YOU MUSTN'T FIGHT URUKI!!

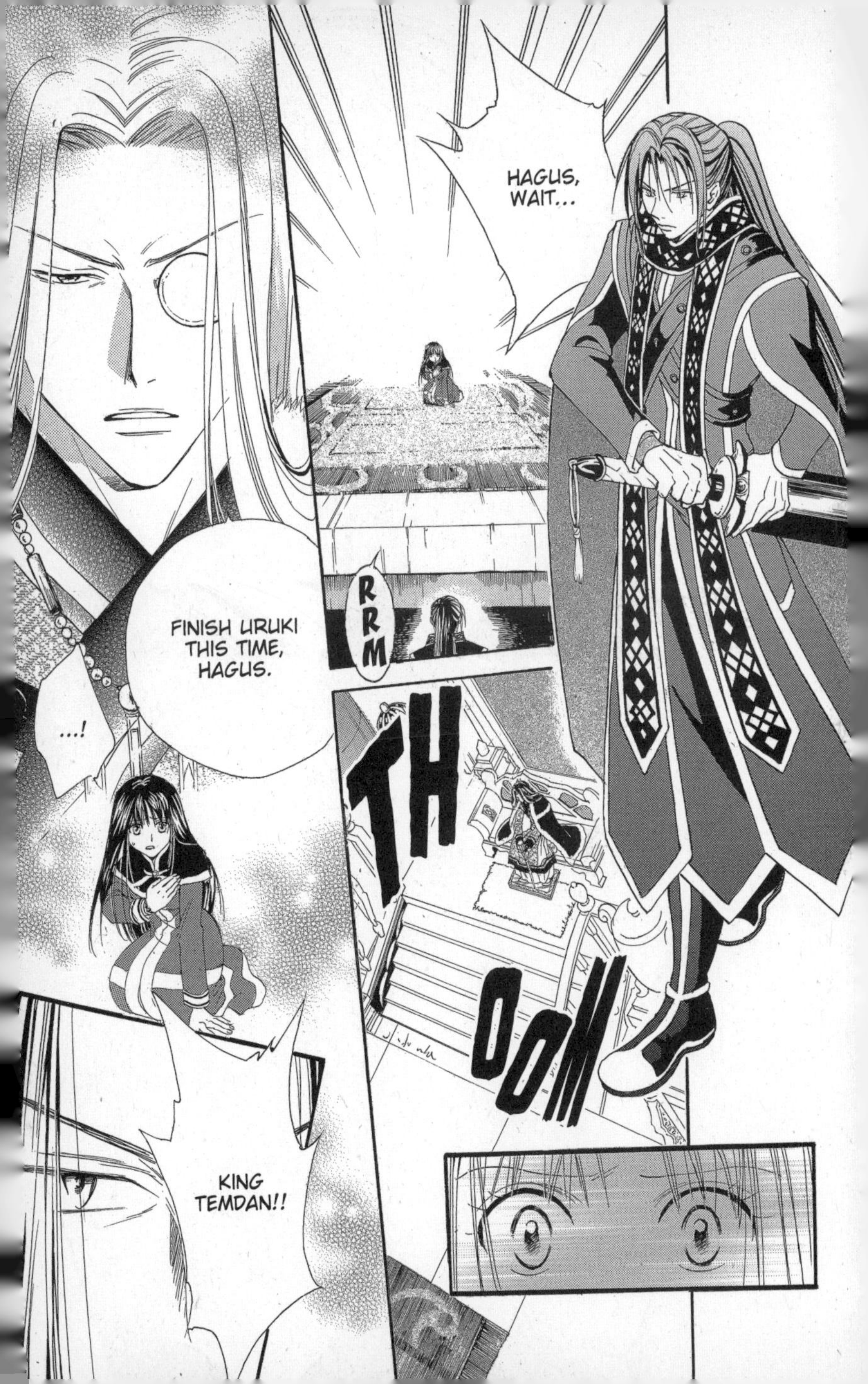
HAGUS, WAIT...
RRM
THOOM
FINISH URUKI THIS TIME, HAGUS.
...!
KING TEMDAN!!

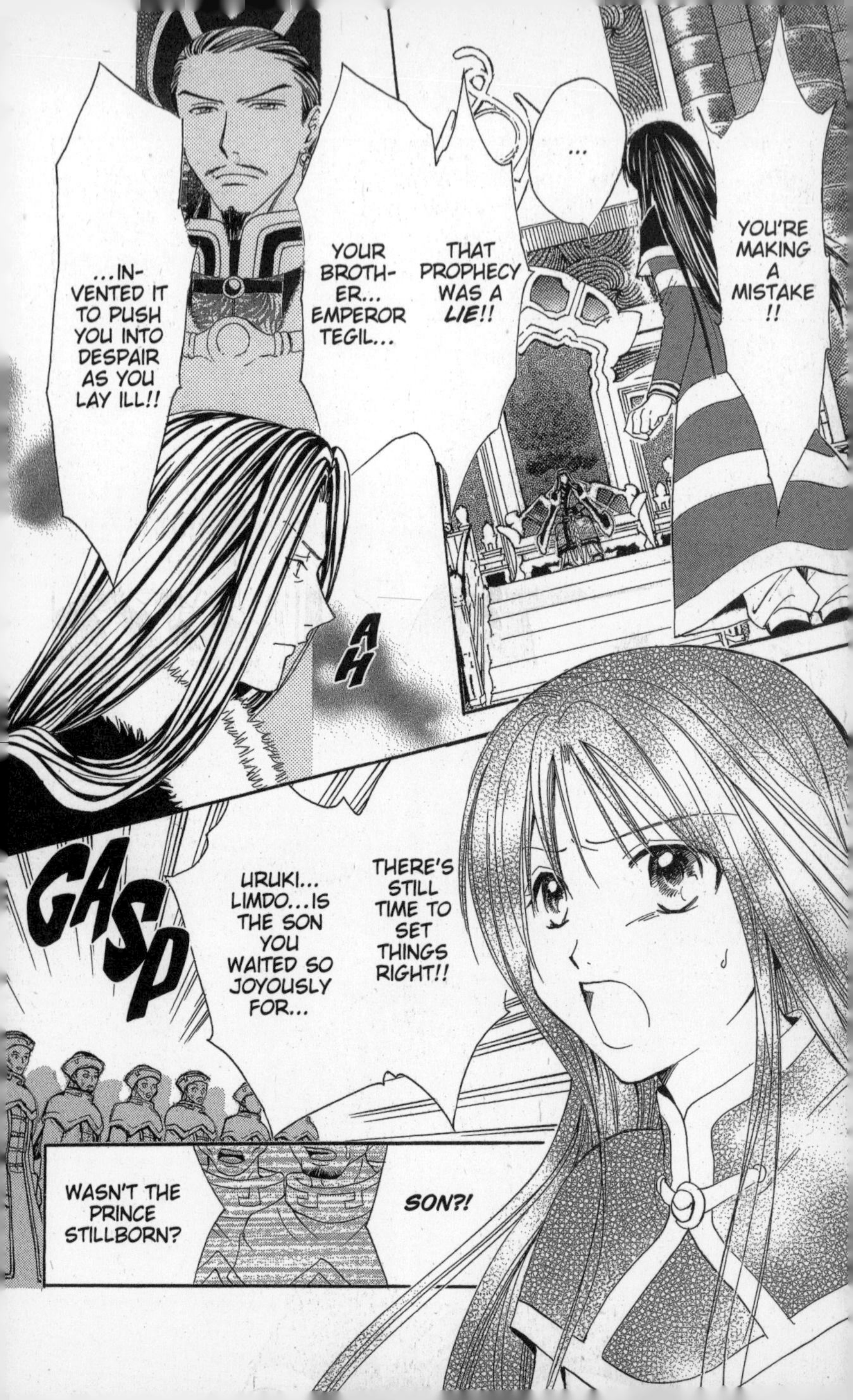
YOU'RE MAKING A MISTAKE!!
...
THAT PROPHECY WAS A LIE!!
YOUR BROTH-ER... EMPEROR TEGIL...
...IN-VENTED IT TO PUSH YOU INTO DESPAIR AS YOU LAY ILL!!
AH
THERE'S STILL TIME TO SET THINGS RIGHT!!
URUKI... LIMDO...IS THE SON YOU WAITED SO JOYOUSLY FOR...
GASP
SON?!
WASN'T THE PRINCE STILLBORN?

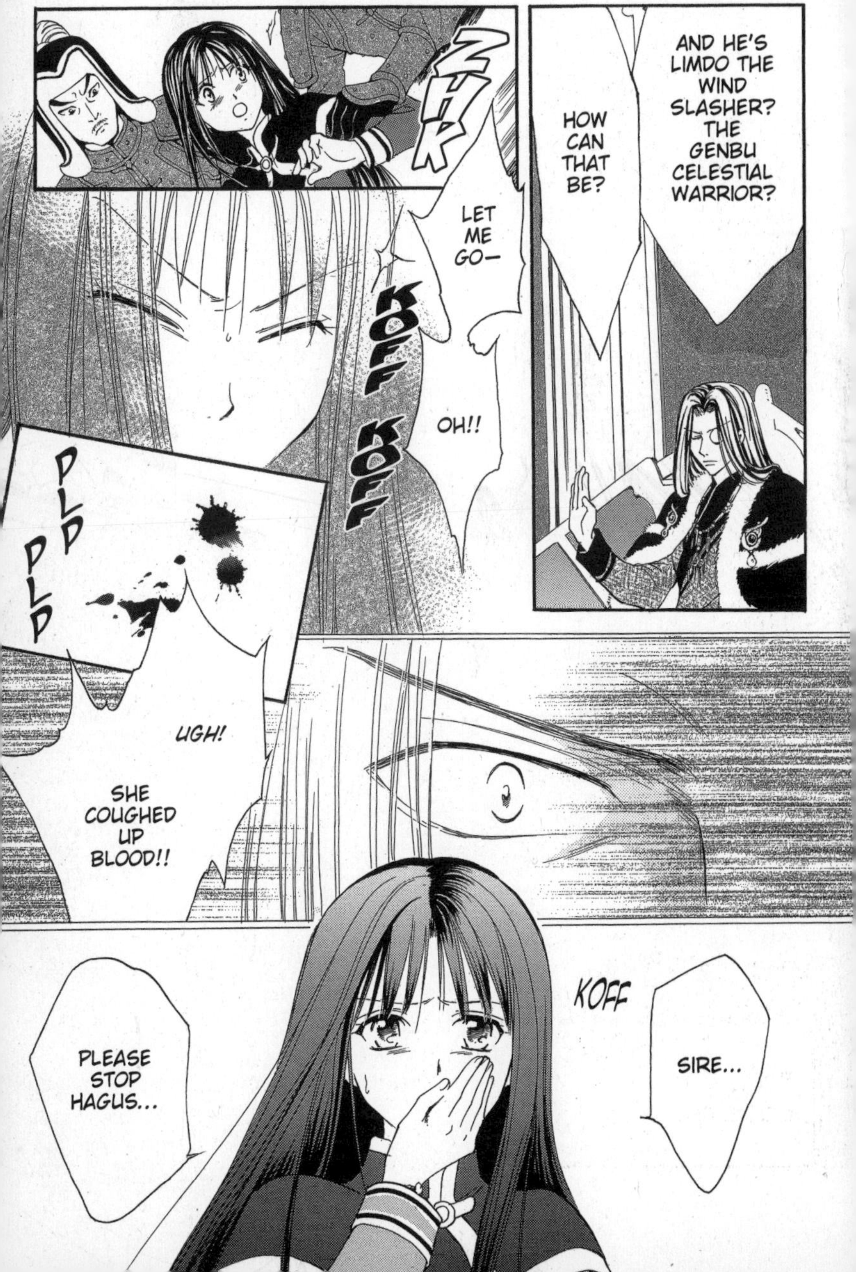
AND HE'S LIMDO THE WIND SLASHER? THE GENBU CELESTIAL WARRIOR?
HOW CAN THAT BE?
ZHK
LET ME GO—
KOFF KOFF
OH!!
PLD PLD
UGH!
SHE COUGHED UP BLOOD!!
KOFF
SIRE...
PLEASE STOP HAGUS...

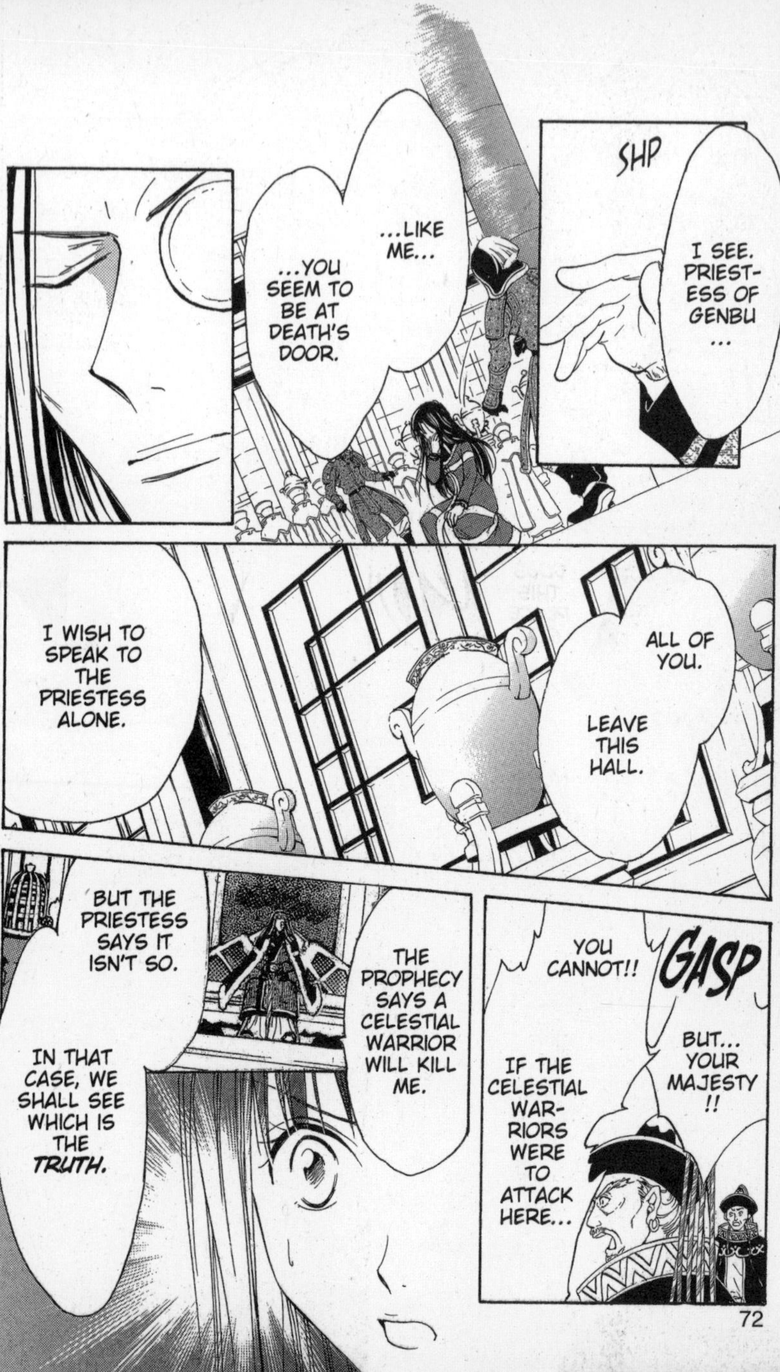
SHP
I SEE. PRIESTESS OF GENBU ...
...YOU SEEM TO BE AT DEATH'S DOOR. ...LIKE ME...
ALL OF YOU. LEAVE THIS HALL.
I WISH TO SPEAK TO THE PRIESTESS ALONE.
GASP
BUT... YOUR MAJESTY !!
YOU CANNOT!!
IF THE CELESTIAL WARRIORS WERE TO ATTACK HERE...
THE PROPHECY SAYS A CELESTIAL WARRIOR WILL KILL ME.
BUT THE PRIESTESS SAYS IT ISN'T SO.
IN THAT CASE, WE SHALL SEE WHICH IS THE *TRUTH*.

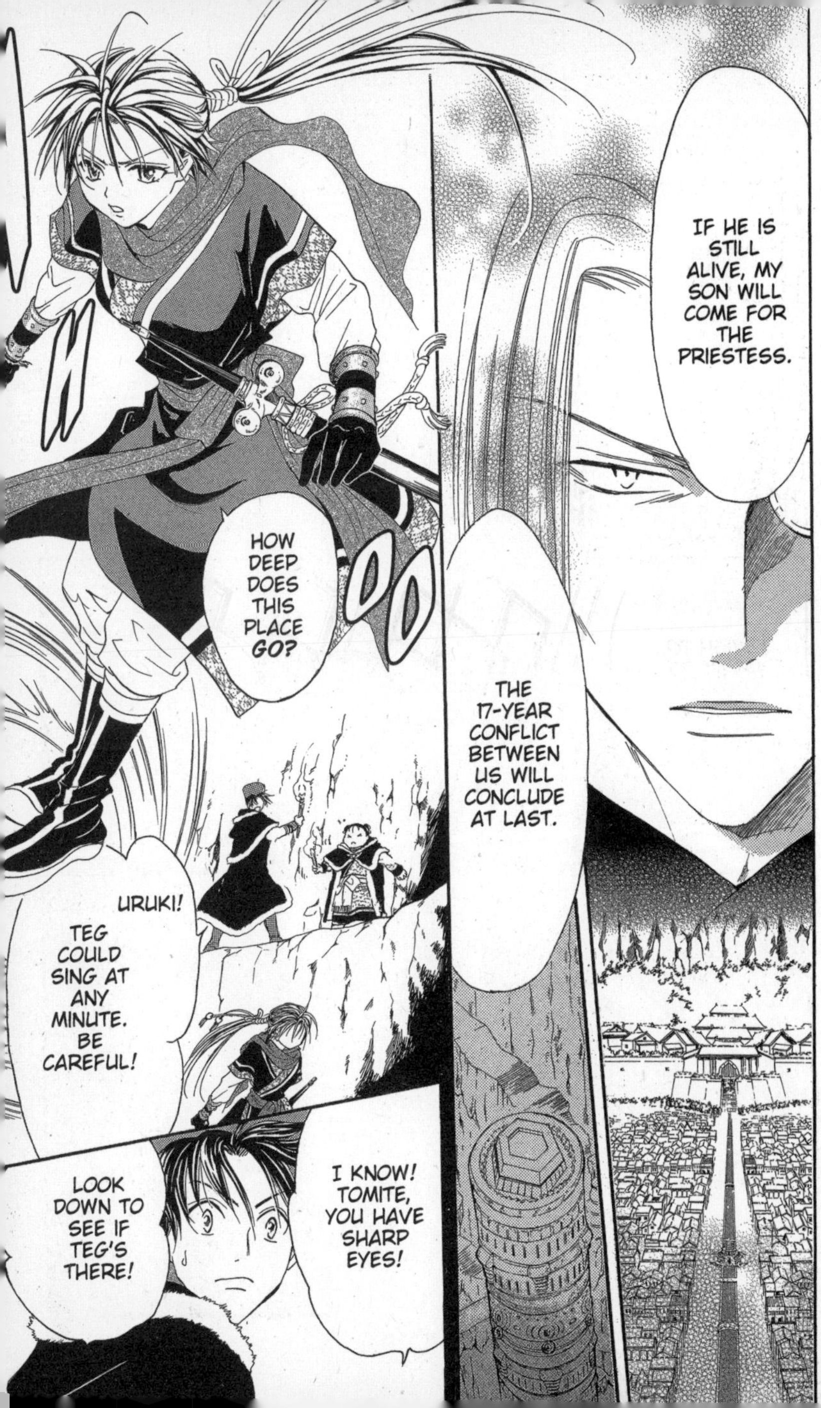
IF HE IS STILL ALIVE, MY SON WILL COME FOR THE PRIESTESS.
THE 17-YEAR CONFLICT BETWEEN US WILL CONCLUDE AT LAST.
HOW DEEP DOES THIS PLACE GO?
URUKI!
TEG COULD SING AT ANY MINUTE. BE CAREFUL!
I KNOW! TOMITE, YOU HAVE SHARP EYES!
LOOK DOWN TO SEE IF TEG'S THERE!

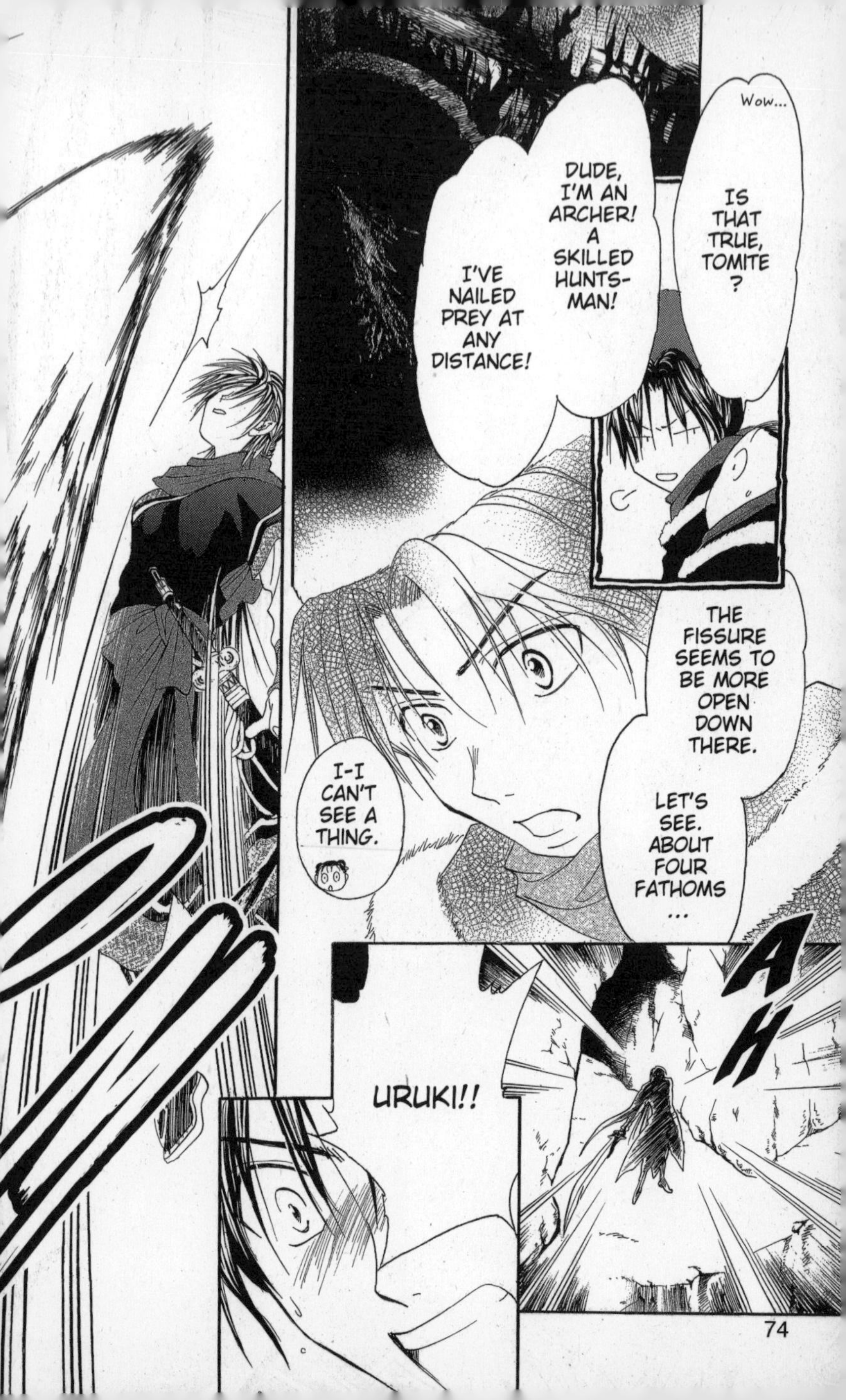
Wow...
IS THAT TRUE, TOMITE?
DUDE, I'M AN ARCHER! A SKILLED HUNTSMAN!
I'VE NAILED PREY AT ANY DISTANCE!
THE FISSURE SEEMS TO BE MORE OPEN DOWN THERE.
LET'S SEE. ABOUT FOUR FATHOMS...
I-I CAN'T SEE A THING.
AH
URUKI!!

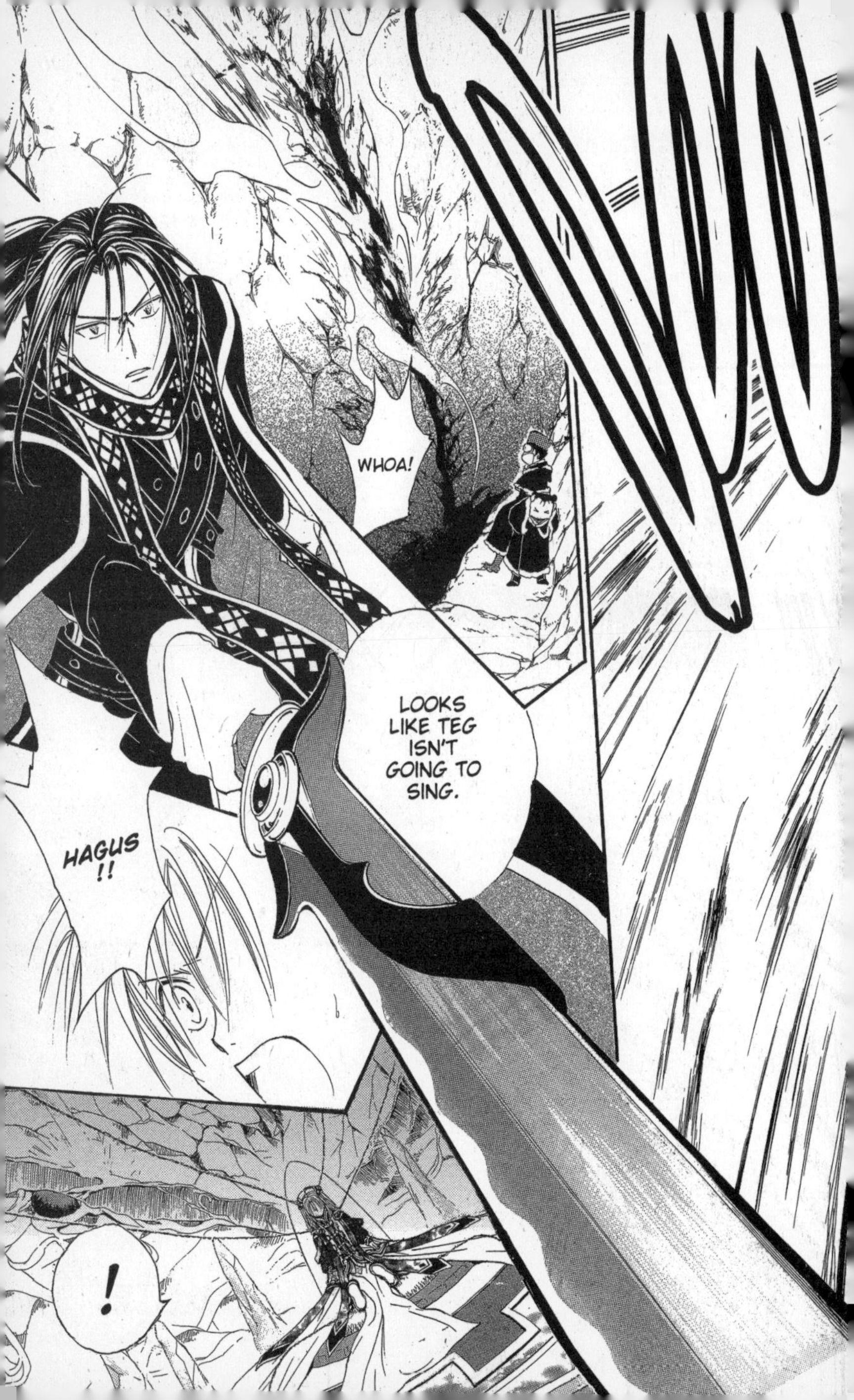
WHOA!
LOOKS LIKE TEG ISN'T GOING TO SING.
HAGUS !!
!

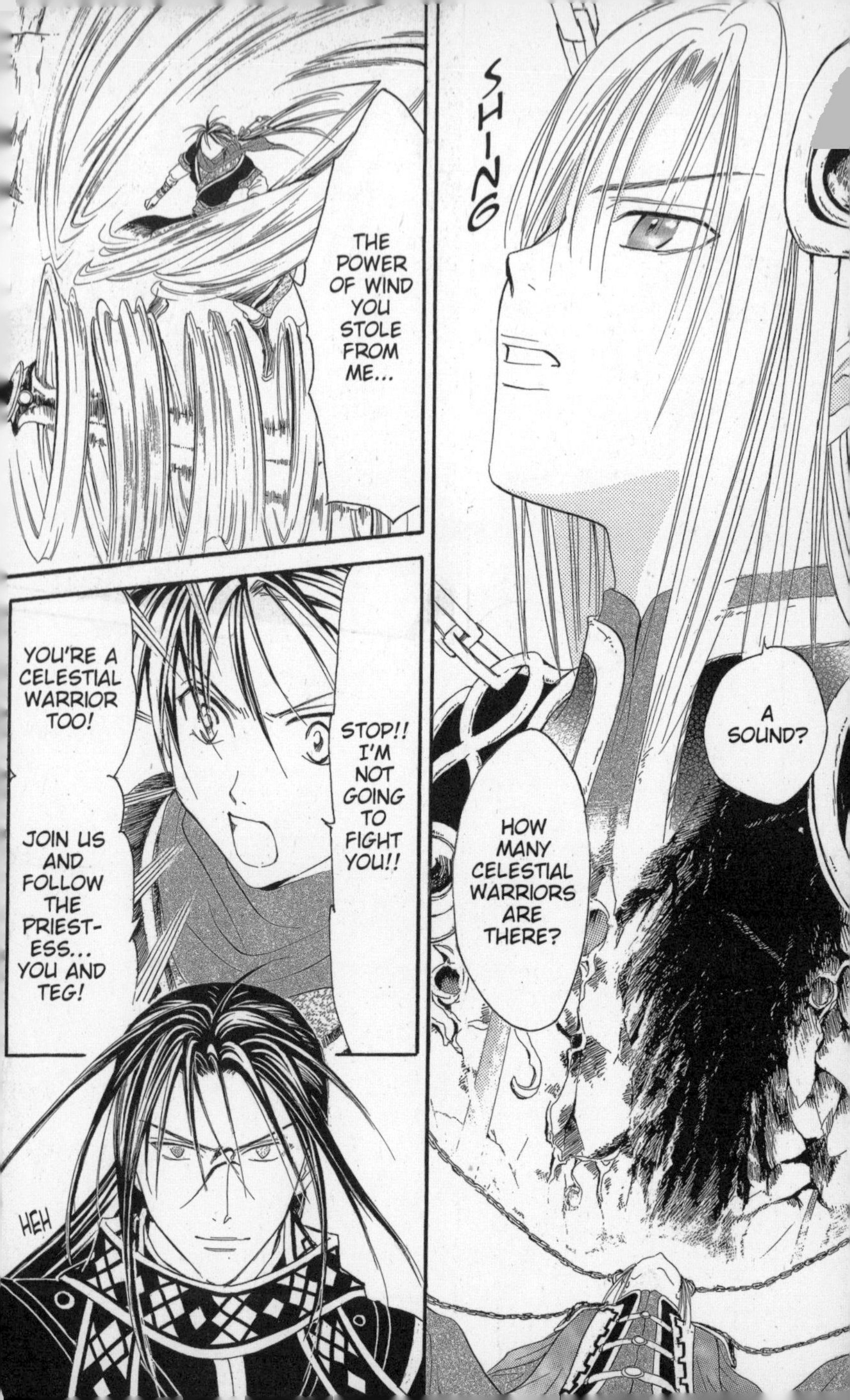
SHING
A SOUND?
HOW MANY CELESTIAL WARRIORS ARE THERE?
THE POWER OF WIND YOU STOLE FROM ME...
STOP!! I'M NOT GOING TO FIGHT YOU!!
YOU'RE A CELESTIAL WARRIOR TOO!
JOIN US AND FOLLOW THE PRIEST-ESS... YOU AND TEG!
HEH

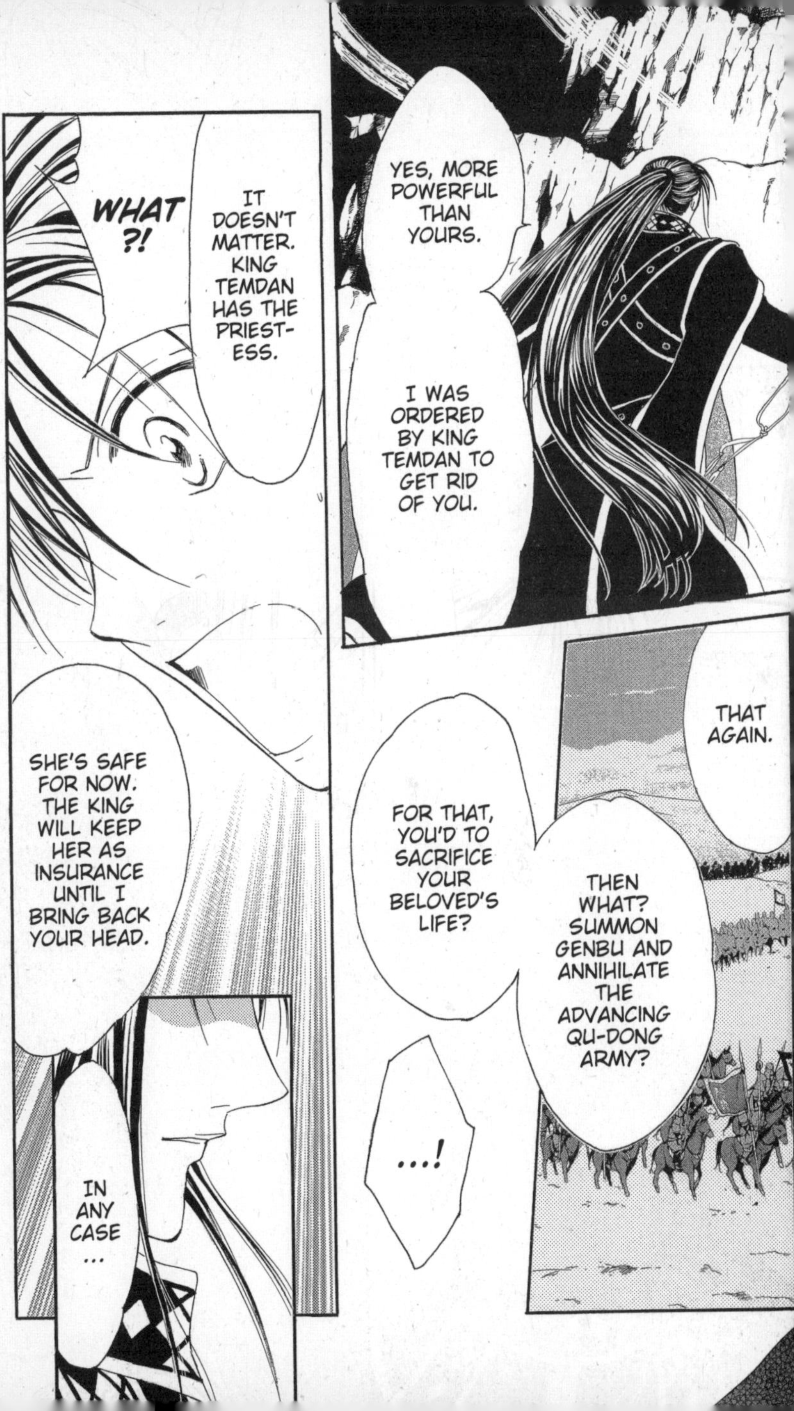
YES, MORE POWERFUL THAN YOURS.
I WAS ORDERED BY KING TEMDAN TO GET RID OF YOU.
IT DOESN'T MATTER. KING TEMDAN HAS THE PRIEST-ESS.
WHAT ?!
SHE'S SAFE FOR NOW. THE KING WILL KEEP HER AS INSURANCE UNTIL I BRING BACK YOUR HEAD.
THAT AGAIN.
THEN WHAT? SUMMON GENBU AND ANNIHILATE THE ADVANCING QU-DONG ARMY?
FOR THAT, YOU'D TO SACRIFICE YOUR BELOVED'S LIFE?
...!
IN ANY CASE ...

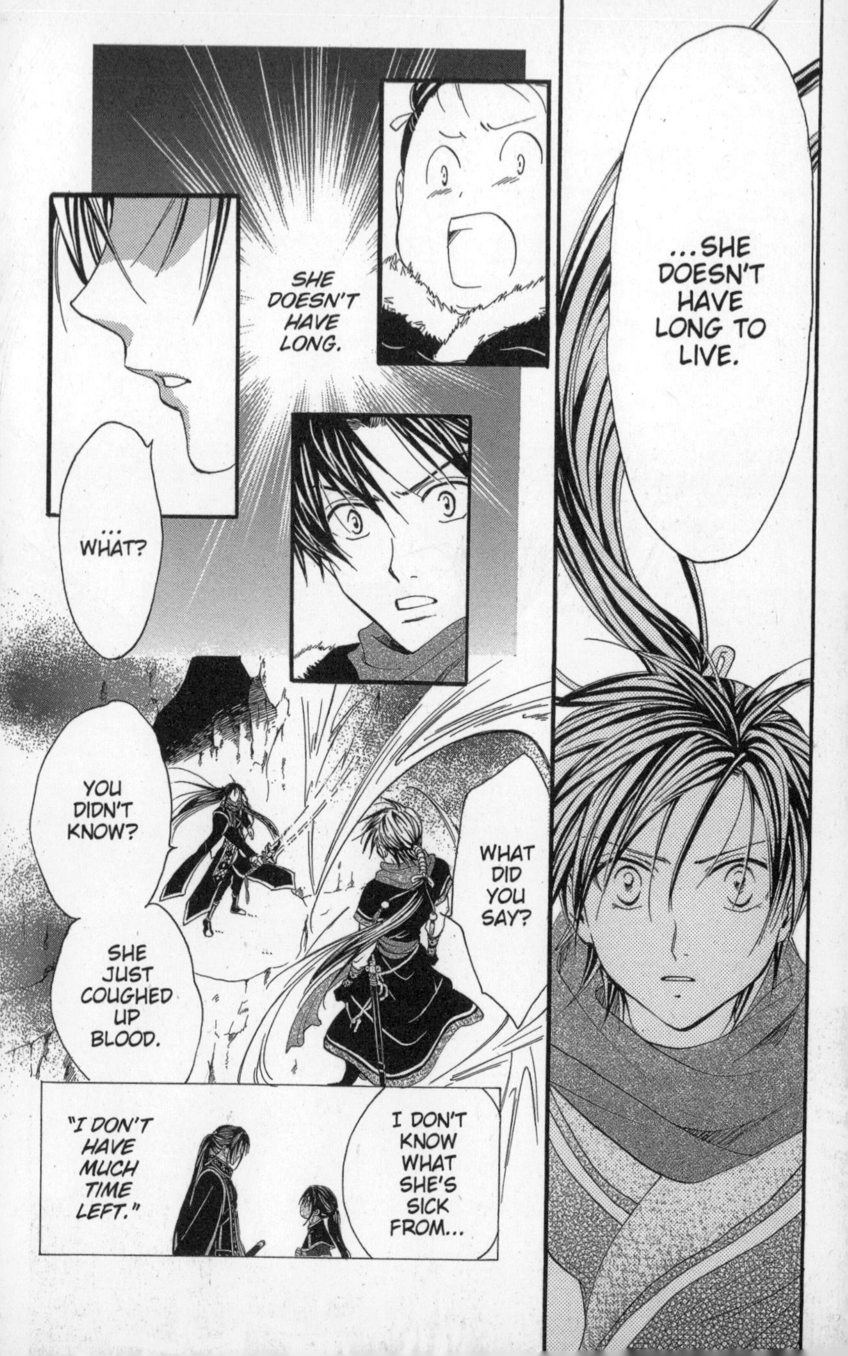
...SHE DOESN'T HAVE LONG TO LIVE.
SHE DOESN'T HAVE LONG.
...WHAT?
WHAT DID YOU SAY?
YOU DIDN'T KNOW?
SHE JUST COUGHED UP BLOOD.
I DON'T KNOW WHAT SHE'S SICK FROM...
"I DON'T HAVE MUCH TIME LEFT."

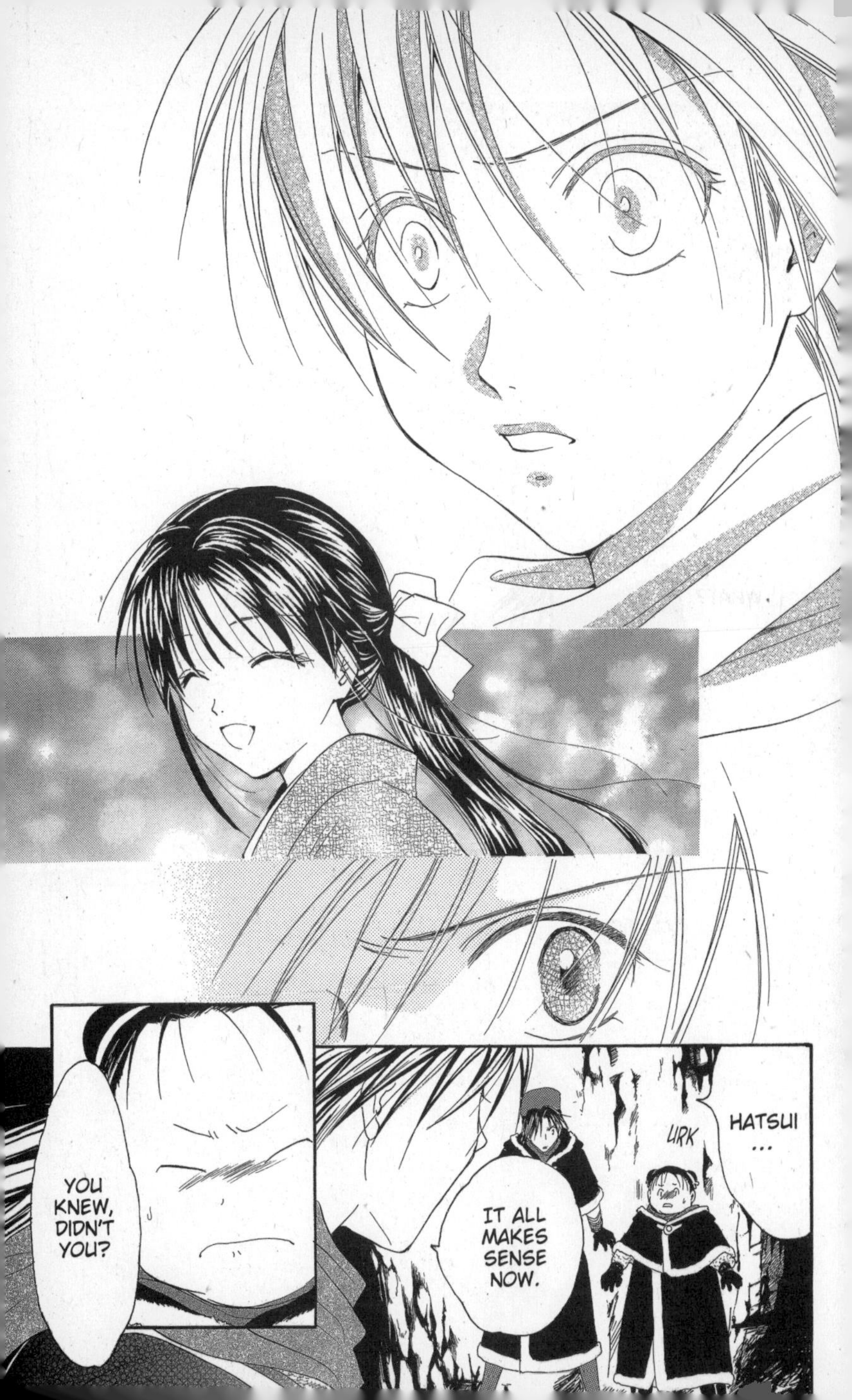
HATSUI...
URK
IT ALL MAKES SENSE NOW.
YOU KNEW, DIDN'T YOU?

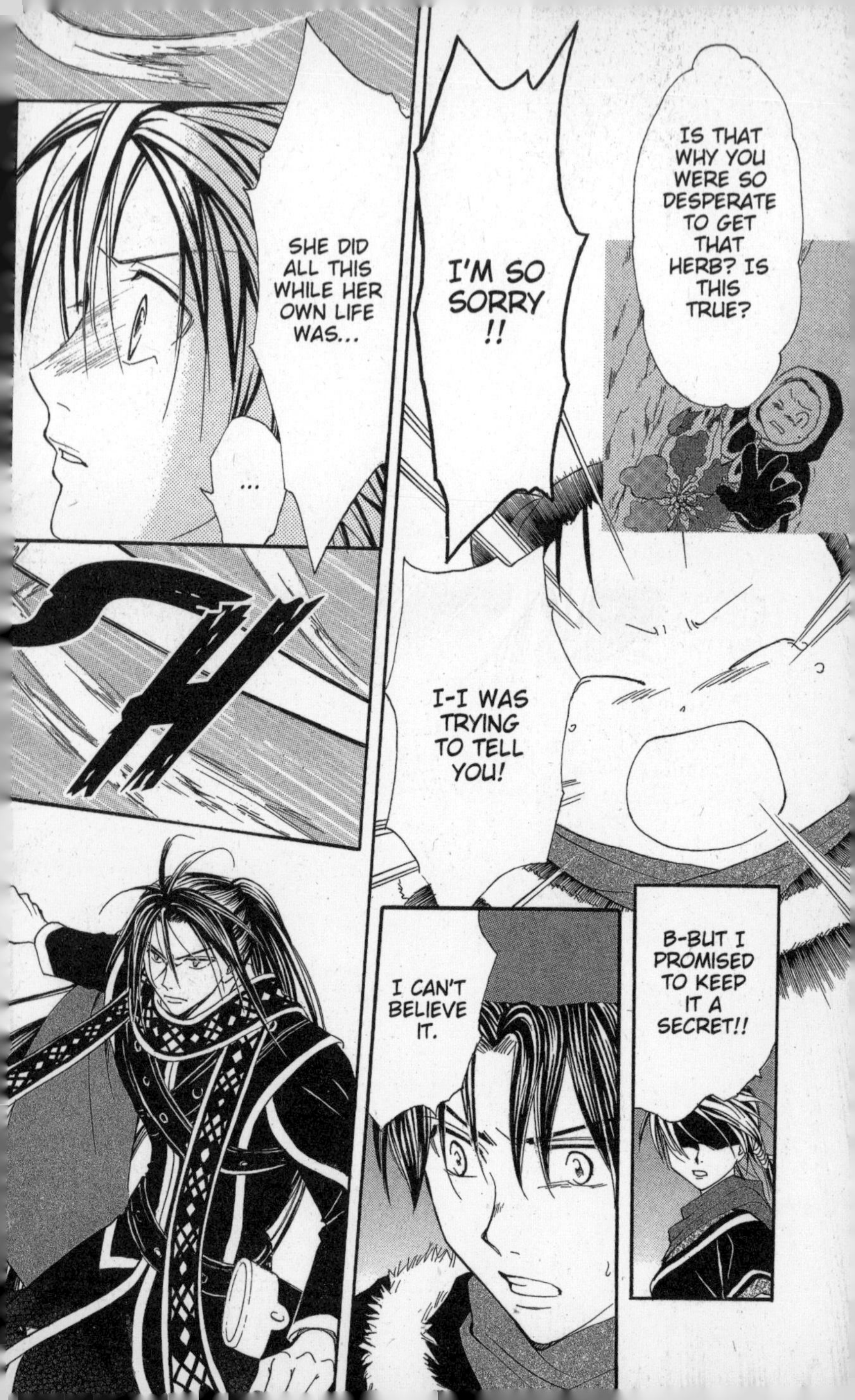
IS THAT WHY YOU WERE SO DESPERATE TO GET THAT HERB? IS THIS TRUE?
I'M SO SORRY!!
I-I WAS TRYING TO TELL YOU!
B-BUT I PROMISED TO KEEP IT A SECRET!!
I CAN'T BELIEVE IT.
SHE DID ALL THIS WHILE HER OWN LIFE WAS...
...

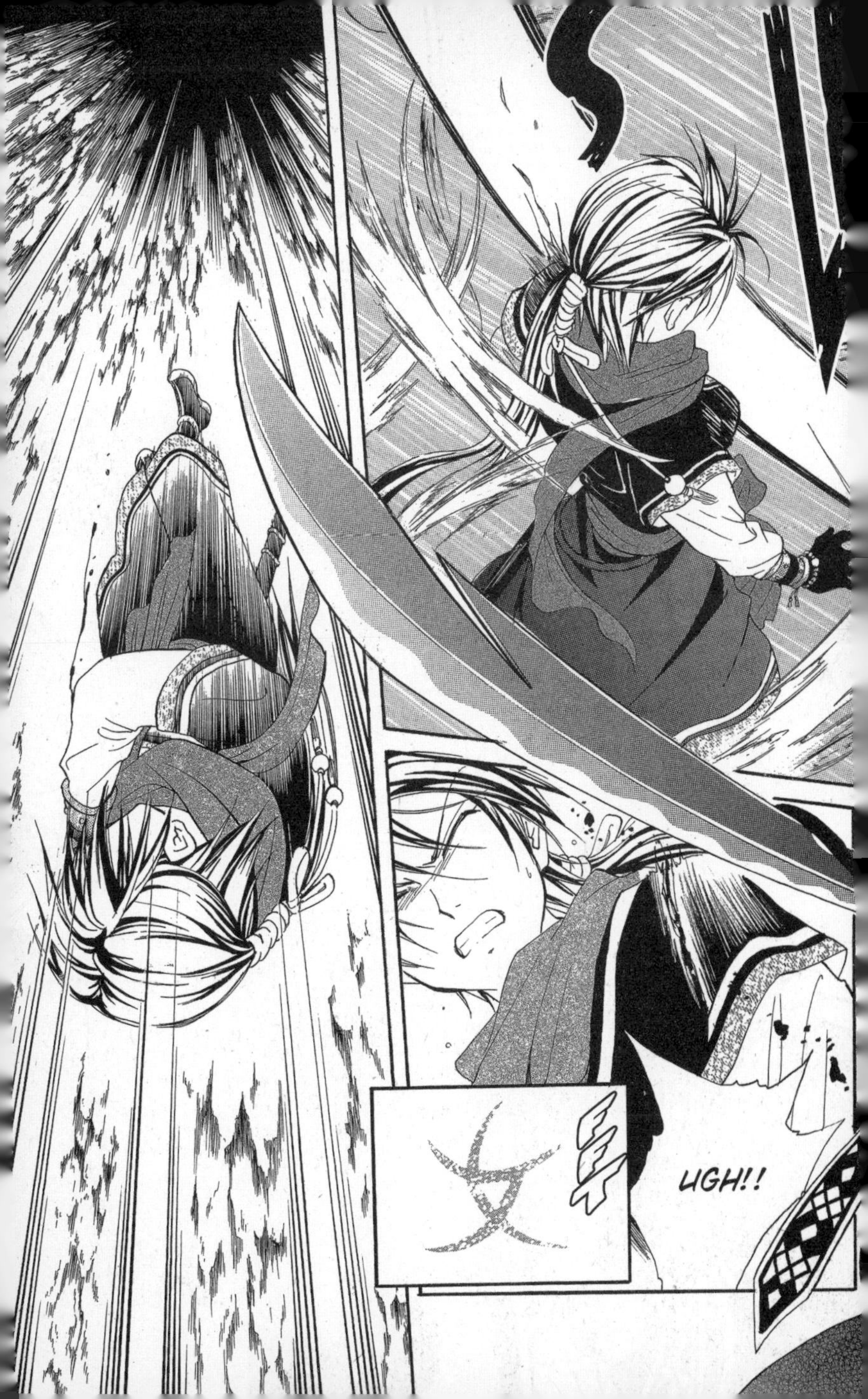
UGH!!

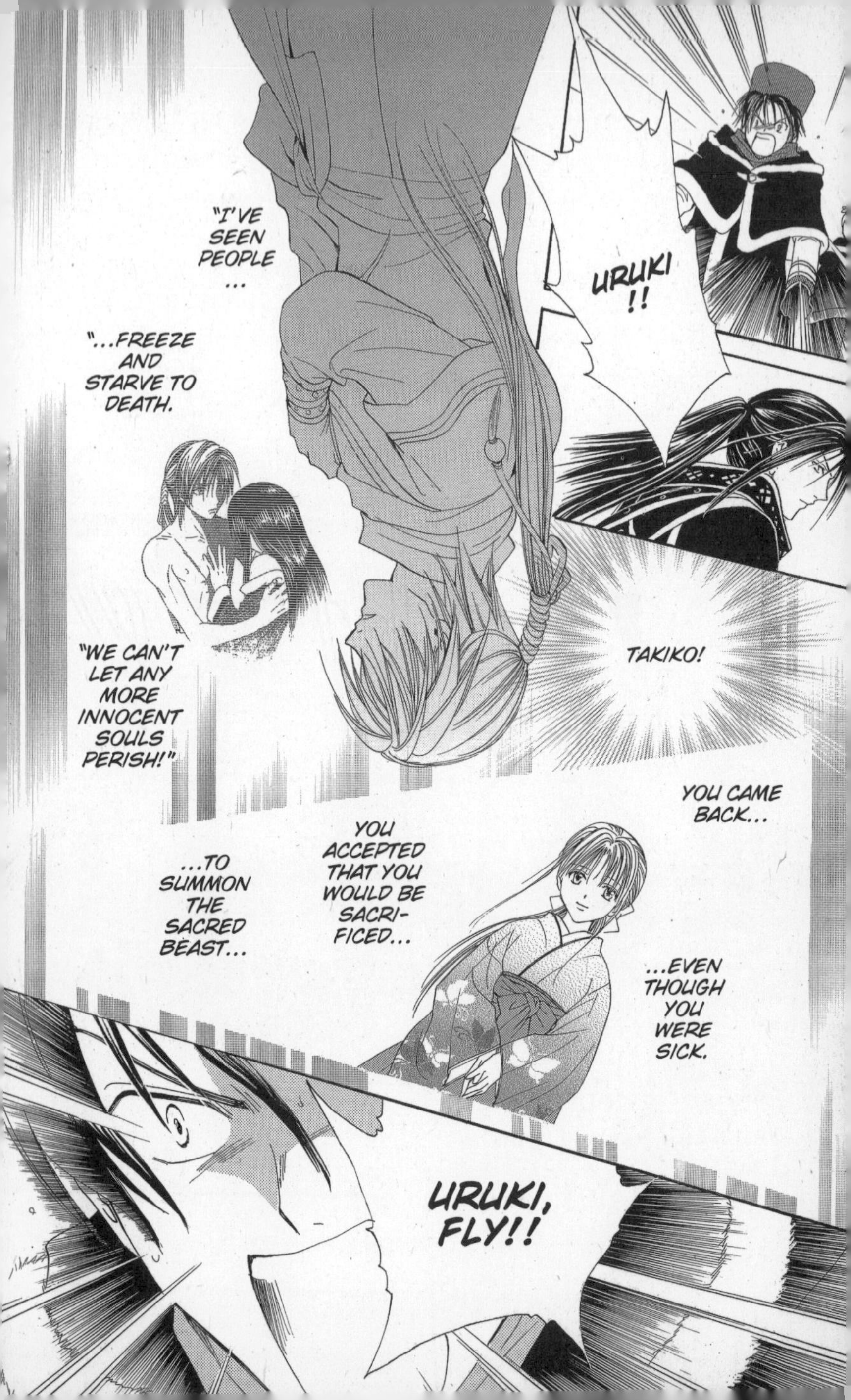
URUKI!!
"I'VE SEEN PEOPLE...
"...FREEZE AND STARVE TO DEATH.
TAKIKO!
"WE CAN'T LET ANY MORE INNOCENT SOULS PERISH!"
YOU CAME BACK...
...EVEN THOUGH YOU WERE SICK.
YOU ACCEPTED THAT YOU WOULD BE SACRI-FICED...
...TO SUMMON THE SACRED BEAST...
URUKI, FLY!!

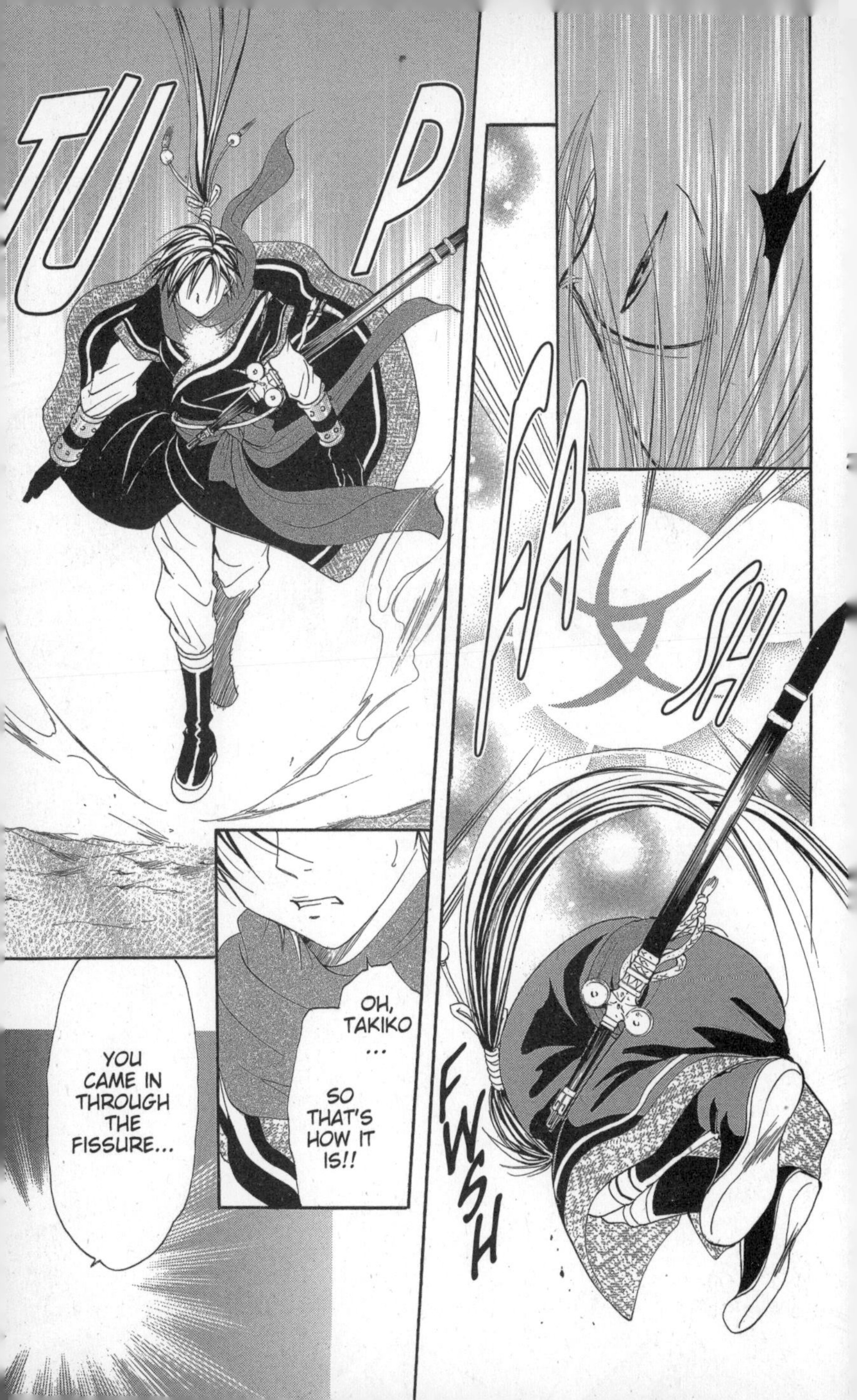
FASH
FWSH
TUP
OH, TAKIKO...
SO THAT'S HOW IT IS!!
YOU CAME IN THROUGH THE FISSURE...

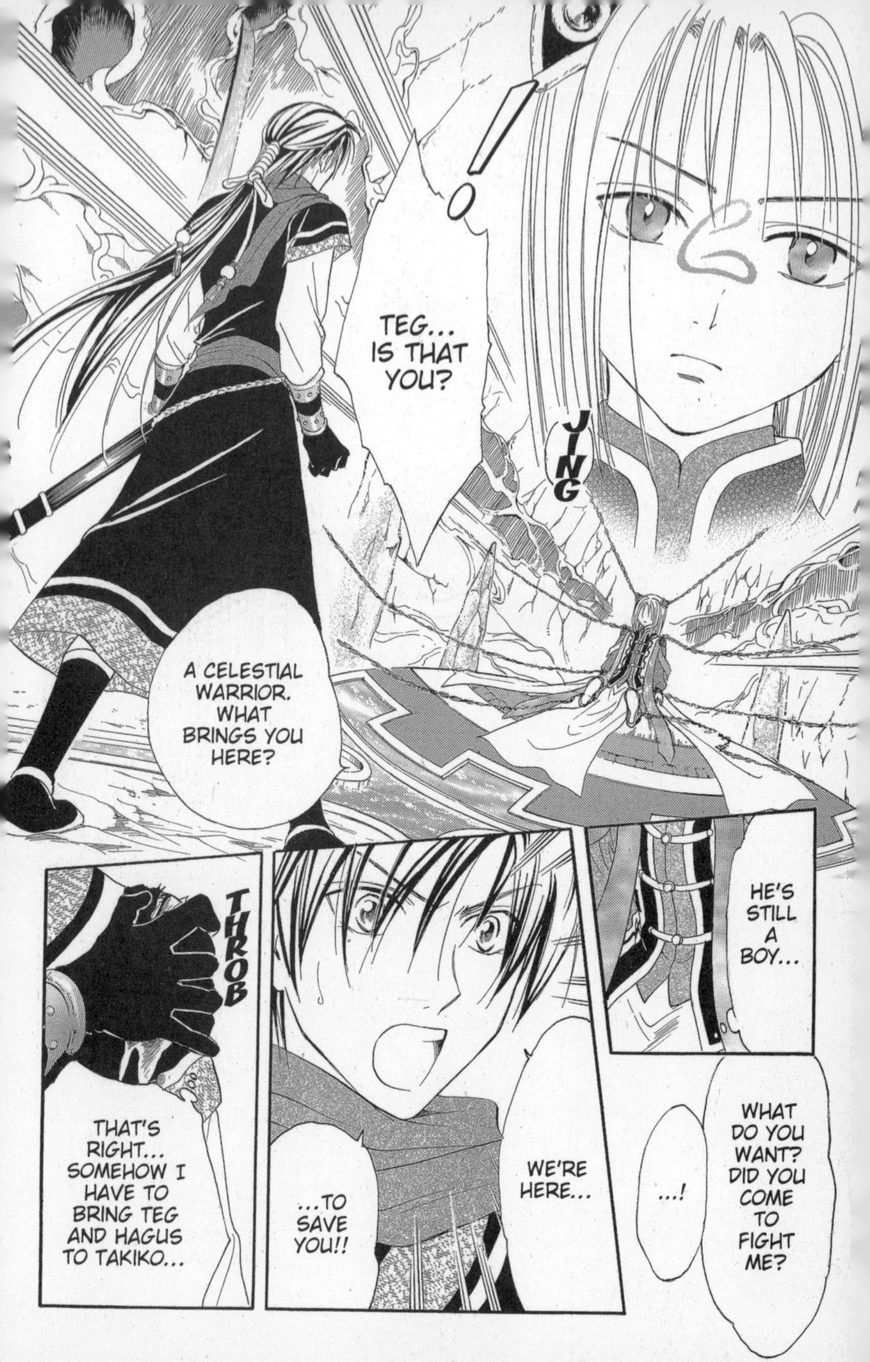
!
TEG... IS THAT YOU?
JING
A CELESTIAL WARRIOR. WHAT BRINGS YOU HERE?
HE'S STILL A BOY...
WHAT DO YOU WANT? DID YOU COME TO FIGHT ME?
...!
WE'RE HERE...
...TO SAVE YOU!!
THROB
THAT'S RIGHT... SOMEHOW I HAVE TO BRING TEG AND HAGUS TO TAKIKO...

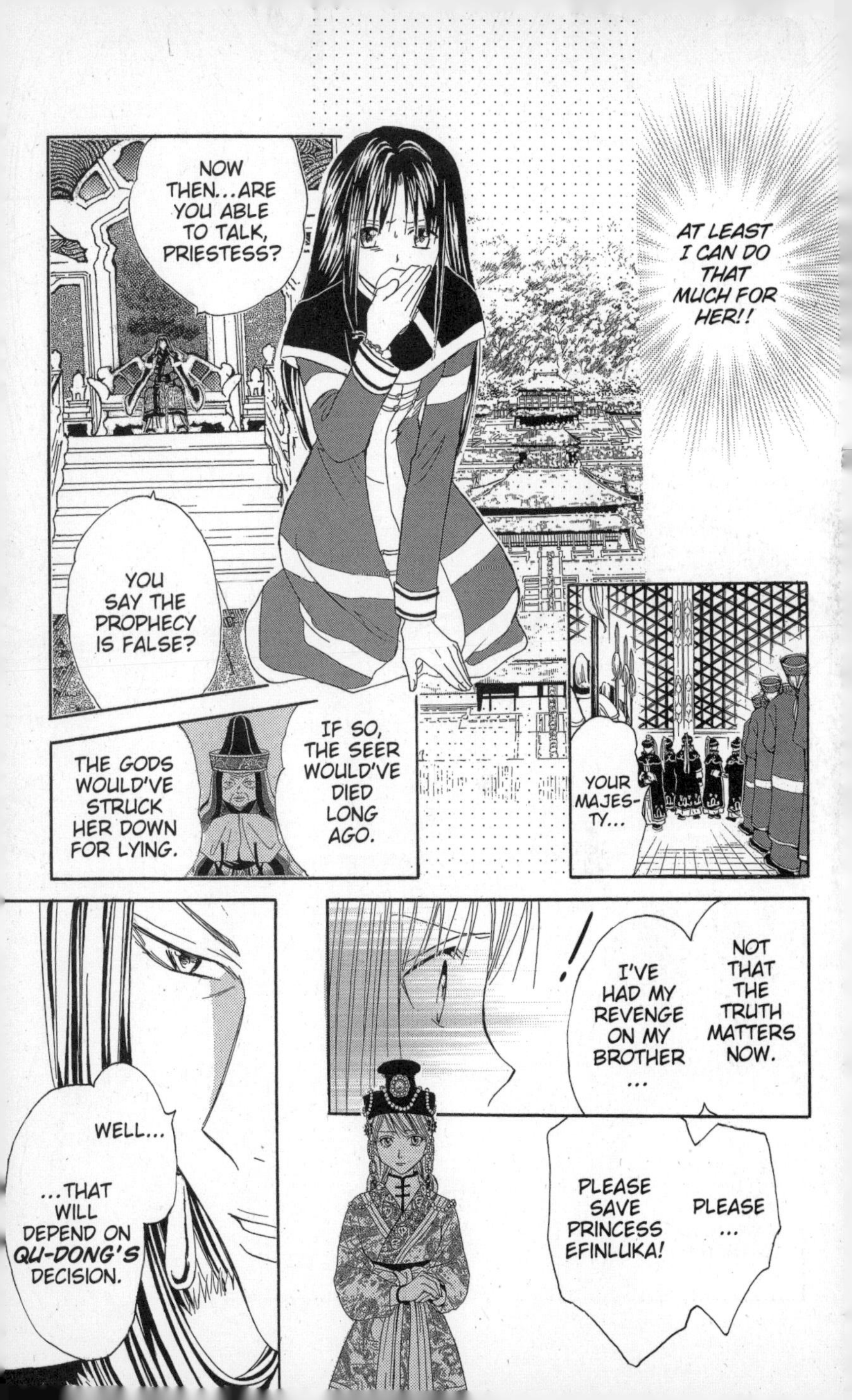
AT LEAST I CAN DO THAT MUCH FOR HER!!
NOW THEN...ARE YOU ABLE TO TALK, PRIESTESS?
YOU SAY THE PROPHECY IS FALSE?
YOUR MAJESTY...
IF SO, THE SEER WOULD'VE DIED LONG AGO.
THE GODS WOULD'VE STRUCK HER DOWN FOR LYING.
NOT THAT THE TRUTH MATTERS NOW.
I'VE HAD MY REVENGE ON MY BROTHER...
!
PLEASE...
PLEASE SAVE PRINCESS EFINLUKA!
WELL...
...THAT WILL DEPEND ON QU-DONG'S DECISION.

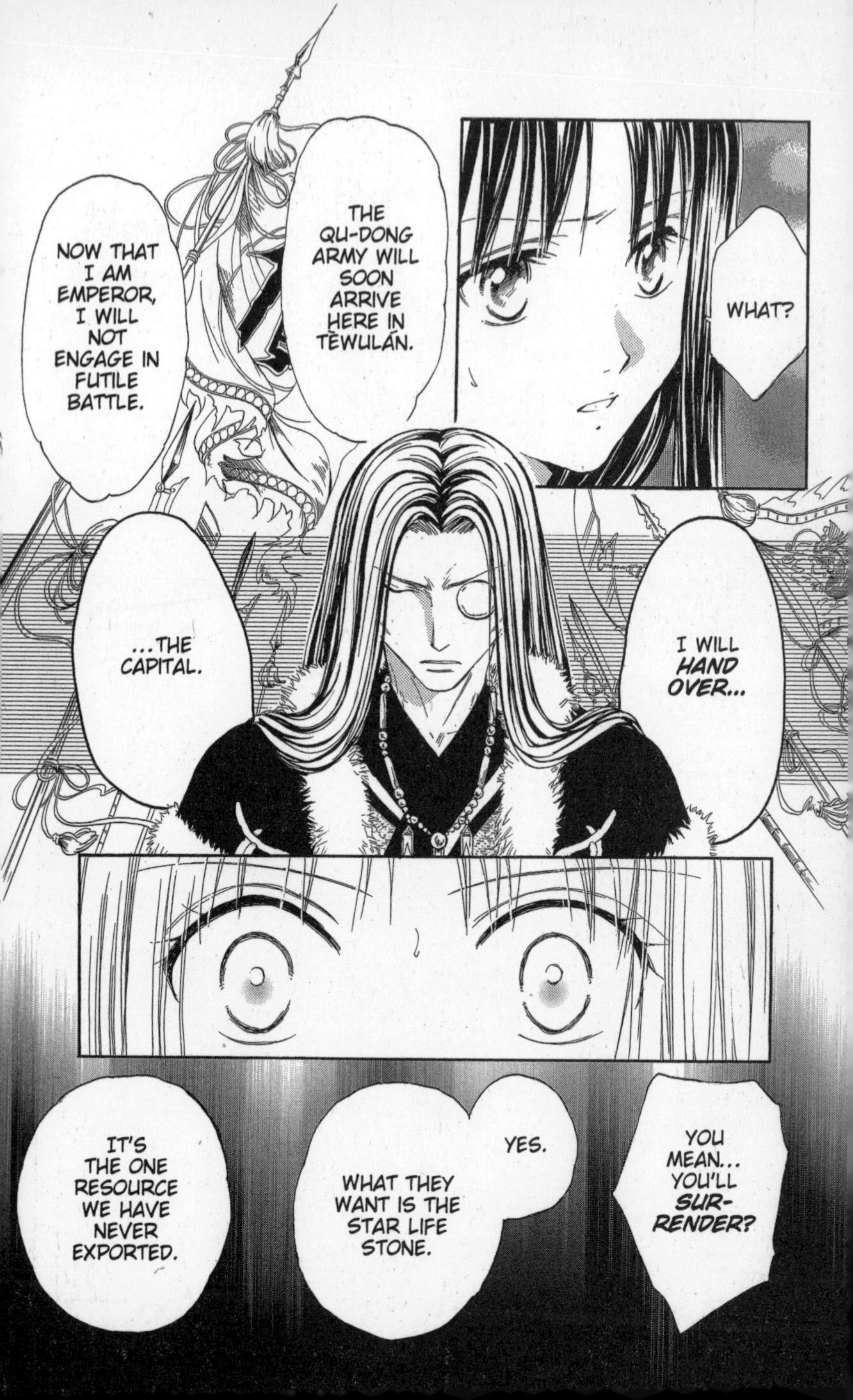
WHAT?
THE QU-DONG ARMY WILL SOON ARRIVE HERE IN TÈWULÁN.
NOW THAT I AM EMPEROR, I WILL NOT ENGAGE IN FUTILE BATTLE.
I WILL *HAND OVER...*
...THE CAPITAL.
YOU MEAN... YOU'LL *SUR-RENDER?*
YES.
WHAT THEY WANT IS THE STAR LIFE STONE.
IT'S THE ONE RESOURCE WE HAVE NEVER EXPORTED.

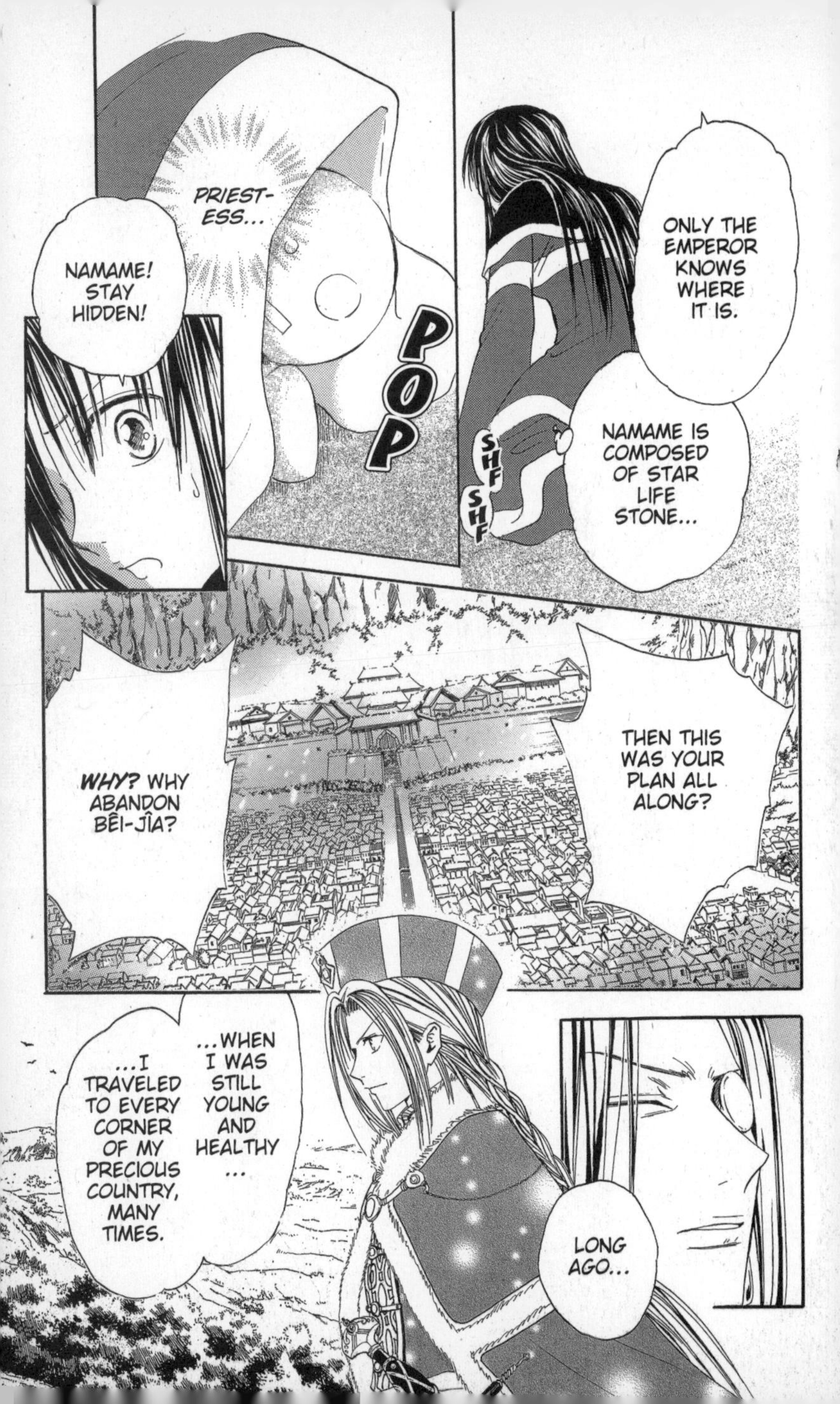
ONLY THE EMPEROR KNOWS WHERE IT IS.
NAMAME IS COMPOSED OF STAR LIFE STONE...
SHF SHF
PRIEST-ESS...
POP
NAMAME! STAY HIDDEN!
THEN THIS WAS YOUR PLAN ALL ALONG?
WHY? WHY ABANDON BÊI-JÎA?
LONG AGO...
...WHEN I WAS STILL YOUNG AND HEALTHY...
...I TRAVELED TO EVERY CORNER OF MY PRECIOUS COUNTRY, MANY TIMES.

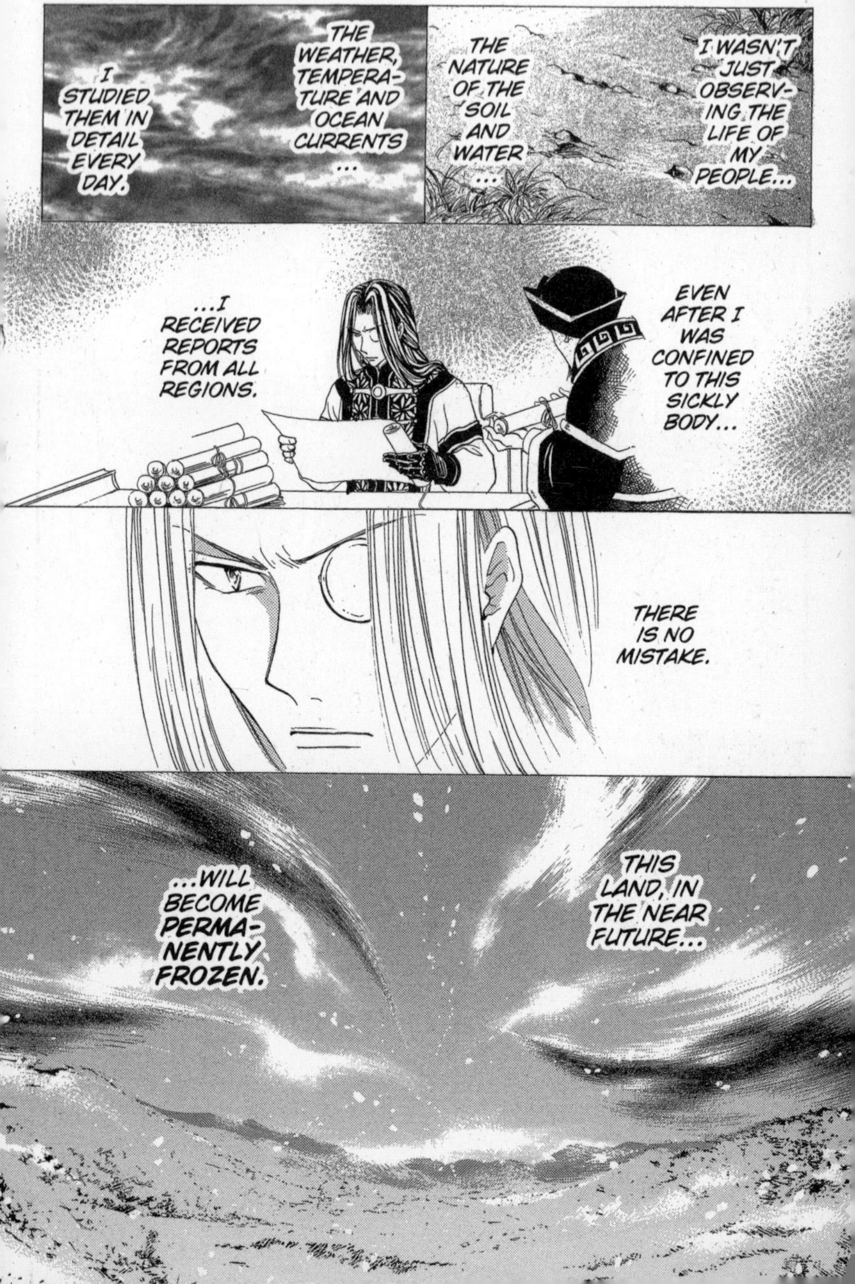
I WASN'T JUST OBSERVING THE LIFE OF MY PEOPLE...
THE NATURE OF THE SOIL AND WATER...
THE WEATHER, TEMPERATURE AND OCEAN CURRENTS...
I STUDIED THEM IN DETAIL EVERY DAY.
EVEN AFTER I WAS CONFINED TO THIS SICKLY BODY...
...I RECEIVED REPORTS FROM ALL REGIONS.
THERE IS NO MISTAKE.
THIS LAND, IN THE NEAR FUTURE...
...WILL BECOME PERMANENTLY FROZEN.

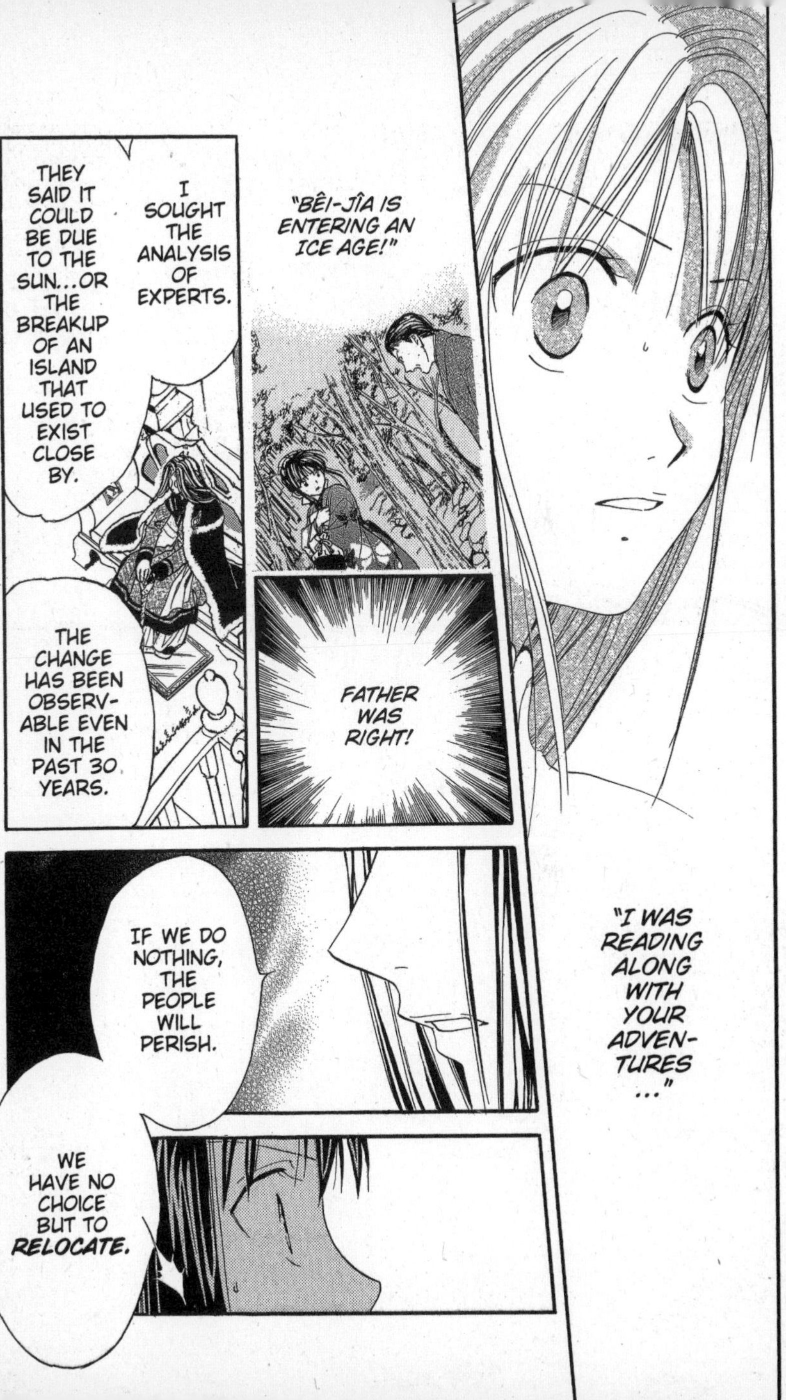
"I WAS READING ALONG WITH YOUR ADVENTURES..."
"BÊI-JÍA IS ENTERING AN ICE AGE!"
FATHER WAS RIGHT!
I SOUGHT THE ANALYSIS OF EXPERTS.
THEY SAID IT COULD BE DUE TO THE SUN...OR THE BREAKUP OF AN ISLAND THAT USED TO EXIST CLOSE BY.
THE CHANGE HAS BEEN OBSERVABLE EVEN IN THE PAST 30 YEARS.
IF WE DO NOTHING, THE PEOPLE WILL PERISH.
WE HAVE NO CHOICE BUT TO RELOCATE.

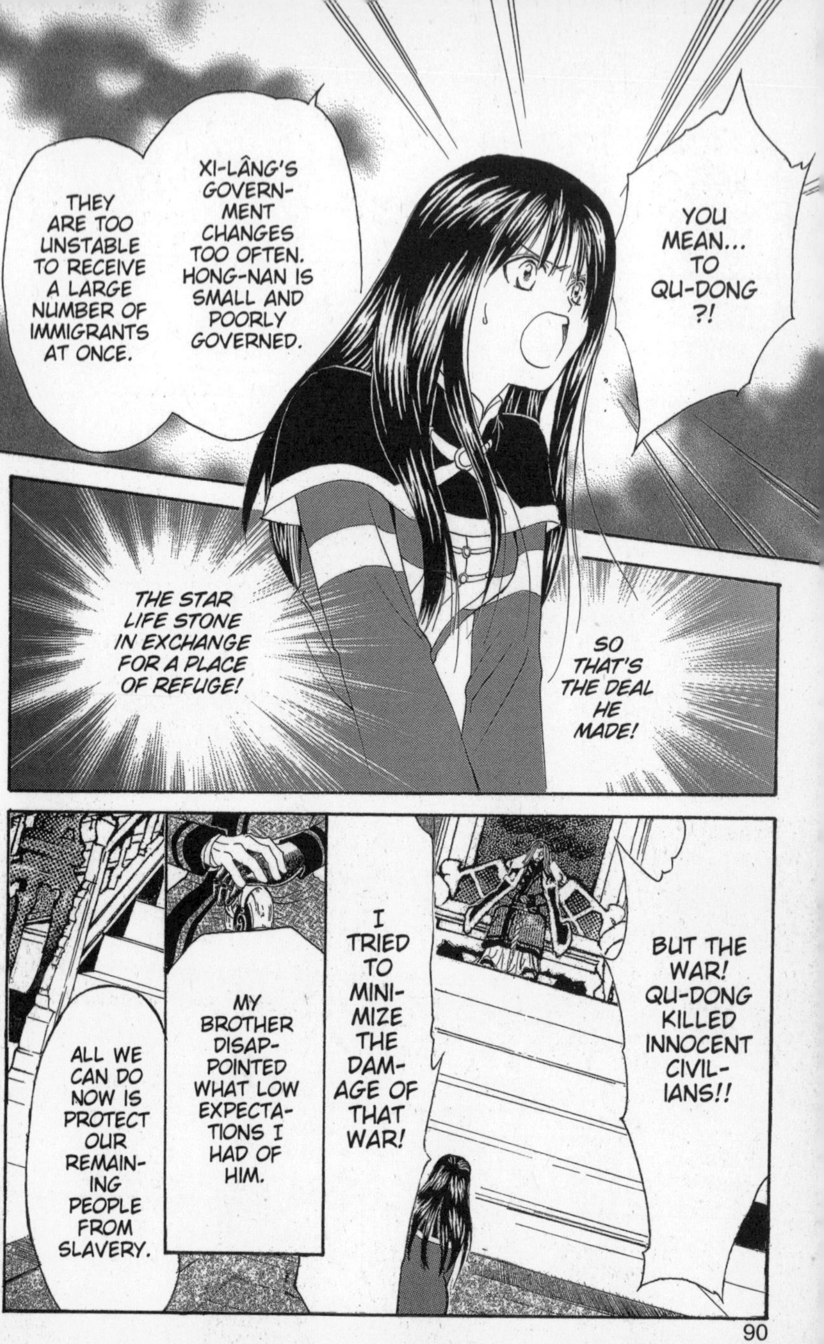

YOU MEAN... TO QU-DONG?!
XI-LÂNG'S GOVERNMENT CHANGES TOO OFTEN. HONG-NAN IS SMALL AND POORLY GOVERNED.
THEY ARE TOO UNSTABLE TO RECEIVE A LARGE NUMBER OF IMMIGRANTS AT ONCE.
SO THAT'S THE DEAL HE MADE!
THE STAR LIFE STONE IN EXCHANGE FOR A PLACE OF REFUGE!
BUT THE WAR! QU-DONG KILLED INNOCENT CIVILIANS!!
I TRIED TO MINIMIZE THE DAMAGE OF THAT WAR!
MY BROTHER DISAPPOINTED WHAT LOW EXPECTATIONS I HAD OF HIM.
ALL WE CAN DO NOW IS PROTECT OUR REMAINING PEOPLE FROM SLAVERY.

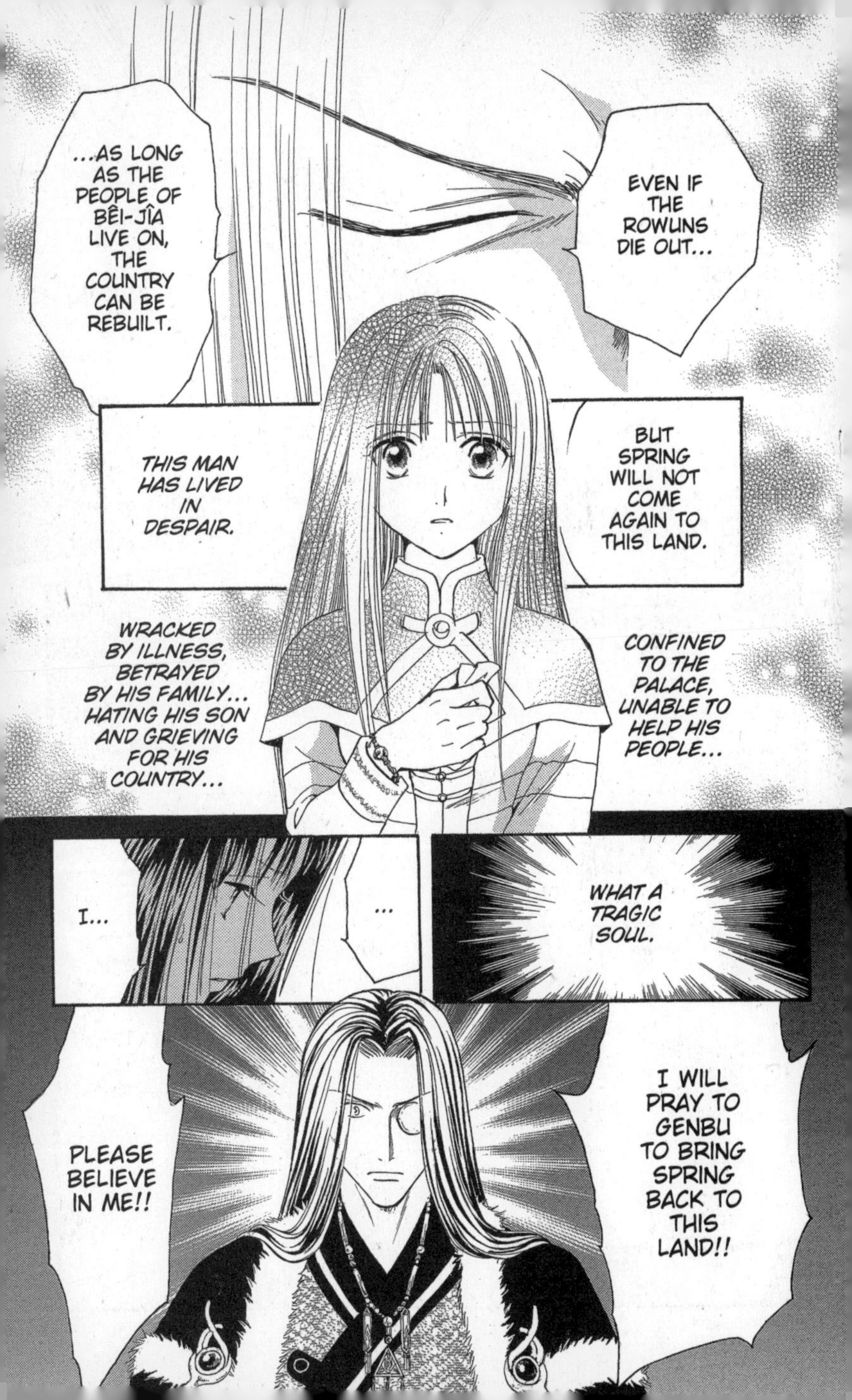
EVEN IF THE ROWUNS DIE OUT...
...AS LONG AS THE PEOPLE OF BÊI-JÎA LIVE ON, THE COUNTRY CAN BE REBUILT.
BUT SPRING WILL NOT COME AGAIN TO THIS LAND.
THIS MAN HAS LIVED IN DESPAIR.
CONFINED TO THE PALACE, UNABLE TO HELP HIS PEOPLE...
WRACKED BY ILLNESS, BETRAYED BY HIS FAMILY... HATING HIS SON AND GRIEVING FOR HIS COUNTRY...
WHAT A TRAGIC SOUL.
...
I...
I WILL PRAY TO GENBU TO BRING SPRING BACK TO THIS LAND!!
PLEASE BELIEVE IN ME!!

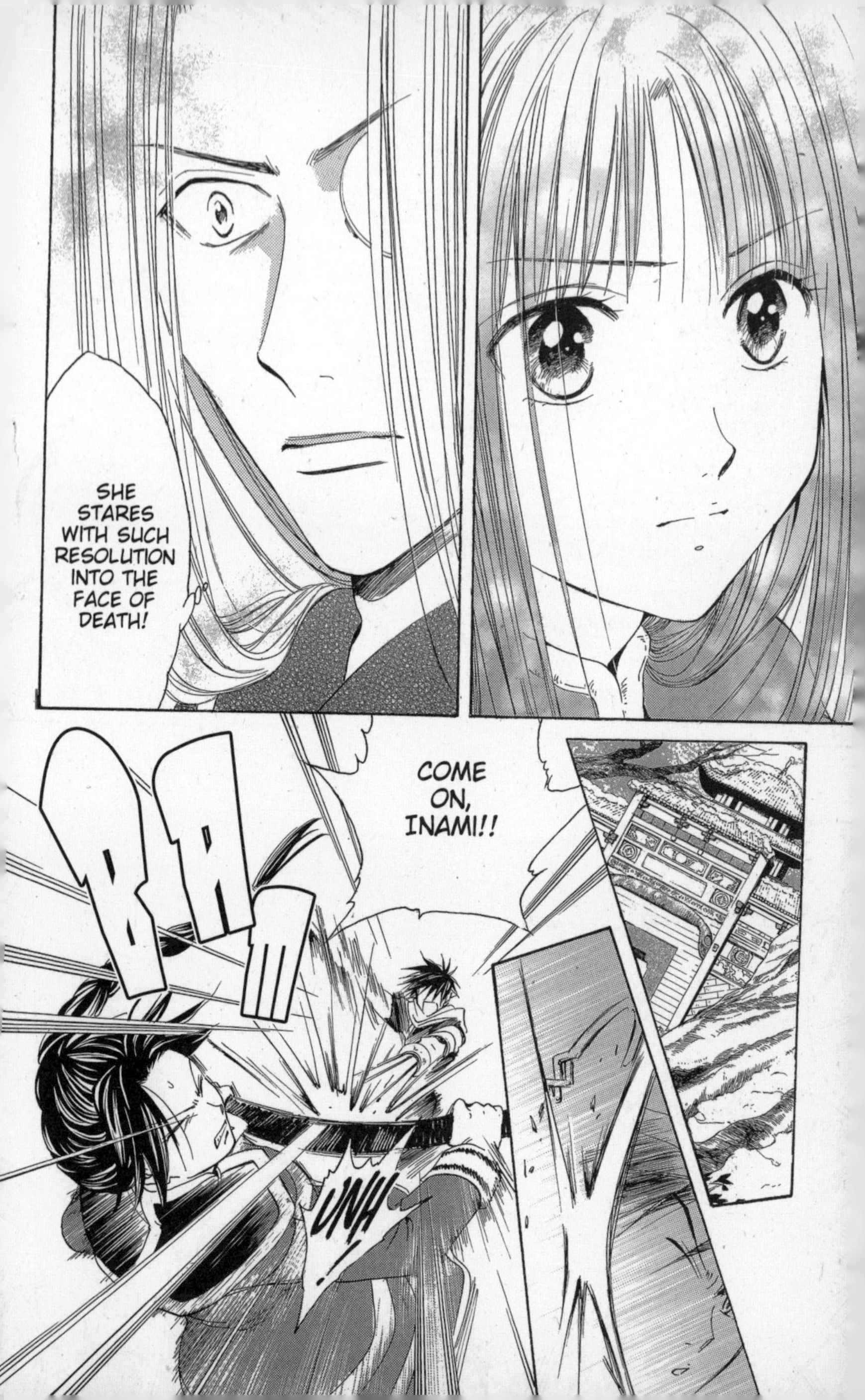
SHE STARES WITH SUCH RESOLUTION INTO THE FACE OF DEATH!
COME ON, INAMI!!
BAM
UNH!

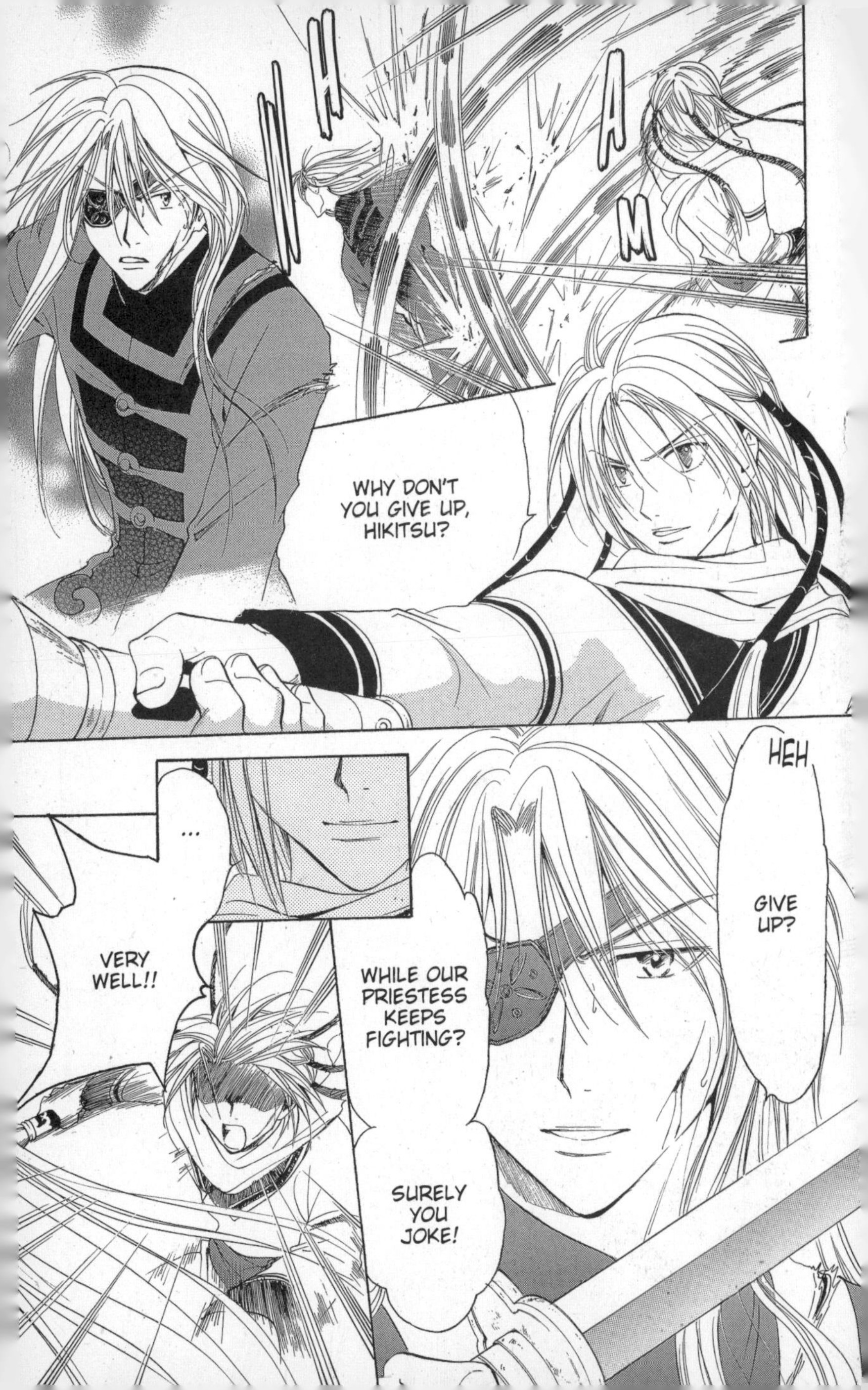
WHAM
WHY DON'T YOU GIVE UP, HIKITSU?
HEH
GIVE UP?
WHILE OUR PRIESTESS KEEPS FIGHTING?
SURELY YOU JOKE!
...
VERY WELL!!

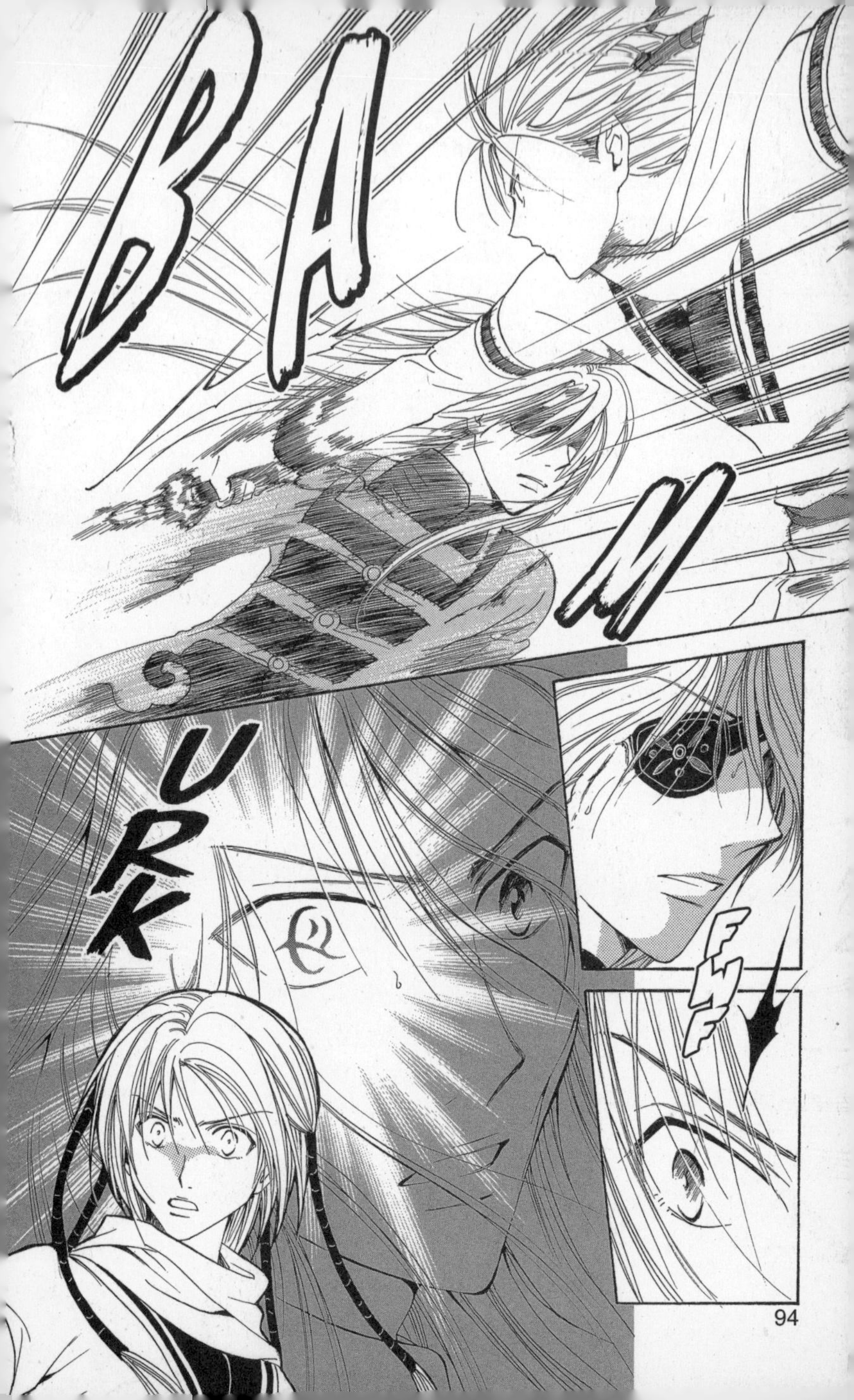
BAM
FWF
URK

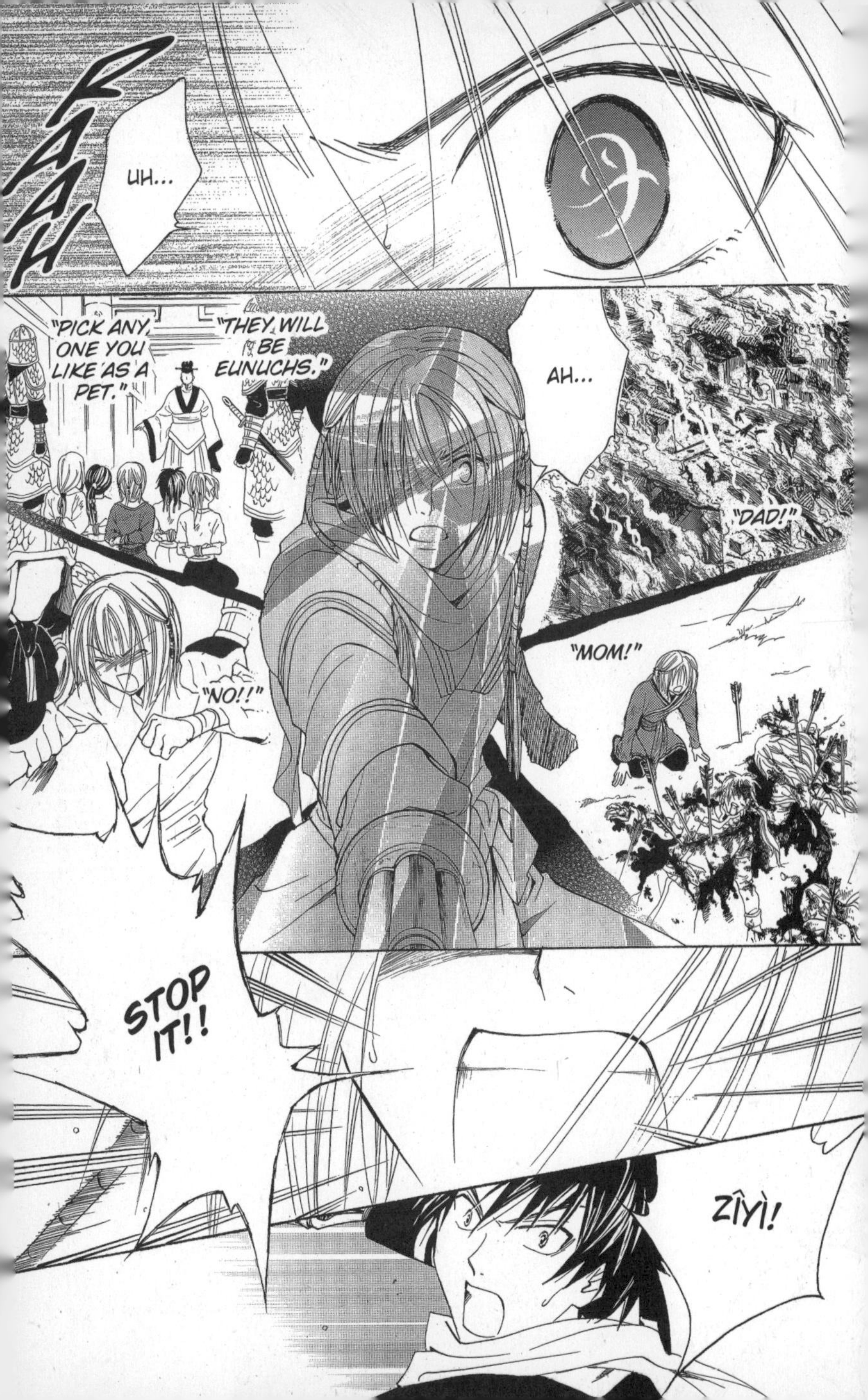
UH...
RAAAH
AH...
"DAD!"
"MOM!"
"THEY WILL BE EUNUCHS."
"PICK ANY ONE YOU LIKE AS A PET."
"NO!!"
ZÎYÌ!
STOP IT!!

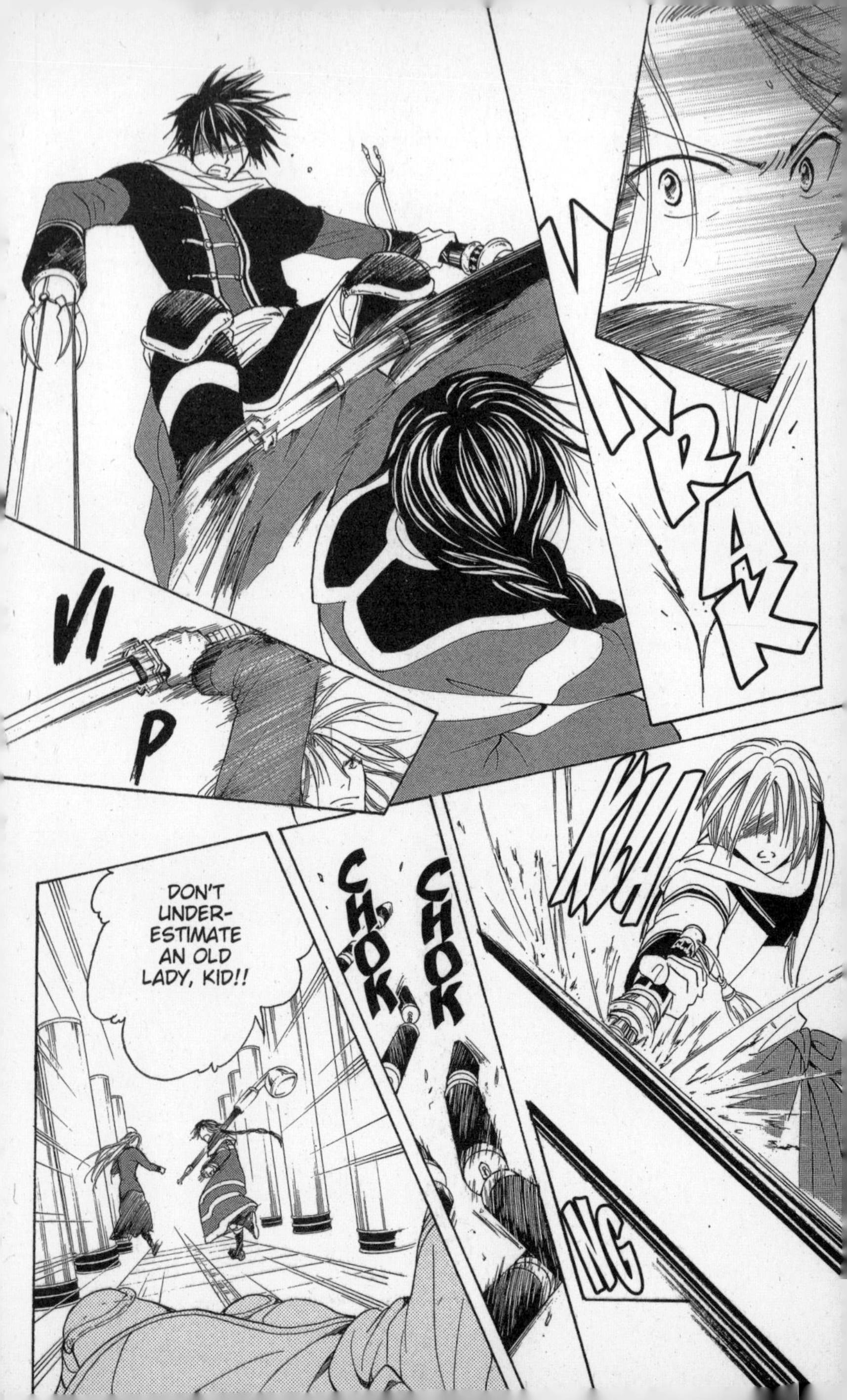
KRAK
VIP
KWA
NG
CHOK
CHOK
DON'T UNDER-ESTIMATE AN OLD LADY, KID!!

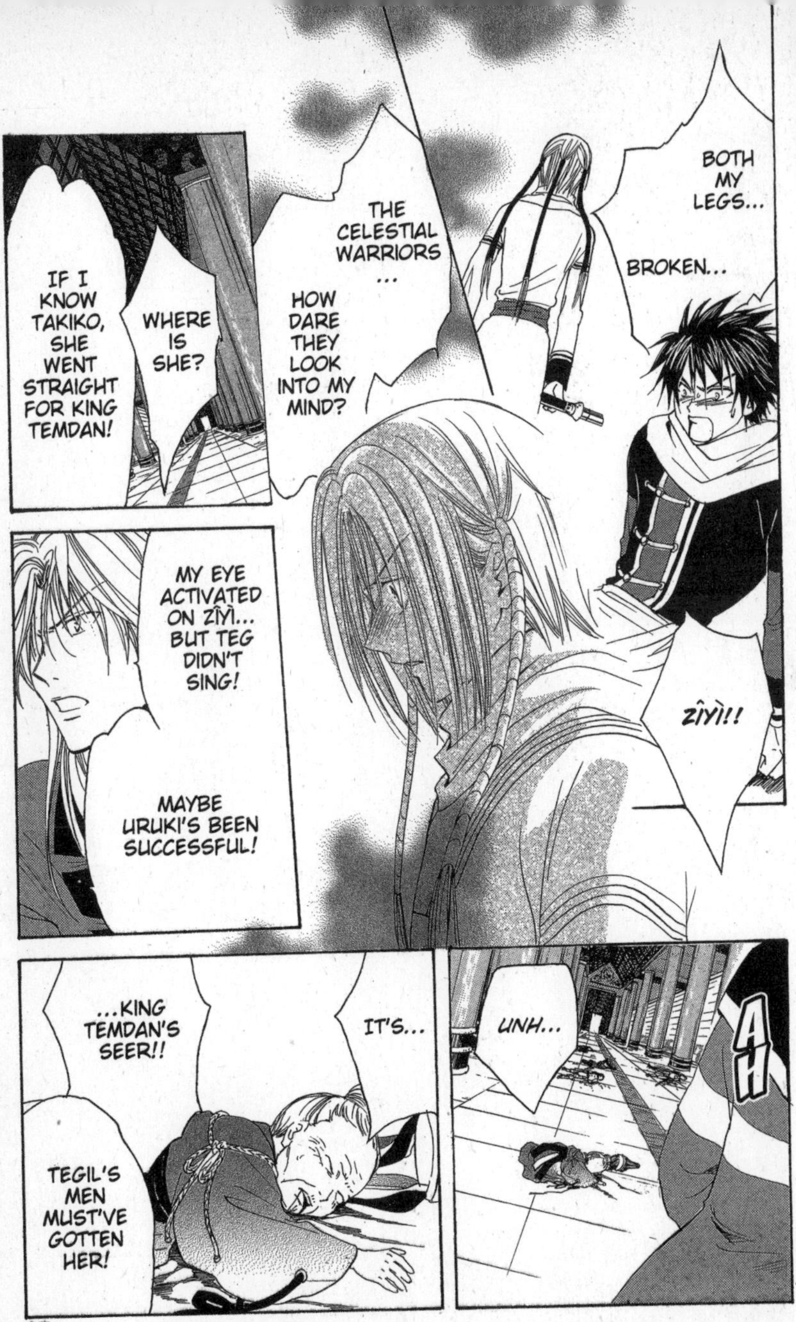

BOTH MY LEGS...
BROKEN...
THE CELESTIAL WARRIORS ...
HOW DARE THEY LOOK INTO MY MIND?
ZÎYÌ!!
WHERE IS SHE?
IF I KNOW TAKIKO, SHE WENT STRAIGHT FOR KING TEMDAN!
MY EYE ACTIVATED ON ZÎYÌ... BUT TEG DIDN'T SING!
MAYBE URUKI'S BEEN SUCCESSFUL!
AH
UNH...
IT'S...
...KING TEMDAN'S SEER!!
TEGIL'S MEN MUST'VE GOTTEN HER!

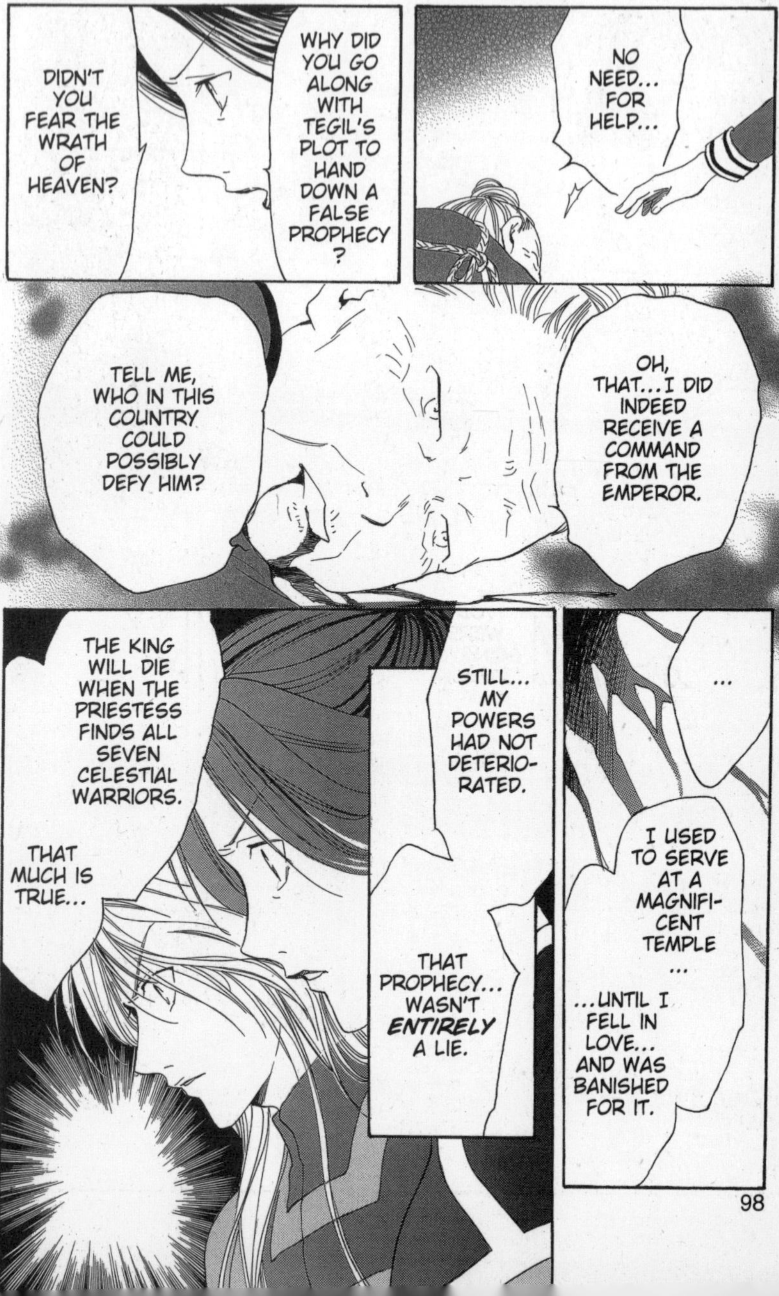
NO NEED... FOR HELP...
WHY DID YOU GO ALONG WITH TEGIL'S PLOT TO HAND DOWN A FALSE PROPHECY?
DIDN'T YOU FEAR THE WRATH OF HEAVEN?
OH, THAT... I DID INDEED RECEIVE A COMMAND FROM THE EMPEROR.
TELL ME, WHO IN THIS COUNTRY COULD POSSIBLY DEFY HIM?
...
I USED TO SERVE AT A MAGNIFICENT TEMPLE...
...UNTIL I FELL IN LOVE... AND WAS BANISHED FOR IT.
STILL... MY POWERS HAD NOT DETERIORATED.
THE KING WILL DIE WHEN THE PRIESTESS FINDS ALL SEVEN CELESTIAL WARRIORS.
THAT MUCH IS TRUE...
THAT PROPHECY... WASN'T *ENTIRELY* A LIE.

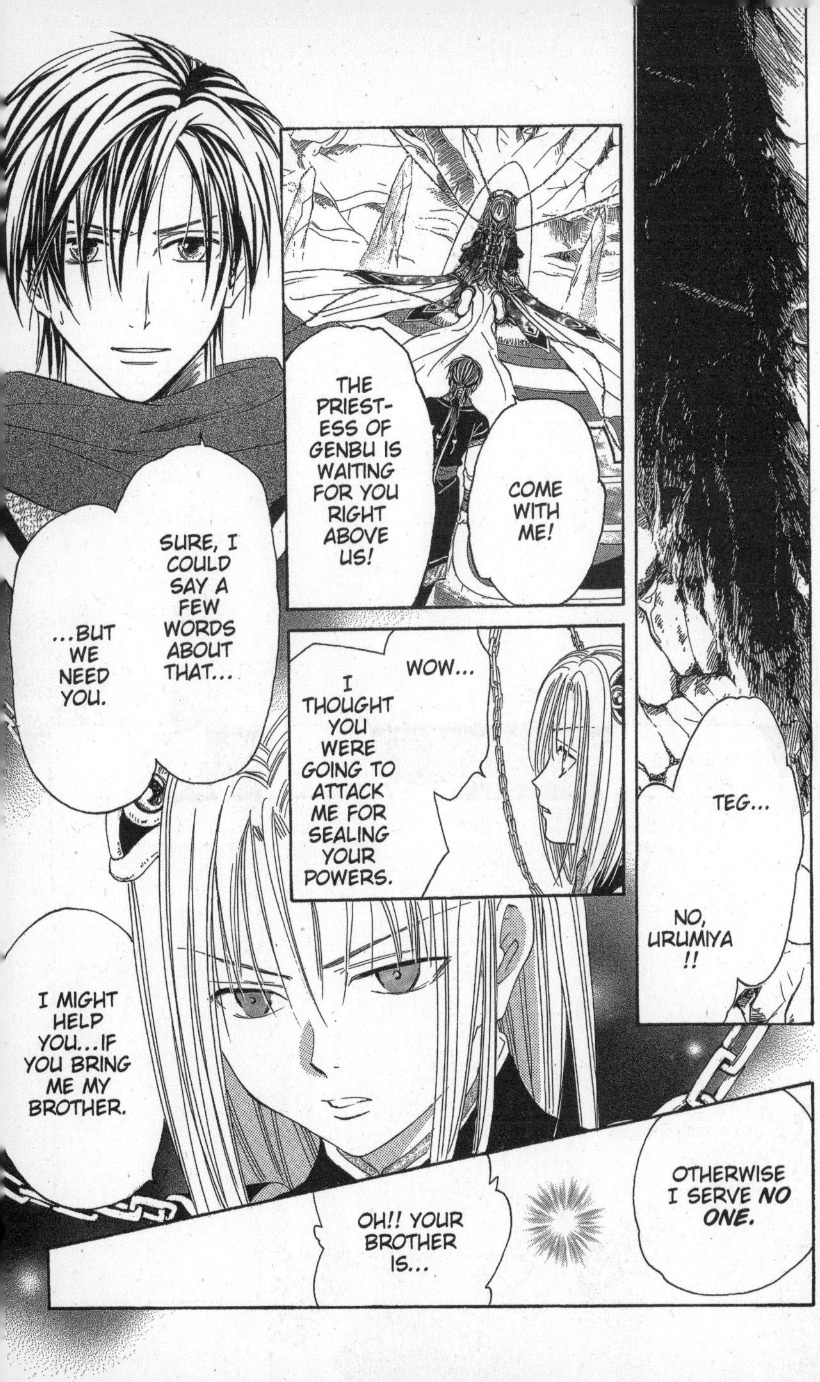
TEG...
NO, URUMIYA!!
COME WITH ME!
THE PRIESTESS OF GENBU IS WAITING FOR YOU RIGHT ABOVE US!
SURE, I COULD SAY A FEW WORDS ABOUT THAT...
...BUT WE NEED YOU.
WOW...
I THOUGHT YOU WERE GOING TO ATTACK ME FOR SEALING YOUR POWERS.
I MIGHT HELP YOU...IF YOU BRING ME MY BROTHER.
OTHERWISE I SERVE *NO ONE.*
OH!! YOUR BROTHER IS...

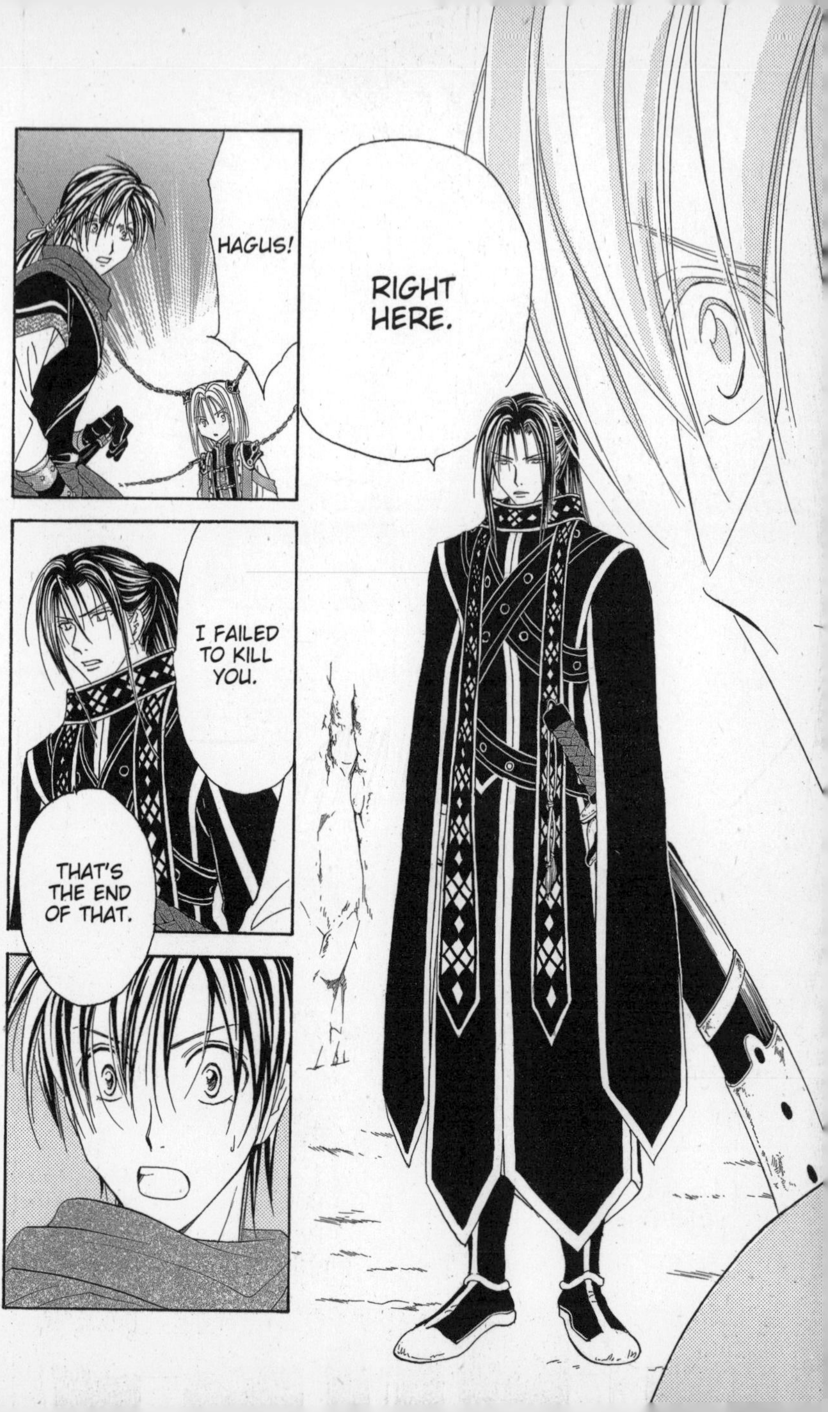
RIGHT HERE.
HAGUS!
I FAILED TO KILL YOU.
THAT'S THE END OF THAT.

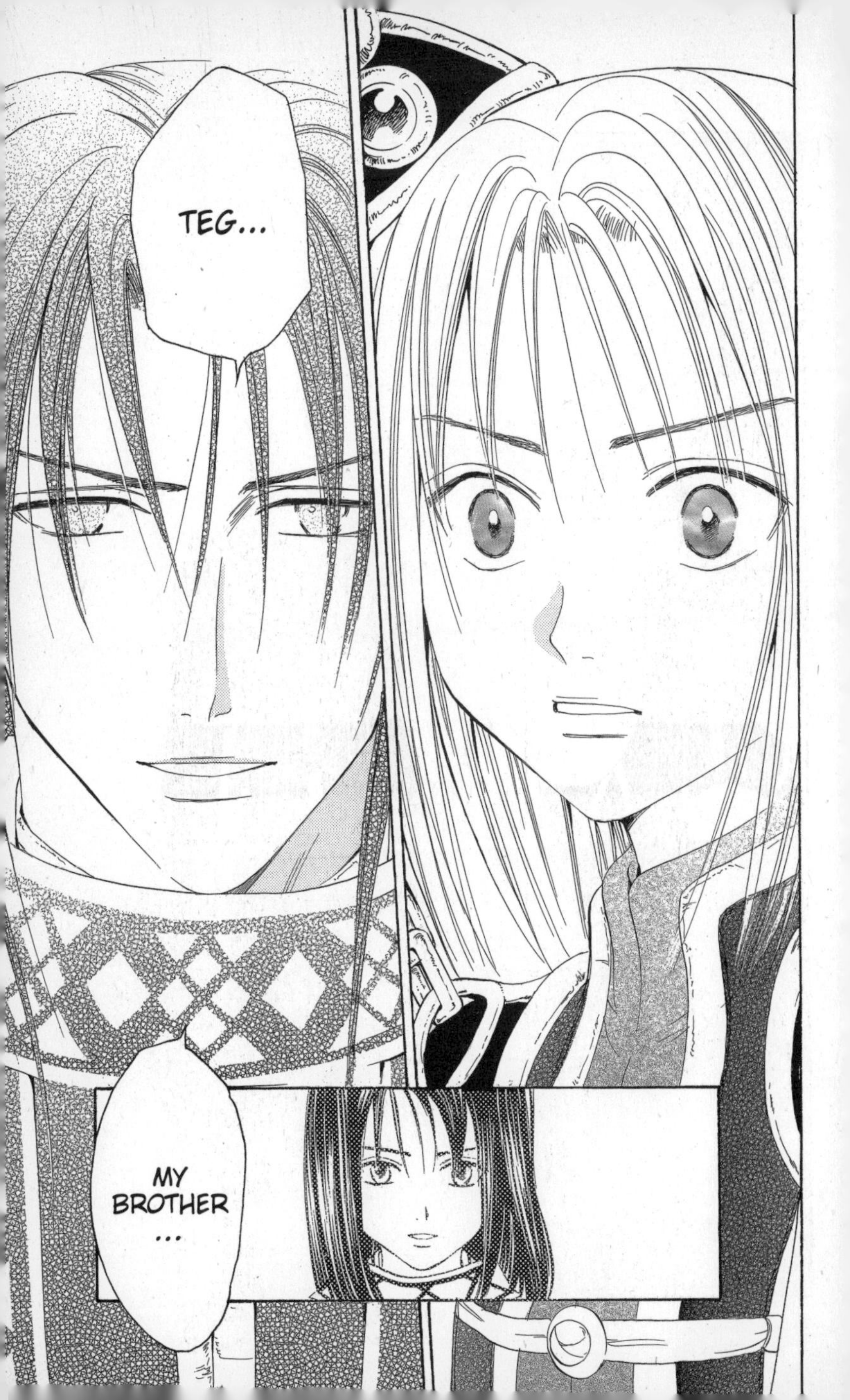
TEG...
MY BROTHER ...

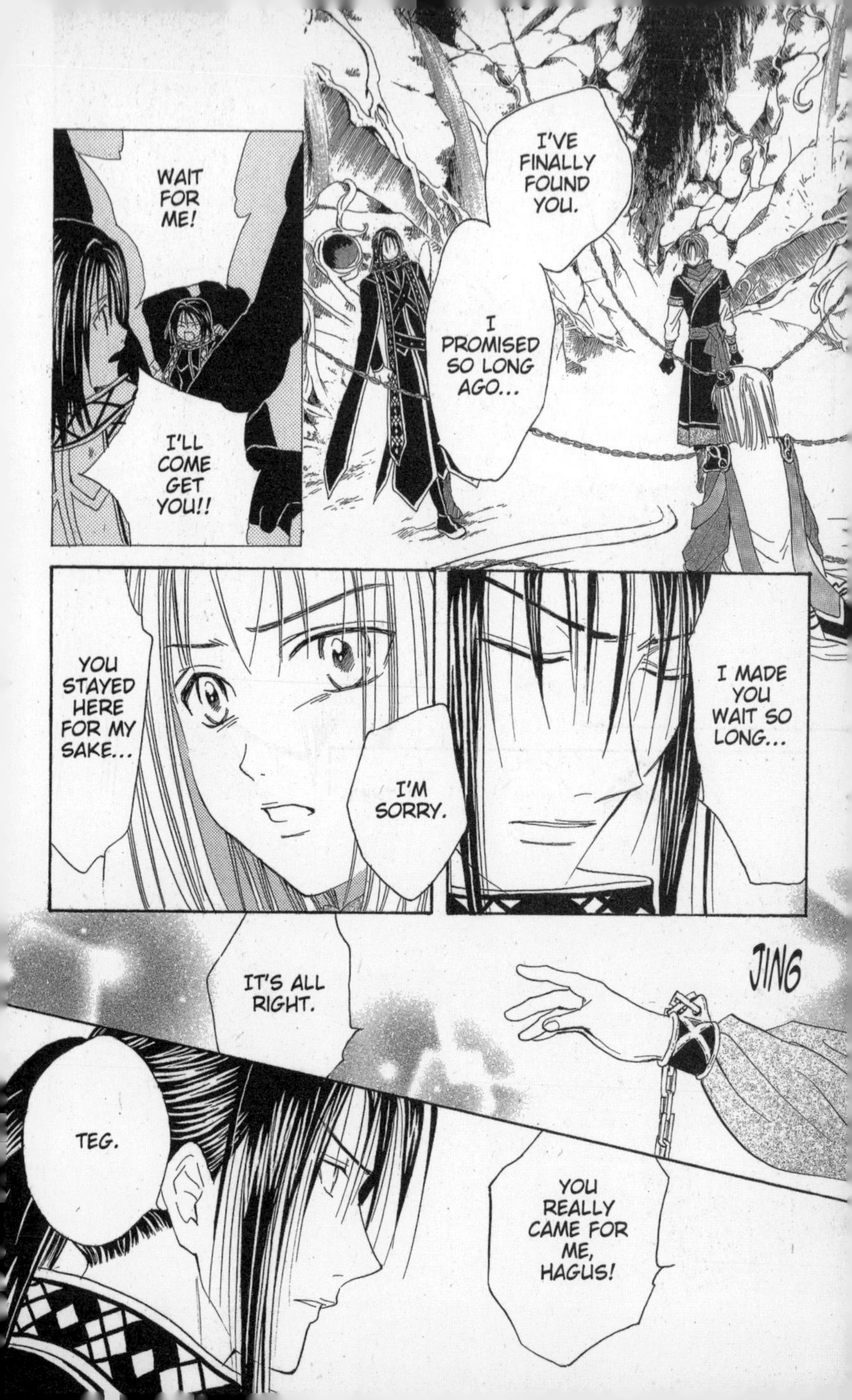
I'VE FINALLY FOUND YOU.
I PROMISED SO LONG AGO...
WAIT FOR ME!
I'LL COME GET YOU!!
I MADE YOU WAIT SO LONG...
YOU STAYED HERE FOR MY SAKE...
I'M SORRY.
JING
IT'S ALL RIGHT.
YOU REALLY CAME FOR ME, HAGUS!
TEG.

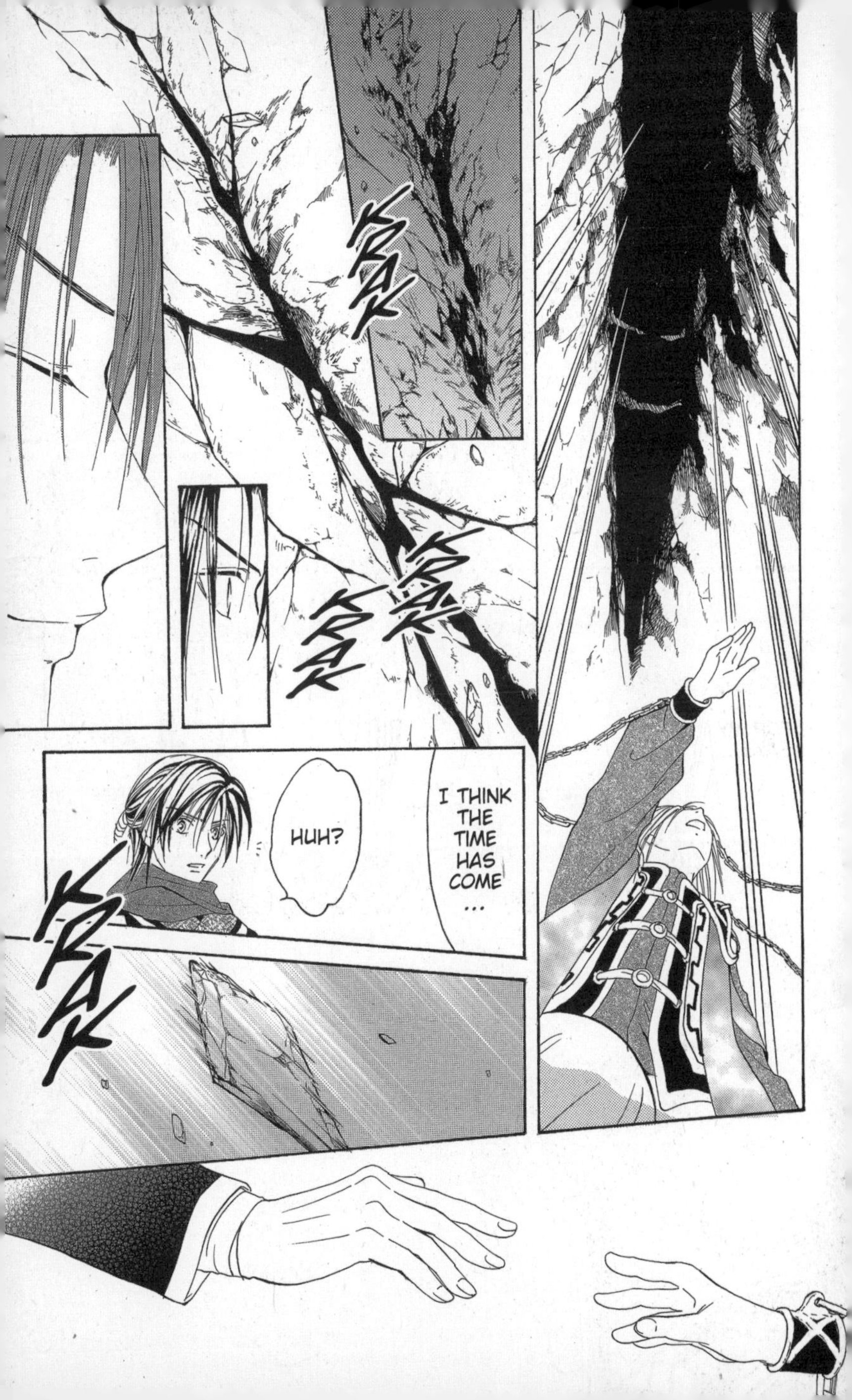
KRAK
KRAK
KRAK
I THINK THE TIME HAS COME ...
HUH?
KRAK

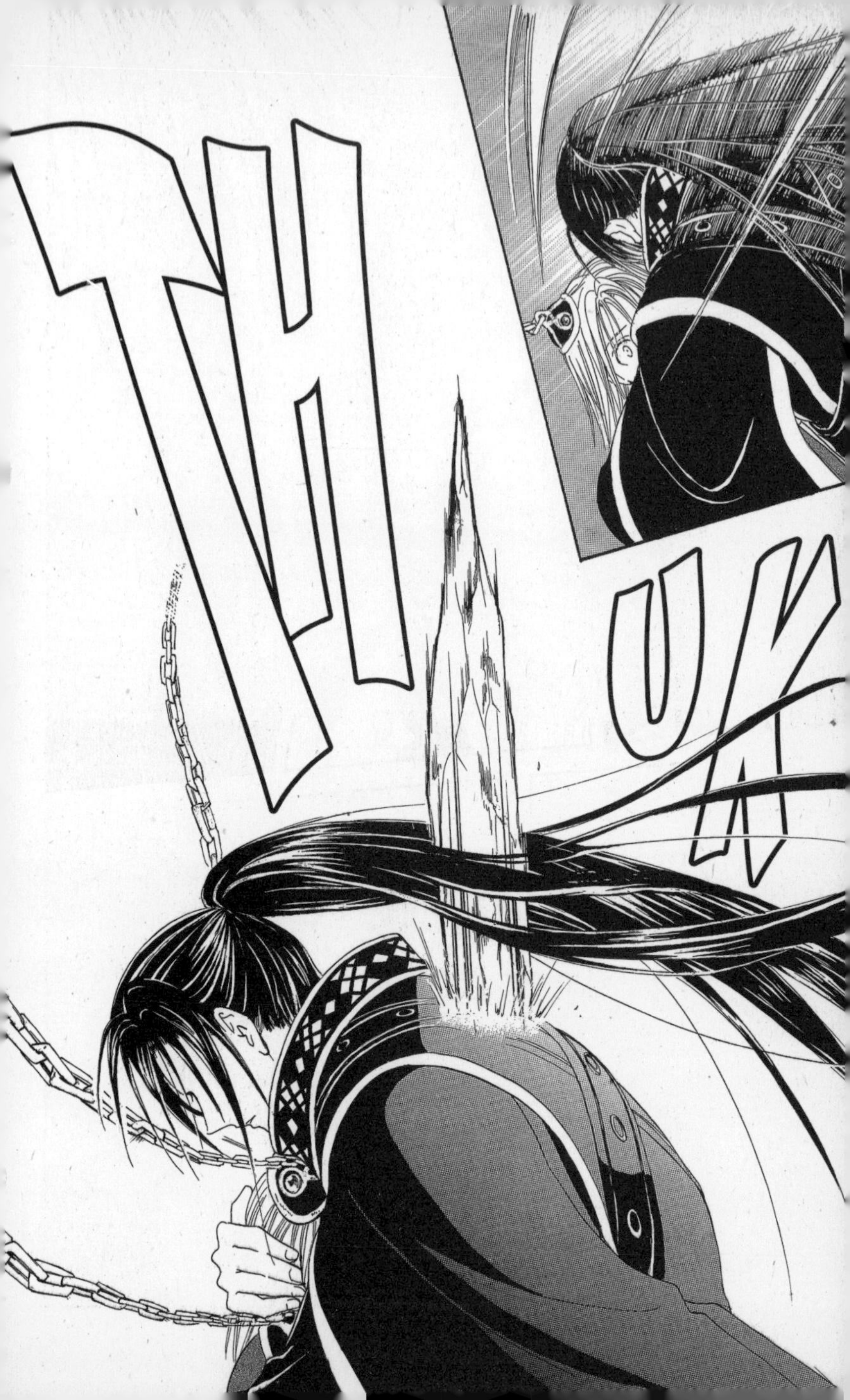
THUNK

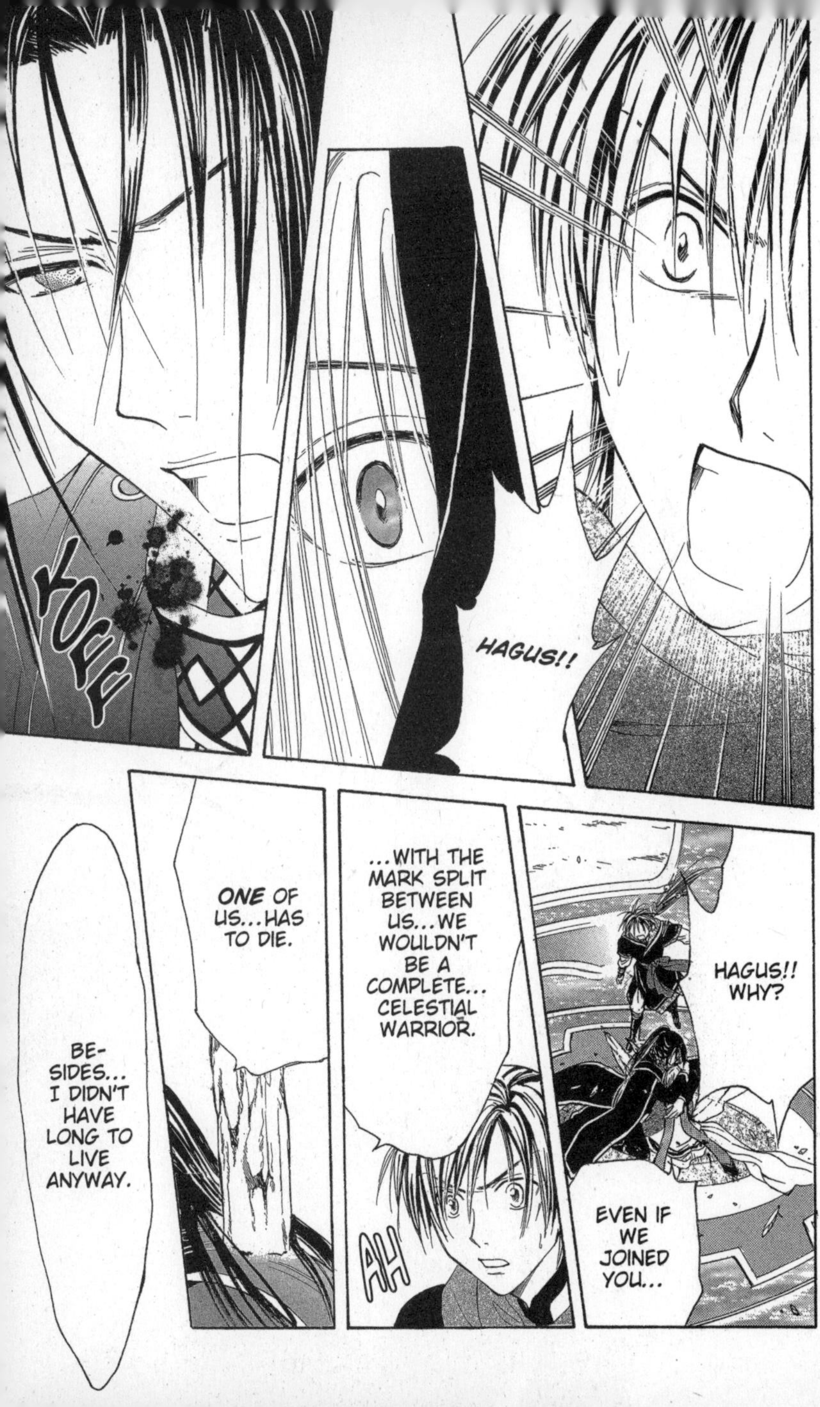
HAGUS!!
KOFF
HAGUS!! WHY?
EVEN IF WE JOINED YOU...
...WITH THE MARK SPLIT BETWEEN US...WE WOULDN'T BE A COMPLETE... CELESTIAL WARRIOR.
AH
ONE OF US...HAS TO DIE.
BE-SIDES... I DIDN'T HAVE LONG TO LIVE ANYWAY.

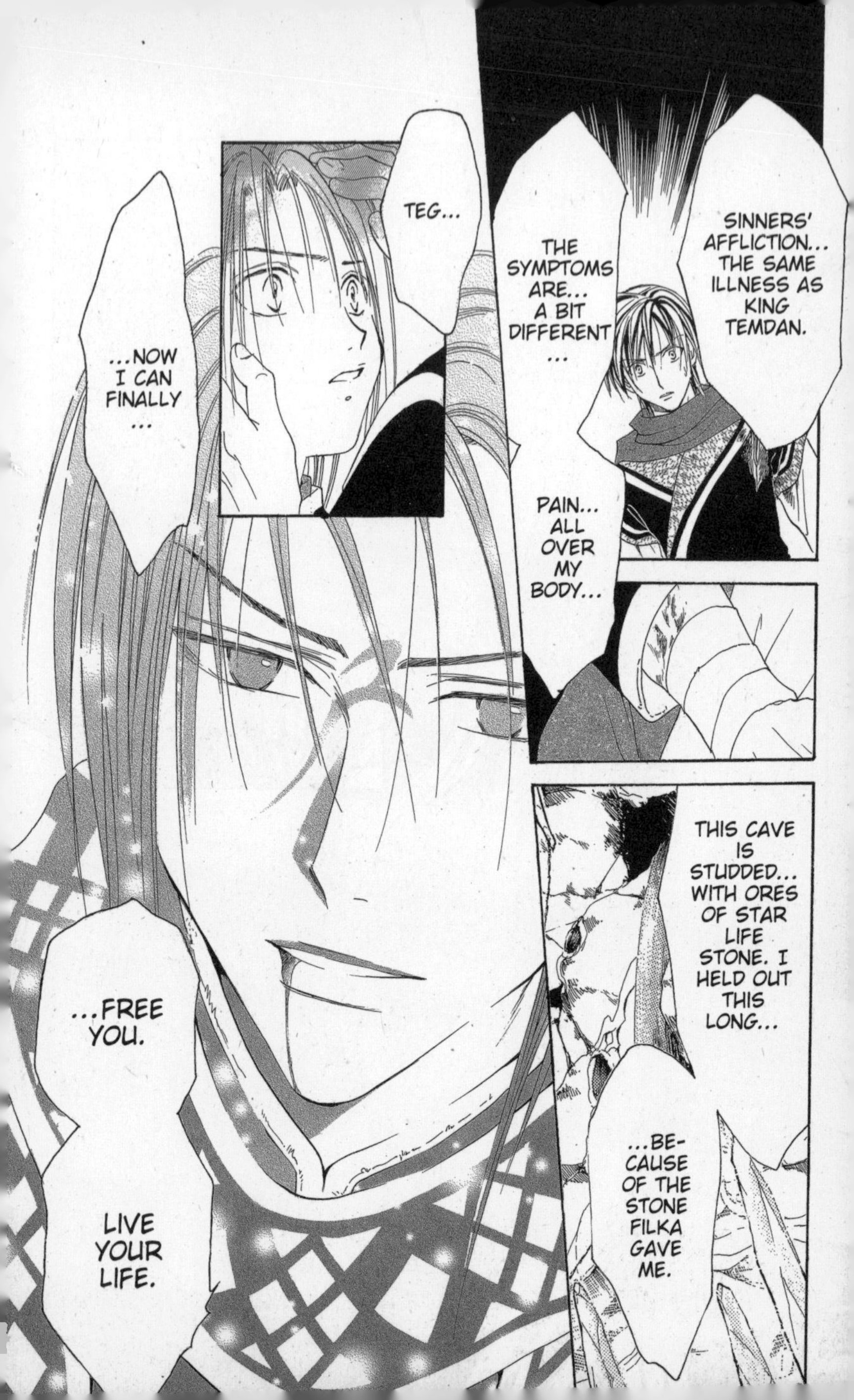
SINNERS' AFFLICTION... THE SAME ILLNESS AS KING TEMDAN.
THE SYMPTOMS ARE... A BIT DIFFERENT...
PAIN... ALL OVER MY BODY...
THIS CAVE IS STUDDED... WITH ORES OF STAR LIFE STONE. I HELD OUT THIS LONG...
...BE-CAUSE OF THE STONE FILKA GAVE ME.
TEG...
...NOW I CAN FINALLY...
...FREE YOU.
LIVE YOUR LIFE.

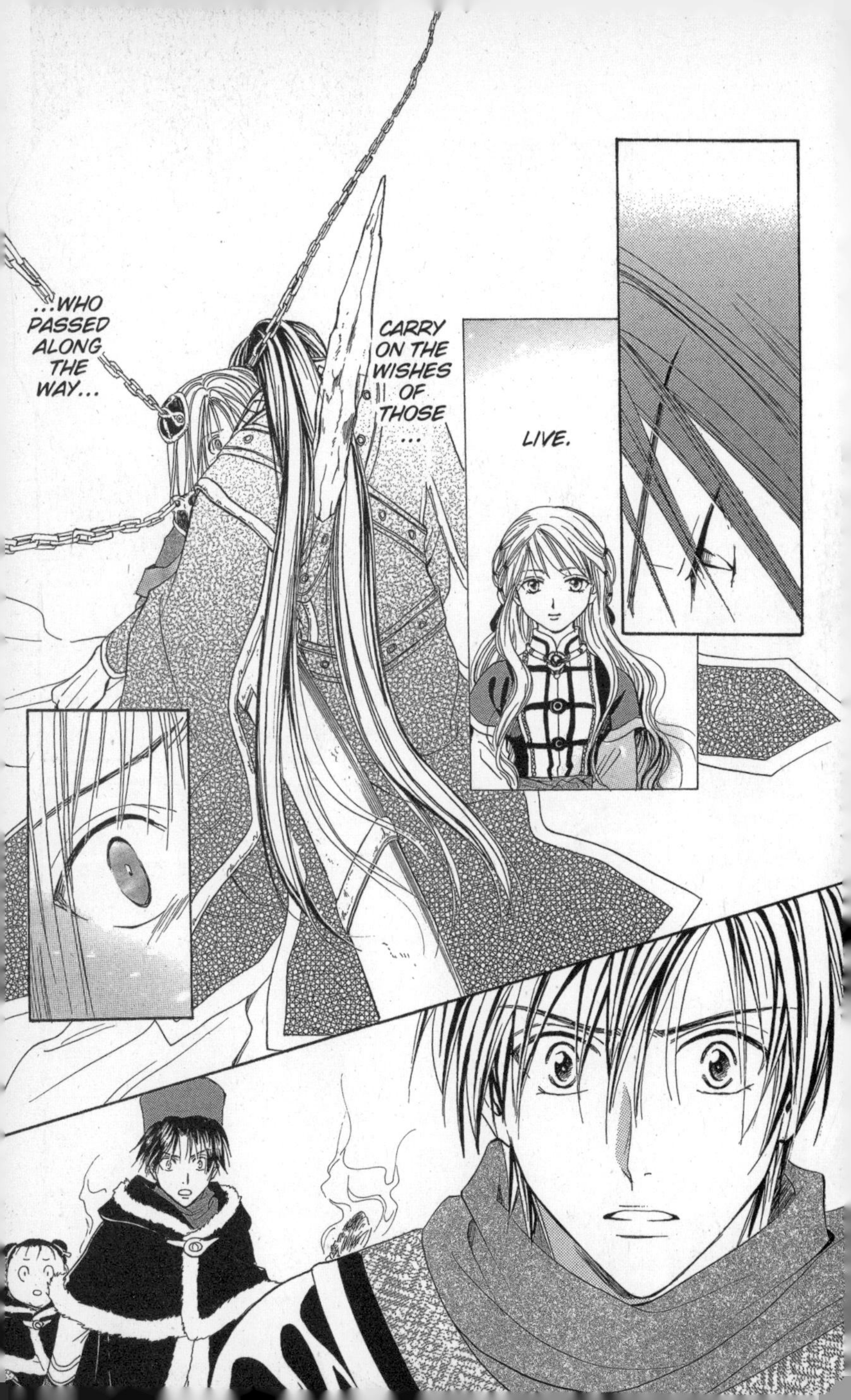
LIVE.
CARRY ON THE WISHES OF THOSE...
...WHO PASSED ALONG THE WAY...

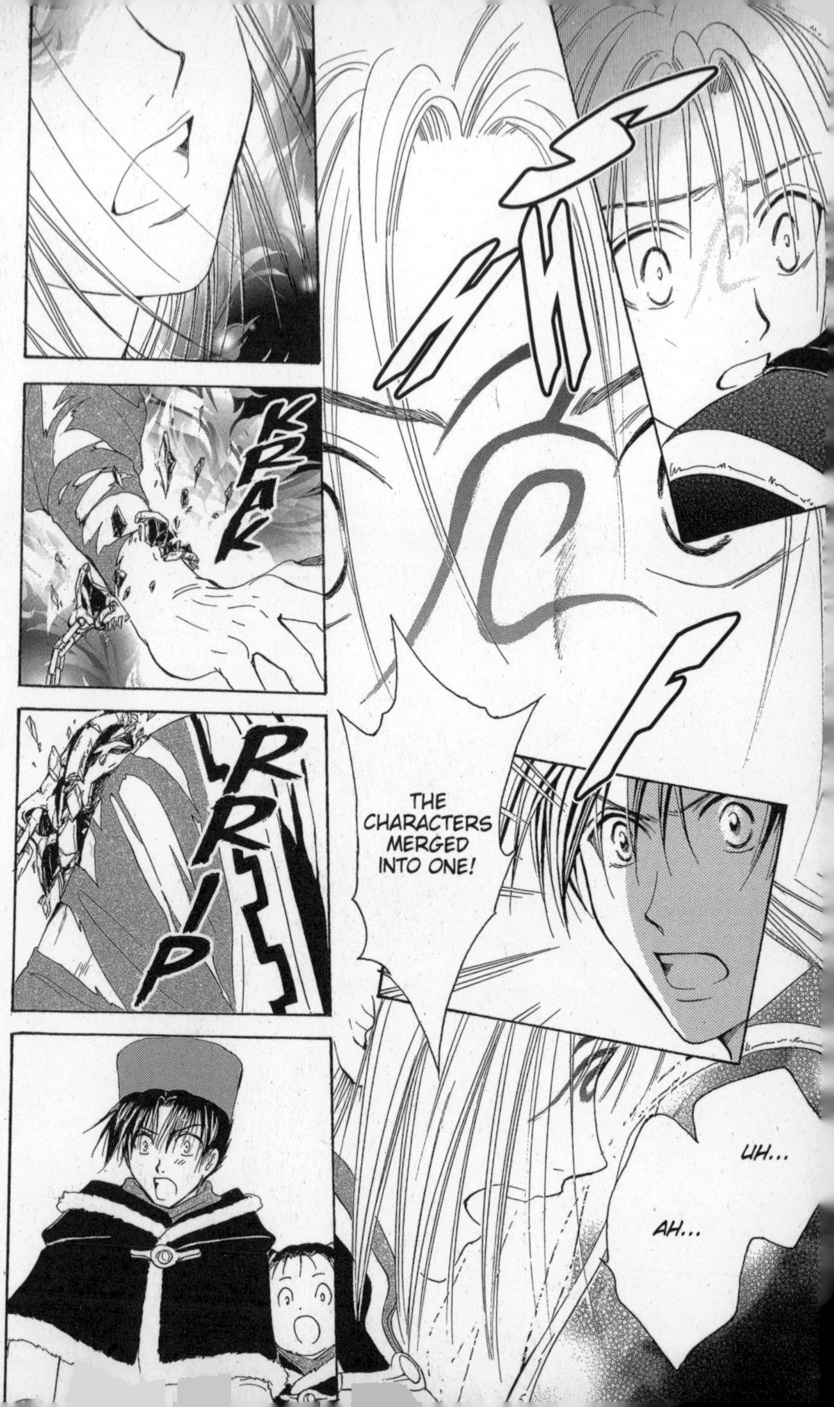
SHHF
THE CHARACTERS MERGED INTO ONE!
UH...
AH...
KRAK
RRIP

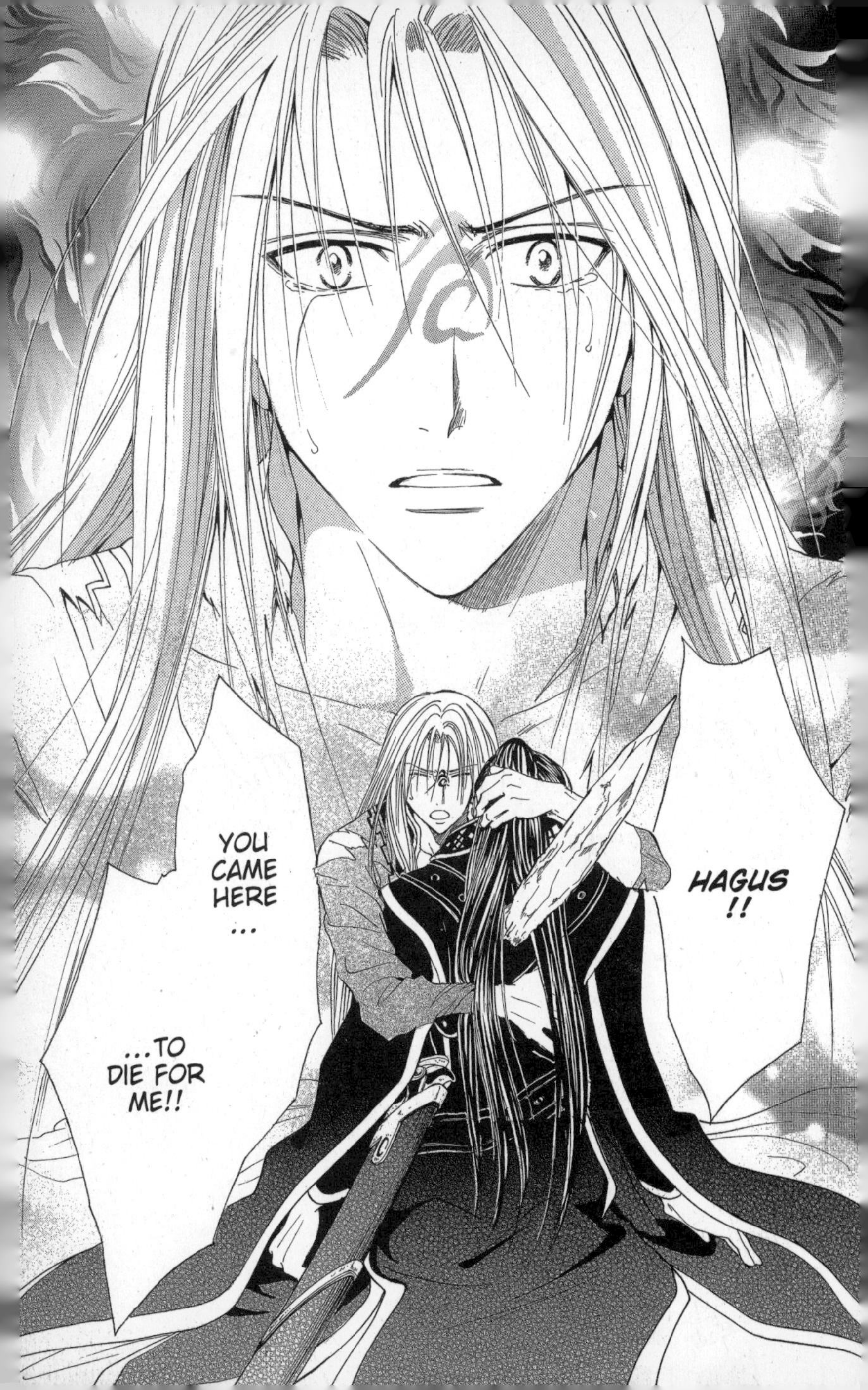
HAGUS!!
YOU CAME HERE...
...TO DIE FOR ME!!

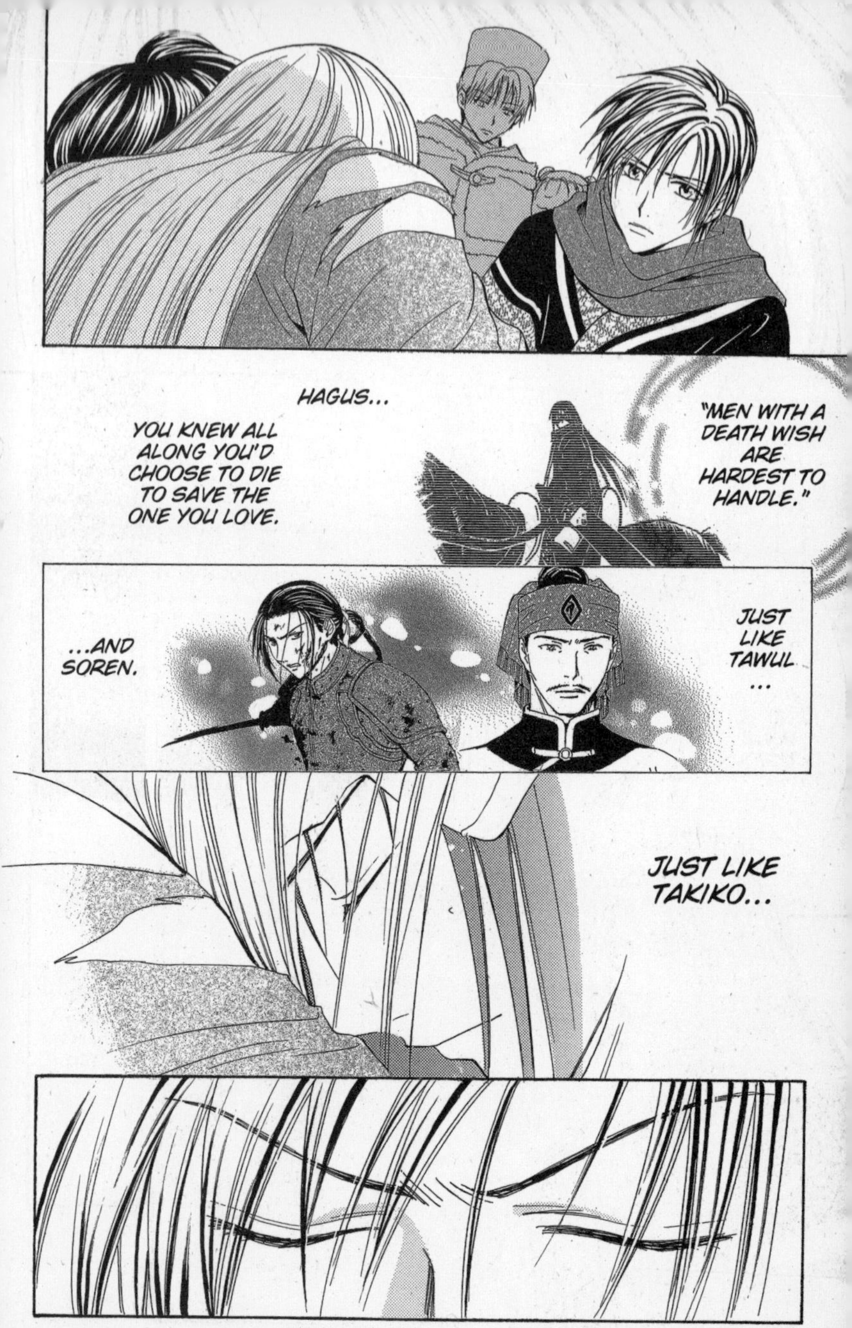
"MEN WITH A DEATH WISH ARE HARDEST TO HANDLE."
HAGUS...
YOU KNEW ALL ALONG YOU'D CHOOSE TO DIE TO SAVE THE ONE YOU LOVE.
JUST LIKE TAWUL...
...AND SOREN.
JUST LIKE TAKIKO...

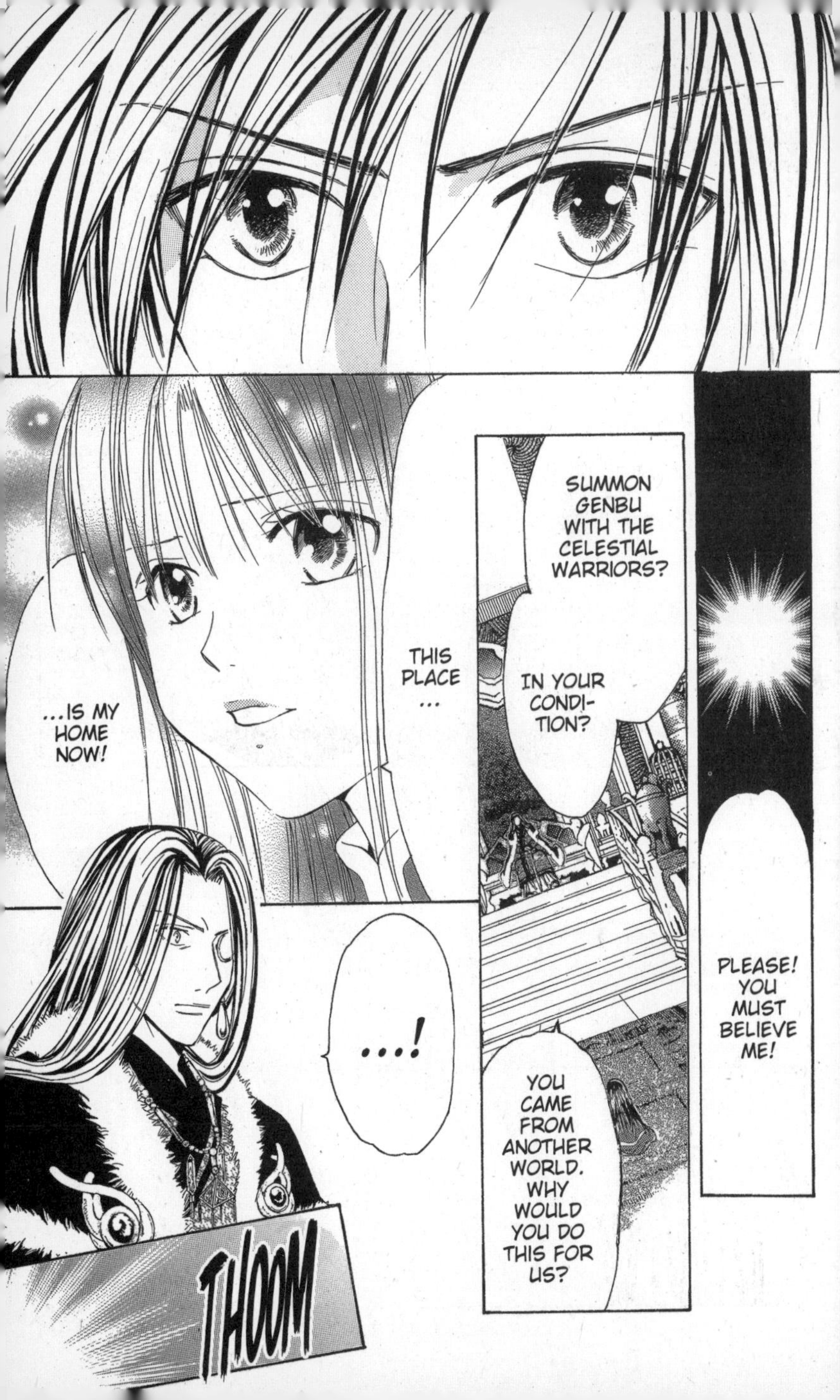
PLEASE! YOU MUST BELIEVE ME!
SUMMON GENBU WITH THE CELESTIAL WARRIORS?
IN YOUR CONDITION?
YOU CAME FROM ANOTHER WORLD. WHY WOULD YOU DO THIS FOR US?
THIS PLACE ...
...IS MY HOME NOW!
...!
THOOM

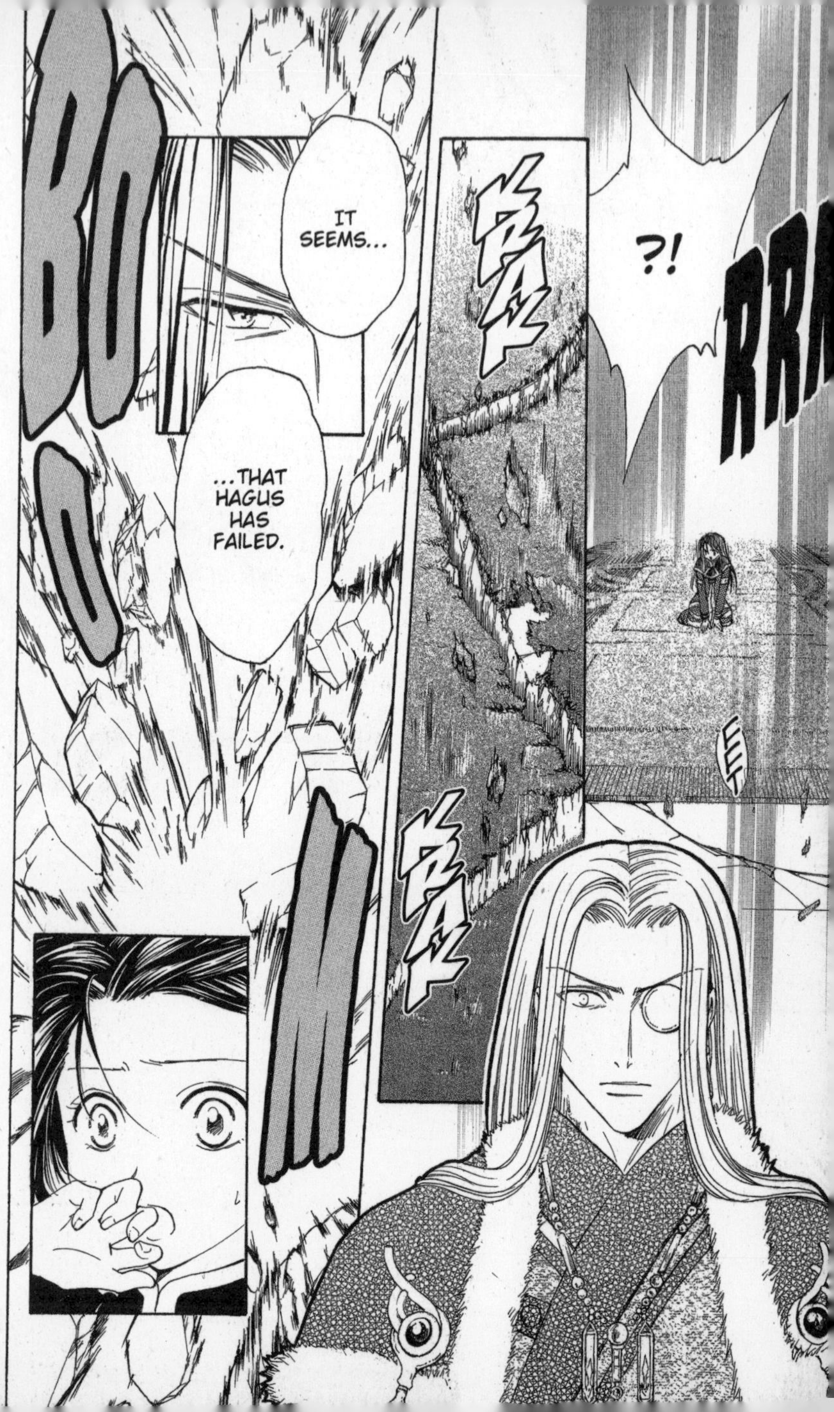
?!
IT SEEMS...
...THAT HAGUS HAS FAILED.
BOOM

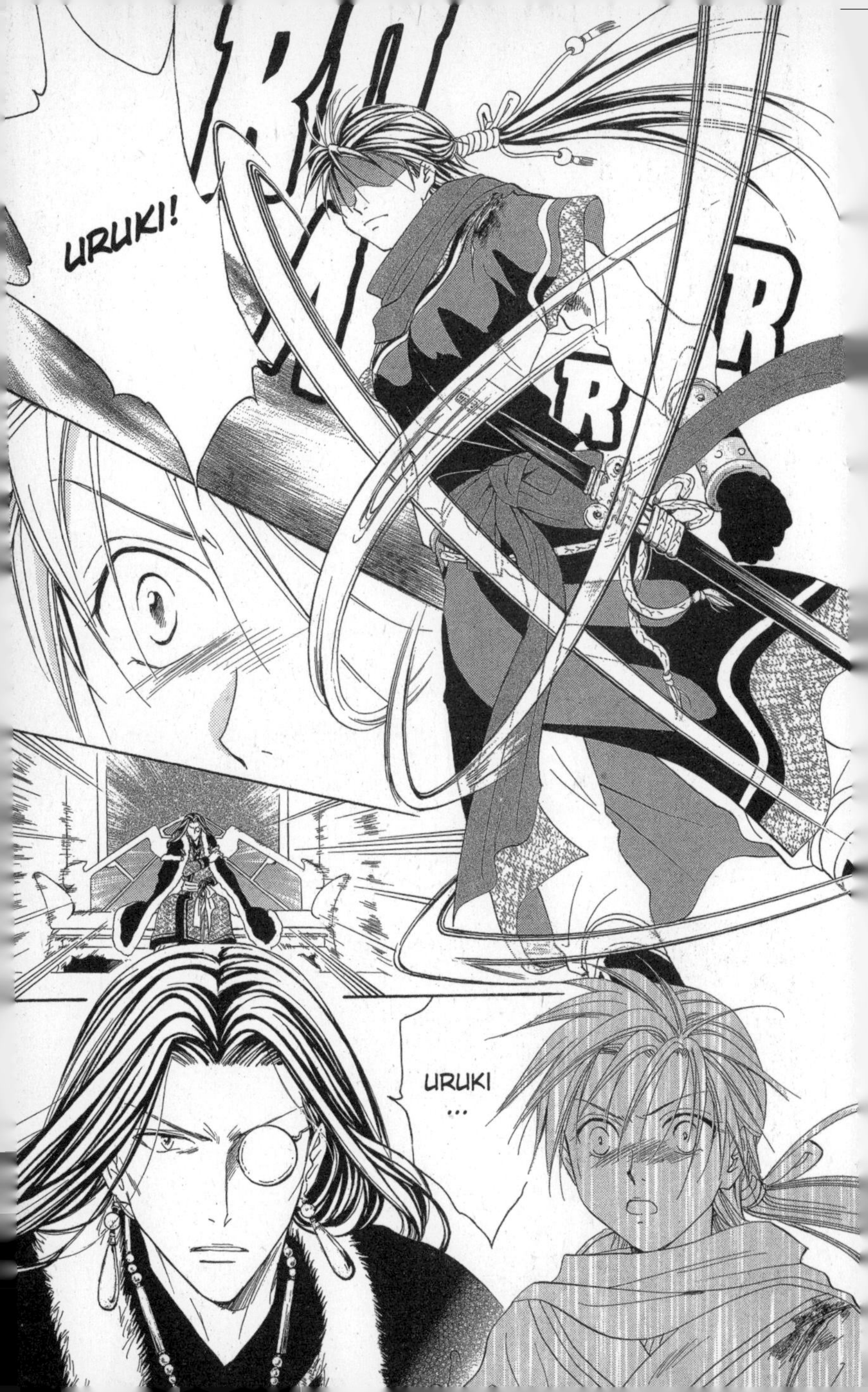
URUKI!
URUKI
...

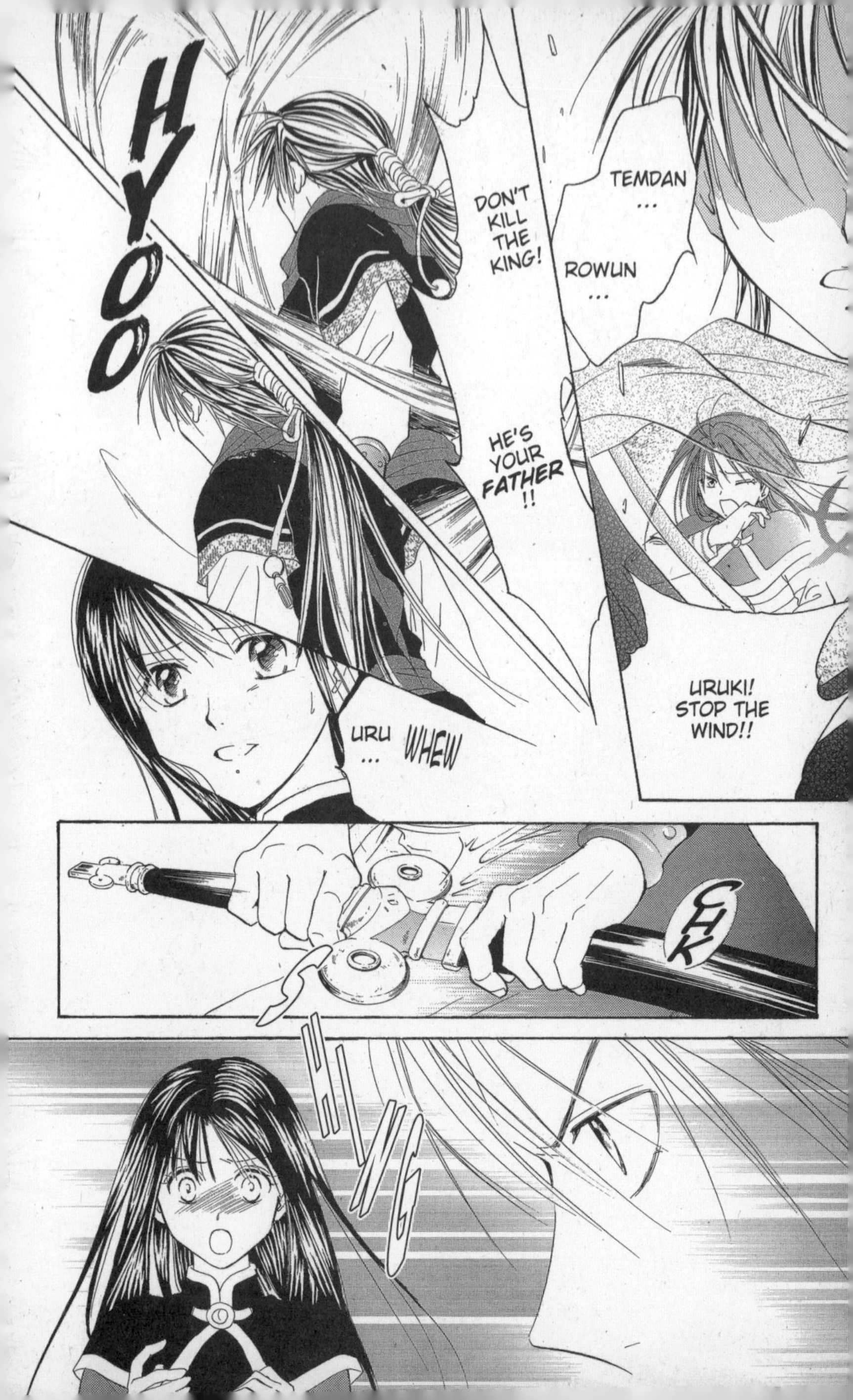
TEMDAN ...
ROWUN ...
URUKI! STOP THE WIND!!
HYOO
DON'T KILL THE KING!
HE'S YOUR FATHER !!
URU ...
WHEW
CHK
HING

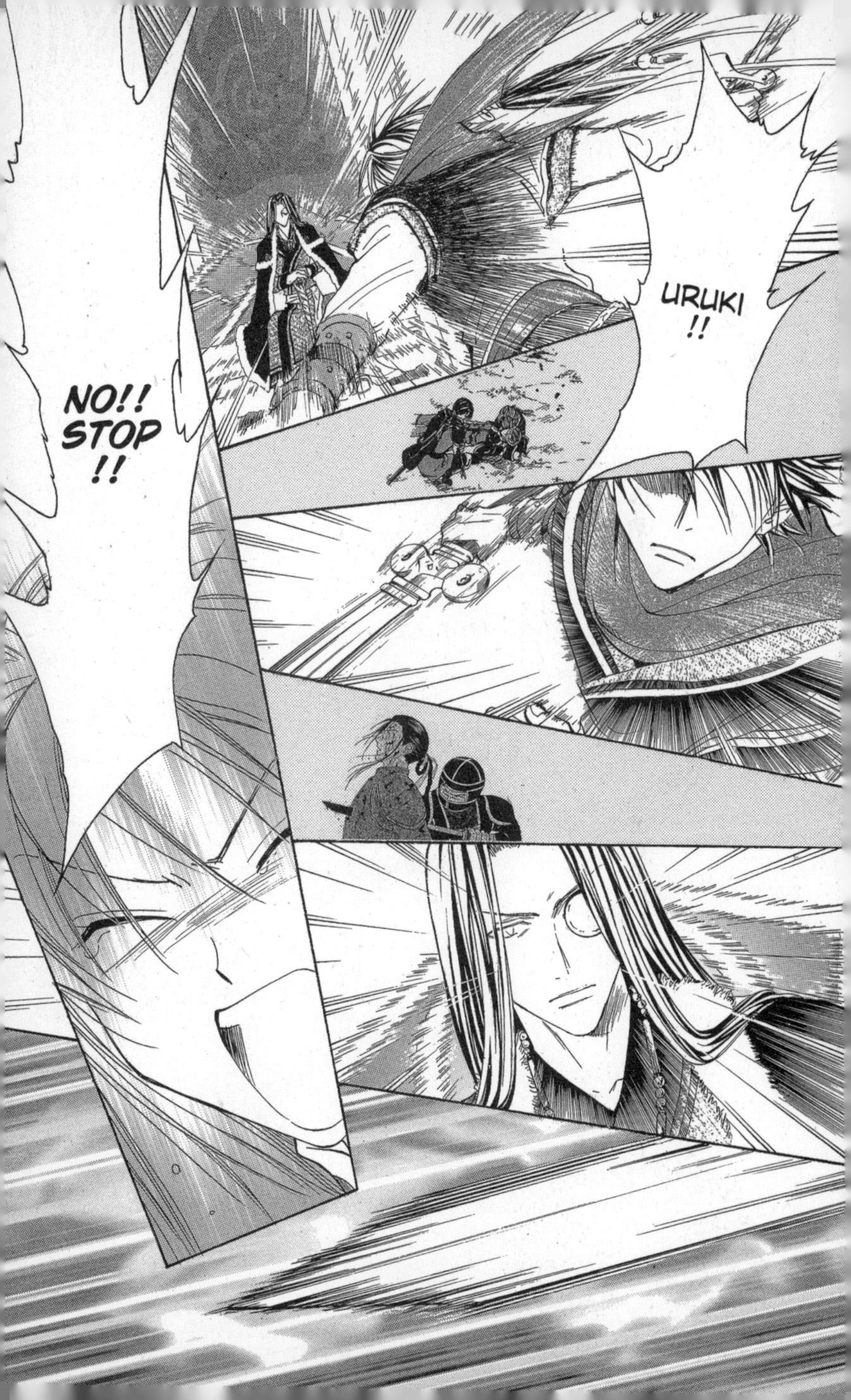
URUKI !!
NO!! STOP !!

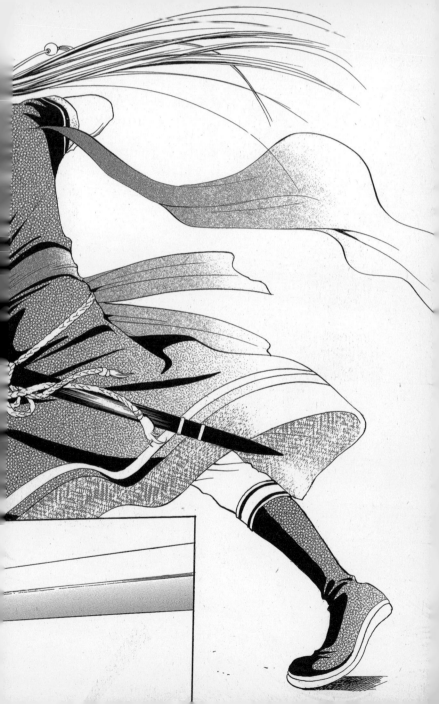

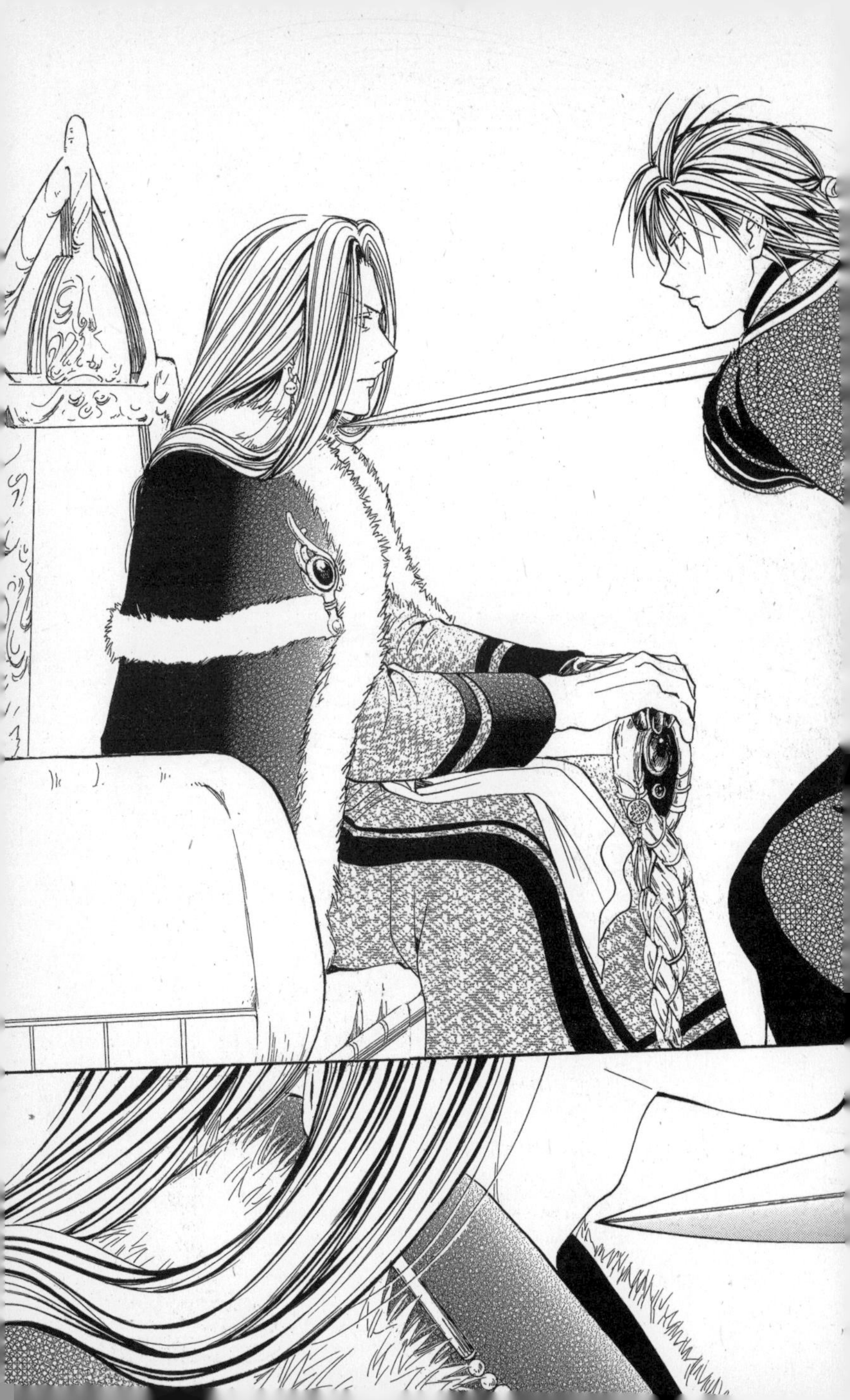

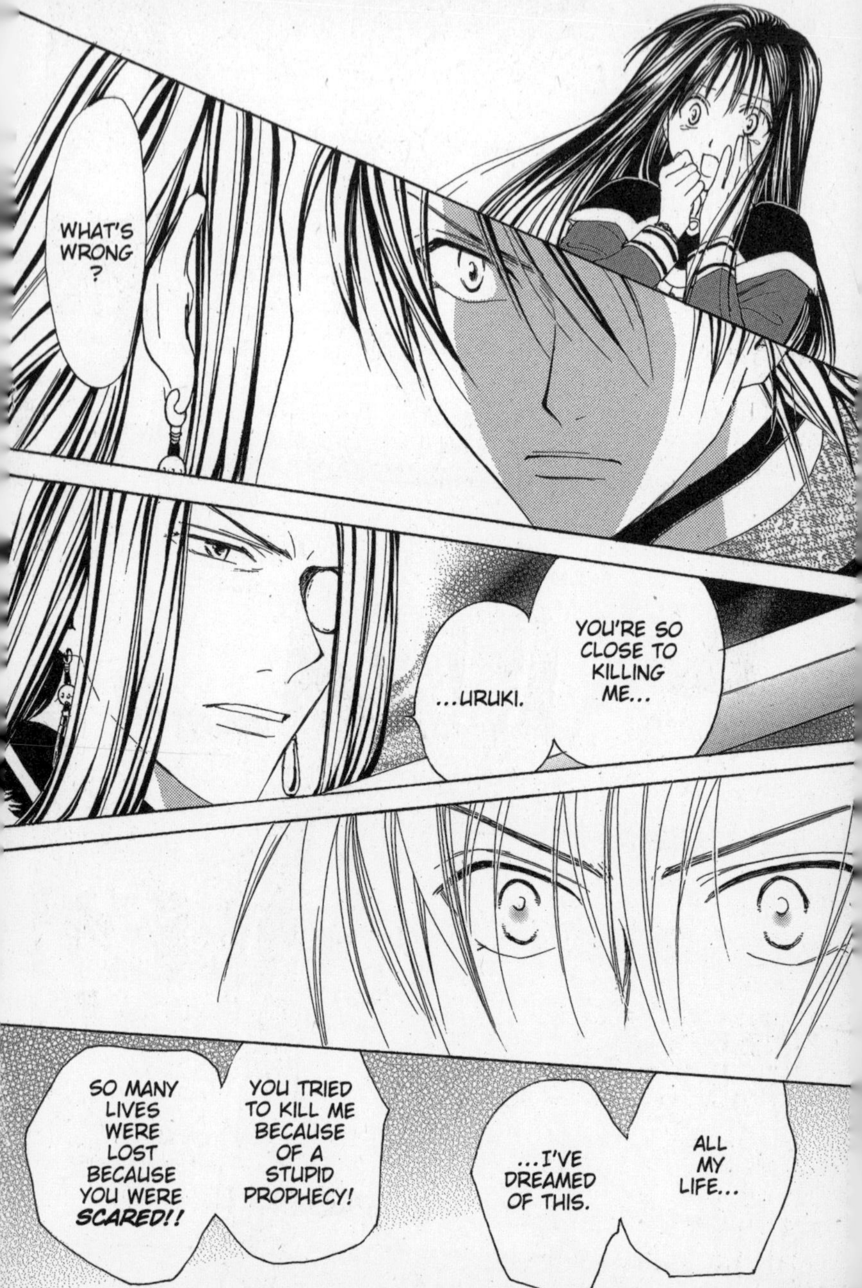
WHAT'S WRONG?
YOU'RE SO CLOSE TO KILLING ME...
...URUKI.
ALL MY LIFE...
...I'VE DREAMED OF THIS.
YOU TRIED TO KILL ME BECAUSE OF A STUPID PROPHECY!
SO MANY LIVES WERE LOST BECAUSE YOU WERE ***SCARED!!***

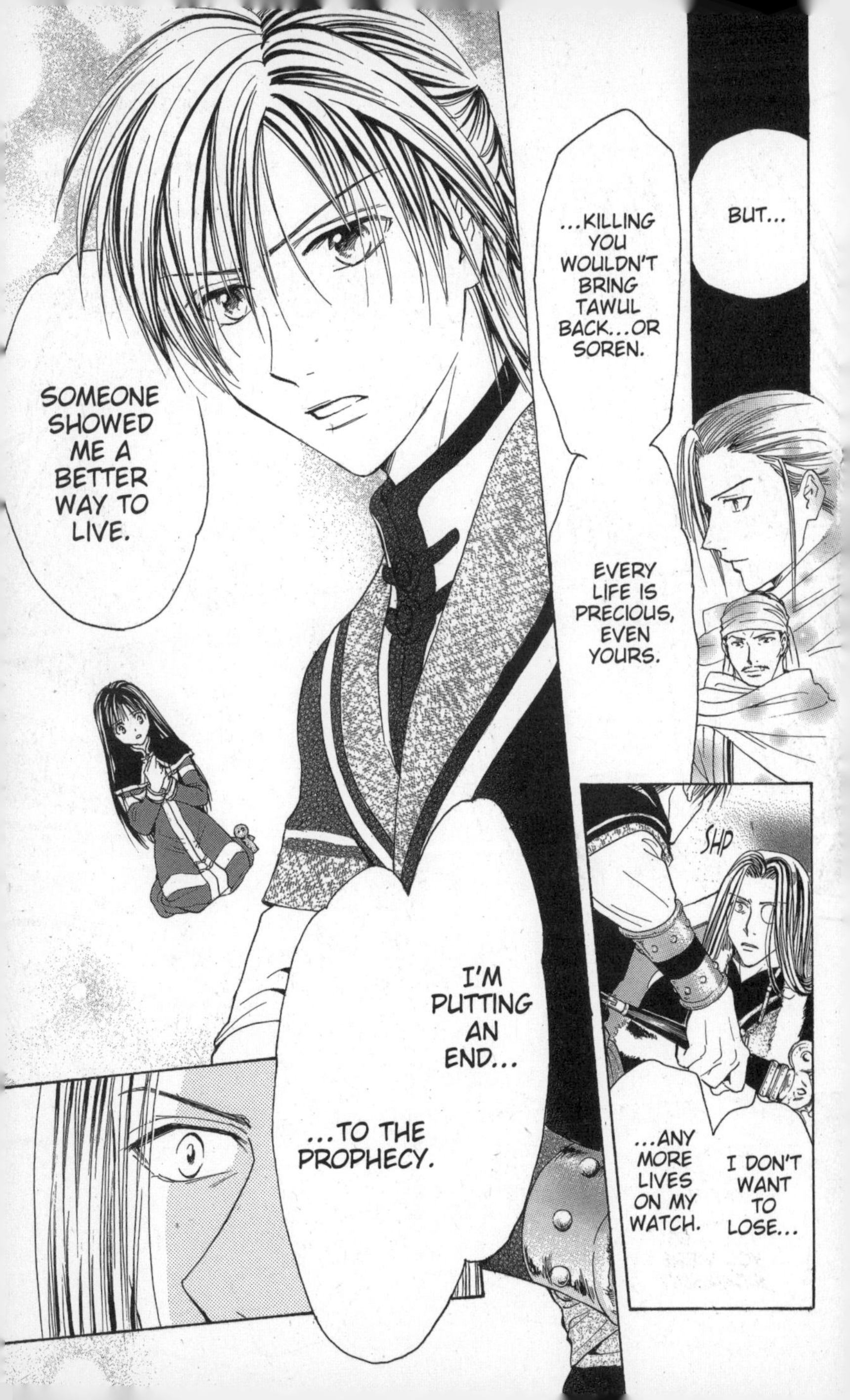
BUT...
...KILLING YOU WOULDN'T BRING TAWUL BACK...OR SOREN.
EVERY LIFE IS PRECIOUS, EVEN YOURS.
SHP
I DON'T WANT TO LOSE...
...ANY MORE LIVES ON MY WATCH.
SOMEONE SHOWED ME A BETTER WAY TO LIVE.
I'M PUTTING AN END...
...TO THE PROPHECY.

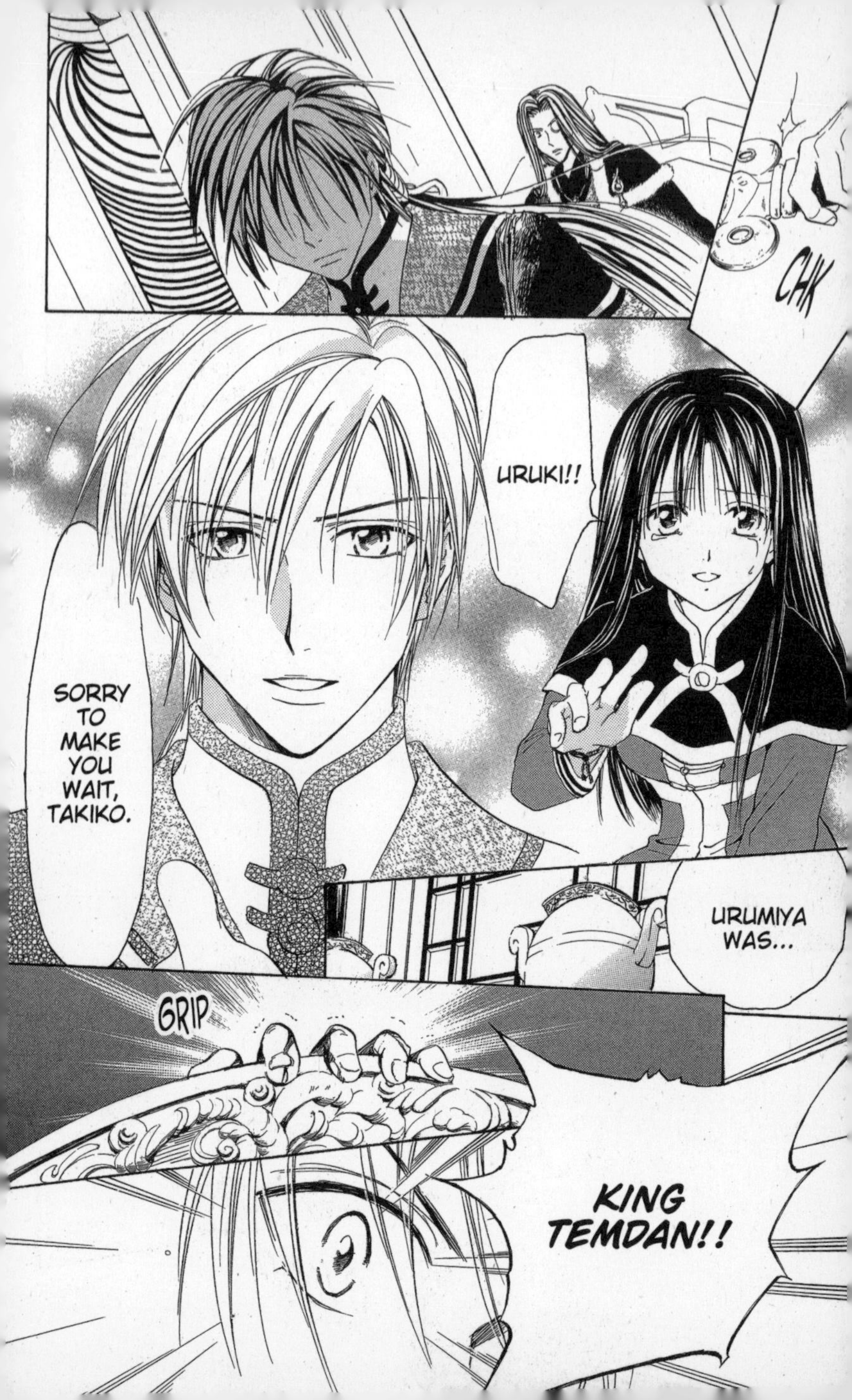
CHK
URUKI!!
SORRY TO MAKE YOU WAIT, TAKIKO.
URUMIYA WAS...
GRIP
KING TEMDAN!!

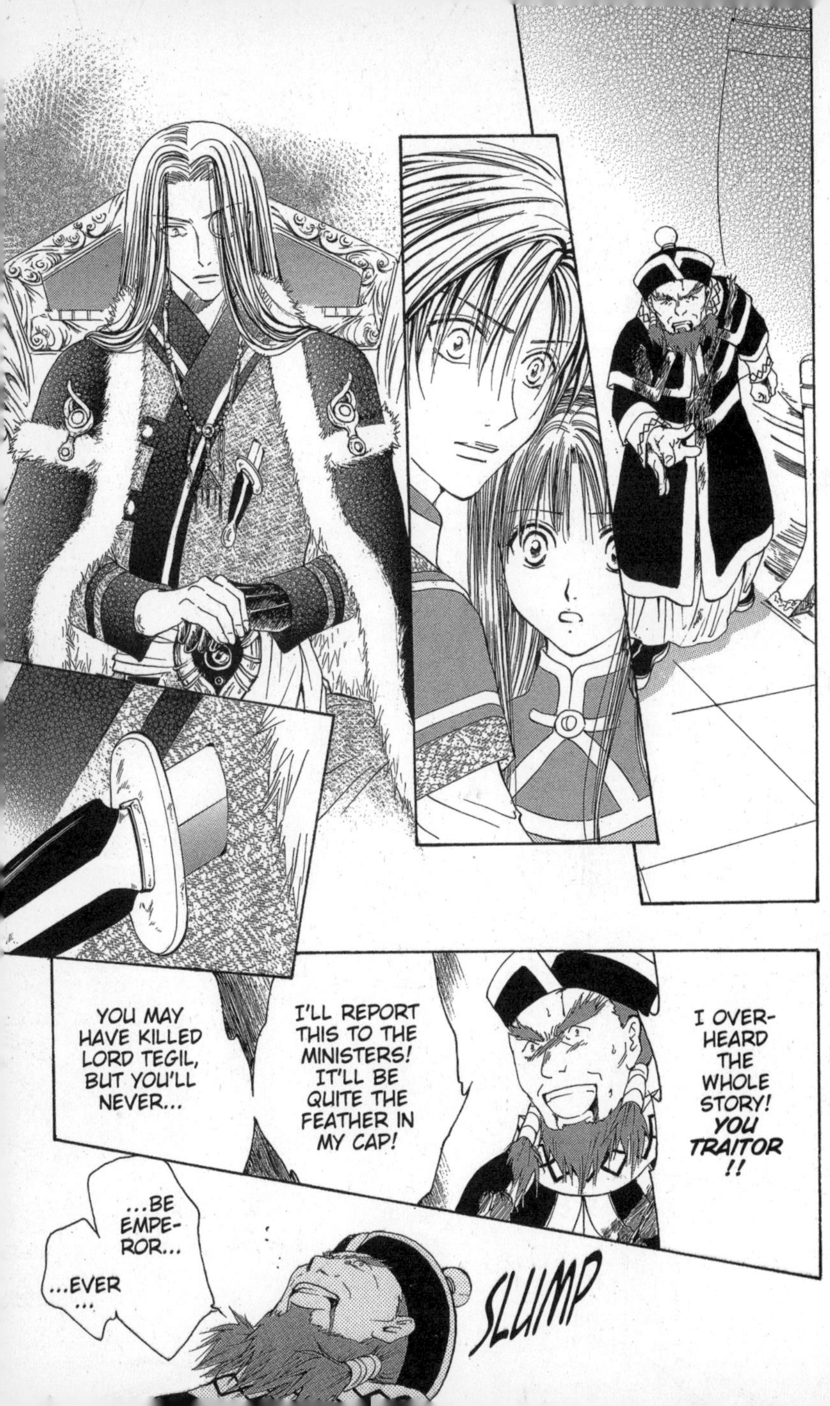
I OVER-HEARD THE WHOLE STORY! *YOU TRAITOR* !!
I'LL REPORT THIS TO THE MINISTERS! IT'LL BE QUITE THE FEATHER IN MY CAP!
YOU MAY HAVE KILLED LORD TEGIL, BUT YOU'LL NEVER...
...BE EMPE-ROR...
...EVER ...
SLUMP

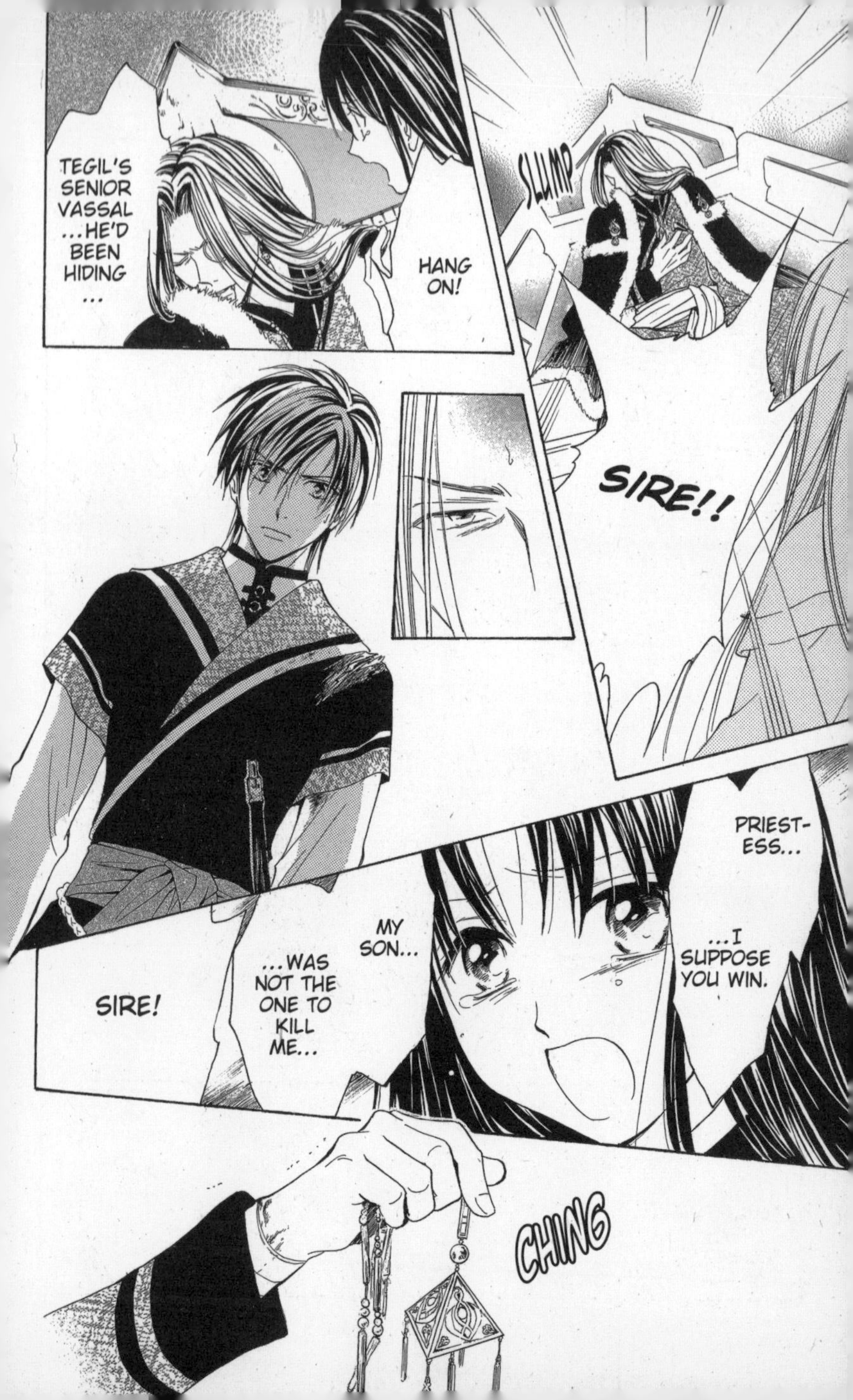
SLUMP
SIRE!!
HANG ON!
TEGIL'S SENIOR VASSAL ...HE'D BEEN HIDING ...
PRIEST-ESS...
...I SUPPOSE YOU WIN.
MY SON...
...WAS NOT THE ONE TO KILL ME...
SIRE!
CHING

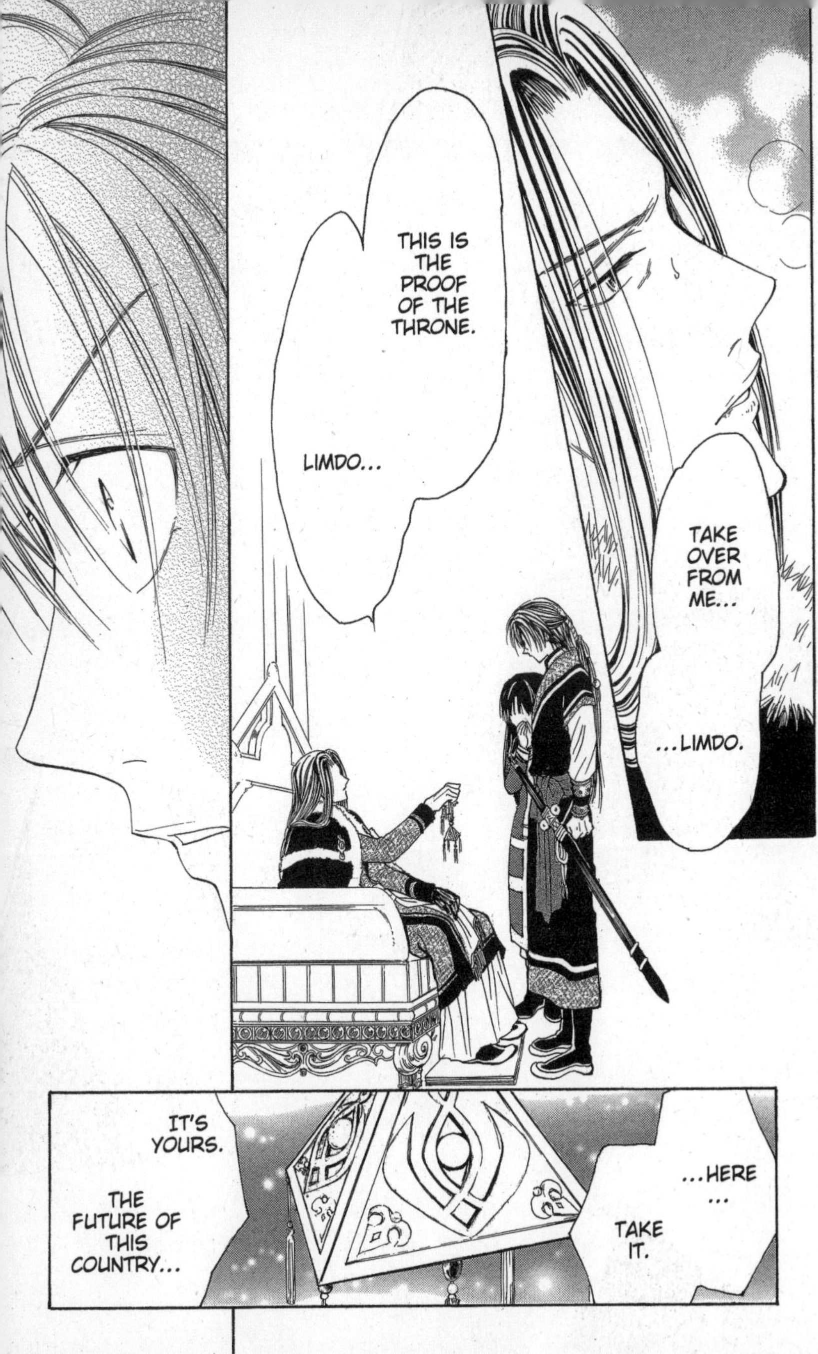
TAKE OVER FROM ME...
...LIMDO.
THIS IS THE PROOF OF THE THRONE.
LIMDO...
...HERE ...
TAKE IT.
IT'S YOURS.
THE FUTURE OF THIS COUNTRY...

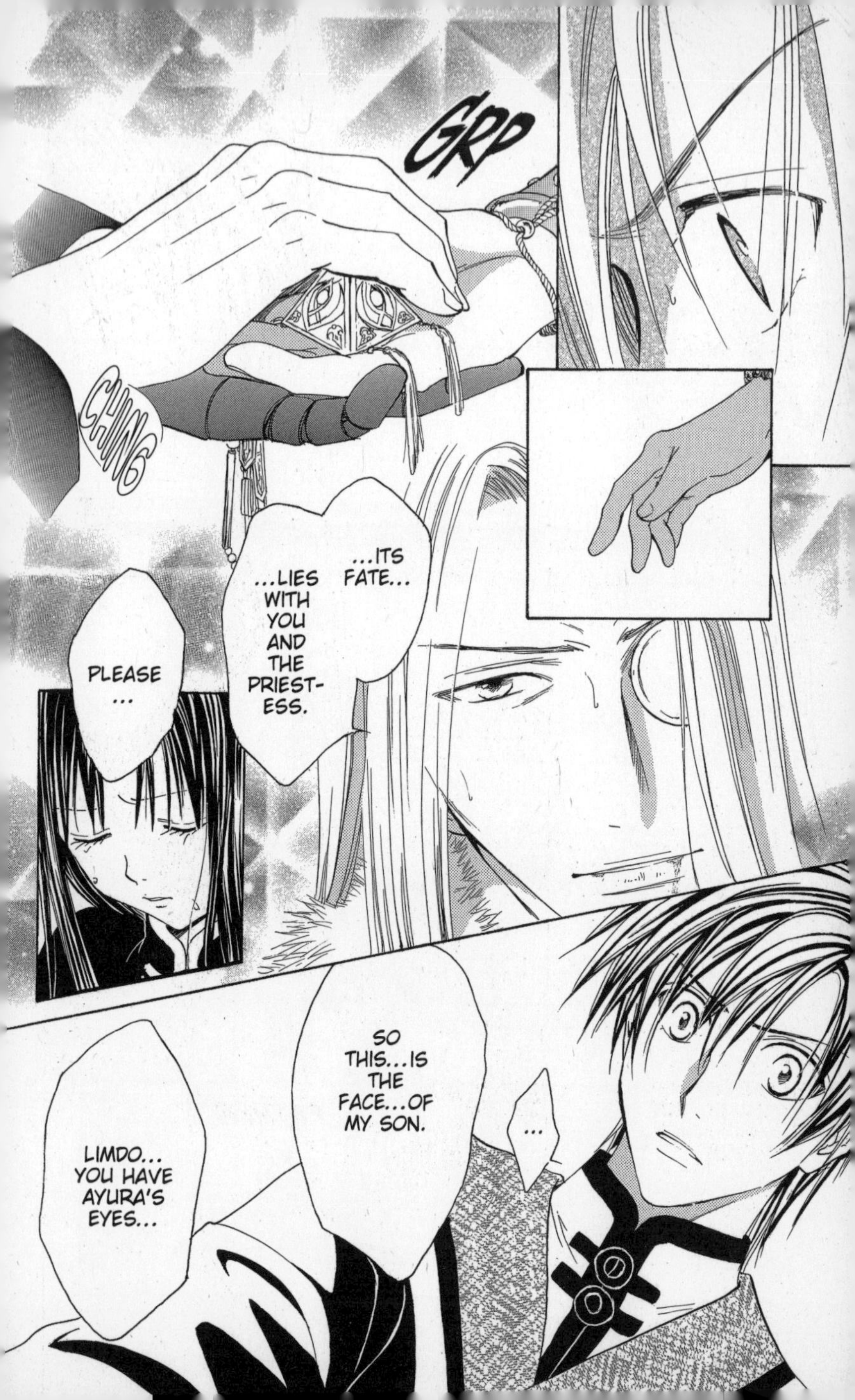
GRP
CHING
...ITS FATE...
...LIES WITH YOU AND THE PRIESTESS.
PLEASE...
...
SO THIS...IS THE FACE...OF MY SON.
LIMDO... YOU HAVE AYURA'S EYES...

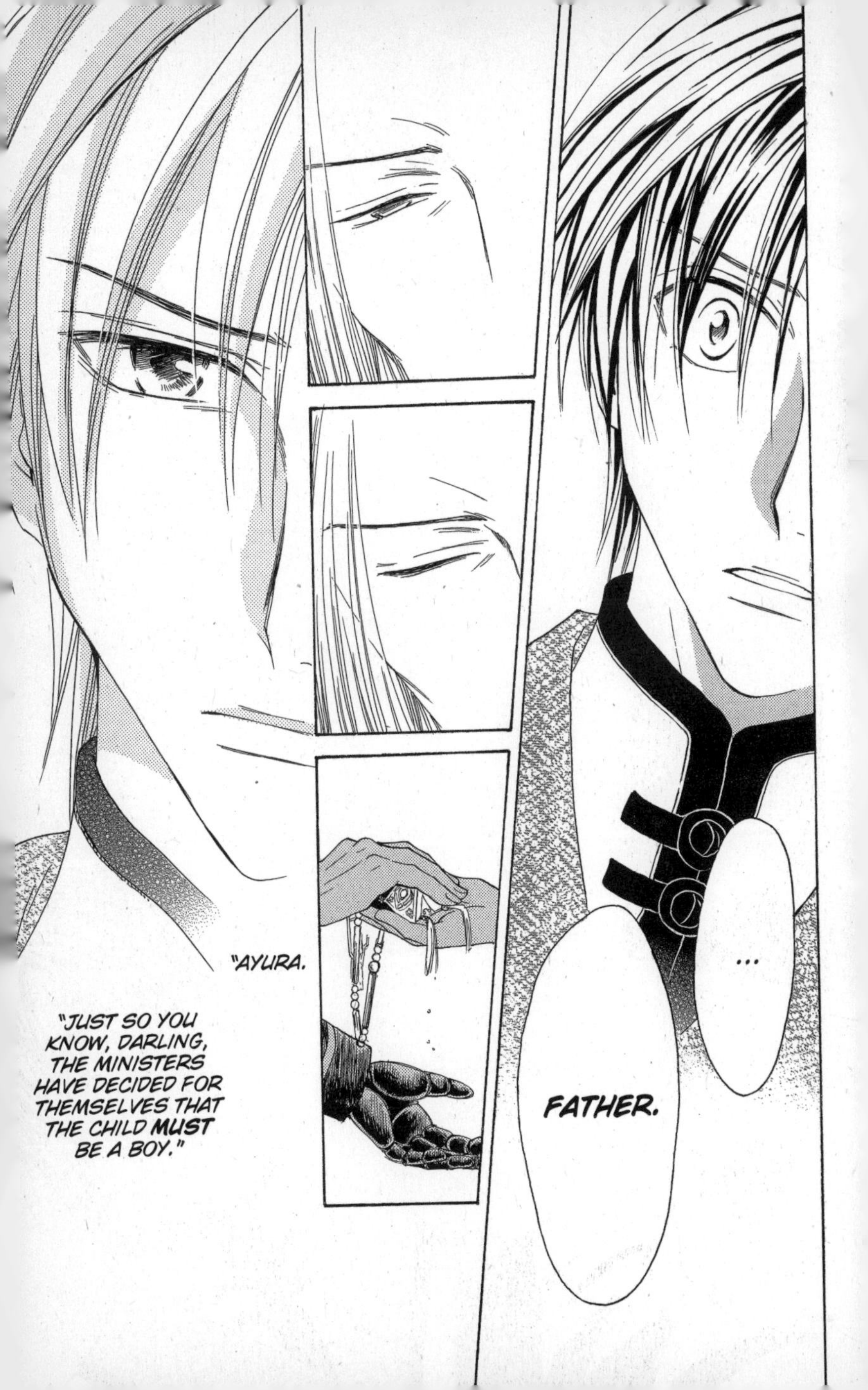
...
FATHER.
"AYURA.
"JUST SO YOU KNOW, DARLING, THE MINISTERS HAVE DECIDED FOR THEMSELVES THAT THE CHILD MUST BE A BOY."

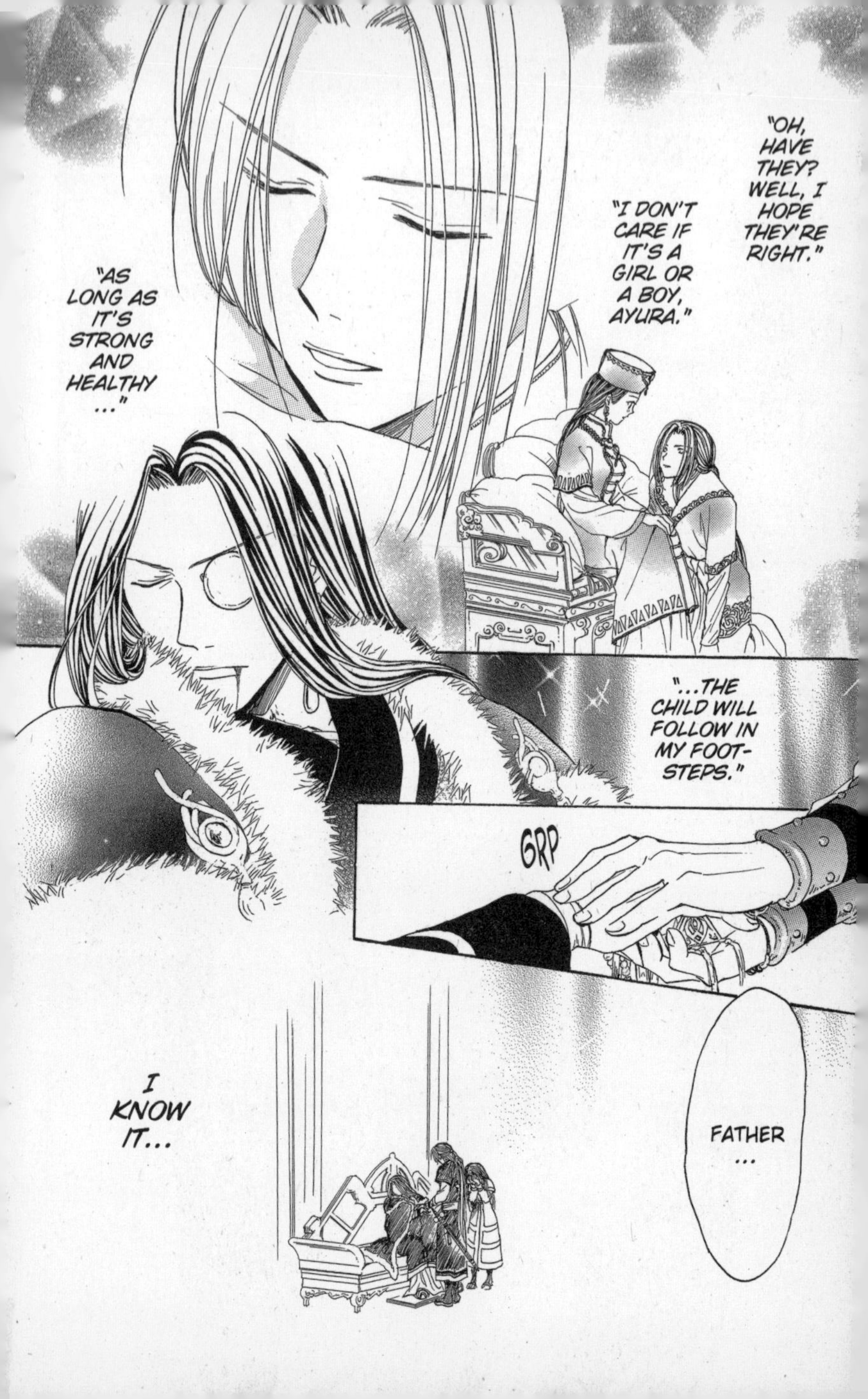

"OH, HAVE THEY? WELL, I HOPE THEY'RE RIGHT."
"I DON'T CARE IF IT'S A GIRL OR A BOY, AYURA."
"AS LONG AS IT'S STRONG AND HEALTHY..."
"...THE CHILD WILL FOLLOW IN MY FOOT-STEPS."
GRP
FATHER...
I KNOW IT...

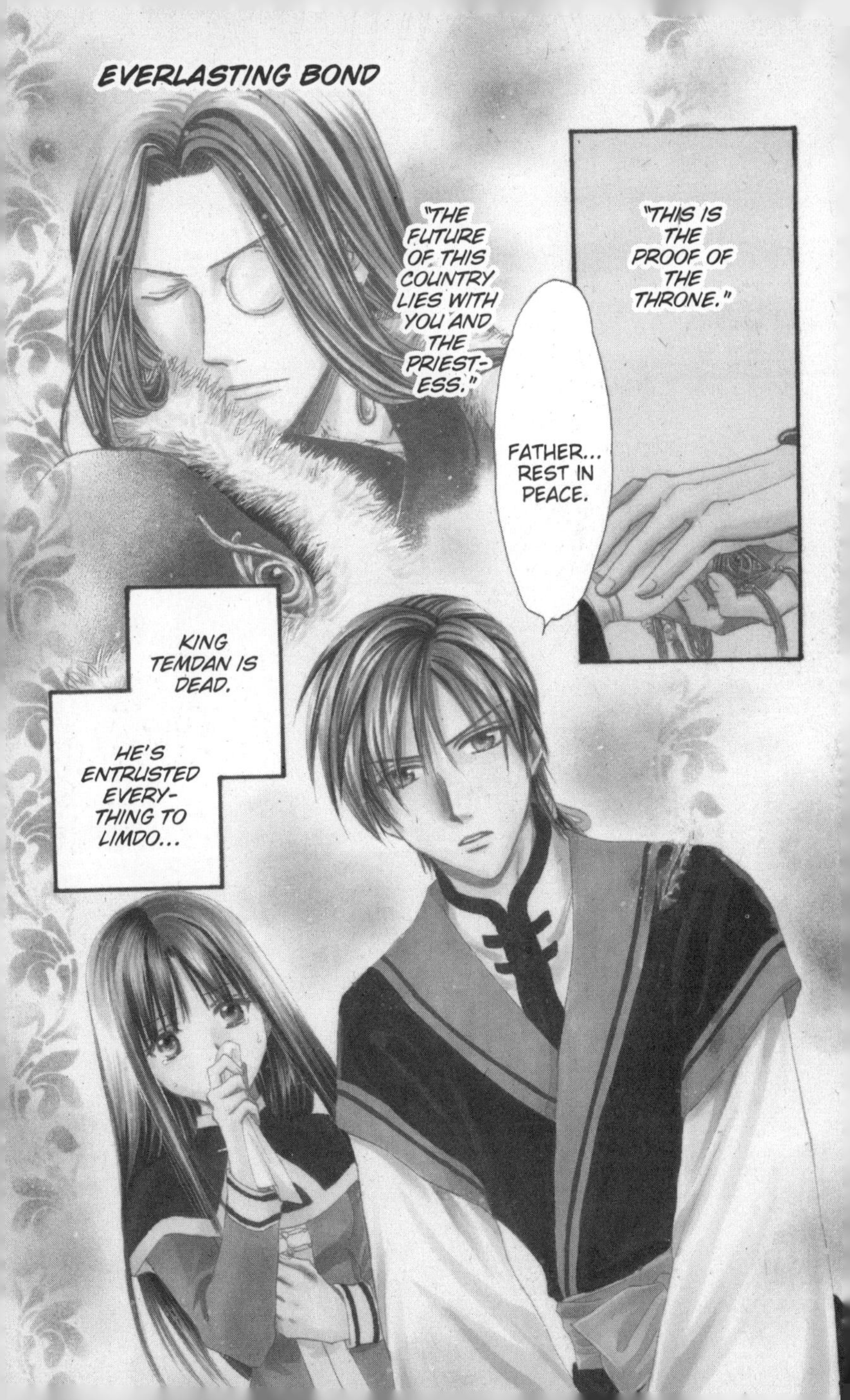
EVERLASTING BOND
"THIS IS THE PROOF OF THE THRONE."
FATHER... REST IN PEACE.
"THE FUTURE OF THIS COUNTRY LIES WITH YOU AND THE PRIEST-ESS."
KING TEMDAN IS DEAD.
HE'S ENTRUSTED EVERY-THING TO LIMDO...

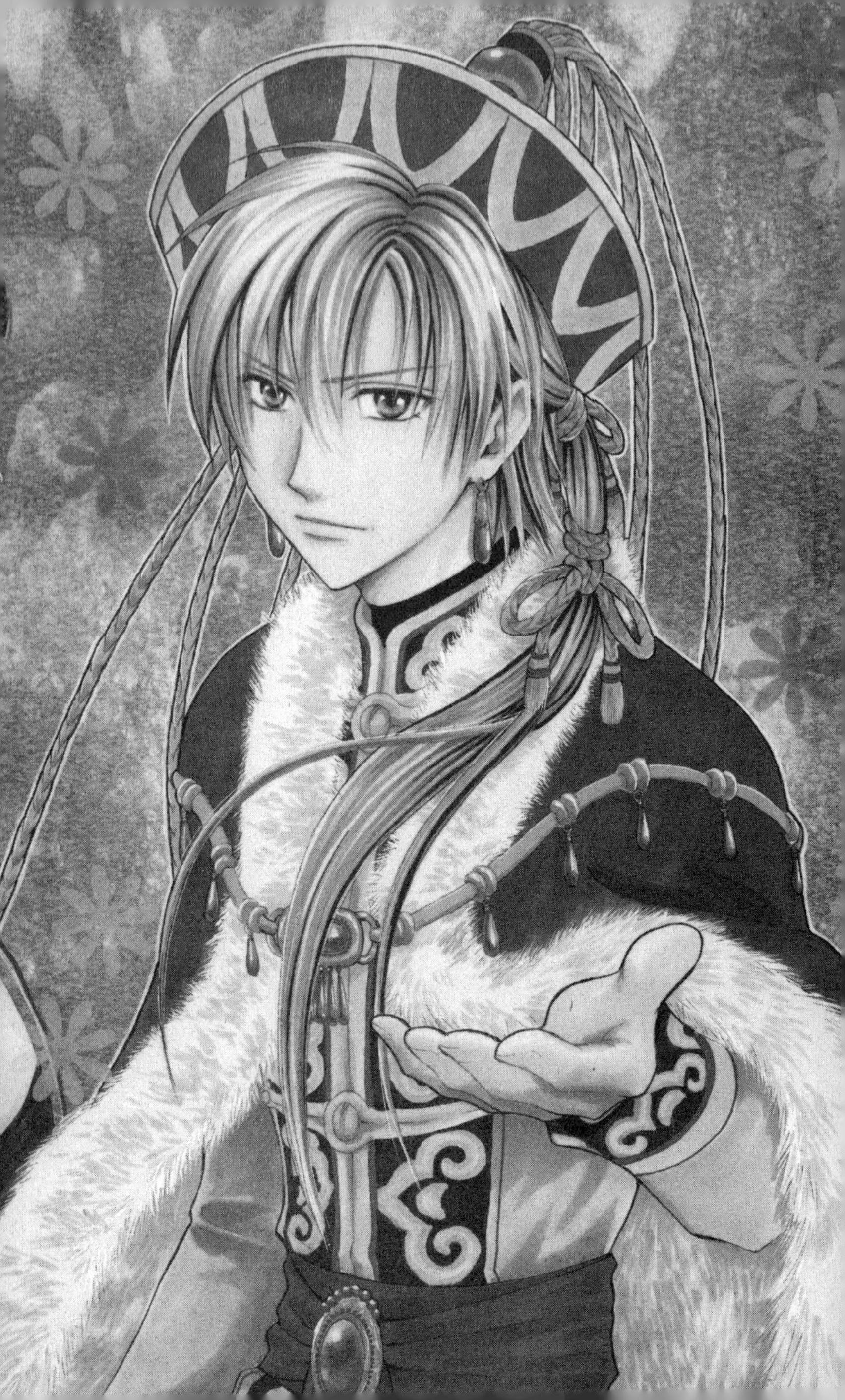

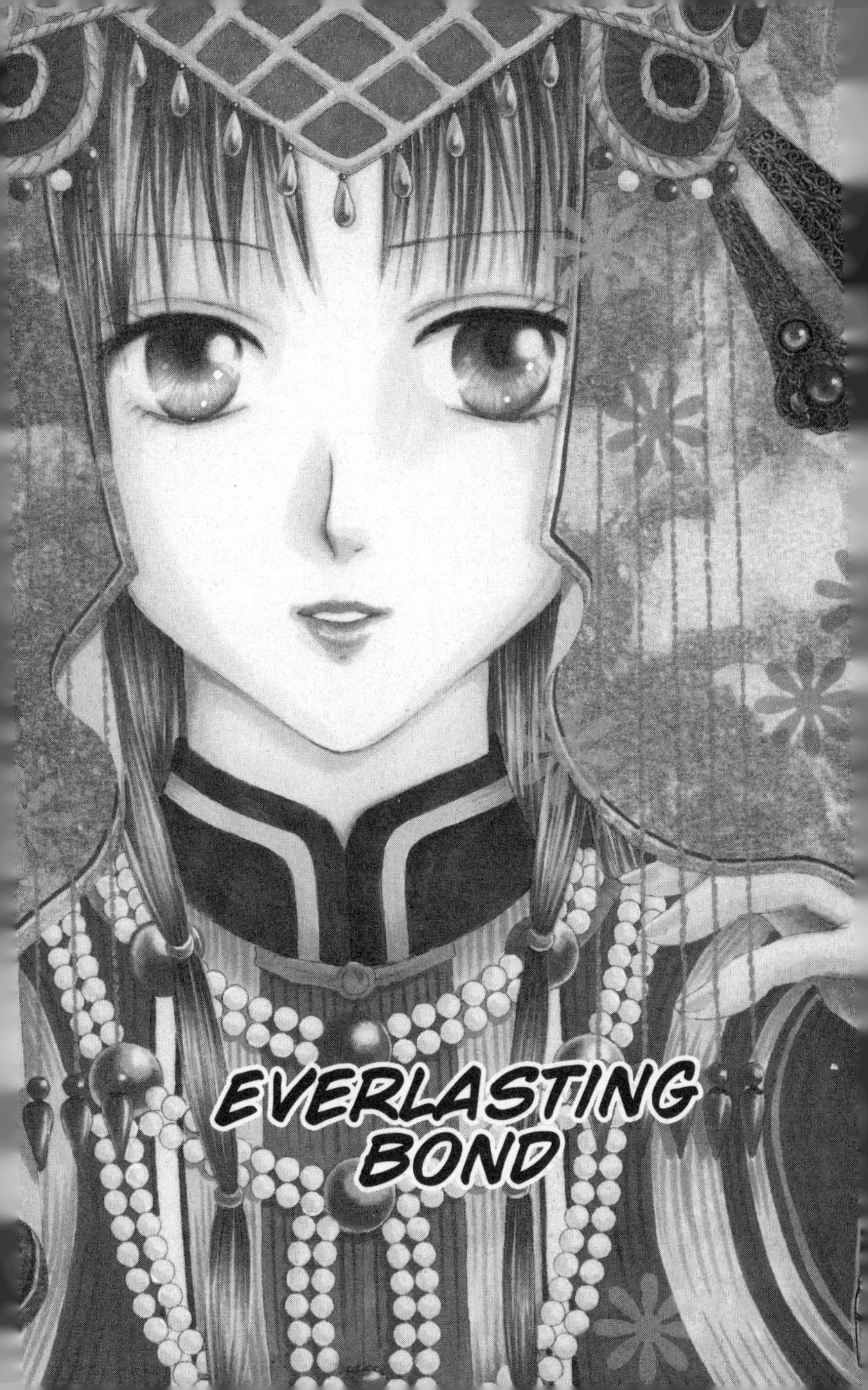
EVERLASTING BOND

How are you, everyone? It's me, Watase. I'm exhausted as usual. 😚

It's been a whole year since the last volume of Genbu. Thank you for checking it out! The story is moving along at a fast clip now. The next volume will be the last! Shock! Finally it's come to this point... 😣

It's taken about ten years. Storylines I plotted years ago are unfolding at last. For me, it's like assembling the pieces of a puzzle. Still, there are new scenes that surprise me. I'm excited and nervous about how it's all going to end...

As longtime readers know, some characters have been fated to die since the original Fushigi Yûgi. When the time comes, I'm sure I'm going to feel the emotions... (sob)

Darn it, I don't have time to be tired!! Well, it's not like I'm tired because I want to be (who am I talking to?). Since you've followed me this far, you'd better prepare yourselves. (°ਊ°) Please stick with me to the end. Hey, I'm wrapping it up!

In other news, the stage version of Fushigi Yûgi has just finished the Seiryu arc! ✨ I was unfortunately unable to get out to see the Suzaku run, so I checked it out on DVD and made sure to go to this one!

Actually, I was 30 minutes late! (I'm such an idiot!) But it was great! 😄 ✧ The DVD will be on sale soon, in case you haven't seen it! ✧ My seat was close to the stage, which made me so happy...though I didn't get any of the official photos. Argh! They're so awesome!!

A live-action version of Absolute Boyfriend is running on Taiwanese TV right now. Even though I have no idea what they're saying, it looks like the story follows the manga faithfully, so it's lots of fun. 😄

There have been a lot of live-action adaptations of my work. I never imagined this would happen. It makes me want to keep working hard. I guess the only things Fushigi Yûgi hasn't been adapted into are a TV drama and a movie. Ha ha, what am I saying? I want to see Genbu in live action... What do you guys think?

It doesn't feel real yet that Genbu is coming to an end. (Actually I'm tired because I just hit a deadline.) I wonder how I'll feel in the final volume. There are so many things I want to say, but I feel it's best to throw my effort into the manga and have you feel it, rather than write about it in a space like this. I currently have two chapters left to draw. I can't believe it. Will I be able to wrap it all up in just two chapters?! :) My manga tends to pick up the tempo as it races to the end, so I'm sure it'll work out! (Am I talking to myself again?) Endings are very important. I'll have to conserve my energy so I can put everything I've got into those two chapters. Can I do it? 😶 I'll probably be able to get it to you around this time next year. If you can't wait for the graphic novel, check out the serial in Rinka magazine. :) It's about to switch to quarterly publication. I'll have to start thinking about my next project... 😌

So! See you in volume 12!! ᴍ(--)ɴ

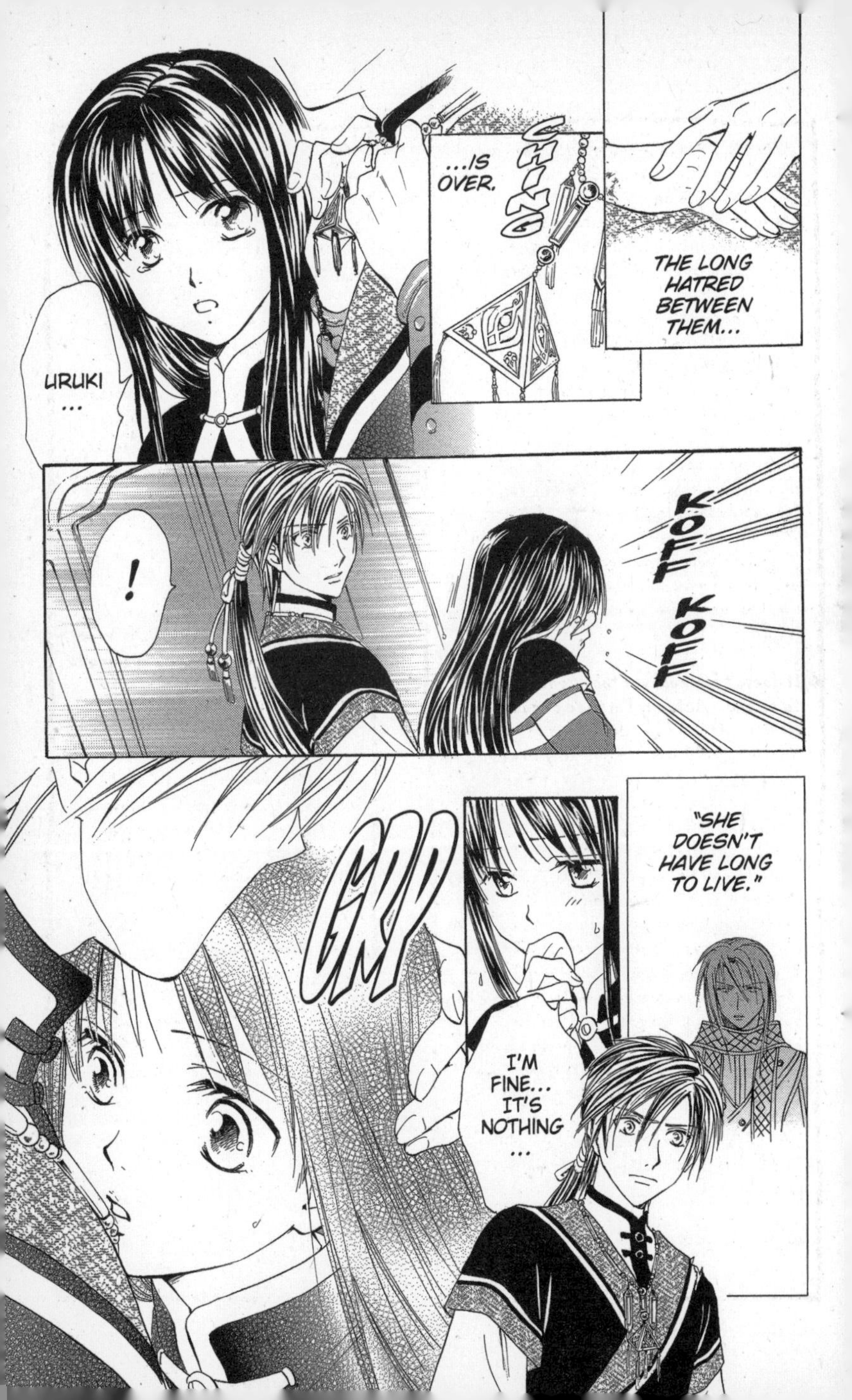
THE LONG HATRED BETWEEN THEM...
...IS OVER.
CHING
URUKI ...
KOFF KOFF
!
"SHE DOESN'T HAVE LONG TO LIVE."
I'M FINE... IT'S NOTHING ...
GRP

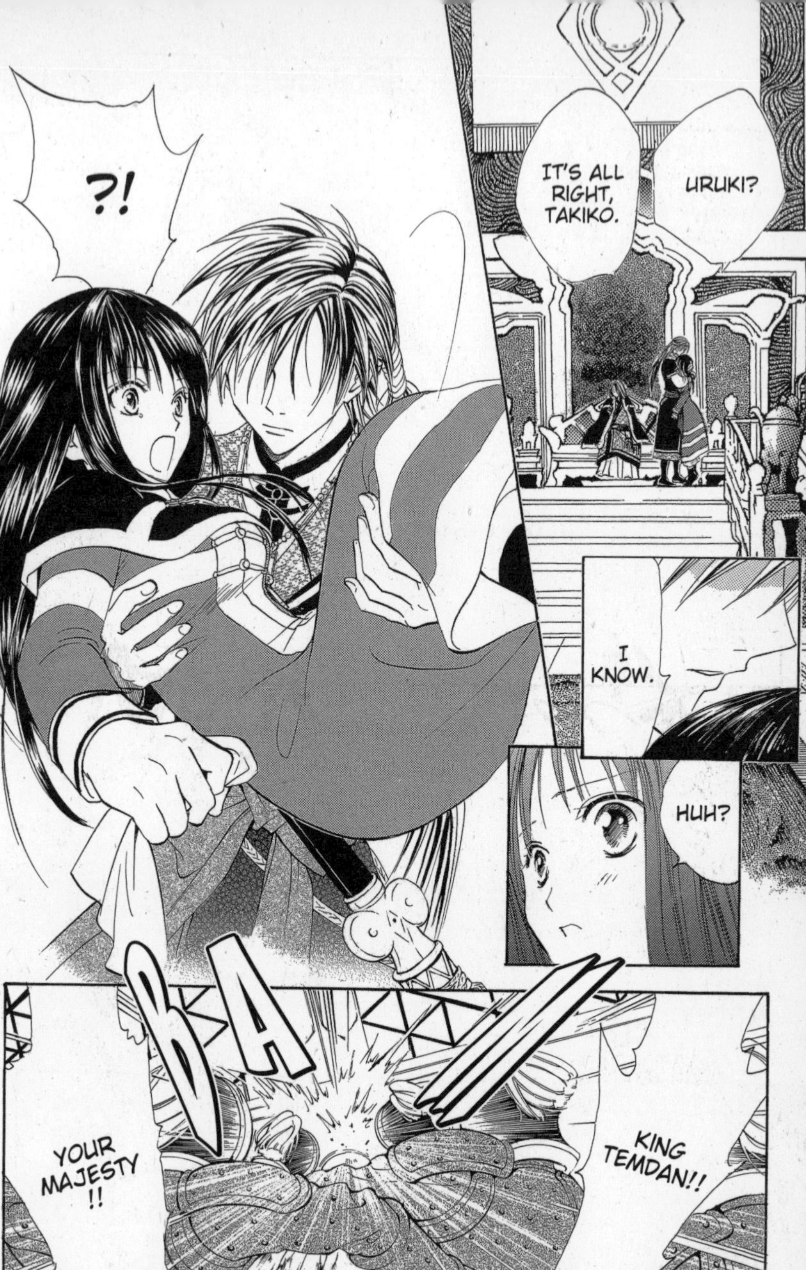
URUKI?
IT'S ALL RIGHT, TAKIKO.
I KNOW.
HUH?
?!
BA
KING TEMDAN!!
YOUR MAJESTY!!

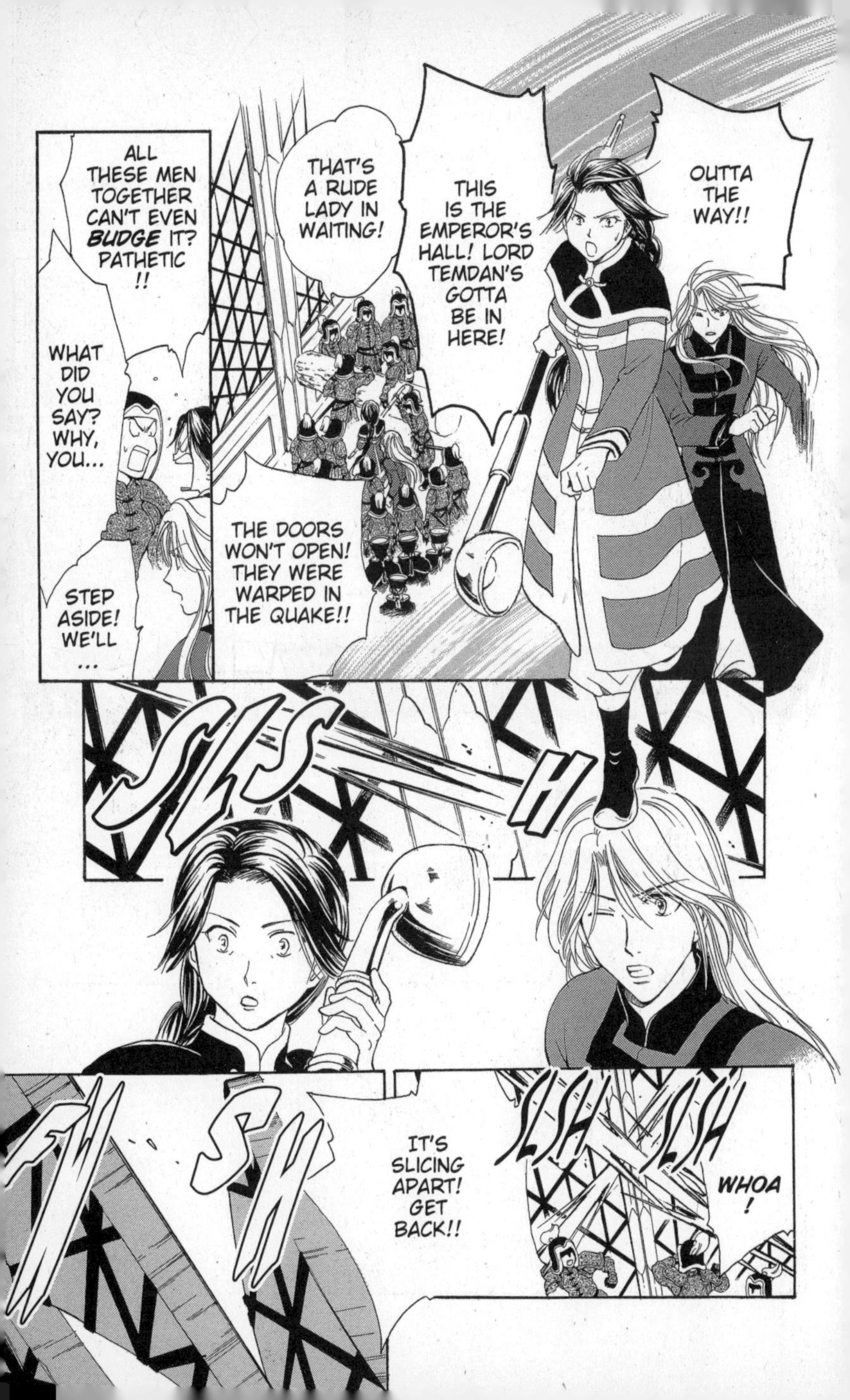
OUTTA THE WAY!!
THIS IS THE EMPEROR'S HALL! LORD TEMDAN'S GOTTA BE IN HERE!
THAT'S A RUDE LADY IN WAITING!
THE DOORS WON'T OPEN! THEY WERE WARPED IN THE QUAKE!!
ALL THESE MEN TOGETHER CAN'T EVEN BUDGE IT? PATHETIC!!
WHAT DID YOU SAY? WHY, YOU...
STEP ASIDE! WE'LL ...
SLISH
SLISH SLISH
WHOA!
IT'S SLICING APART! GET BACK!!
FWSH

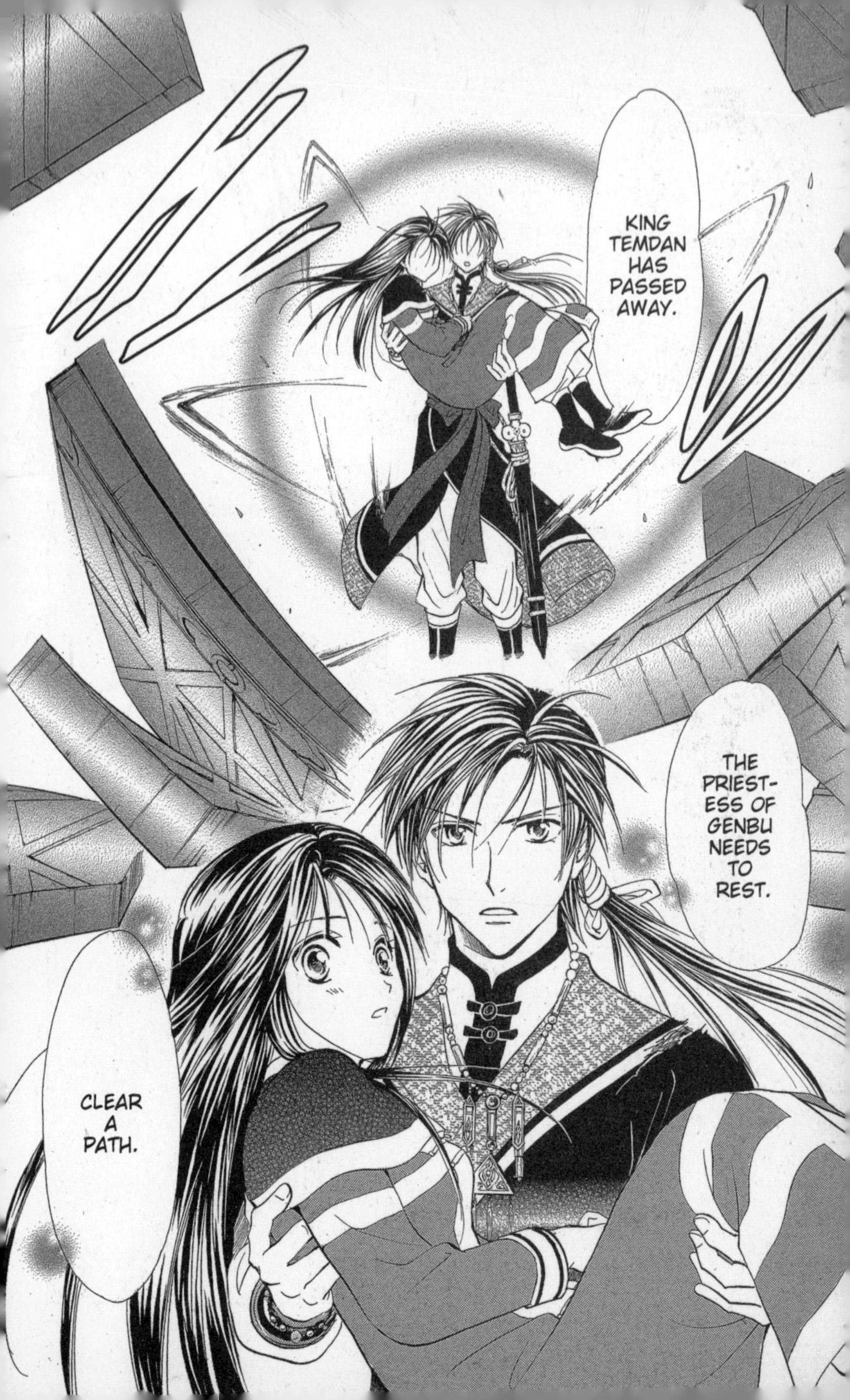
KING TEMDAN HAS PASSED AWAY.
THE PRIESTESS OF GENBU NEEDS TO REST.
CLEAR A PATH.

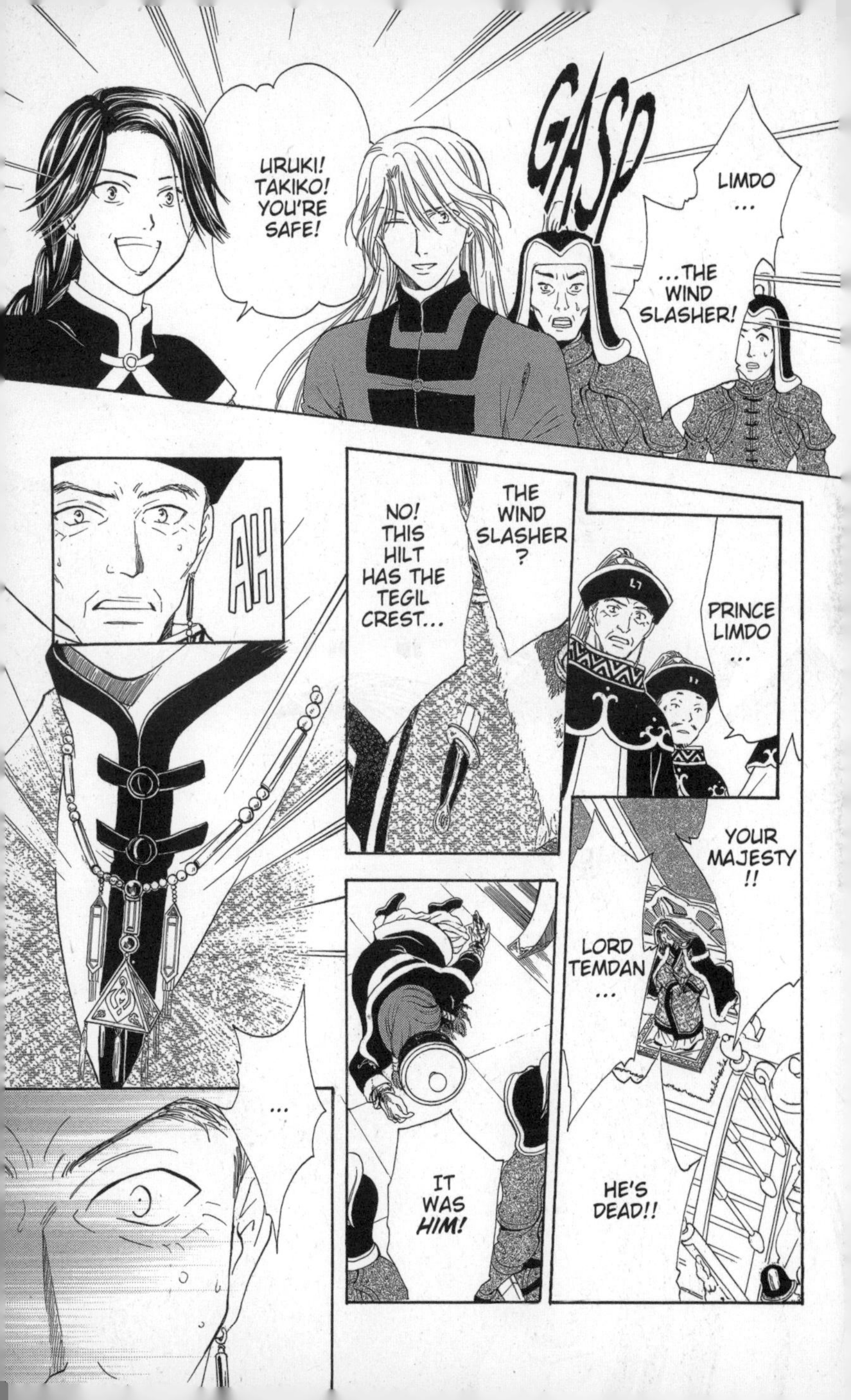
GASP
LIMDO ...
...THE WIND SLASHER!
URUKI! TAKIKO! YOU'RE SAFE!
PRINCE LIMDO ...
THE WIND SLASHER?
NO! THIS HILT HAS THE TEGIL CREST...
AH
YOUR MAJESTY!!
LORD TEMDAN ...
HE'S DEAD!!
IT WAS *HIM!*
...

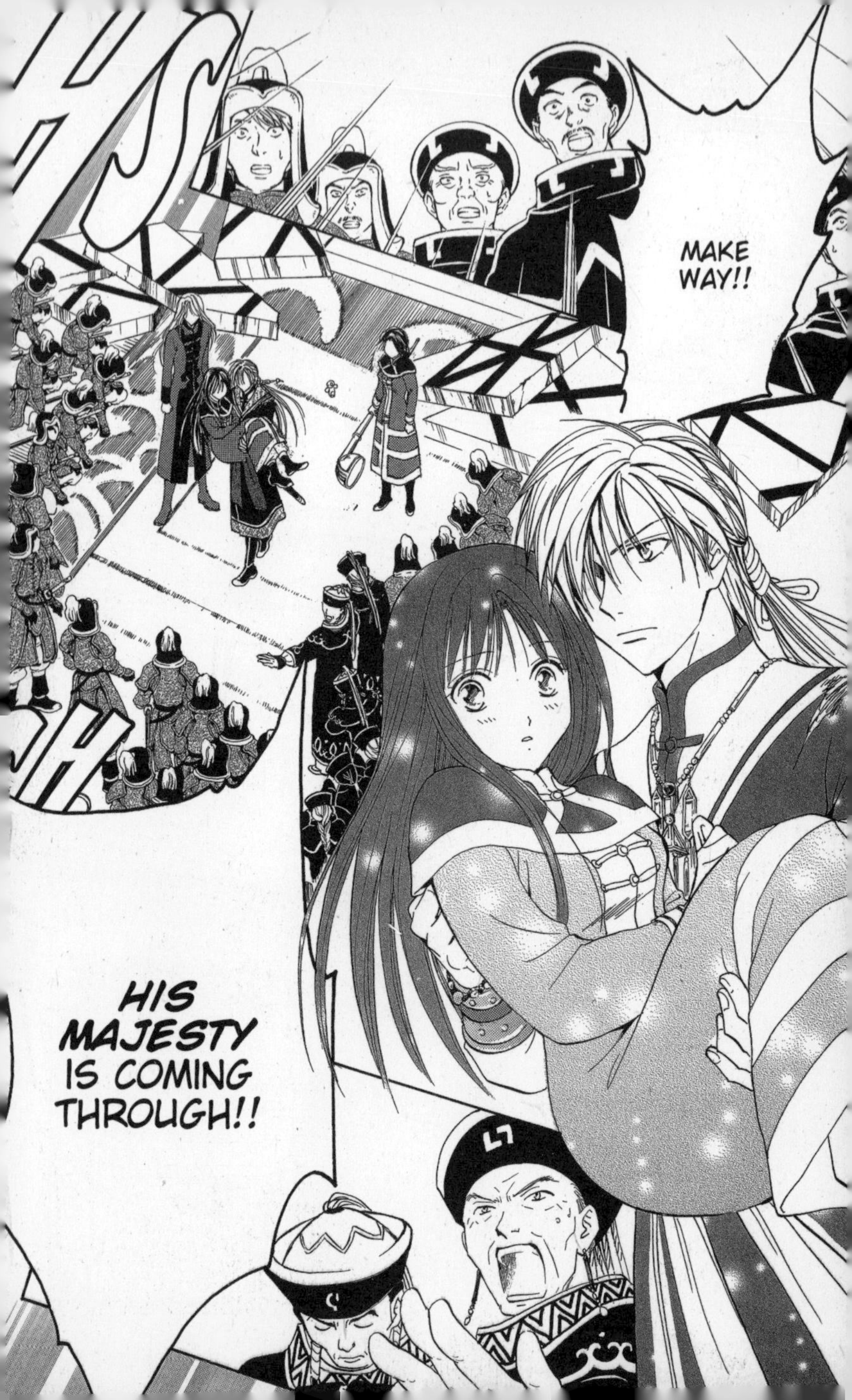
MAKE WAY!!
HIS MAJESTY IS COMING THROUGH!!

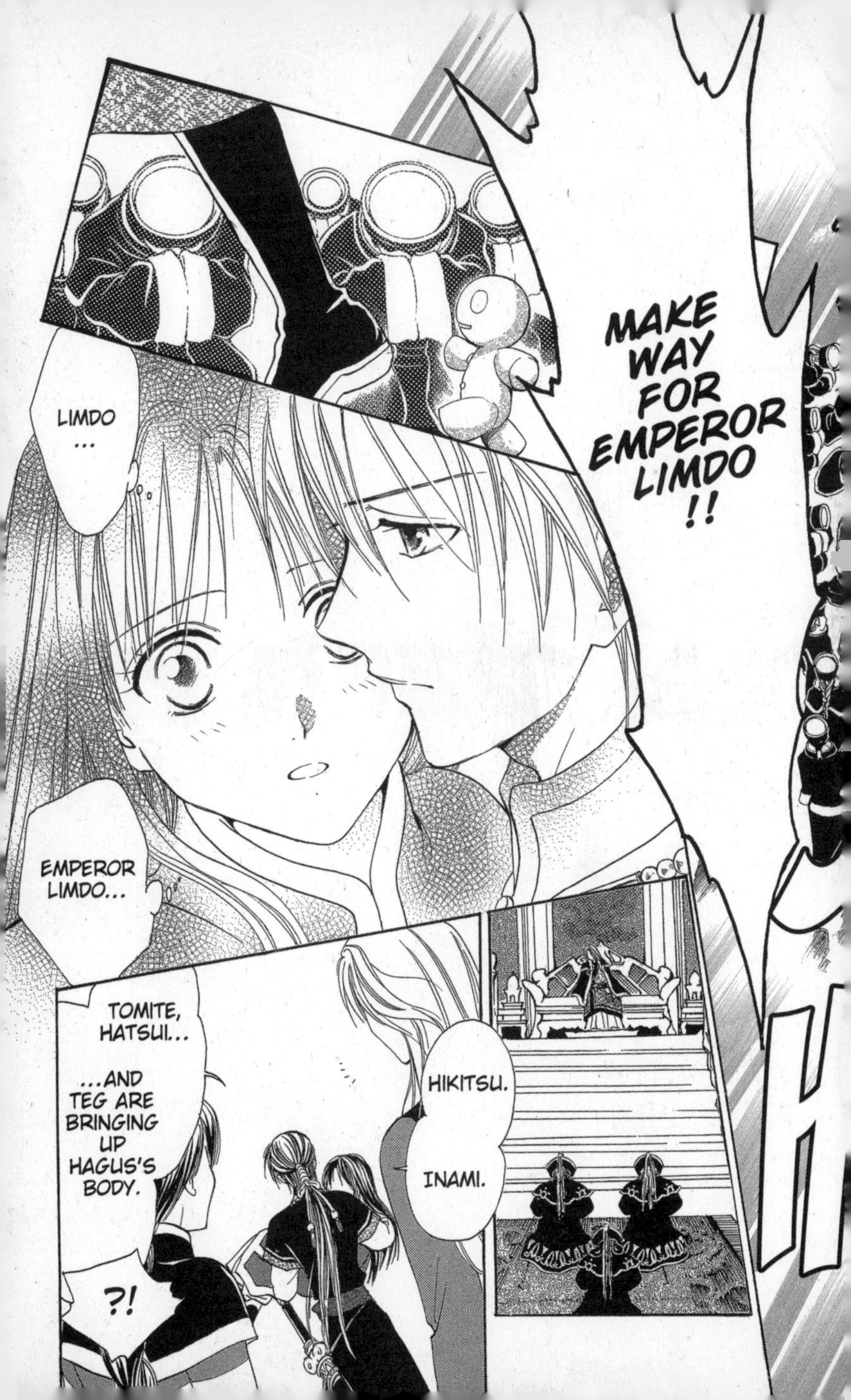
MAKE WAY FOR EMPEROR LIMDO !!
LIMDO ...
EMPEROR LIMDO...
HIKITSU.
INAMI.
TOMITE, HATSUI...
...AND TEG ARE BRINGING UP HAGUS'S BODY.
?!

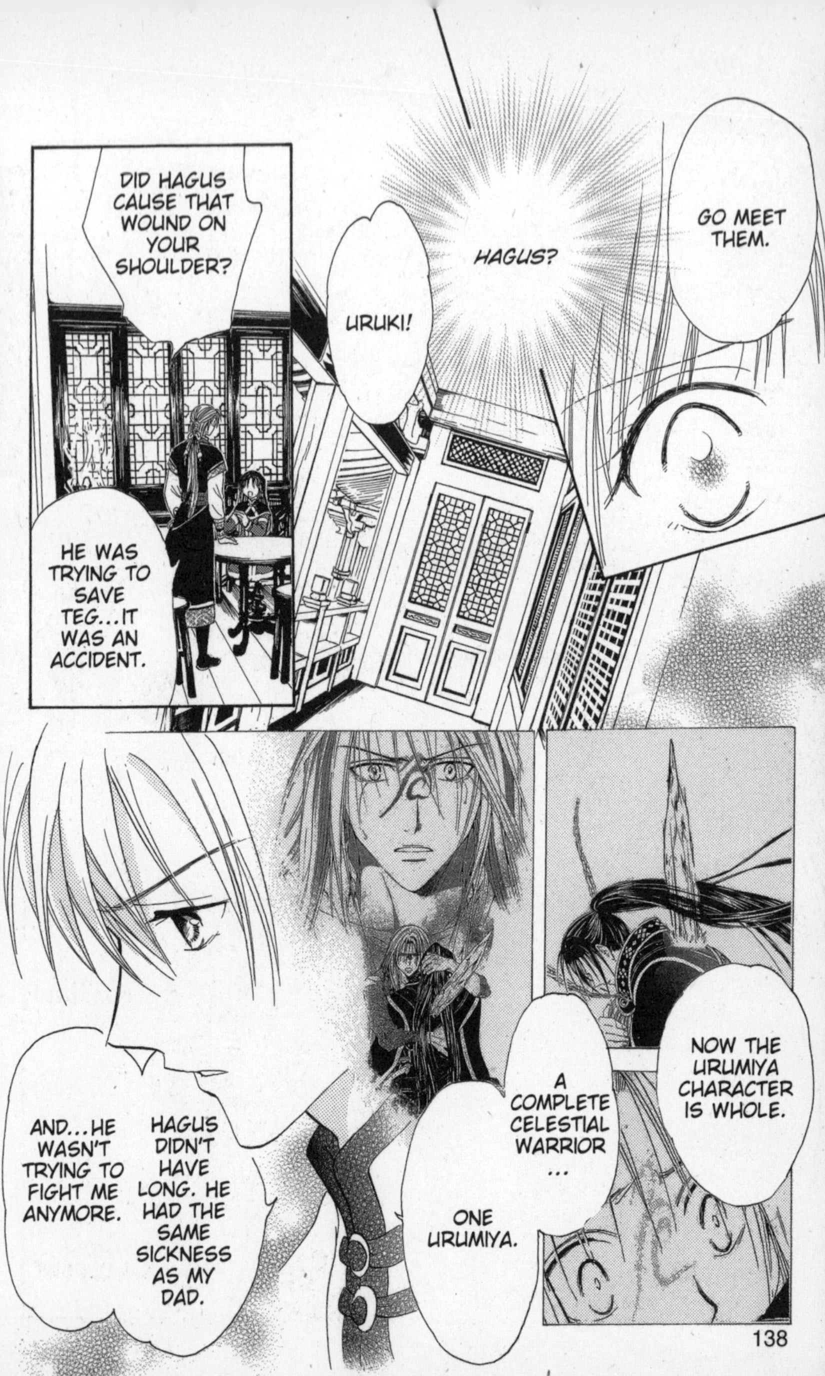
GO MEET THEM.
HAGUS?
URUKI!
DID HAGUS CAUSE THAT WOUND ON YOUR SHOULDER?
HE WAS TRYING TO SAVE TEG...IT WAS AN ACCIDENT.
NOW THE URUMIYA CHARACTER IS WHOLE.
A COMPLETE CELESTIAL WARRIOR...
ONE URUMIYA.
HAGUS DIDN'T HAVE LONG. HE HAD THE SAME SICKNESS AS MY DAD.
AND...HE WASN'T TRYING TO FIGHT ME ANYMORE.

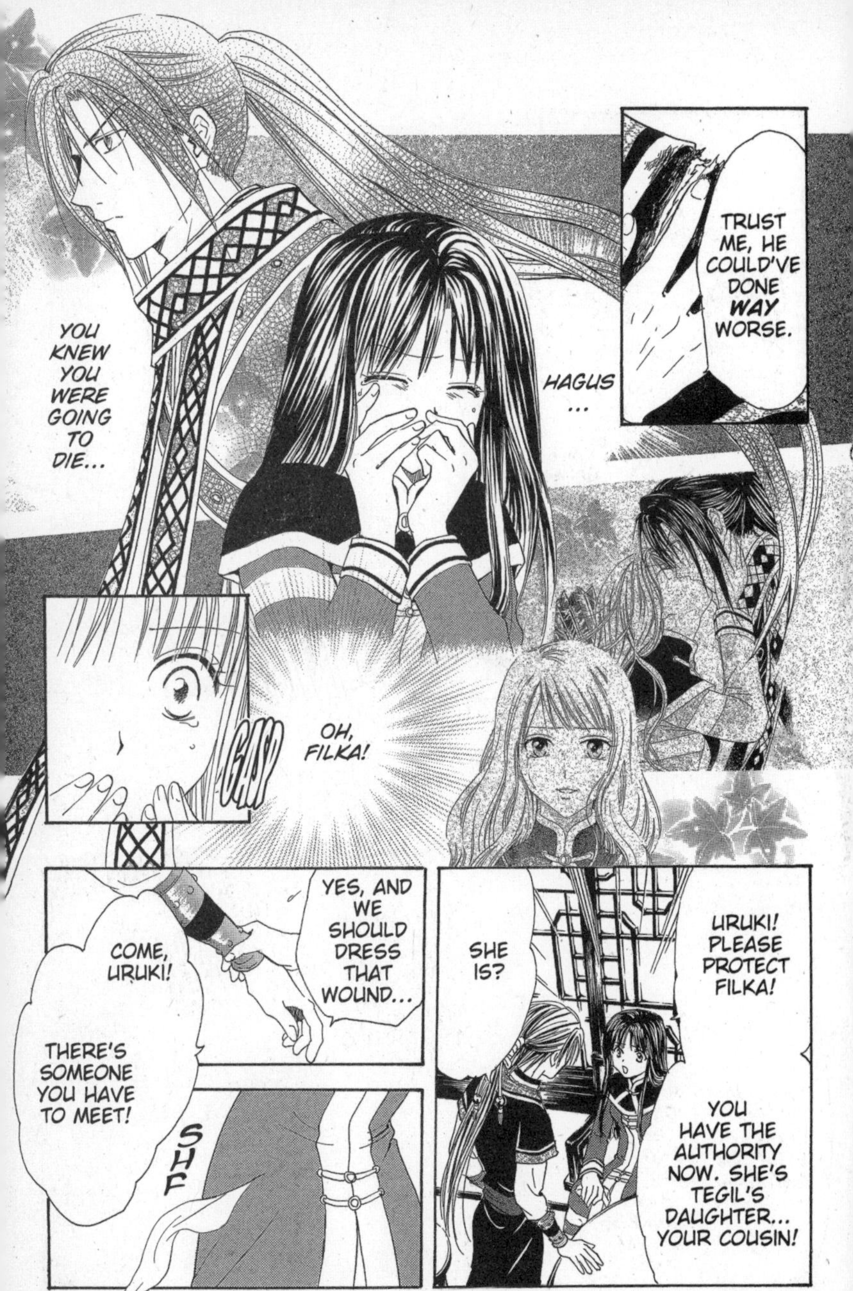
TRUST ME, HE COULD'VE DONE *WAY* WORSE.
HAGUS ...
YOU KNEW YOU WERE GOING TO DIE...
OH, FILKA!
GASP
URUKI! PLEASE PROTECT FILKA!
SHE IS?
YOU HAVE THE AUTHORITY NOW. SHE'S TEGIL'S DAUGHTER... YOUR COUSIN!
YES, AND WE SHOULD DRESS THAT WOUND...
COME, URUKI!
THERE'S SOMEONE YOU HAVE TO MEET!
SHF

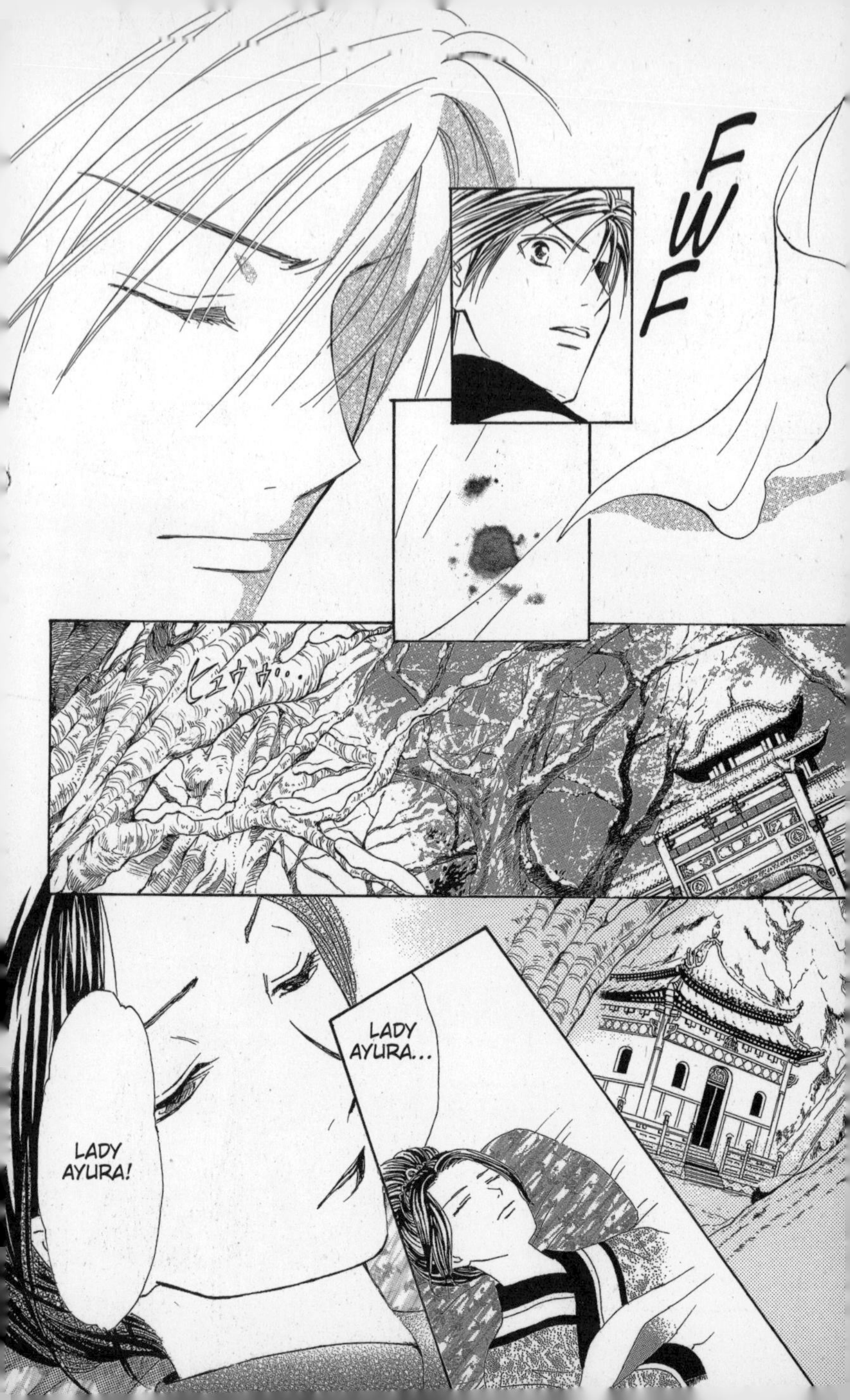
FWF
ヒュウゥ…
LADY AYURA...
LADY AYURA!

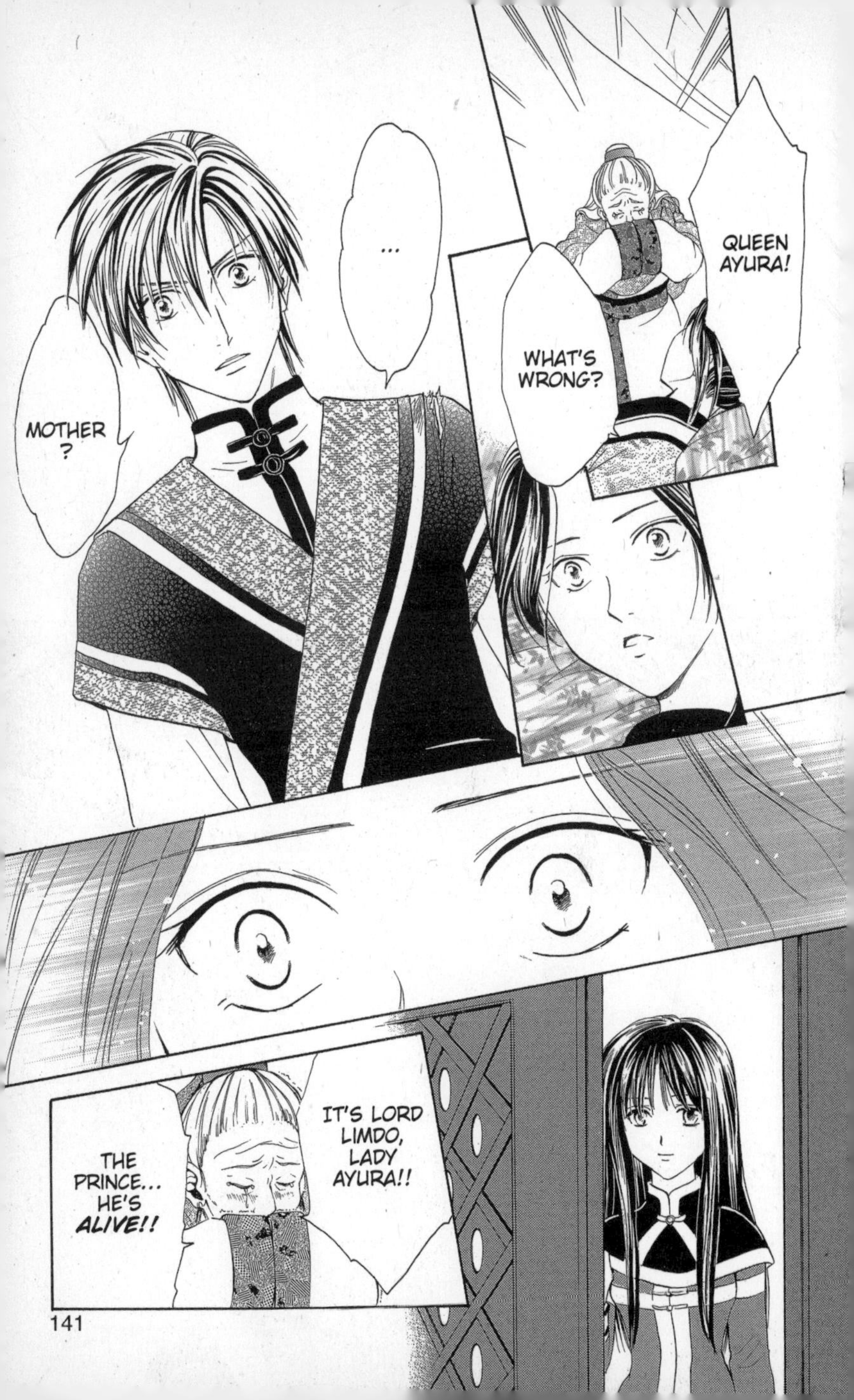
QUEEN AYURA!
WHAT'S WRONG?
...
MOTHER ?
IT'S LORD LIMDO, LADY AYURA!!
THE PRINCE... HE'S *ALIVE!!*

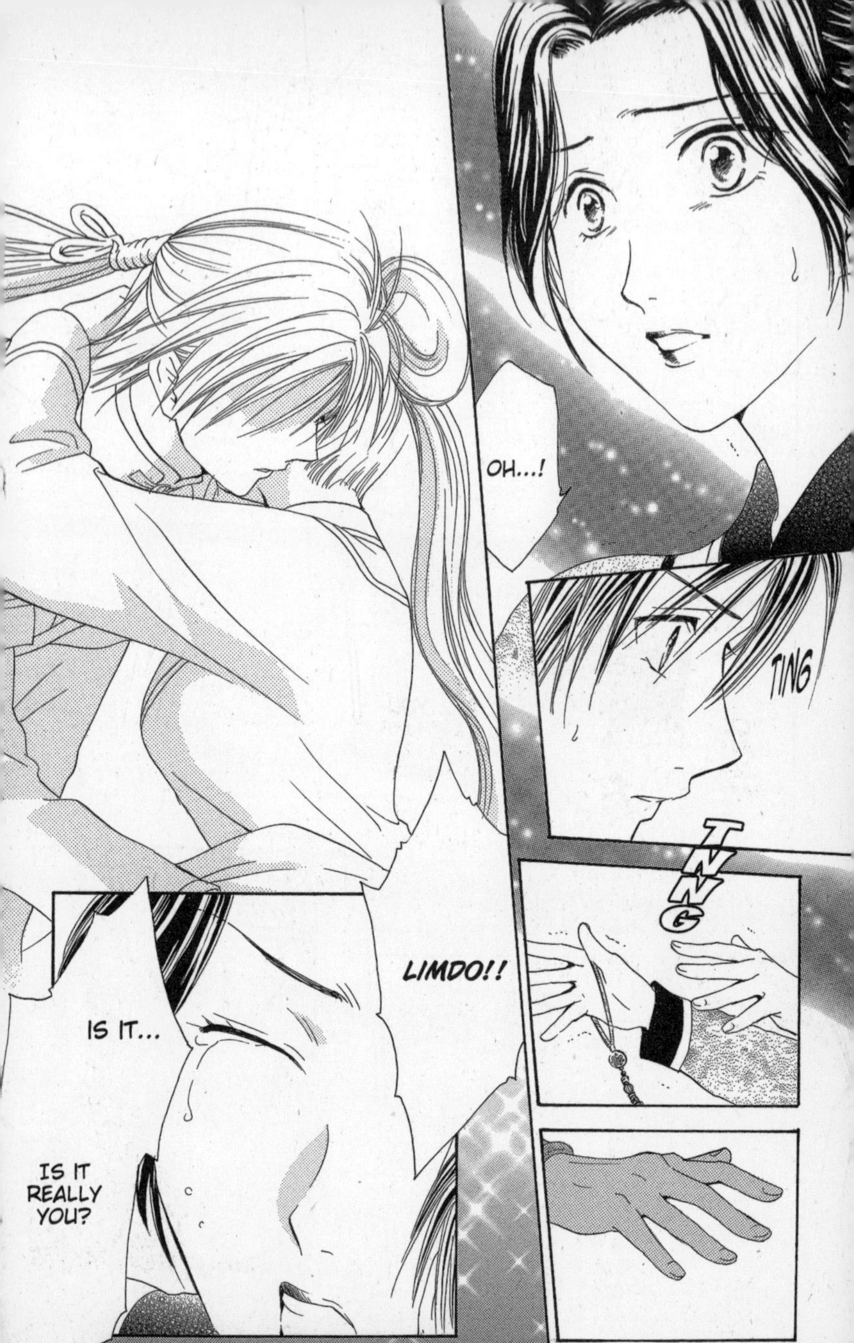
OH...!
TING
TNNG
LIMDO!!
IS IT...
IS IT REALLY YOU?

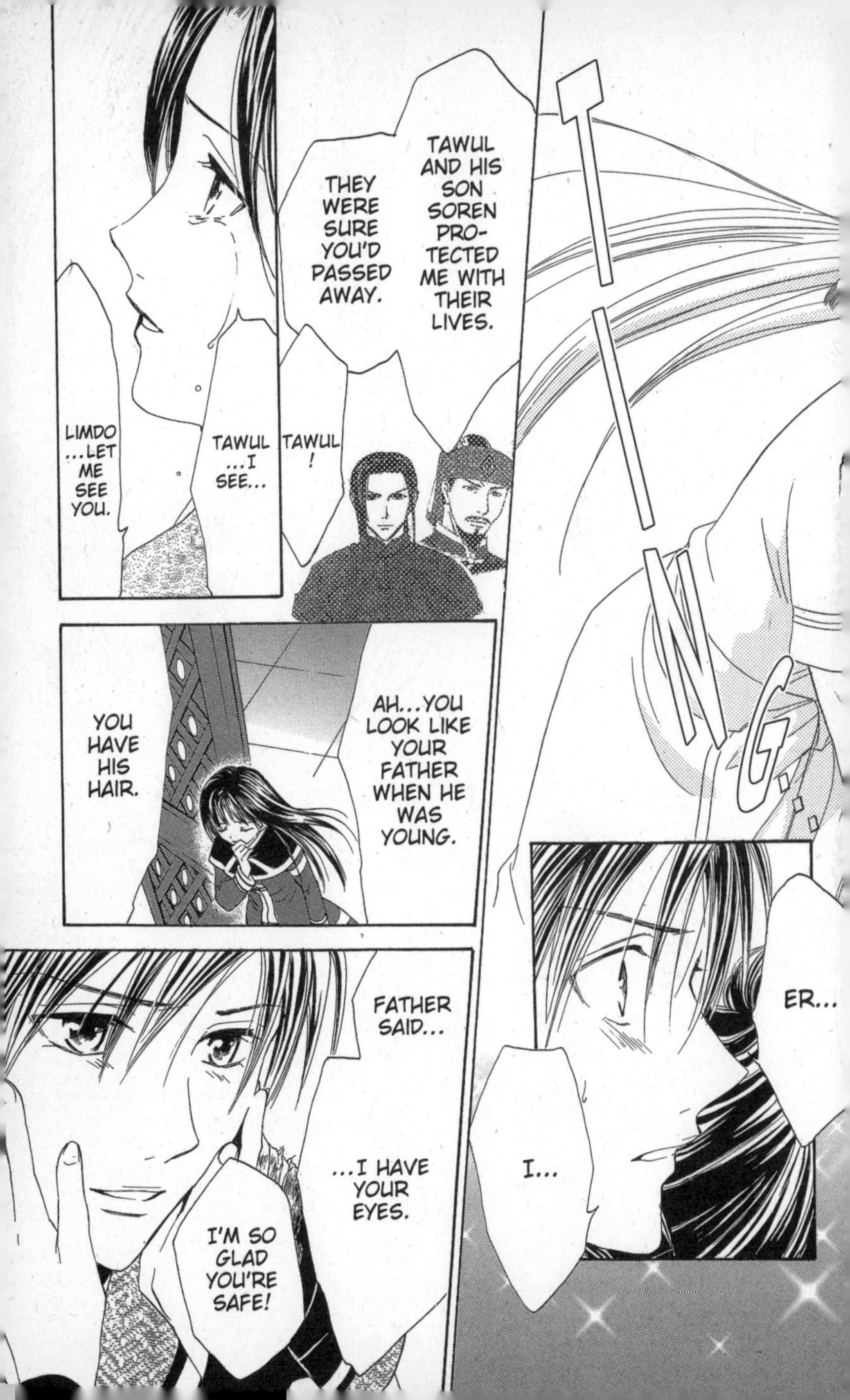
TING
TAWUL AND HIS SON SOREN PRO-TECTED ME WITH THEIR LIVES.
THEY WERE SURE YOU'D PASSED AWAY.
TAWUL!
TAWUL ...I SEE...
LIMDO ...LET ME SEE YOU.
AH...YOU LOOK LIKE YOUR FATHER WHEN HE WAS YOUNG.
YOU HAVE HIS HAIR.
ER...
I...
FATHER SAID...
...I HAVE YOUR EYES.
I'M SO GLAD YOU'RE SAFE!

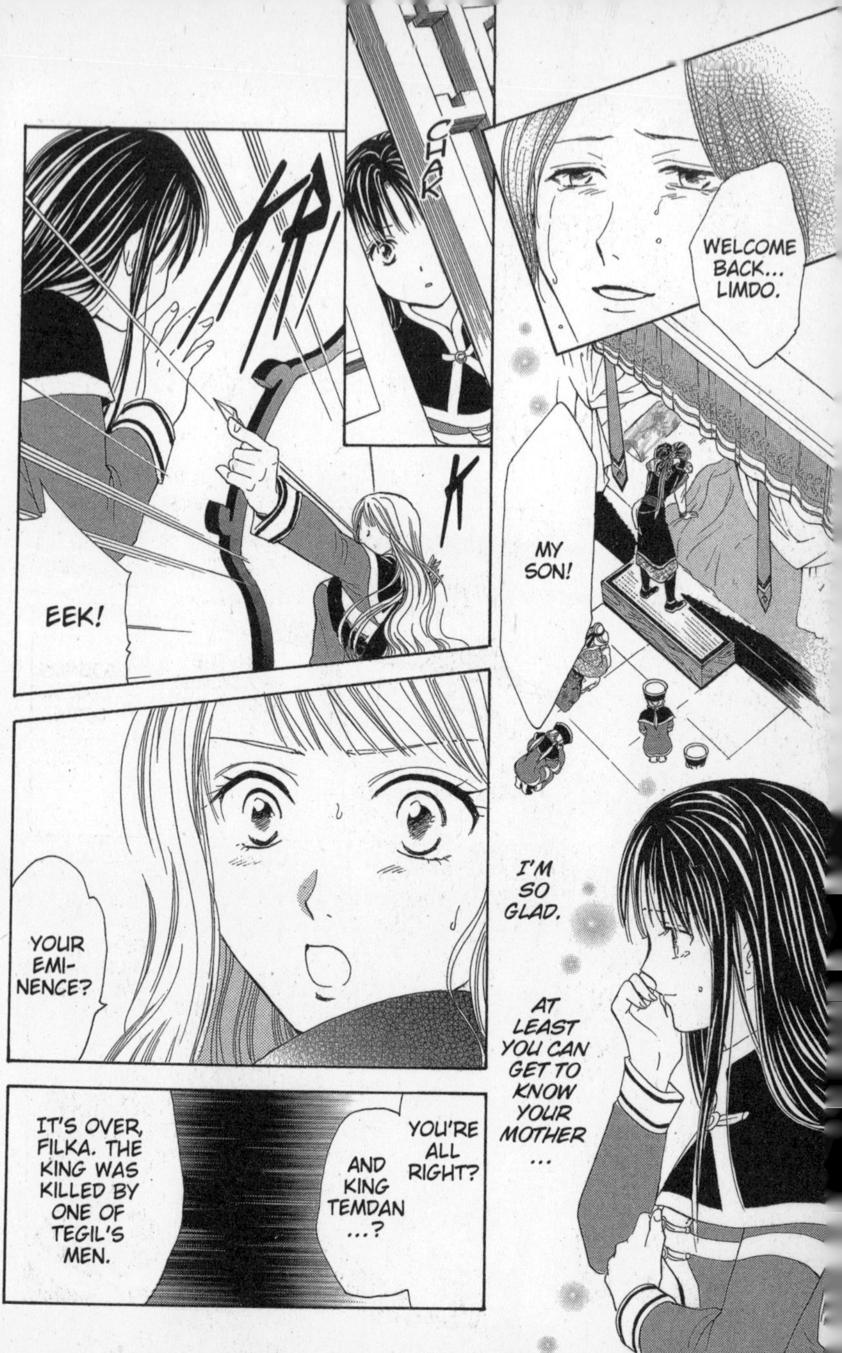
WELCOME BACK... LIMDO.
MY SON!
I'M SO GLAD.
AT LEAST YOU CAN GET TO KNOW YOUR MOTHER ...
CHAK
KR
K
EEK!
YOUR EMINENCE?
YOU'RE ALL RIGHT?
AND KING TEMDAN ...?
IT'S OVER, FILKA. THE KING WAS KILLED BY ONE OF TEGIL'S MEN.

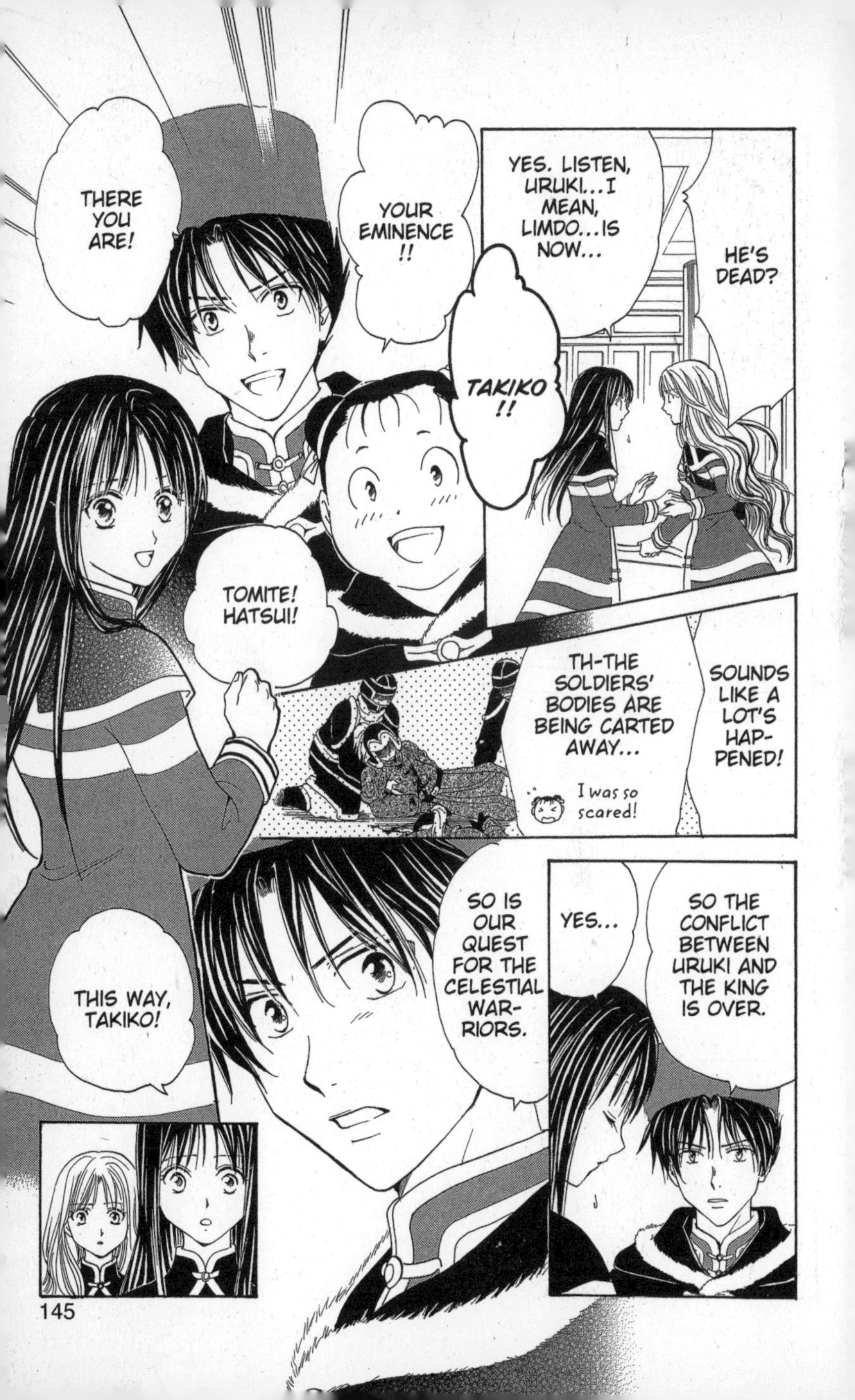
HE'S DEAD?
YES. LISTEN, URUKI...I MEAN, LIMDO...IS NOW...
SOUNDS LIKE A LOT'S HAP-PENED!
TH-THE SOLDIERS' BODIES ARE BEING CARTED AWAY...
I was so scared!
SO THE CONFLICT BETWEEN URUKI AND THE KING IS OVER.
YES...
SO IS OUR QUEST FOR THE CELESTIAL WAR-RIORS.
TAKIKO !!
YOUR EMINENCE !!
THERE YOU ARE!
TOMITE! HATSUI!
THIS WAY, TAKIKO!

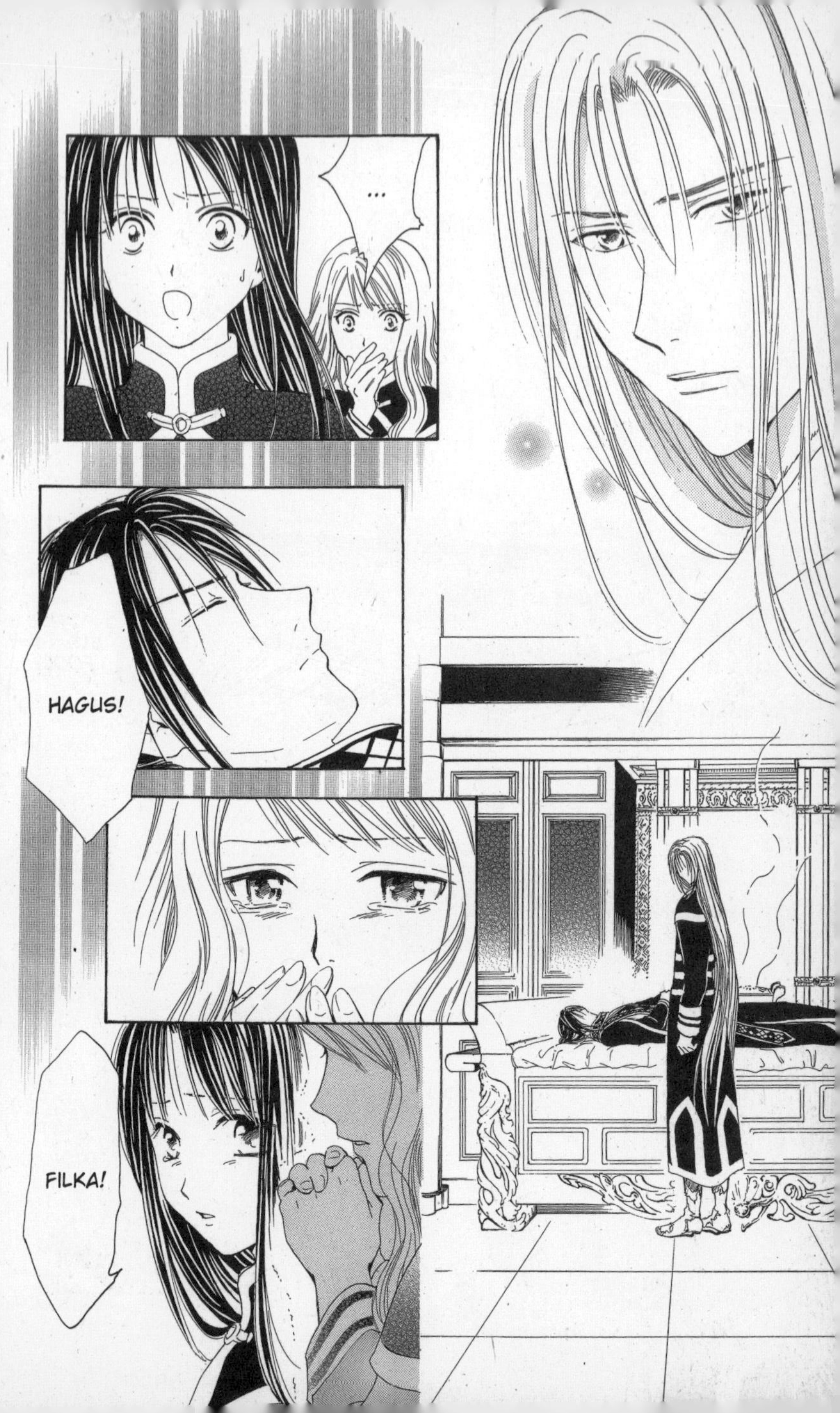
...
HAGUS!
FILKA!

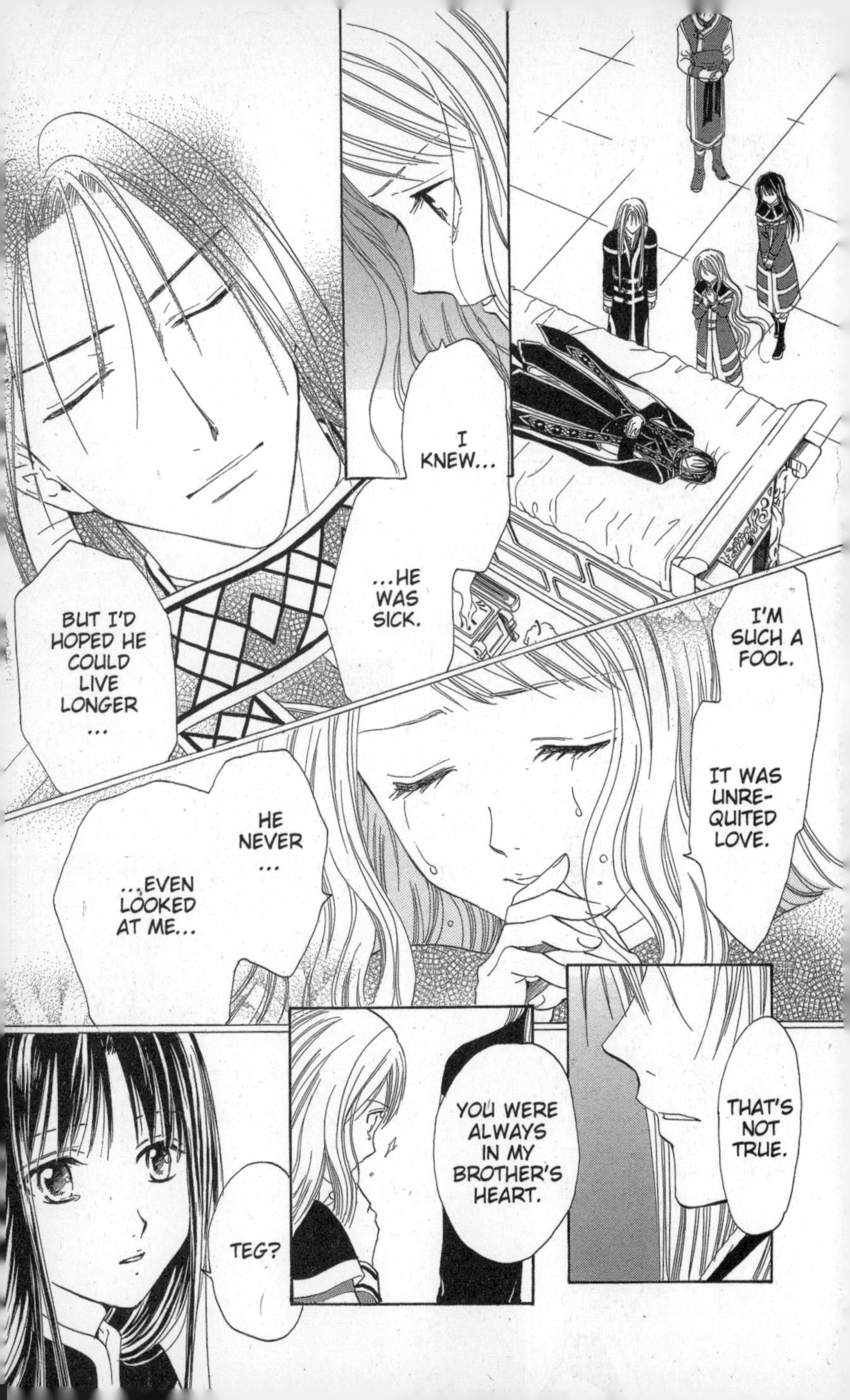
I KNEW...
...HE WAS SICK.
BUT I'D HOPED HE COULD LIVE LONGER ...
I'M SUCH A FOOL.
IT WAS UNREQUITED LOVE.
HE NEVER ...
...EVEN LOOKED AT ME...
THAT'S NOT TRUE.
YOU WERE ALWAYS IN MY BROTHER'S HEART.
TEG?

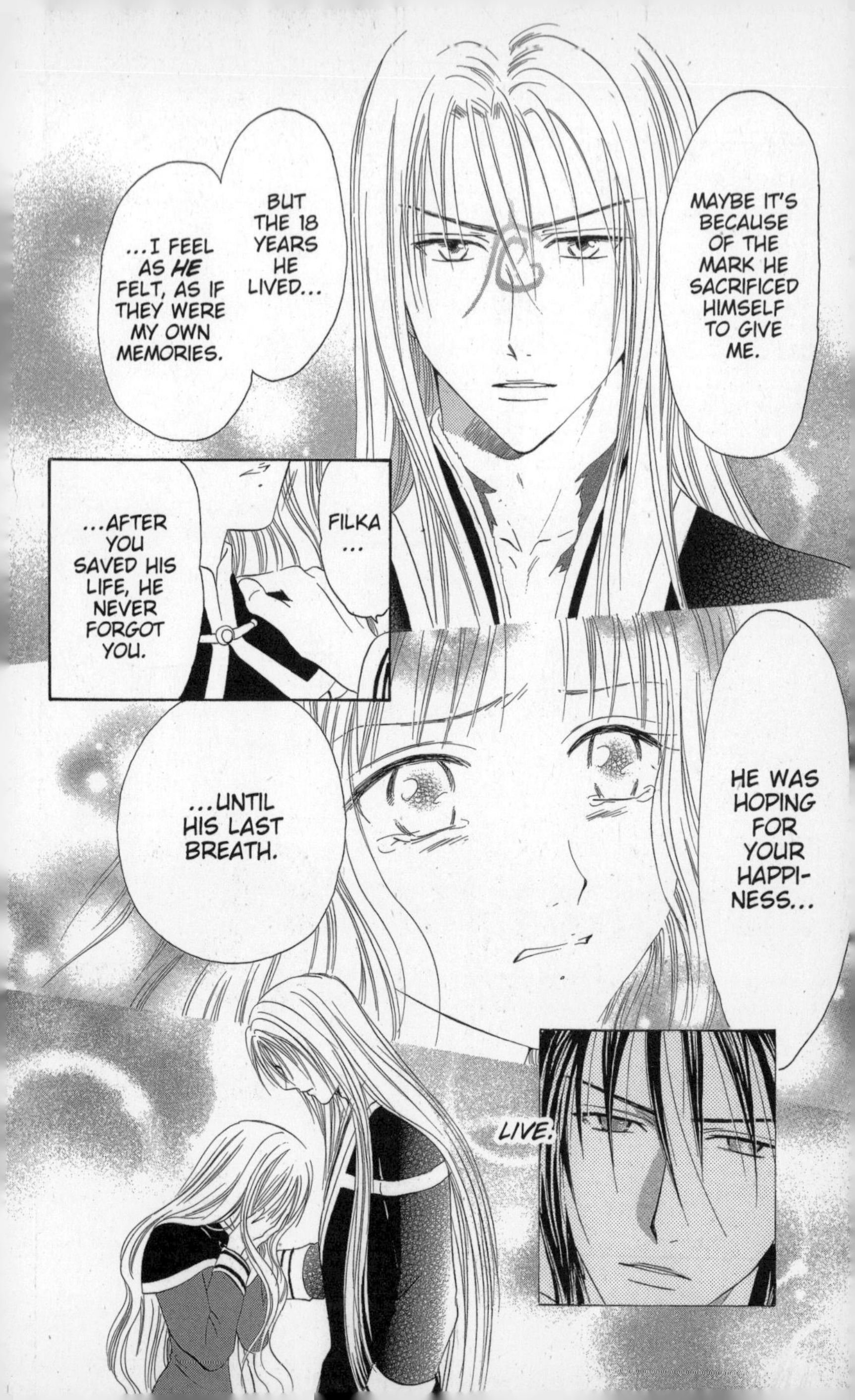
MAYBE IT'S BECAUSE OF THE MARK HE SACRIFICED HIMSELF TO GIVE ME.
BUT THE 18 YEARS HE LIVED...
...I FEEL AS *HE* FELT, AS IF THEY WERE MY OWN MEMORIES.
FILKA ...
...AFTER YOU SAVED HIS LIFE, HE NEVER FORGOT YOU.
HE WAS HOPING FOR YOUR HAPPINESS...
...UNTIL HIS LAST BREATH.
LIVE.

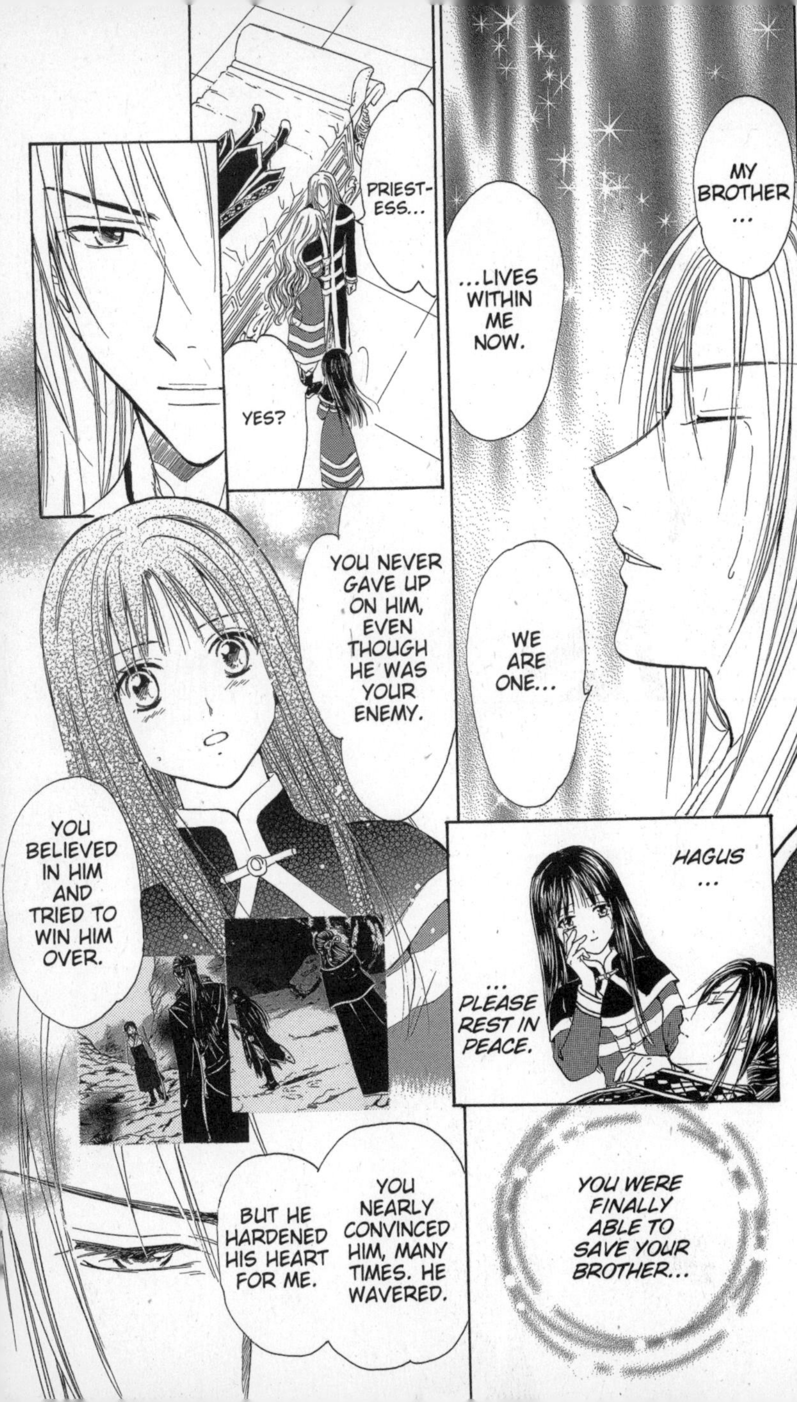
MY BROTHER ...
...LIVES WITHIN ME NOW.
WE ARE ONE...
PRIEST-ESS...
YES?
YOU NEVER GAVE UP ON HIM, EVEN THOUGH HE WAS YOUR ENEMY.
YOU BELIEVED IN HIM AND TRIED TO WIN HIM OVER.
HAGUS ...
... PLEASE REST IN PEACE.
YOU WERE FINALLY ABLE TO SAVE YOUR BROTHER...
YOU NEARLY CONVINCED HIM, MANY TIMES. HE WAVERED.
BUT HE HARDENED HIS HEART FOR ME.

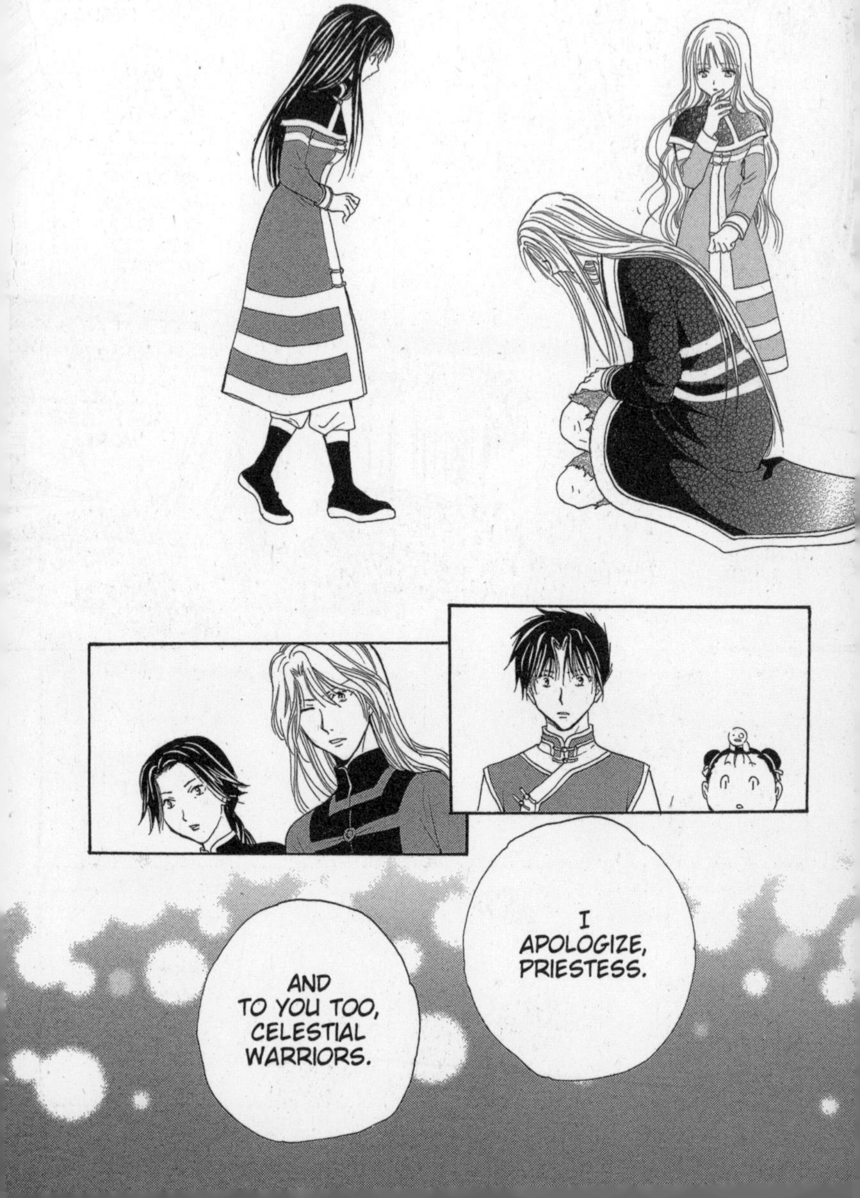
I APOLOGIZE, PRIESTESS.
AND TO YOU TOO, CELESTIAL WARRIORS.

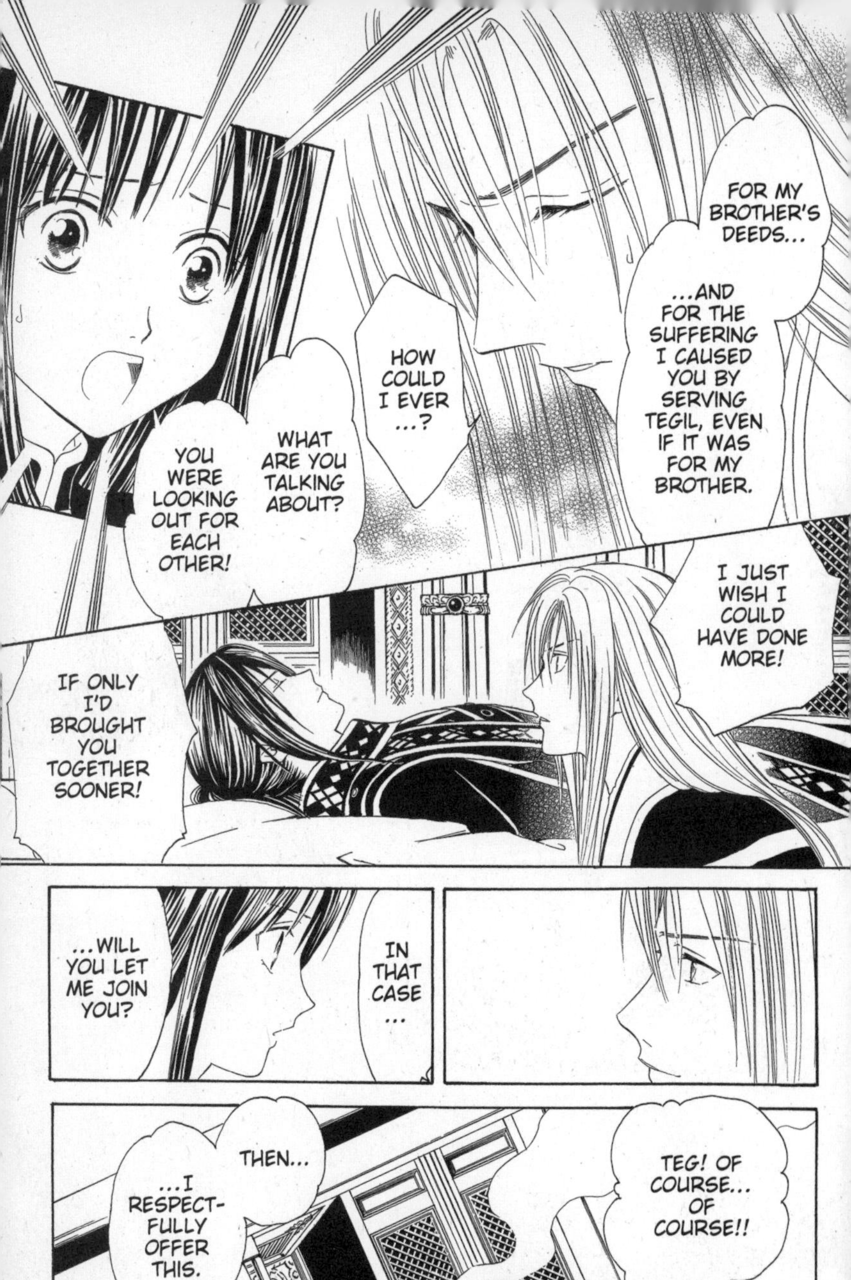
FOR MY BROTHER'S DEEDS...
...AND FOR THE SUFFERING I CAUSED YOU BY SERVING TEGIL, EVEN IF IT WAS FOR MY BROTHER.
HOW COULD I EVER ...?
WHAT ARE YOU TALKING ABOUT?
YOU WERE LOOKING OUT FOR EACH OTHER!
I JUST WISH I COULD HAVE DONE MORE!
IF ONLY I'D BROUGHT YOU TOGETHER SOONER!
IN THAT CASE ...
...WILL YOU LET ME JOIN YOU?
TEG! OF COURSE... OF COURSE!!
THEN...
...I RESPECT-FULLY OFFER THIS.

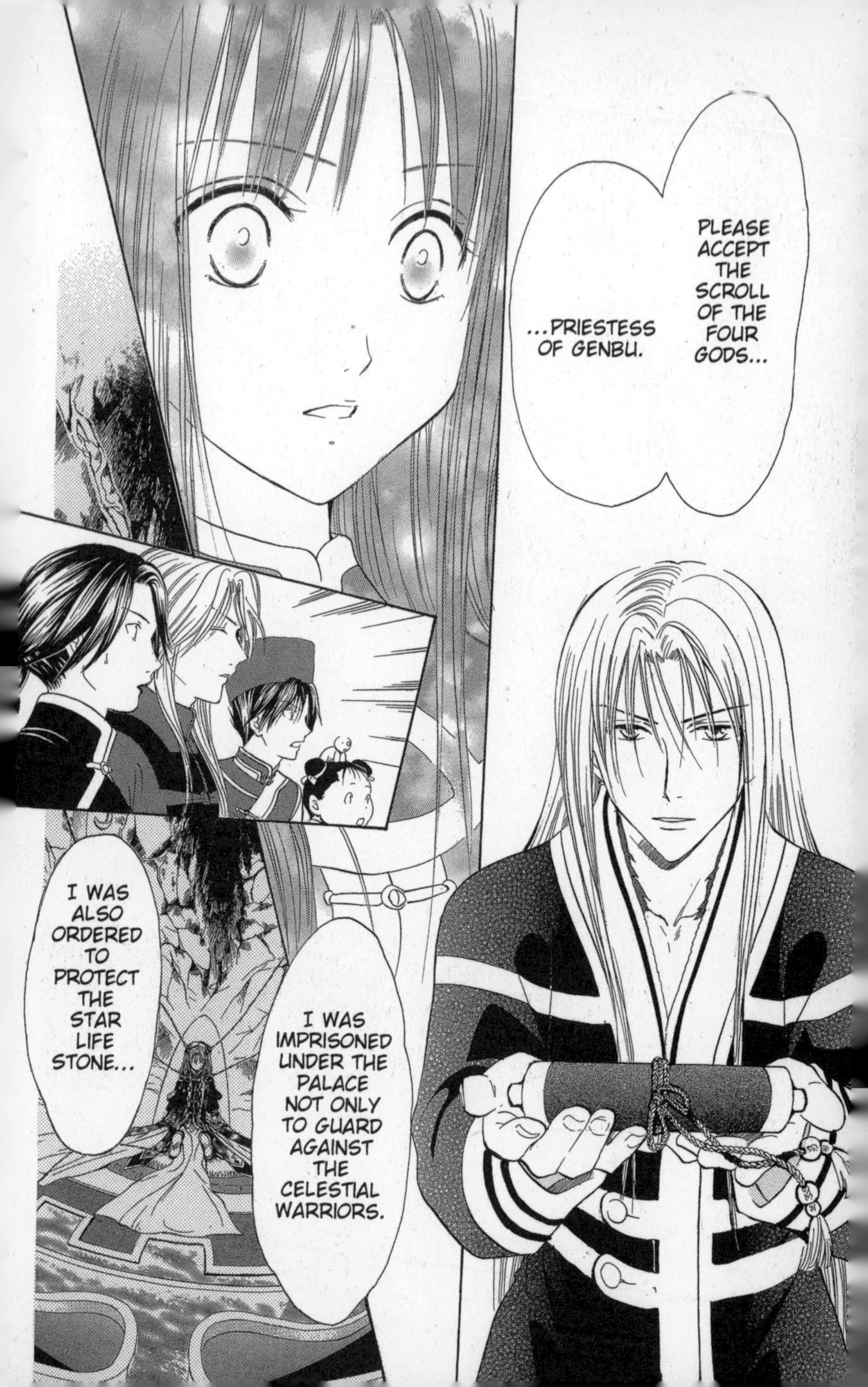
PLEASE ACCEPT THE SCROLL OF THE FOUR GODS...
...PRIESTESS OF GENBU.
I WAS IMPRISONED UNDER THE PALACE NOT ONLY TO GUARD AGAINST THE CELESTIAL WARRIORS.
I WAS ALSO ORDERED TO PROTECT THE STAR LIFE STONE...

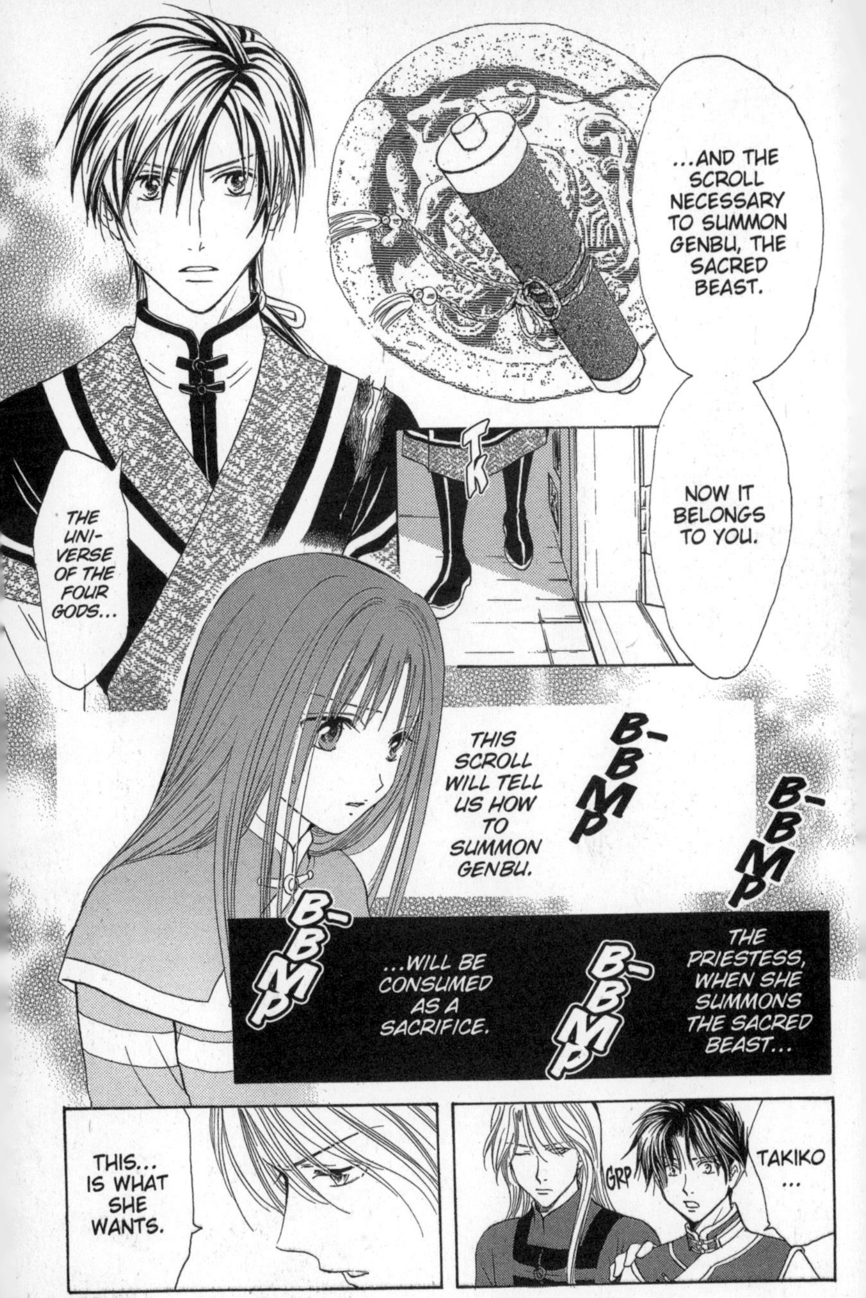
...AND THE SCROLL NECESSARY TO SUMMON GENBU, THE SACRED BEAST.
NOW IT BELONGS TO YOU.
TK
THE UNIVERSE OF THE FOUR GODS...
B-BMP
B-BMP
THIS SCROLL WILL TELL US HOW TO SUMMON GENBU.
THE PRIESTESS, WHEN SHE SUMMONS THE SACRED BEAST...
B-BMP
...WILL BE CONSUMED AS A SACRIFICE.
B-BMP
TAKIKO...
GRP
THIS... IS WHAT SHE WANTS.

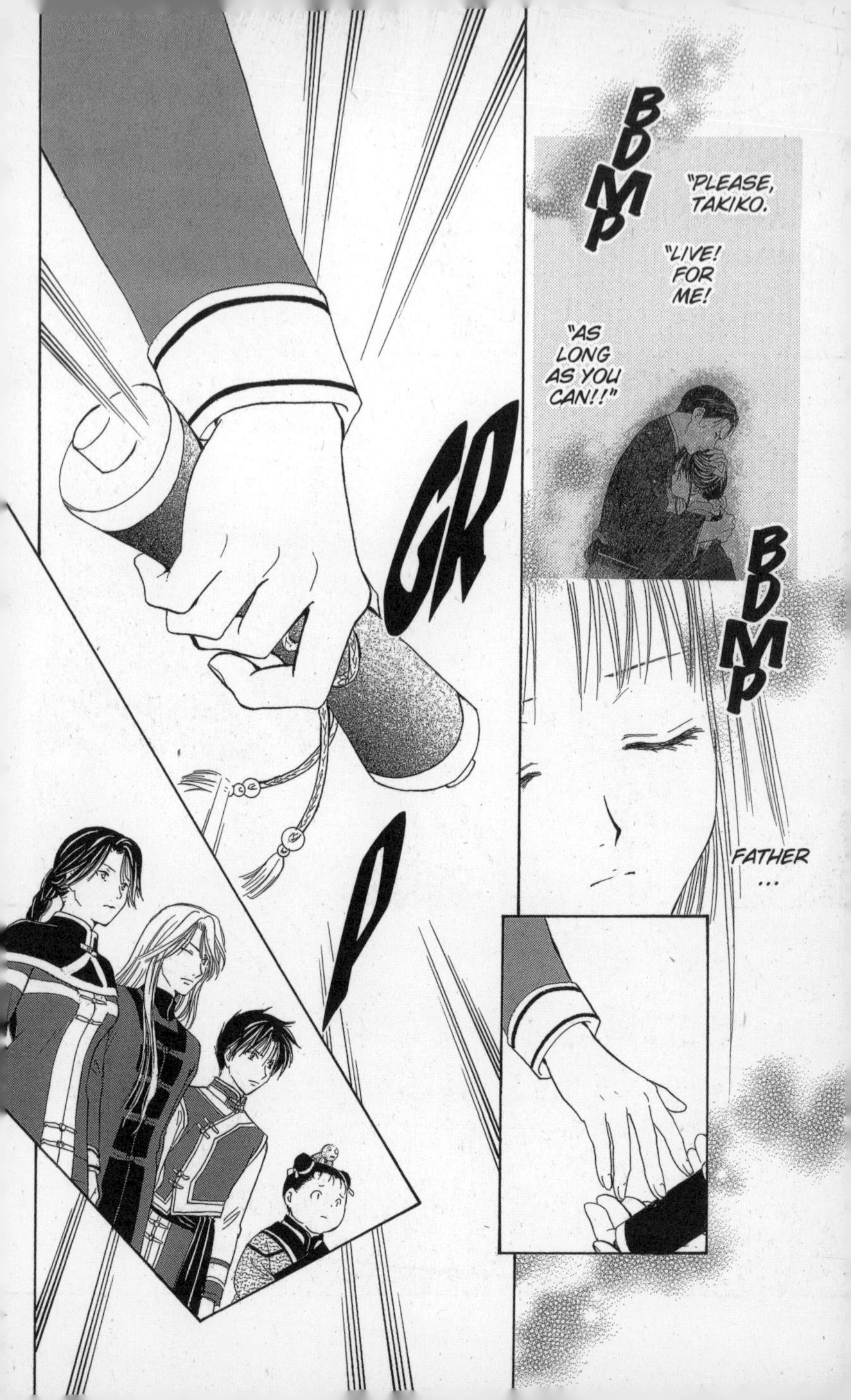
BDMP
"PLEASE, TAKIKO.
"LIVE! FOR ME!
"AS LONG AS YOU CAN!!"
BDMP
FATHER ...
GR
P

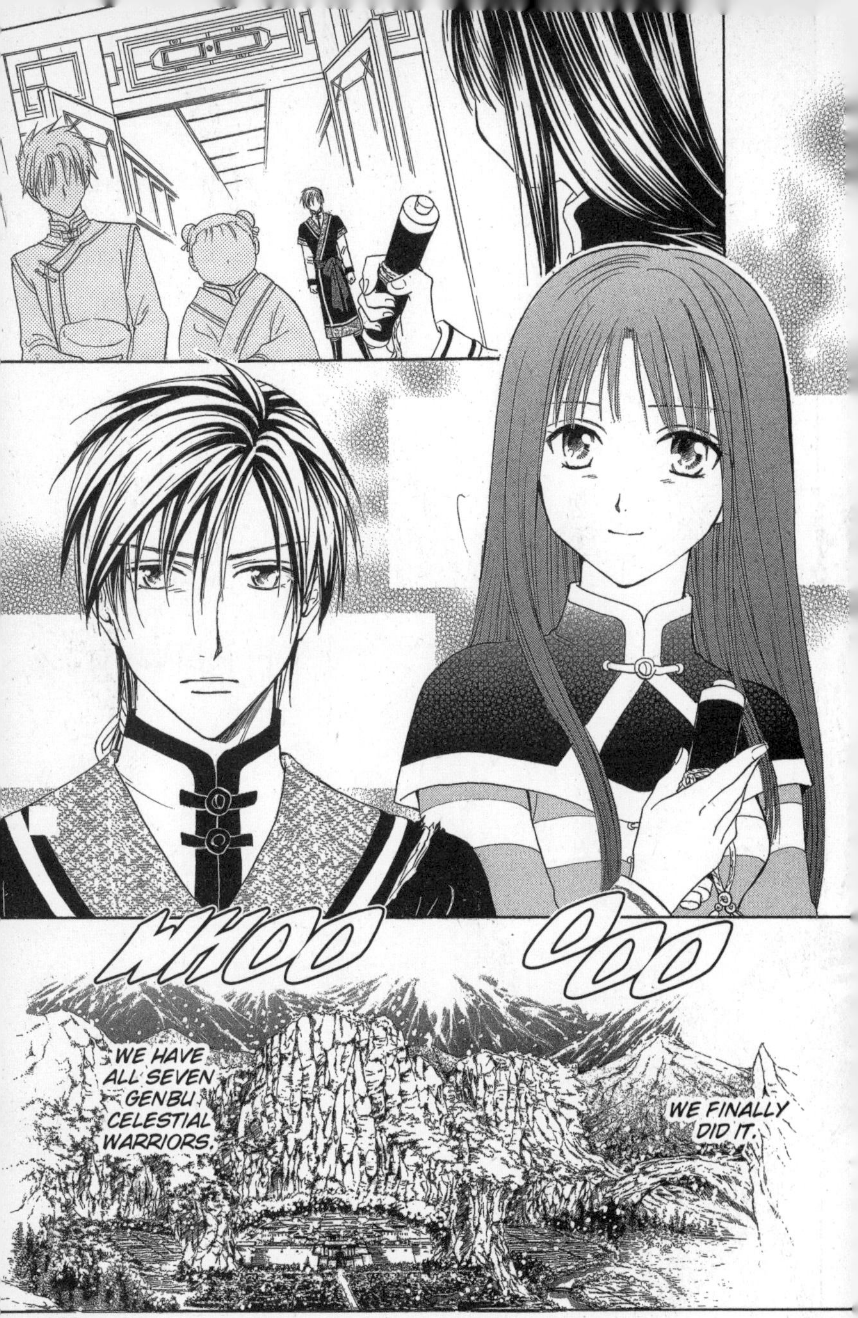
WHOO OOO
WE FINALLY DID IT.
WE HAVE ALL SEVEN GENBU CELESTIAL WARRIORS.

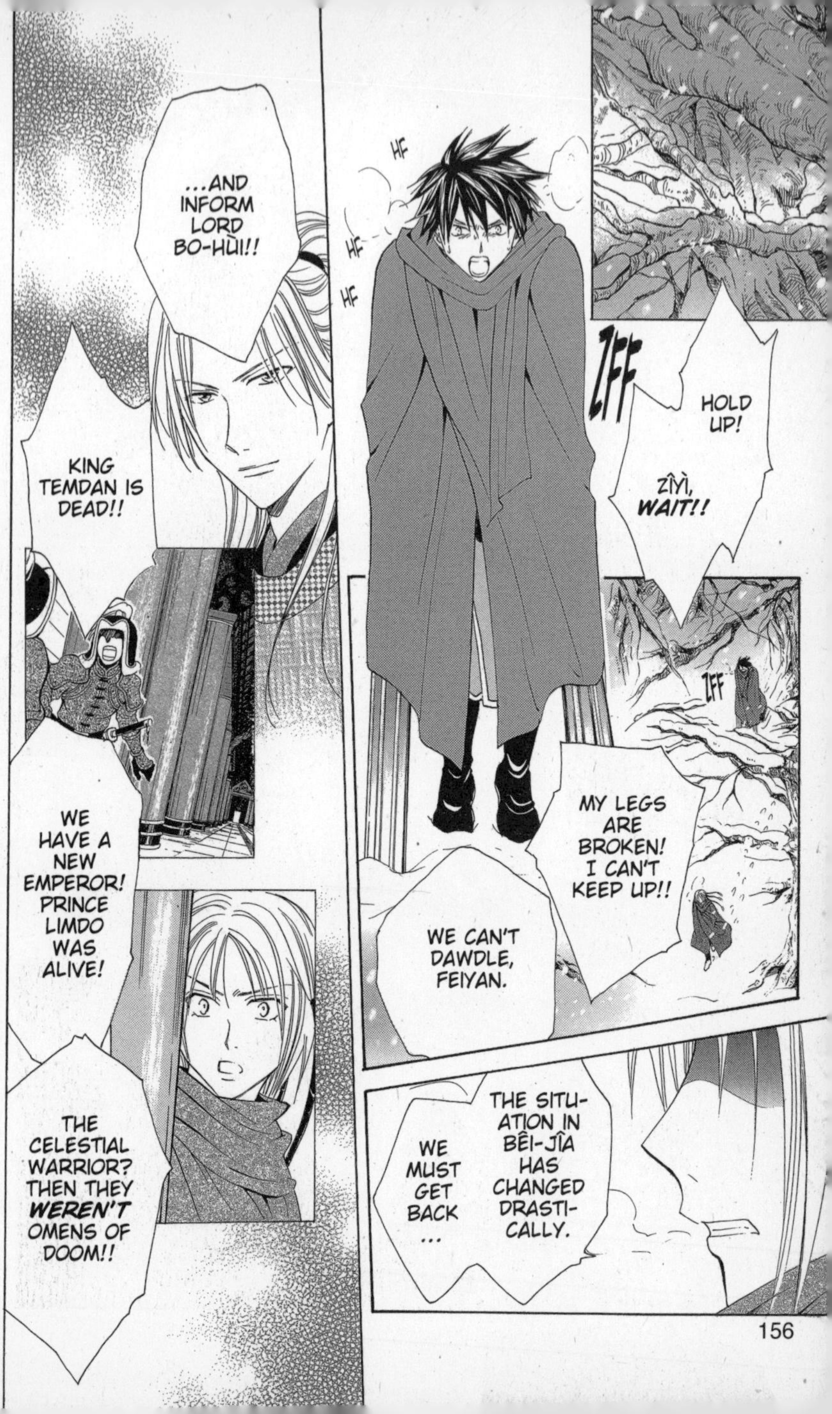
HF
HF
HF
ZFF
HOLD UP!
ZÎYÌ, ***WAIT!!***
ZFF
MY LEGS ARE BROKEN! I CAN'T KEEP UP!!
WE CAN'T DAWDLE, FEIYAN.
THE SITUATION IN BÊI-JÎA HAS CHANGED DRASTICALLY.
WE MUST GET BACK...
...AND INFORM LORD BO-HÙI!!
KING TEMDAN IS DEAD!!
WE HAVE A NEW EMPEROR! PRINCE LIMDO WAS ALIVE!
THE CELESTIAL WARRIOR? THEN THEY ***WEREN'T*** OMENS OF DOOM!!

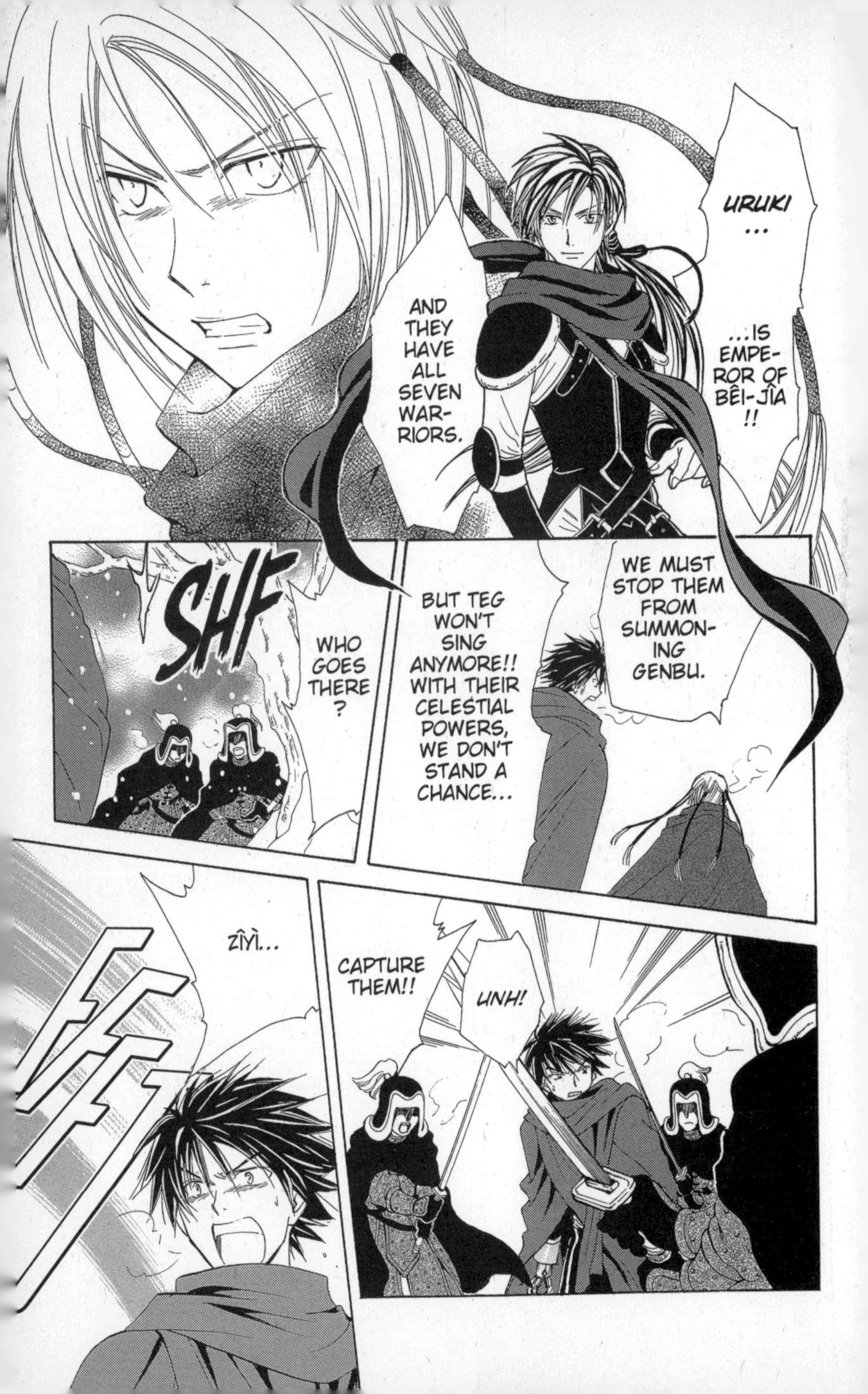
URUKI ...
...IS EMPEROR OF BÊI-JÌA!!
AND THEY HAVE ALL SEVEN WARRIORS.
WE MUST STOP THEM FROM SUMMONING GENBU.
BUT TEG WON'T SING ANYMORE!! WITH THEIR CELESTIAL POWERS, WE DON'T STAND A CHANCE...
SHF
WHO GOES THERE?
CAPTURE THEM!!
UNH!
ZÎYÌ...

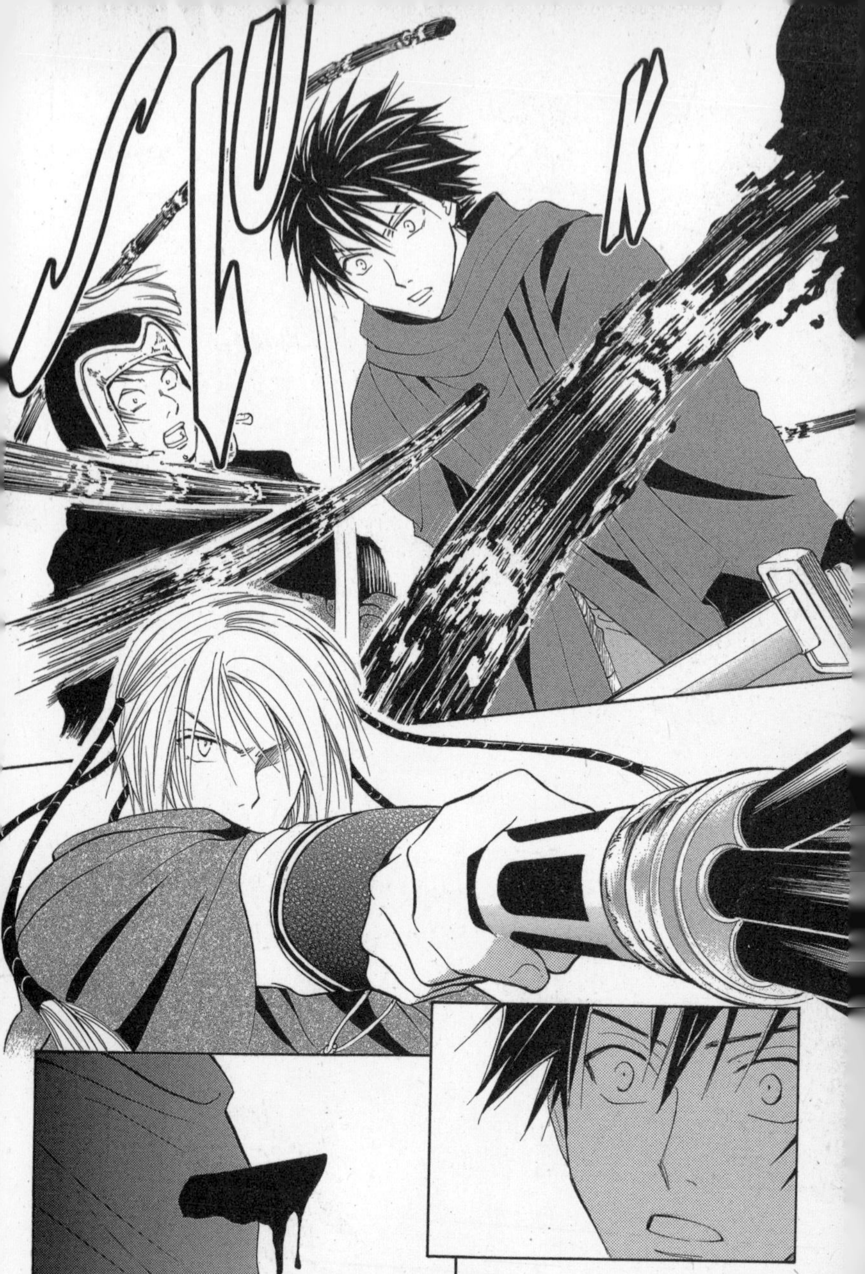
CHUK

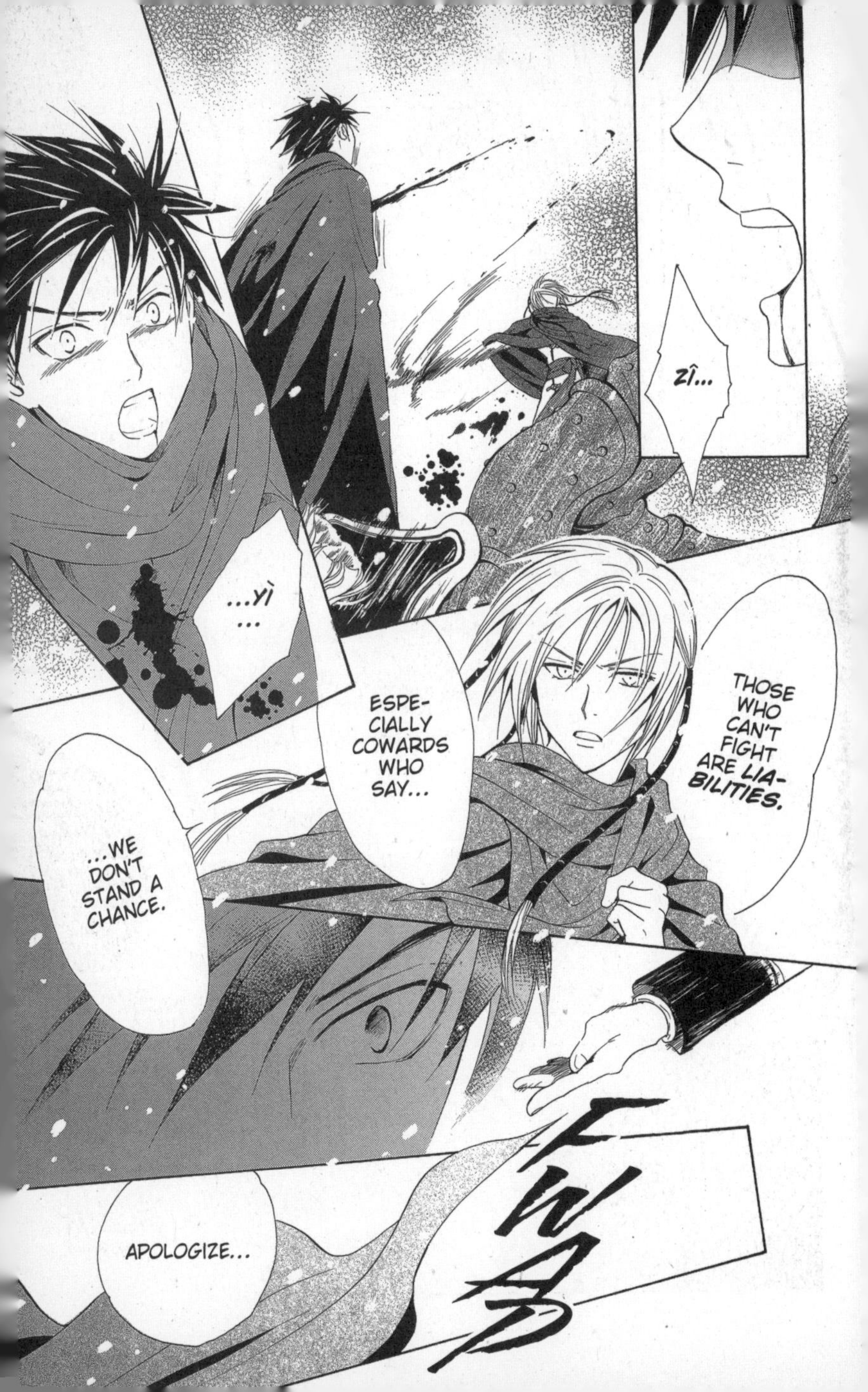
ZÎ...
...YÌ ...
THOSE WHO CAN'T FIGHT ARE LIABILITIES.
ESPECIALLY COWARDS WHO SAY...
...WE DON'T STAND A CHANCE.
FWAP
APOLOGIZE...

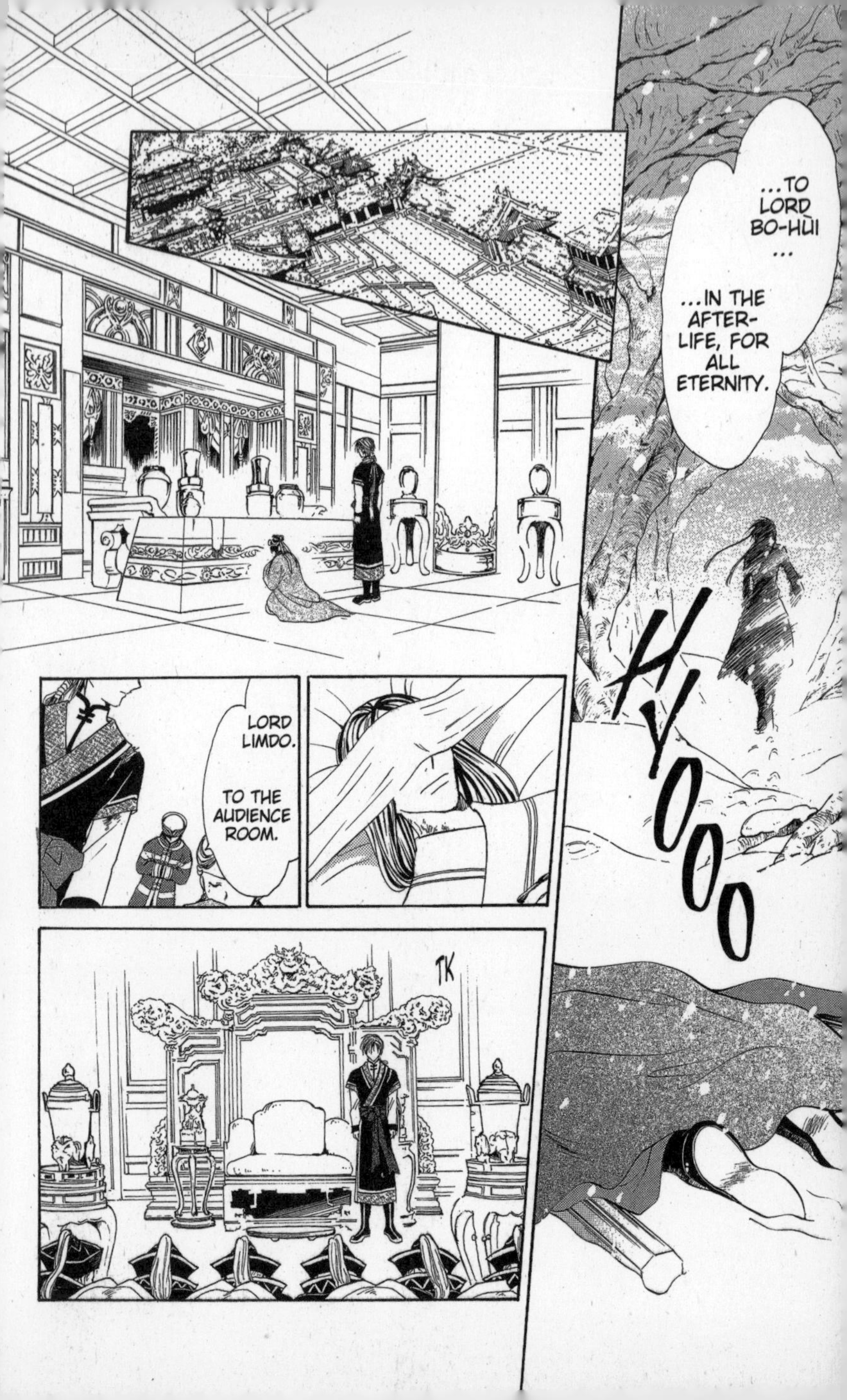
...TO LORD BO-HŪI ...
...IN THE AFTER-LIFE, FOR ALL ETERNITY.
HYOOO
LORD LIMDO.
TO THE AUDIENCE ROOM.
TK

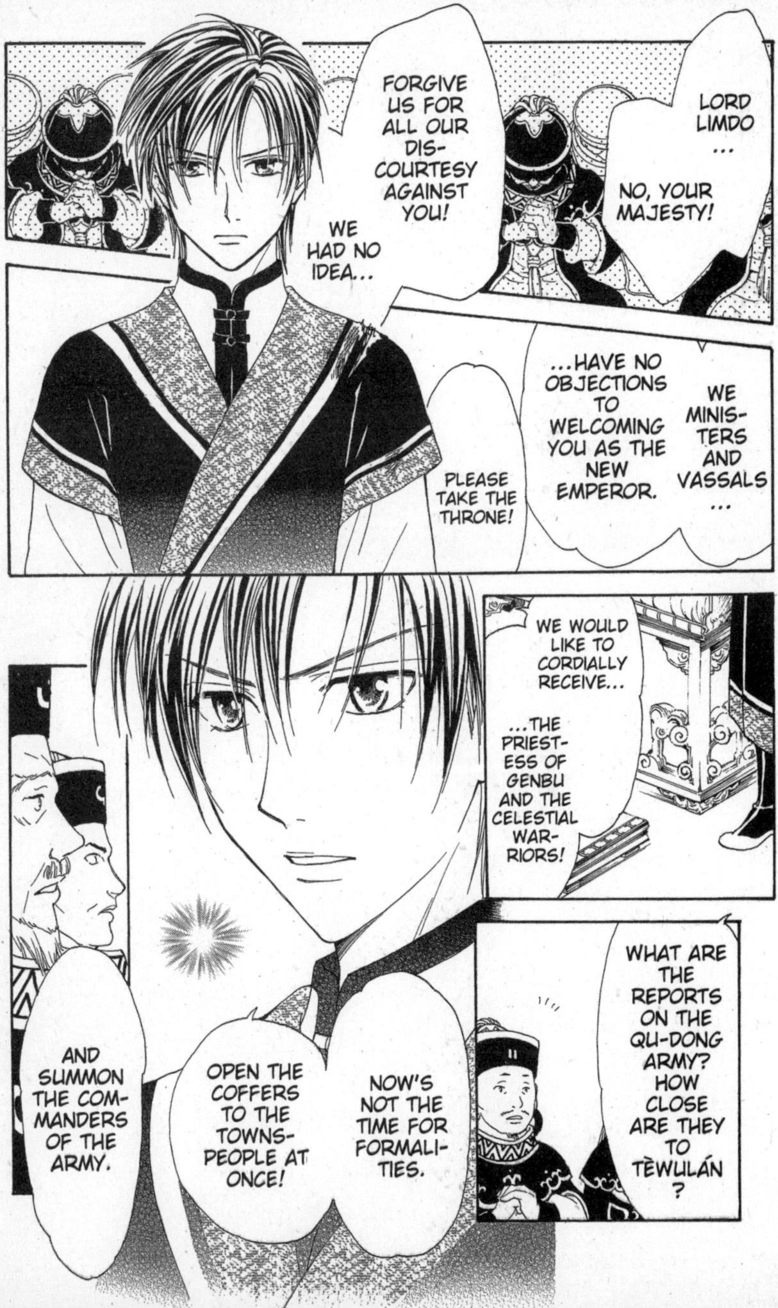

LORD LIMDO...
NO, YOUR MAJESTY!
FORGIVE US FOR ALL OUR DIS-COURTESY AGAINST YOU!
WE HAD NO IDEA...
WE MINIS-TERS AND VASSALS...
...HAVE NO OBJECTIONS TO WELCOMING YOU AS THE NEW EMPEROR.
PLEASE TAKE THE THRONE!
WE WOULD LIKE TO CORDIALLY RECEIVE...
...THE PRIEST-ESS OF GENBU AND THE CELESTIAL WAR-RIORS!
WHAT ARE THE REPORTS ON THE QU-DONG ARMY? HOW CLOSE ARE THEY TO TÈWULÁN?
NOW'S NOT THE TIME FOR FORMALI-TIES.
OPEN THE COFFERS TO THE TOWNS-PEOPLE AT ONCE!
AND SUMMON THE COM-MANDERS OF THE ARMY.

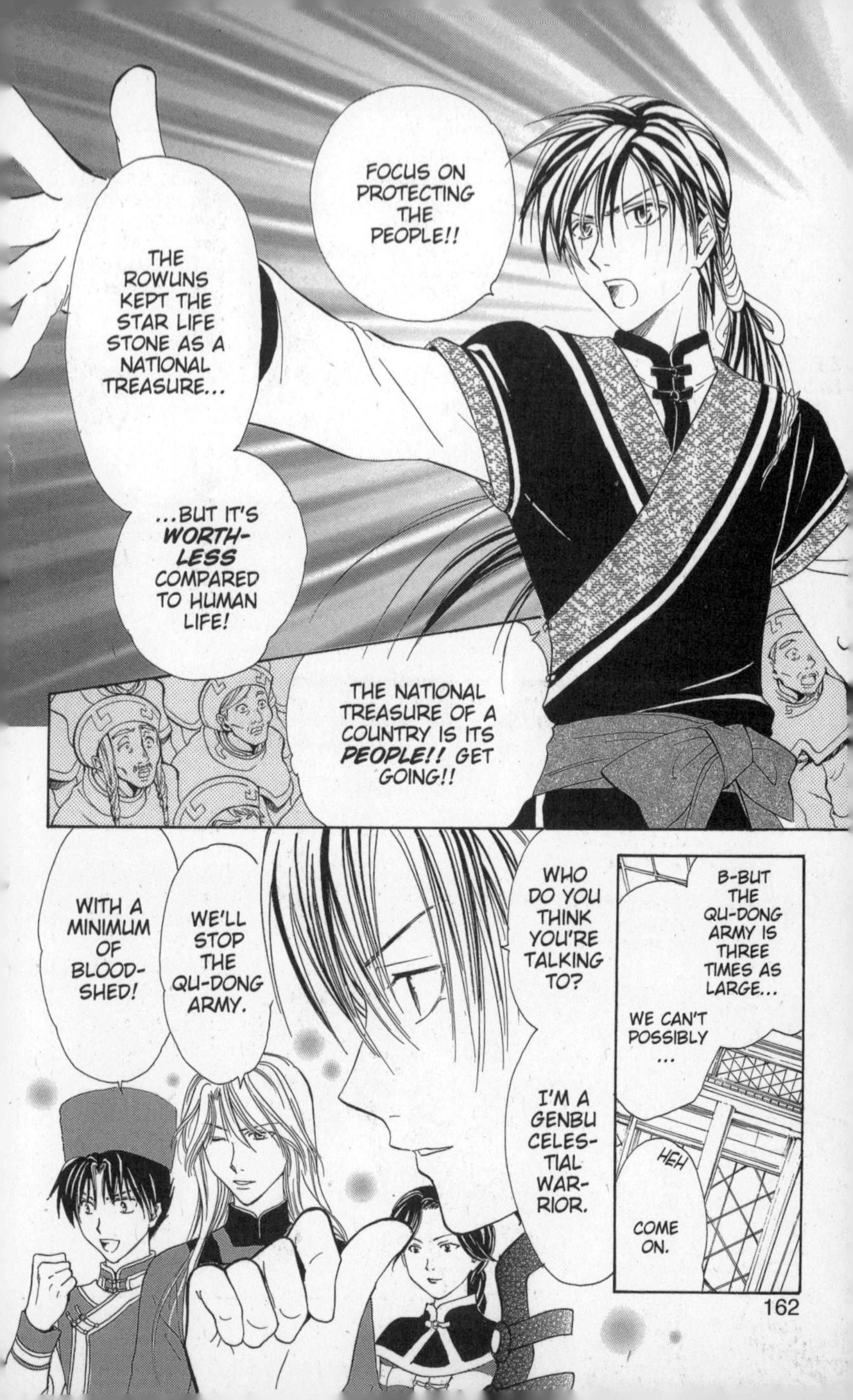
FOCUS ON PROTECTING THE PEOPLE!!
THE ROWUNS KEPT THE STAR LIFE STONE AS A NATIONAL TREASURE...
...BUT IT'S ***WORTH-LESS*** COMPARED TO HUMAN LIFE!
THE NATIONAL TREASURE OF A COUNTRY IS ITS ***PEOPLE!!*** GET GOING!!
B-BUT THE QU-DONG ARMY IS THREE TIMES AS LARGE...
WE CAN'T POSSIBLY ...
HEH
COME ON.
WHO DO YOU THINK YOU'RE TALKING TO?
I'M A GENBU CELES-TIAL WAR-RIOR.
WE'LL STOP THE QU-DONG ARMY.
WITH A MINIMUM OF BLOOD-SHED!

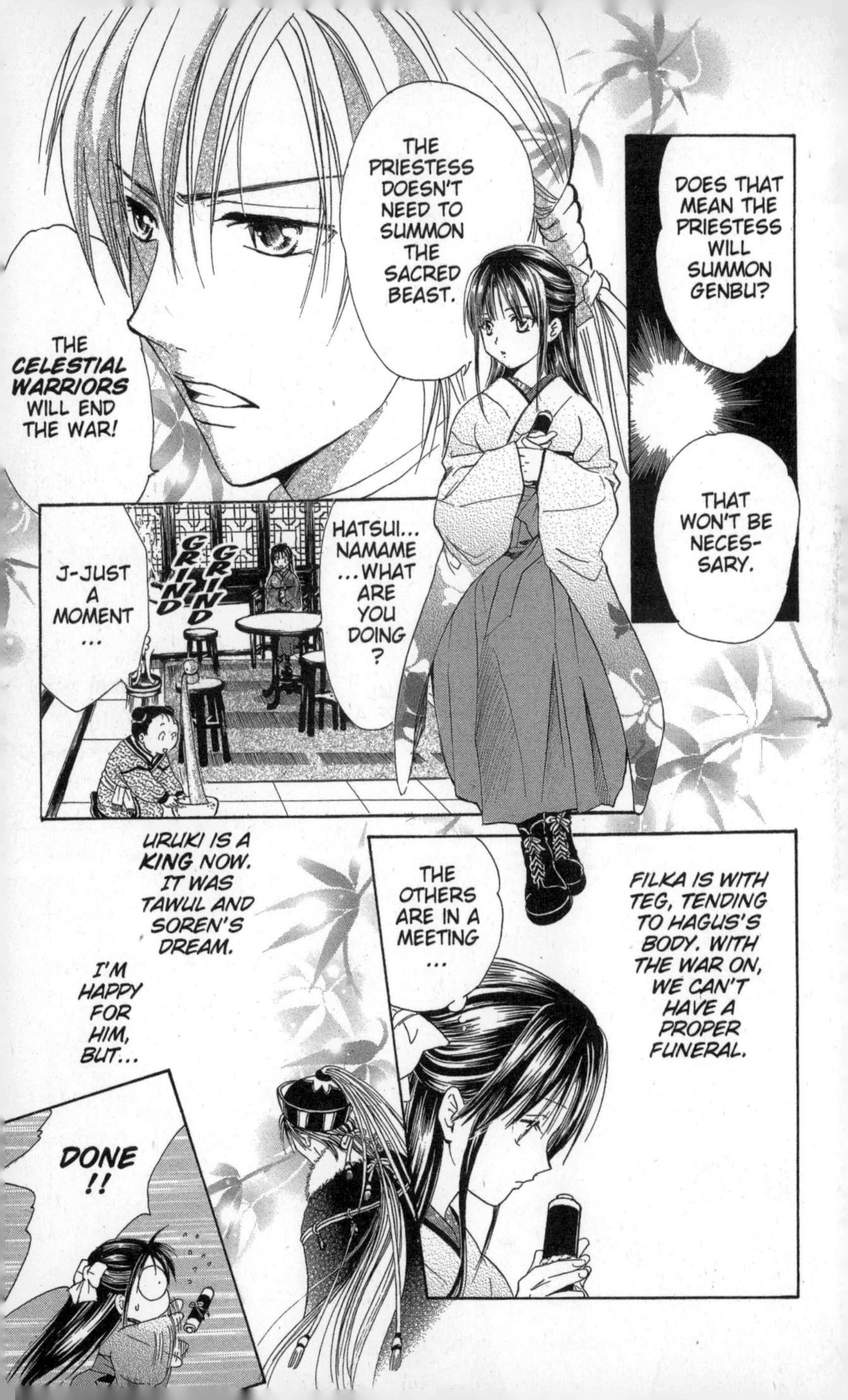
DOES THAT MEAN THE PRIESTESS WILL SUMMON GENBU?
THAT WON'T BE NECESSARY.
THE PRIESTESS DOESN'T NEED TO SUMMON THE SACRED BEAST.
THE **CELESTIAL WARRIORS** WILL END THE WAR!
HATSUI... NAMAME ...WHAT ARE YOU DOING?
GRIND GRIND
J-JUST A MOMENT ...
FILKA IS WITH TEG, TENDING TO HAGUS'S BODY. WITH THE WAR ON, WE CAN'T HAVE A PROPER FUNERAL.
THE OTHERS ARE IN A MEETING ...
*URUKI IS A **KING** NOW. IT WAS TAWUL AND SOREN'S DREAM.*
I'M HAPPY FOR HIM, BUT...
DONE !!

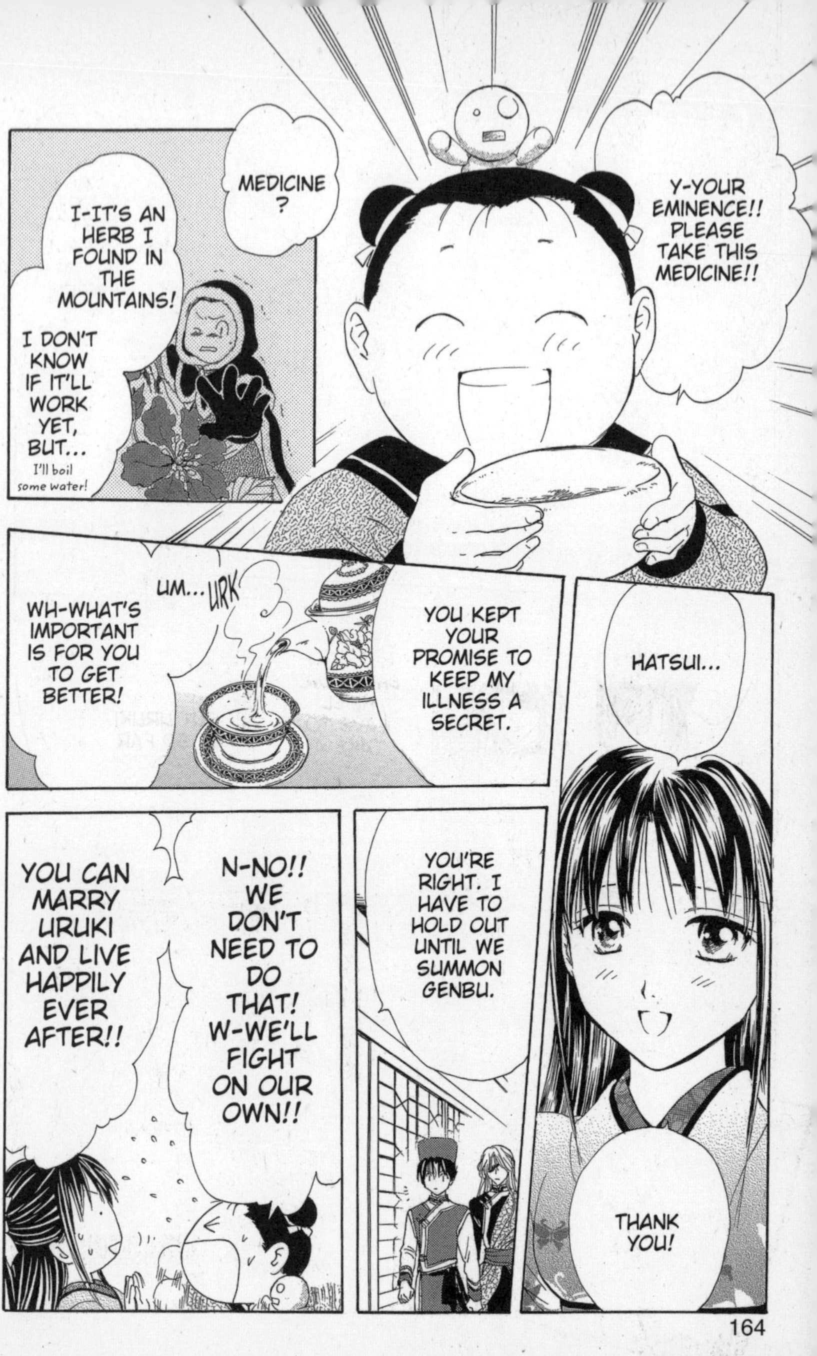
Y-YOUR EMINENCE!! PLEASE TAKE THIS MEDICINE!!
MEDICINE ?
I-IT'S AN HERB I FOUND IN THE MOUNTAINS!
I DON'T KNOW IF IT'LL WORK YET, BUT...
I'll boil some water!
HATSUI...
THANK YOU!
YOU KEPT YOUR PROMISE TO KEEP MY ILLNESS A SECRET.
UM... URK
WH-WHAT'S IMPORTANT IS FOR YOU TO GET BETTER!
YOU'RE RIGHT. I HAVE TO HOLD OUT UNTIL WE SUMMON GENBU.
N-NO!! WE DON'T NEED TO DO THAT! W-WE'LL FIGHT ON OUR OWN!!
YOU CAN MARRY URUKI AND LIVE HAPPILY EVER AFTER!!

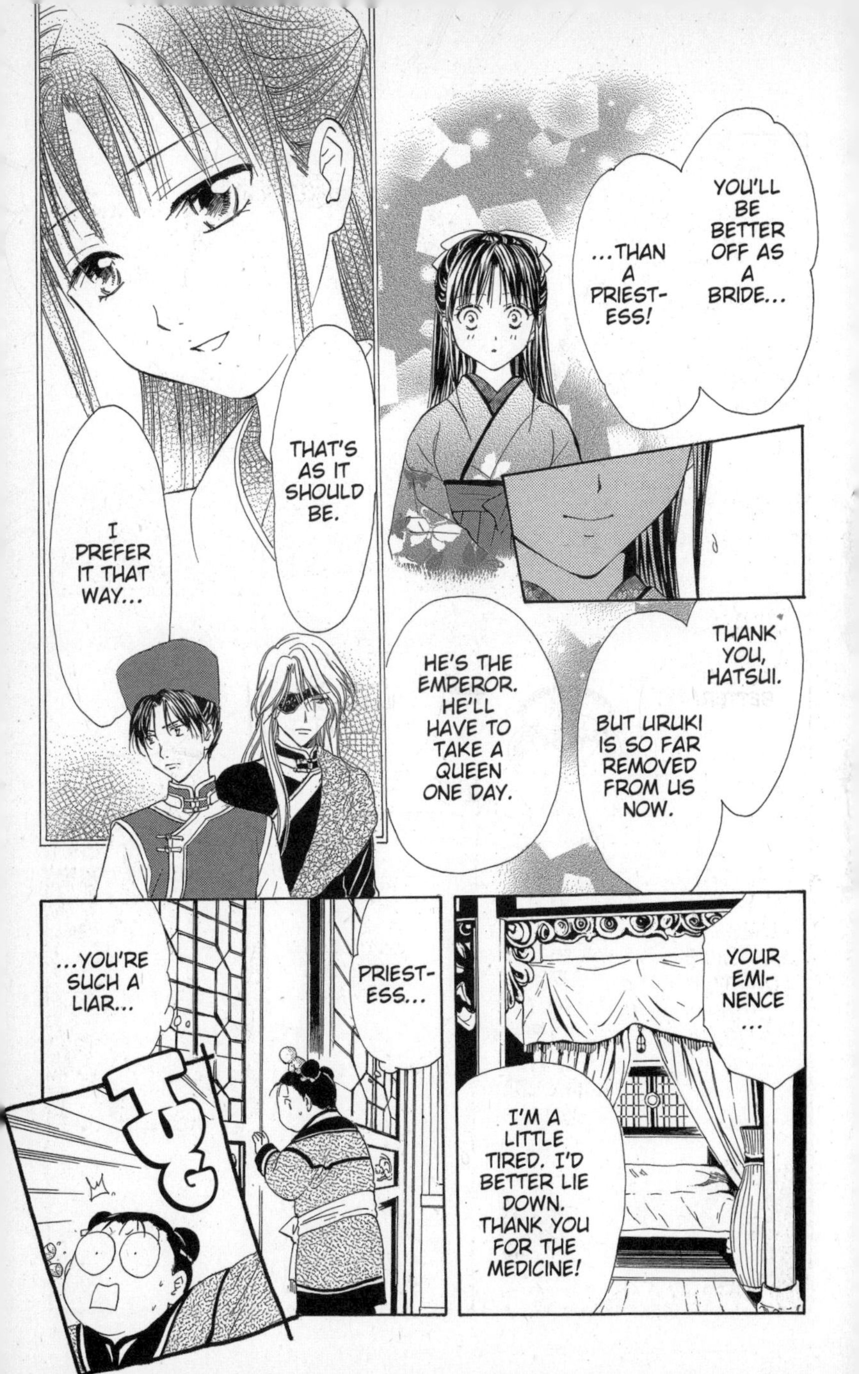
YOU'LL BE BETTER OFF AS A BRIDE...
...THAN A PRIEST-ESS!
THANK YOU, HATSUI.
BUT URUKI IS SO FAR REMOVED FROM US NOW.
HE'S THE EMPEROR. HE'LL HAVE TO TAKE A QUEEN ONE DAY.
THAT'S AS IT SHOULD BE.
I PREFER IT THAT WAY...
YOUR EMI-NENCE...
I'M A LITTLE TIRED. I'D BETTER LIE DOWN. THANK YOU FOR THE MEDICINE!
PRIEST-ESS...
...YOU'RE SUCH A LIAR...
TUG

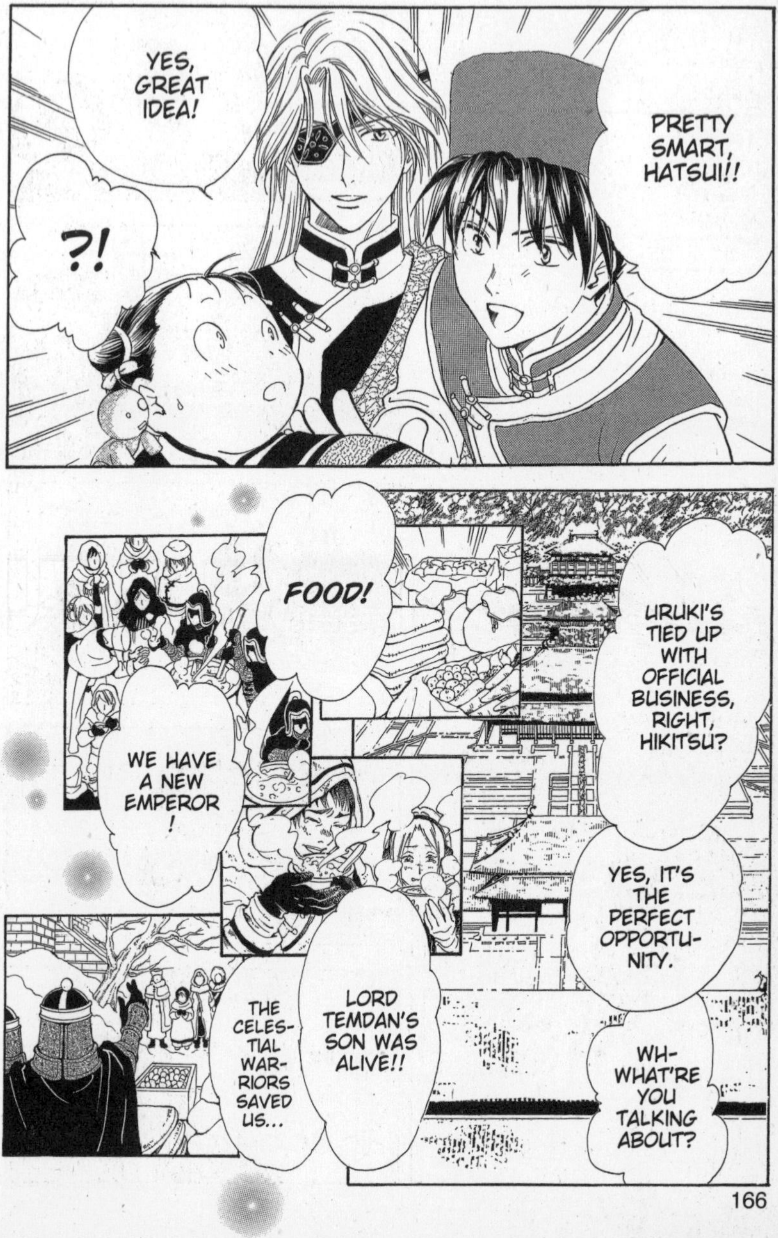
PRETTY SMART, HATSUI!!
YES, GREAT IDEA!
?!
URUKI'S TIED UP WITH OFFICIAL BUSINESS, RIGHT, HIKITSU?
YES, IT'S THE PERFECT OPPORTU-NITY.
WH-WHAT'RE YOU TALKING ABOUT?
FOOD!
WE HAVE A NEW EMPEROR!
LORD TEMDAN'S SON WAS ALIVE!!
THE CELES-TIAL WAR-RIORS SAVED US...

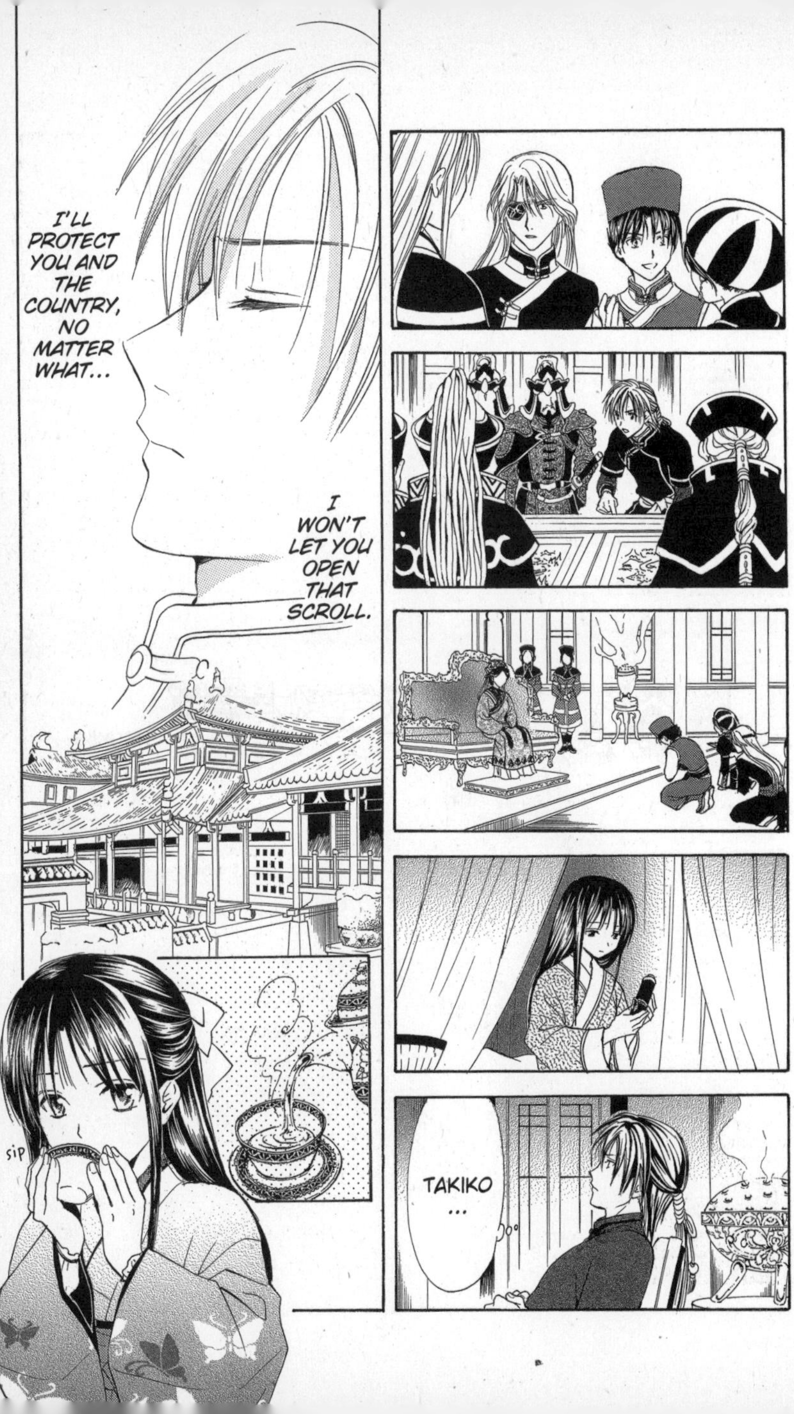
TAKIKO ...
I'LL PROTECT YOU AND THE COUNTRY, NO MATTER WHAT...
I WON'T LET YOU OPEN THAT SCROLL.
sip

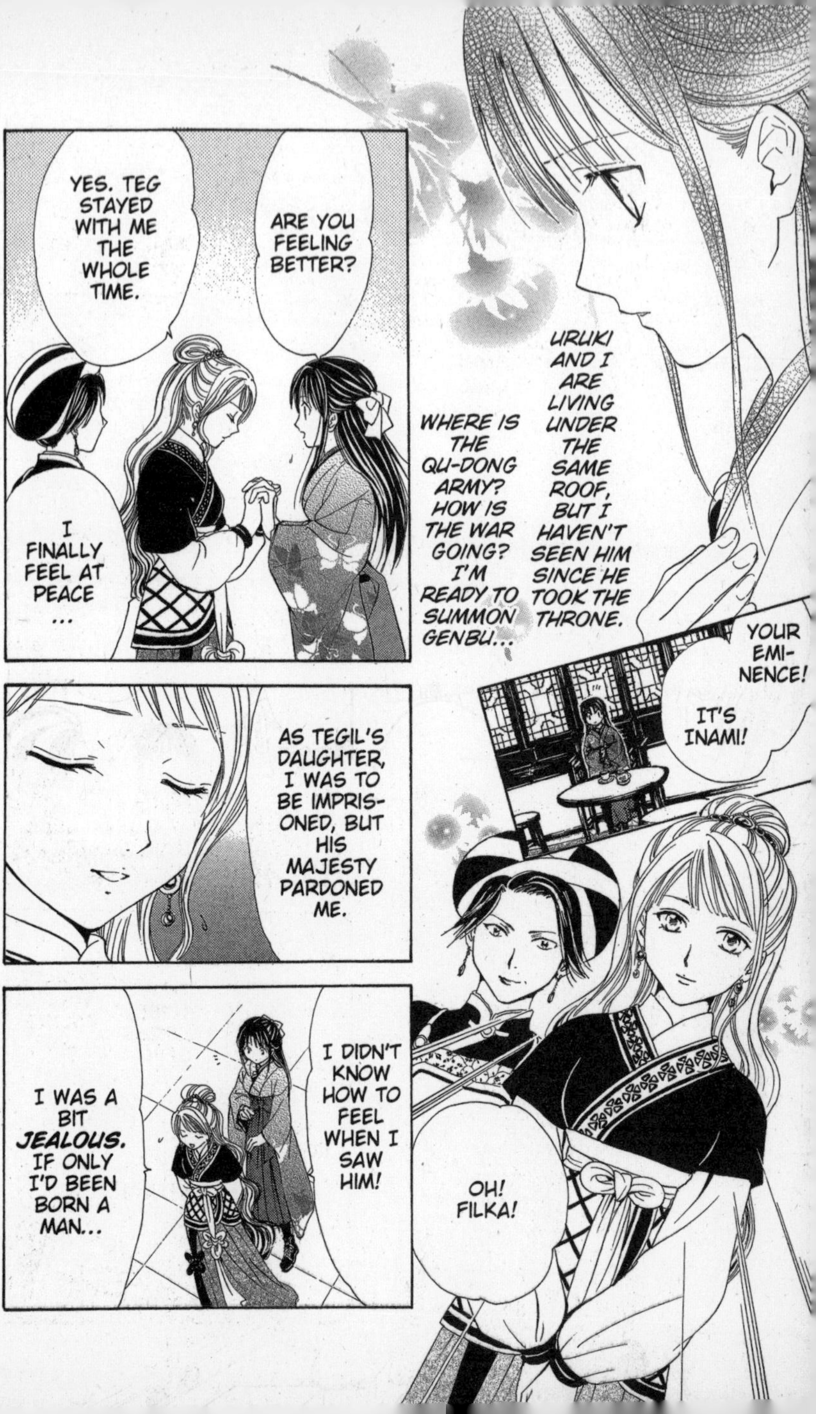
URUKI AND I ARE LIVING UNDER THE SAME ROOF, BUT I HAVEN'T SEEN HIM SINCE HE TOOK THE THRONE.
WHERE IS THE QU-DONG ARMY? HOW IS THE WAR GOING? I'M READY TO SUMMON GENBU...
YOUR EMINENCE!
IT'S INAMI!
OH! FILKA!
ARE YOU FEELING BETTER?
YES. TEG STAYED WITH ME THE WHOLE TIME.
I FINALLY FEEL AT PEACE...
AS TEGIL'S DAUGHTER, I WAS TO BE IMPRISONED, BUT HIS MAJESTY PARDONED ME.
I DIDN'T KNOW HOW TO FEEL WHEN I SAW HIM!
I WAS A BIT JEALOUS. IF ONLY I'D BEEN BORN A MAN...

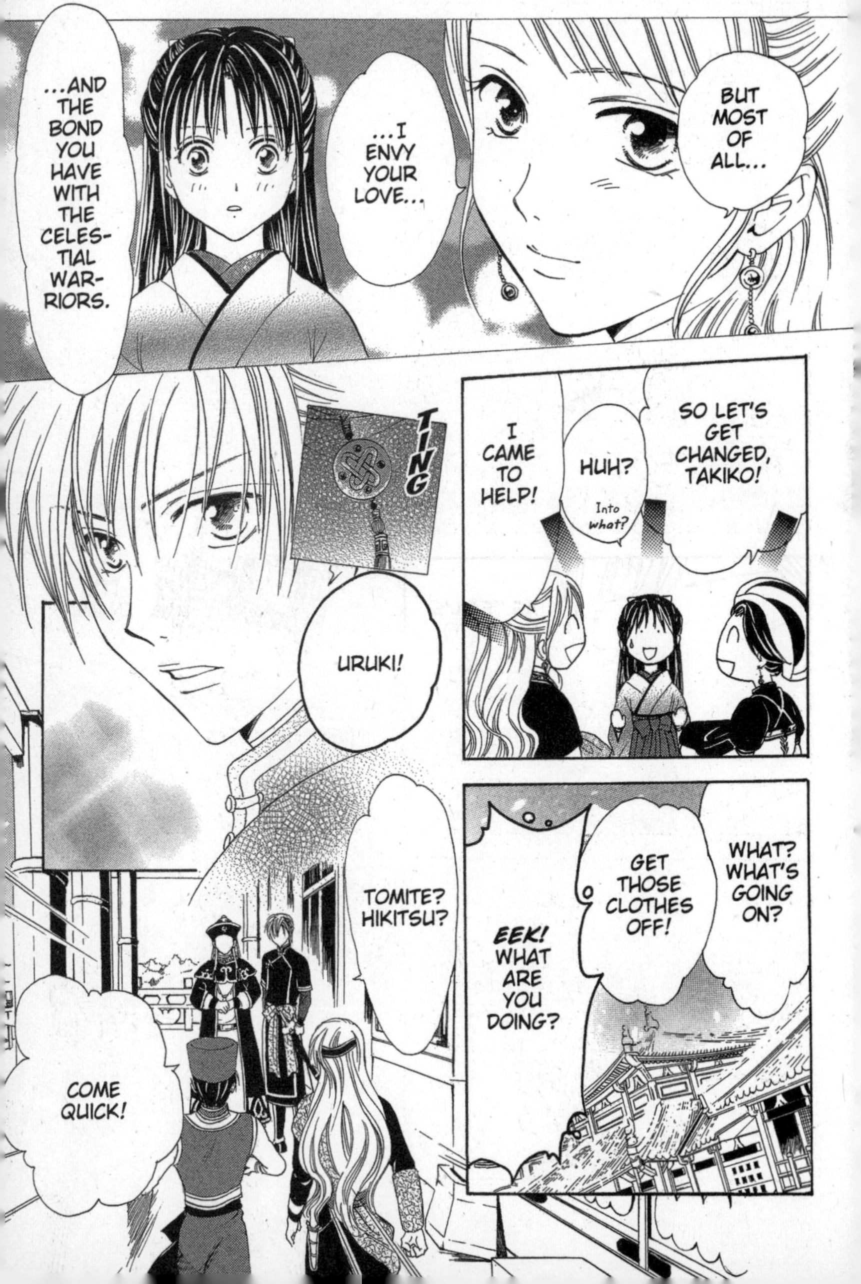
BUT MOST OF ALL...
...I ENVY YOUR LOVE...
...AND THE BOND YOU HAVE WITH THE CELESTIAL WARRIORS.
SO LET'S GET CHANGED, TAKIKO!
HUH?
Into what?
I CAME TO HELP!
WHAT? WHAT'S GOING ON?
GET THOSE CLOTHES OFF!
EEK! WHAT ARE YOU DOING?
TING
URUKI!
TOMITE? HIKITSU?
COME QUICK!

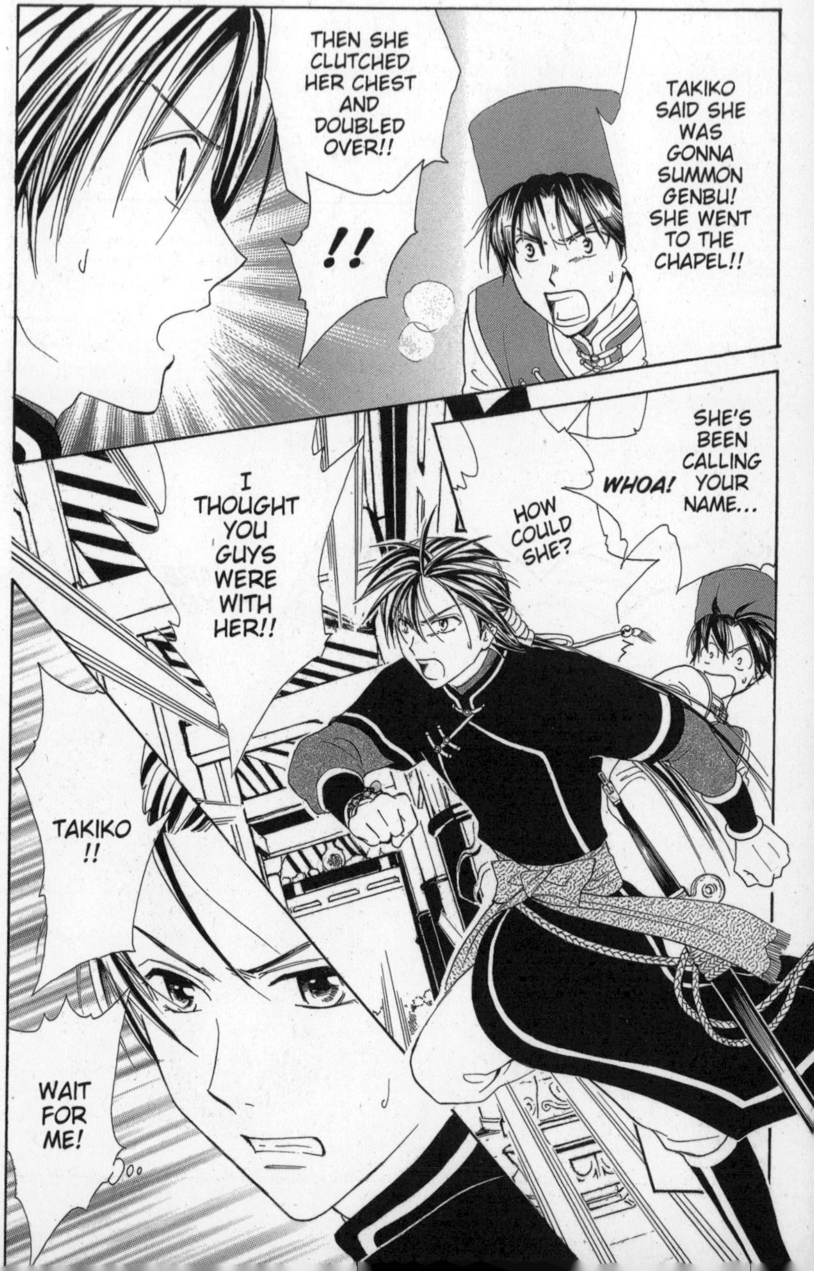
TAKIKO SAID SHE WAS GONNA SUMMON GENBU! SHE WENT TO THE CHAPEL!!
THEN SHE CLUTCHED HER CHEST AND DOUBLED OVER!!
!!
SHE'S BEEN CALLING YOUR NAME...
WHOA!
HOW COULD SHE?
I THOUGHT YOU GUYS WERE WITH HER!!
TAKIKO !!
WAIT FOR ME!

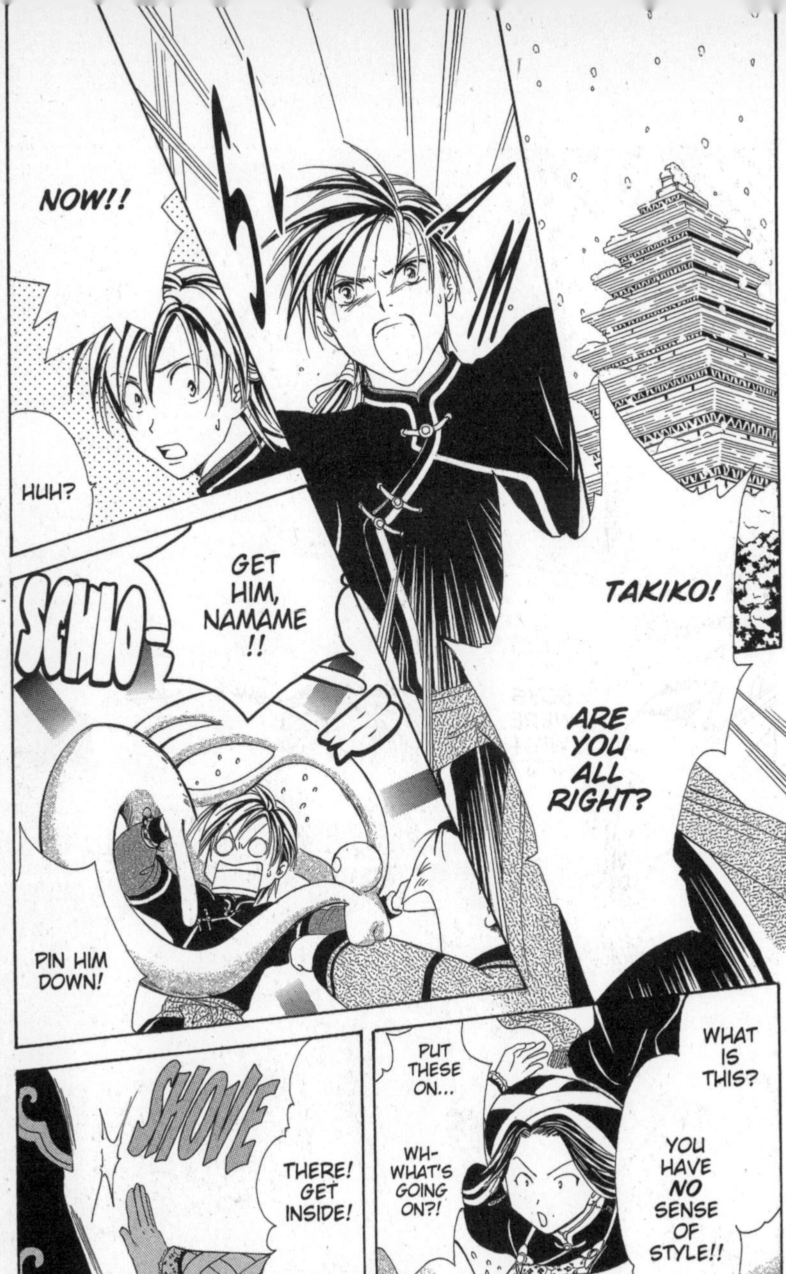

NOW!!
HUH?
TAKIKO!
ARE YOU ALL RIGHT?
GET HIM, NAMAME!!
SCHLO-
PIN HIM DOWN!
WHAT IS THIS?
YOU HAVE NO SENSE OF STYLE!!
PUT THESE ON...
WH-WHAT'S GOING ON?!
THERE! GET INSIDE!
SHOVE

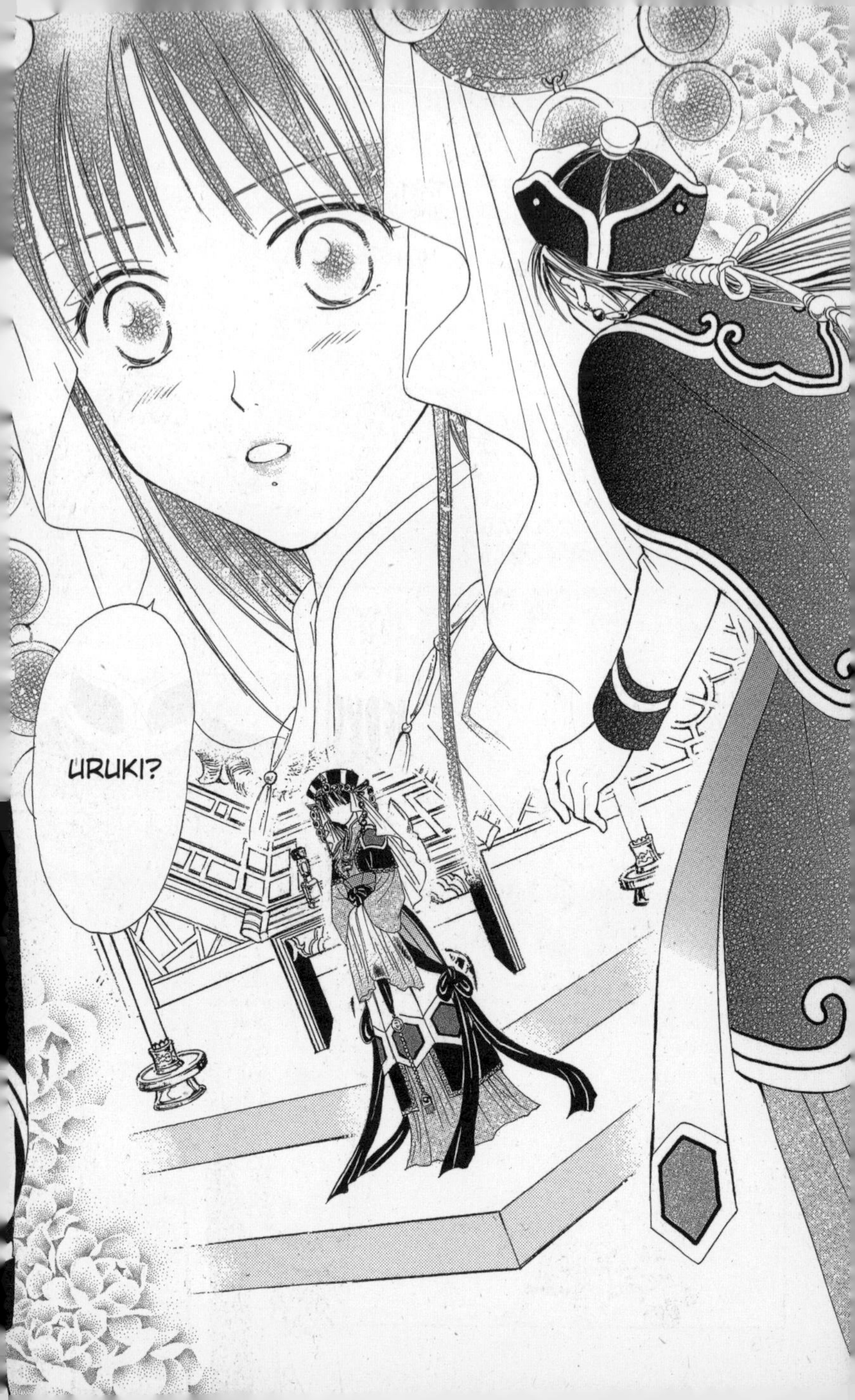
URUKI?

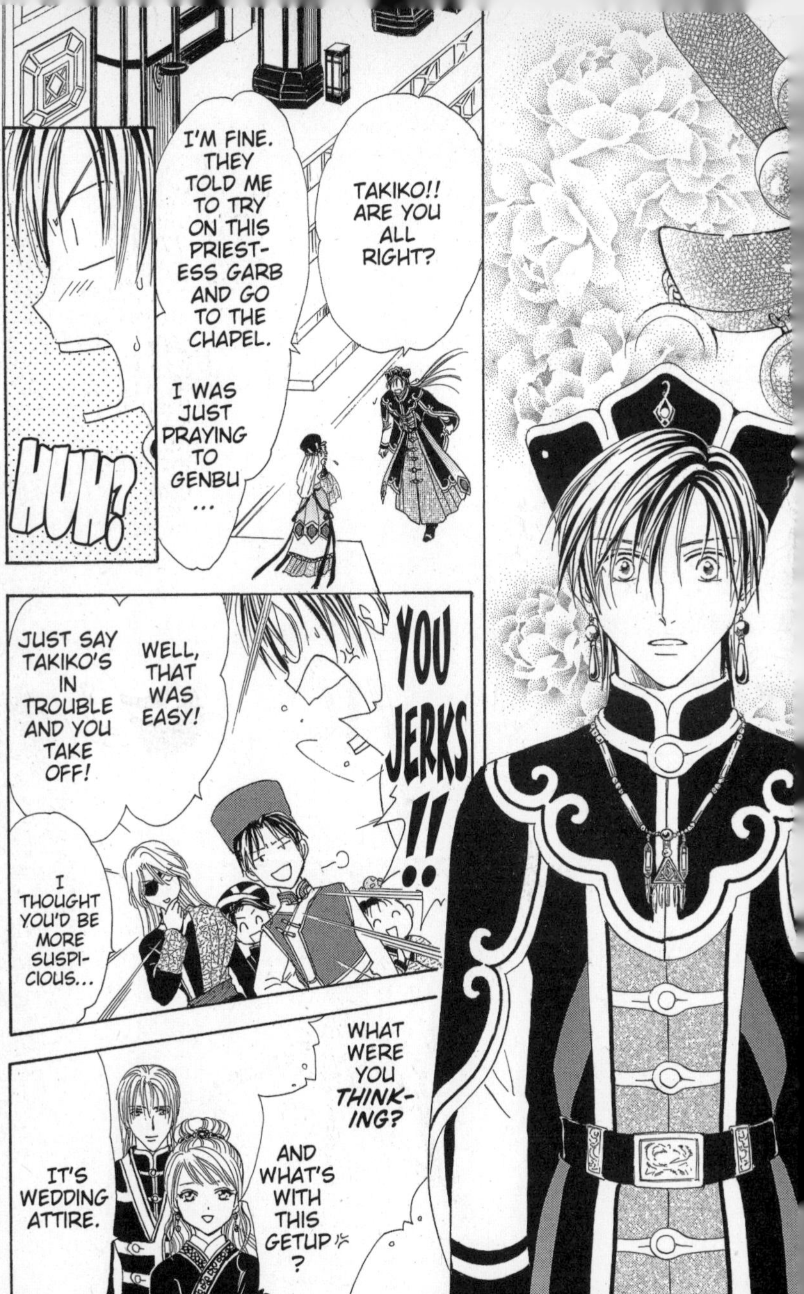
TAKIKO!! ARE YOU ALL RIGHT?
I'M FINE. THEY TOLD ME TO TRY ON THIS PRIEST-ESS GARB AND GO TO THE CHAPEL.
I WAS JUST PRAYING TO GENBU...
HUH?
YOU JERKS!!
WELL, THAT WAS EASY!
JUST SAY TAKIKO'S IN TROUBLE AND YOU TAKE OFF!
I THOUGHT YOU'D BE MORE SUSPICIOUS...
WHAT WERE YOU *THINKING*?
AND WHAT'S WITH THIS GETUP?
IT'S WEDDING ATTIRE.

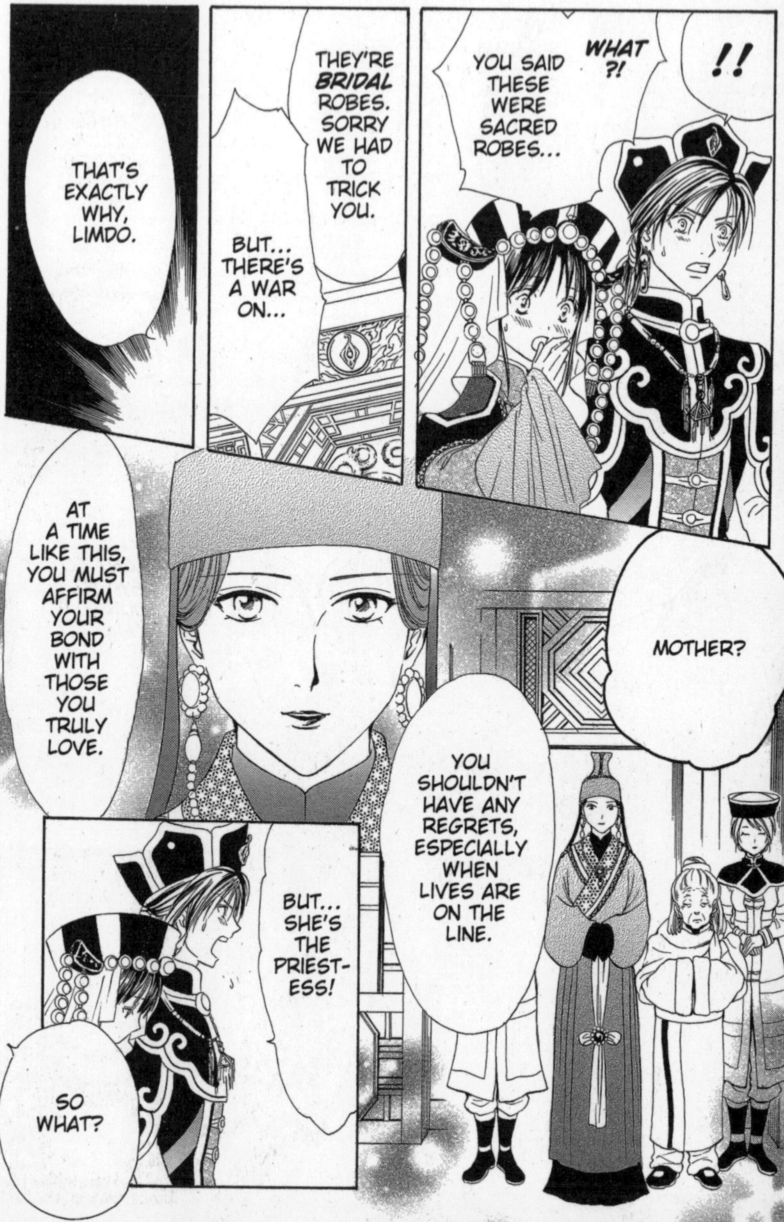
!!
WHAT ?!
YOU SAID THESE WERE SACRED ROBES...
THEY'RE BRIDAL ROBES. SORRY WE HAD TO TRICK YOU.
BUT... THERE'S A WAR ON...
THAT'S EXACTLY WHY, LIMDO.
MOTHER?
YOU SHOULDN'T HAVE ANY REGRETS, ESPECIALLY WHEN LIVES ARE ON THE LINE.
AT A TIME LIKE THIS, YOU MUST AFFIRM YOUR BOND WITH THOSE YOU TRULY LOVE.
BUT... SHE'S THE PRIEST-ESS!
SO WHAT?

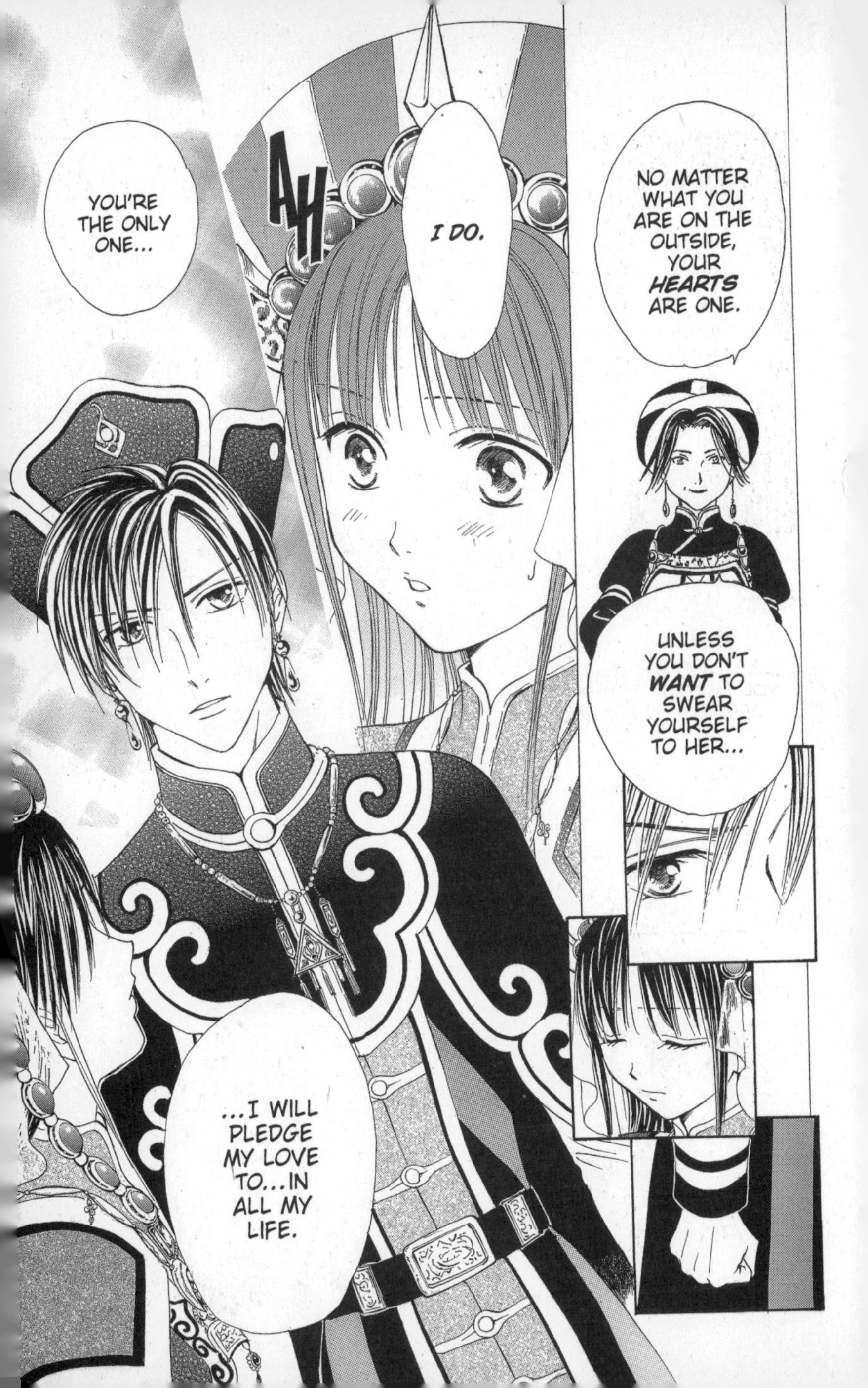
NO MATTER WHAT YOU ARE ON THE OUTSIDE, YOUR HEARTS ARE ONE.
UNLESS YOU DON'T WANT TO SWEAR YOURSELF TO HER...
I DO.
AH
YOU'RE THE ONLY ONE...
...I WILL PLEDGE MY LOVE TO...IN ALL MY LIFE.

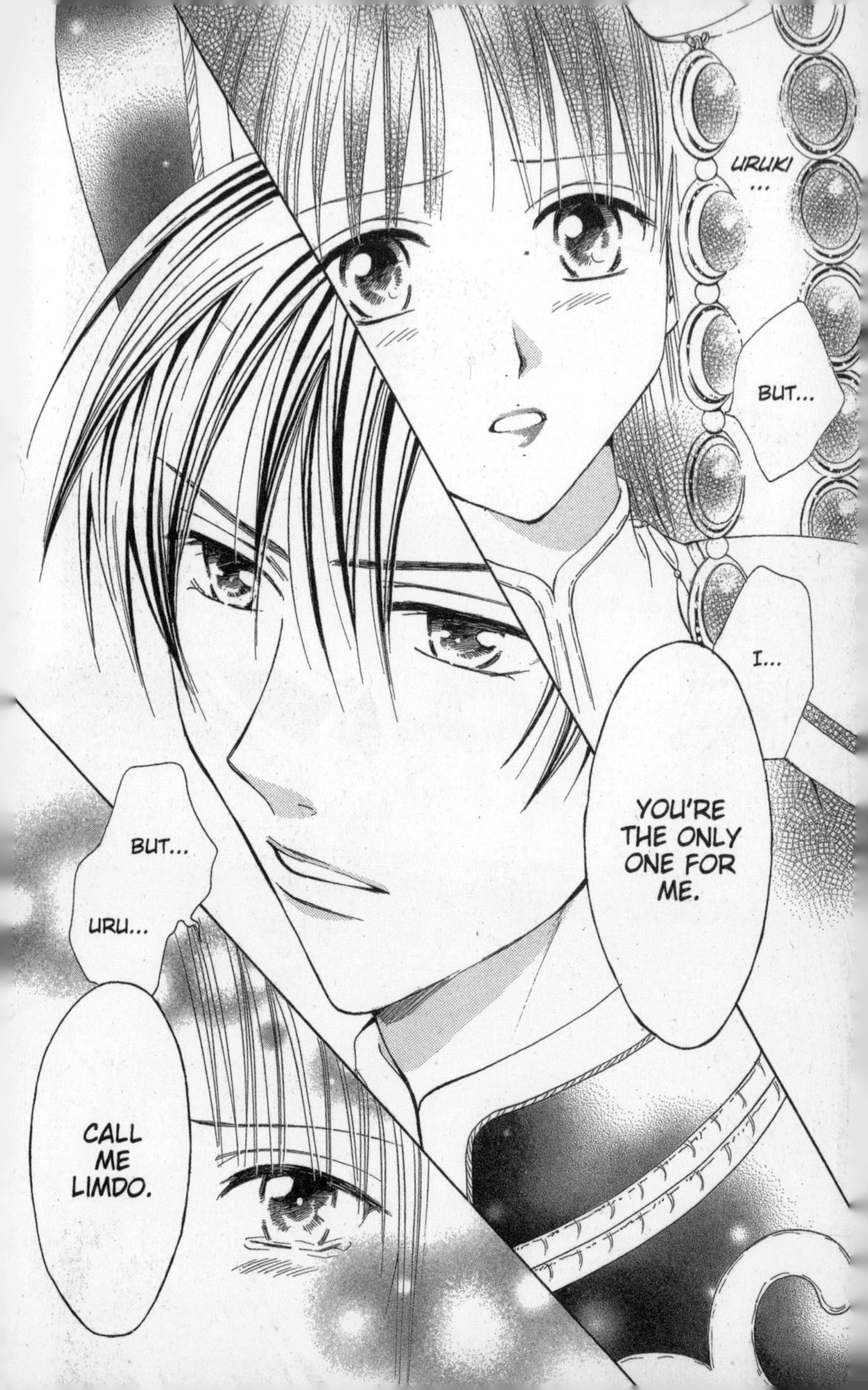
URUKI ...
BUT...
I...
YOU'RE THE ONLY ONE FOR ME.
BUT...
URU...
CALL ME LIMDO.

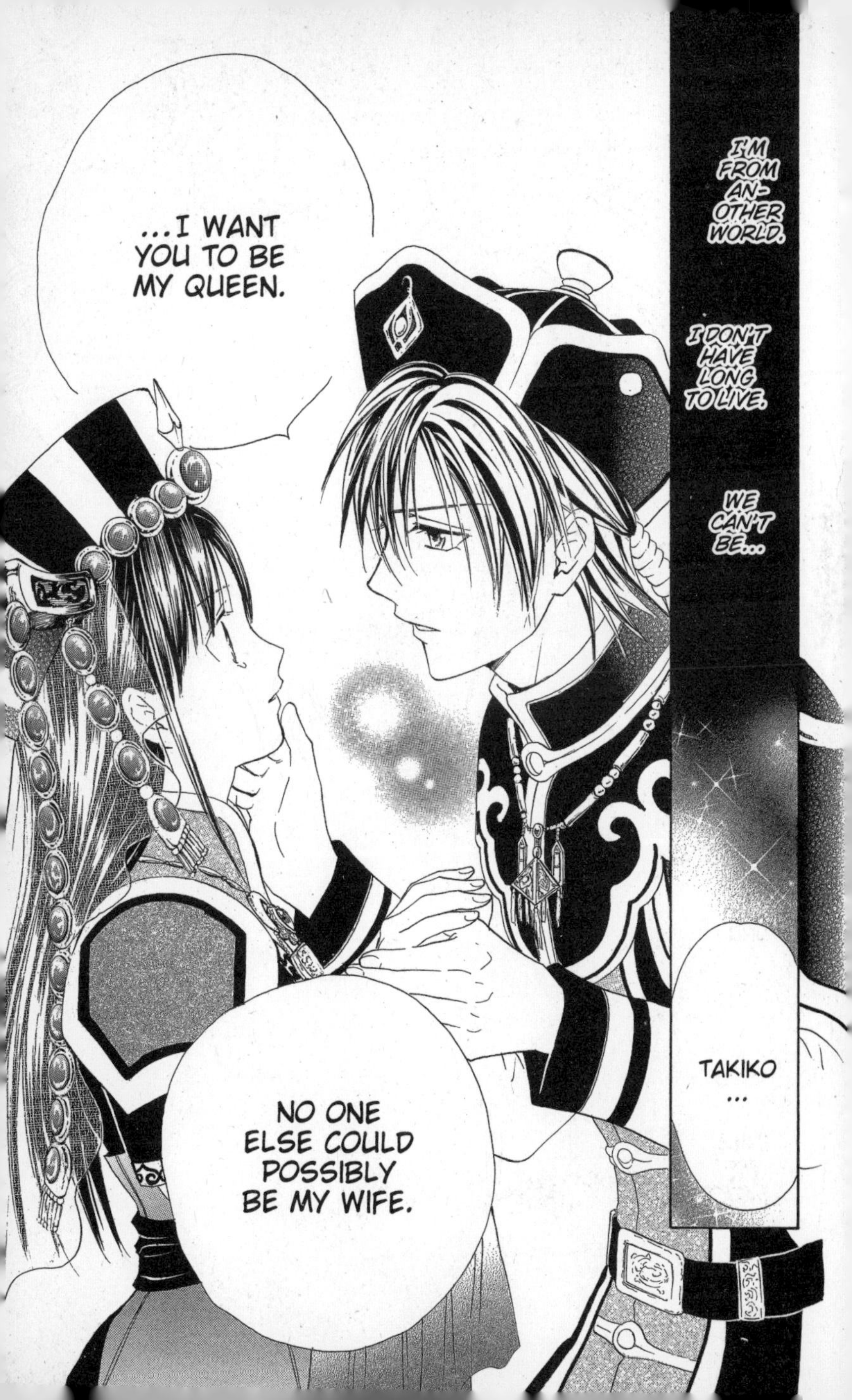
I'M FROM AN-OTHER WORLD.
I DON'T HAVE LONG TO LIVE.
WE CAN'T BE...
TAKIKO ...
...I WANT YOU TO BE MY QUEEN.
NO ONE ELSE COULD POSSIBLY BE MY WIFE.

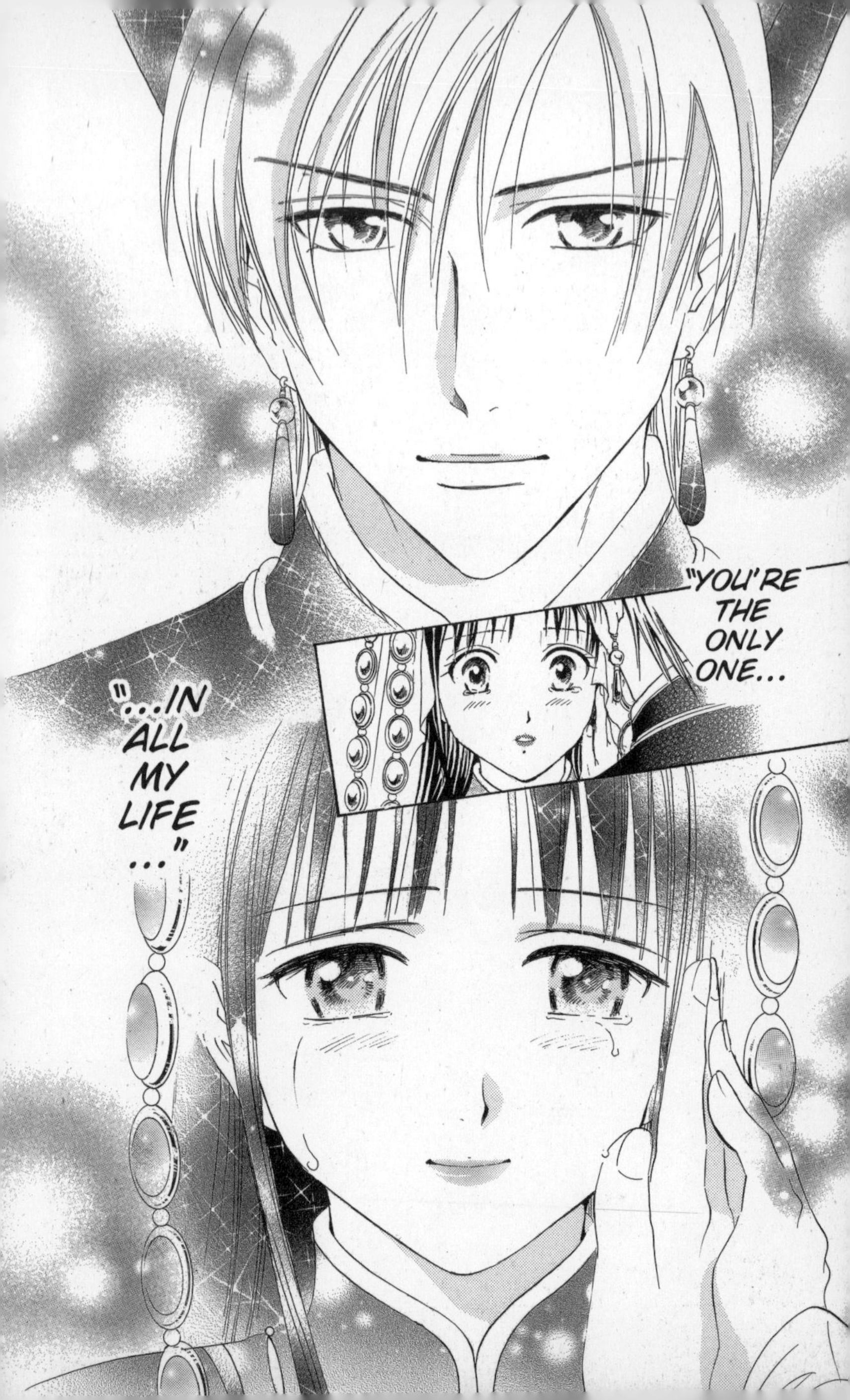
"YOU'RE THE ONLY ONE...
"...IN ALL MY LIFE..."

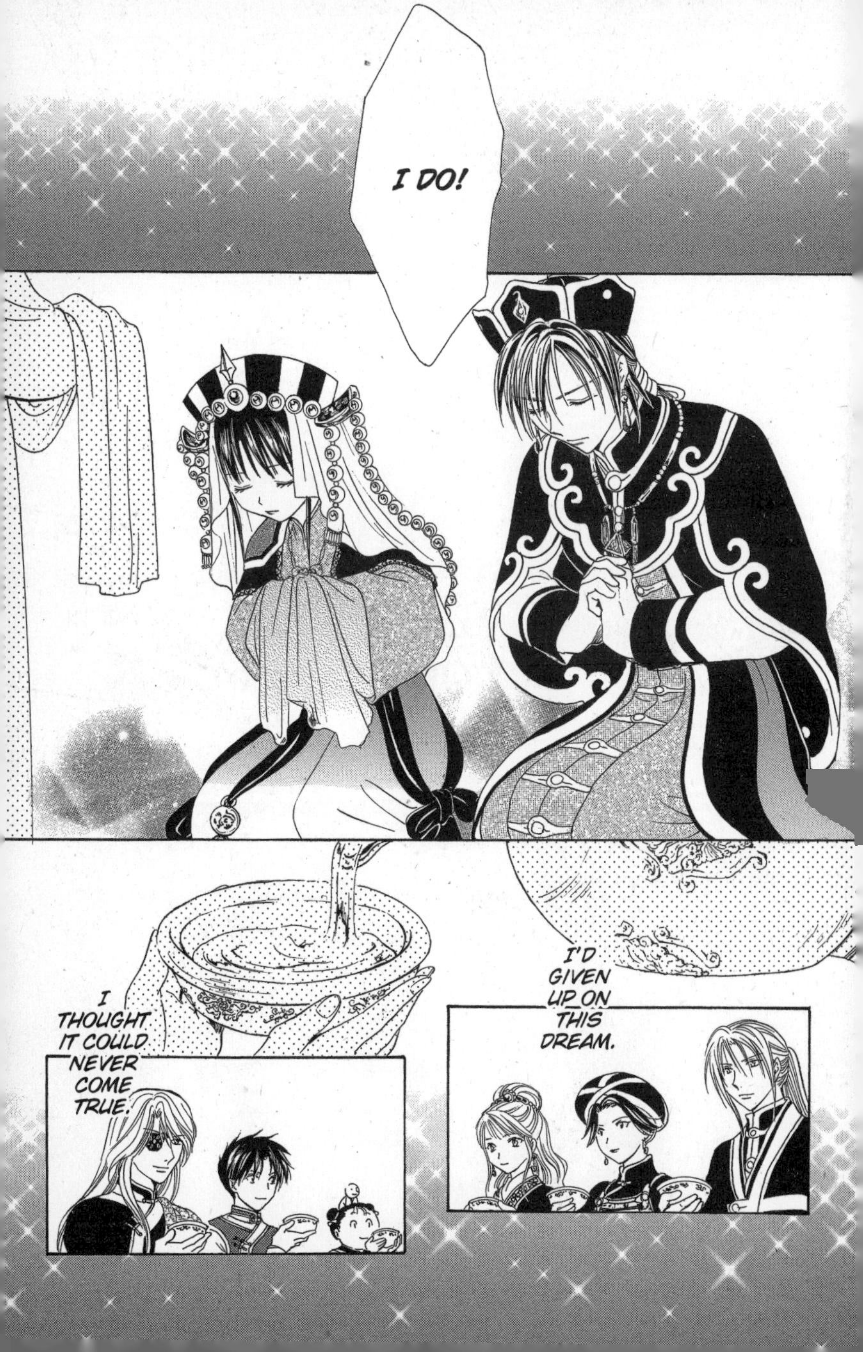
I DO!
I'D GIVEN UP ON THIS DREAM.
I THOUGHT IT COULD NEVER COME TRUE.

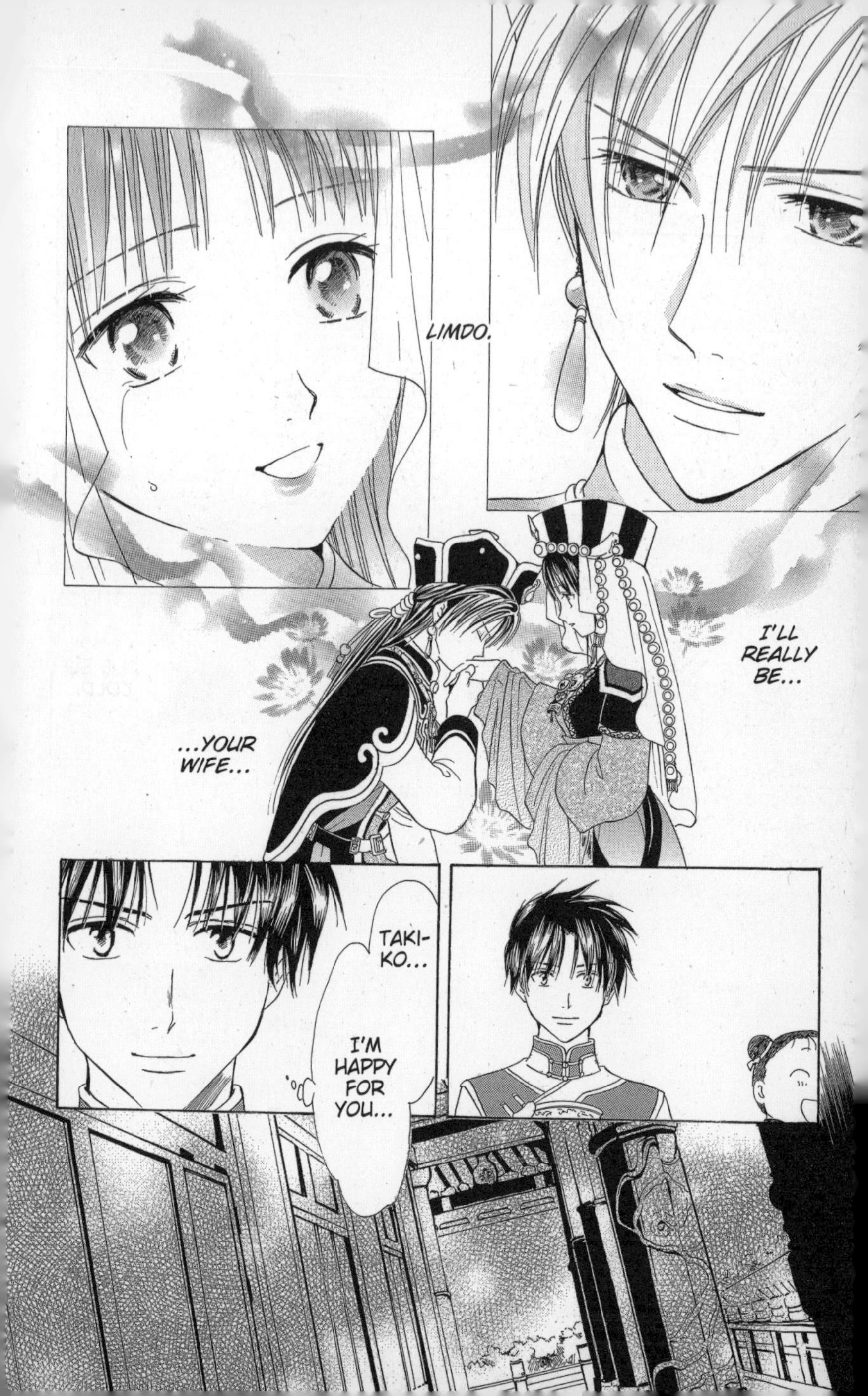
LIMDO.
I'LL REALLY BE...
...YOUR WIFE...
TAKI-KO...
I'M HAPPY FOR YOU...

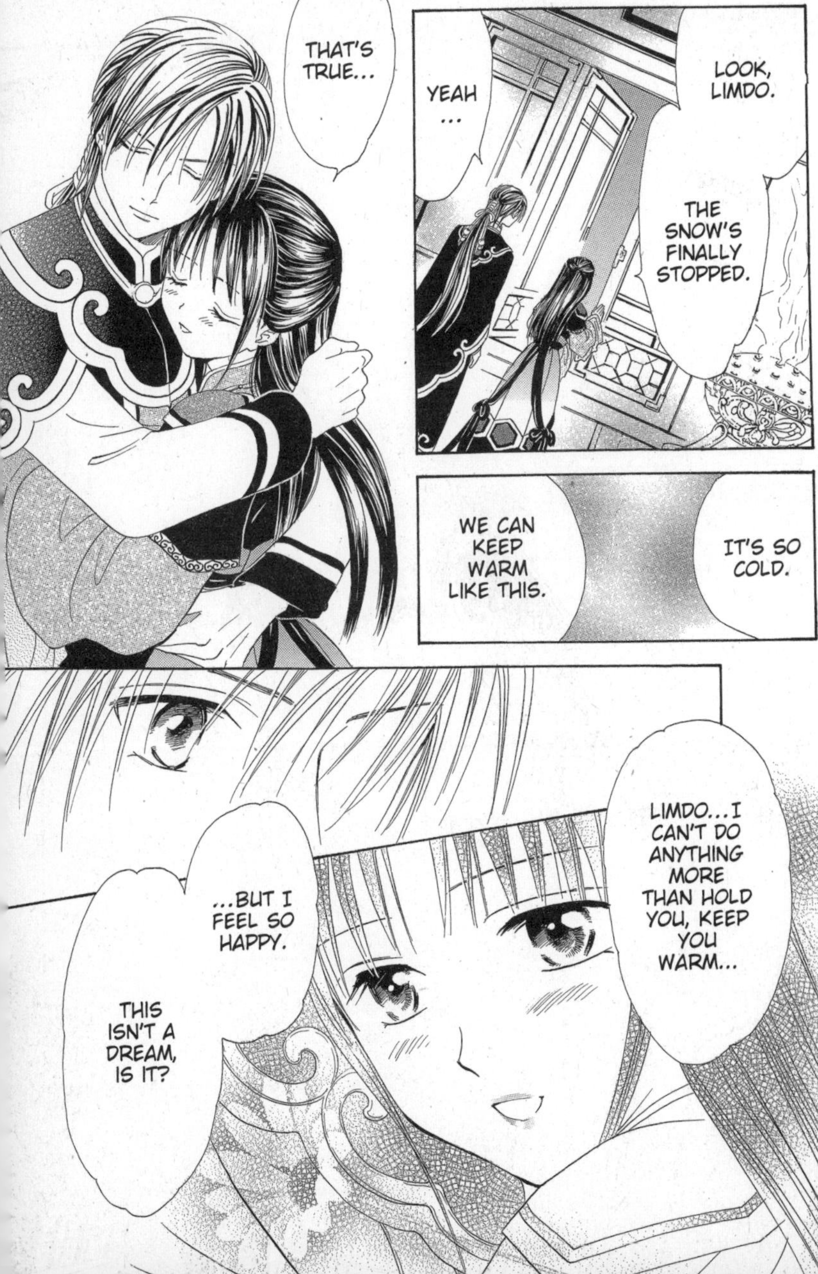
LOOK, LIMDO.
THE SNOW'S FINALLY STOPPED.
YEAH ...
IT'S SO COLD.
WE CAN KEEP WARM LIKE THIS.
THAT'S TRUE...
LIMDO...I CAN'T DO ANYTHING MORE THAN HOLD YOU, KEEP YOU WARM...
...BUT I FEEL SO HAPPY.
THIS ISN'T A DREAM, IS IT?

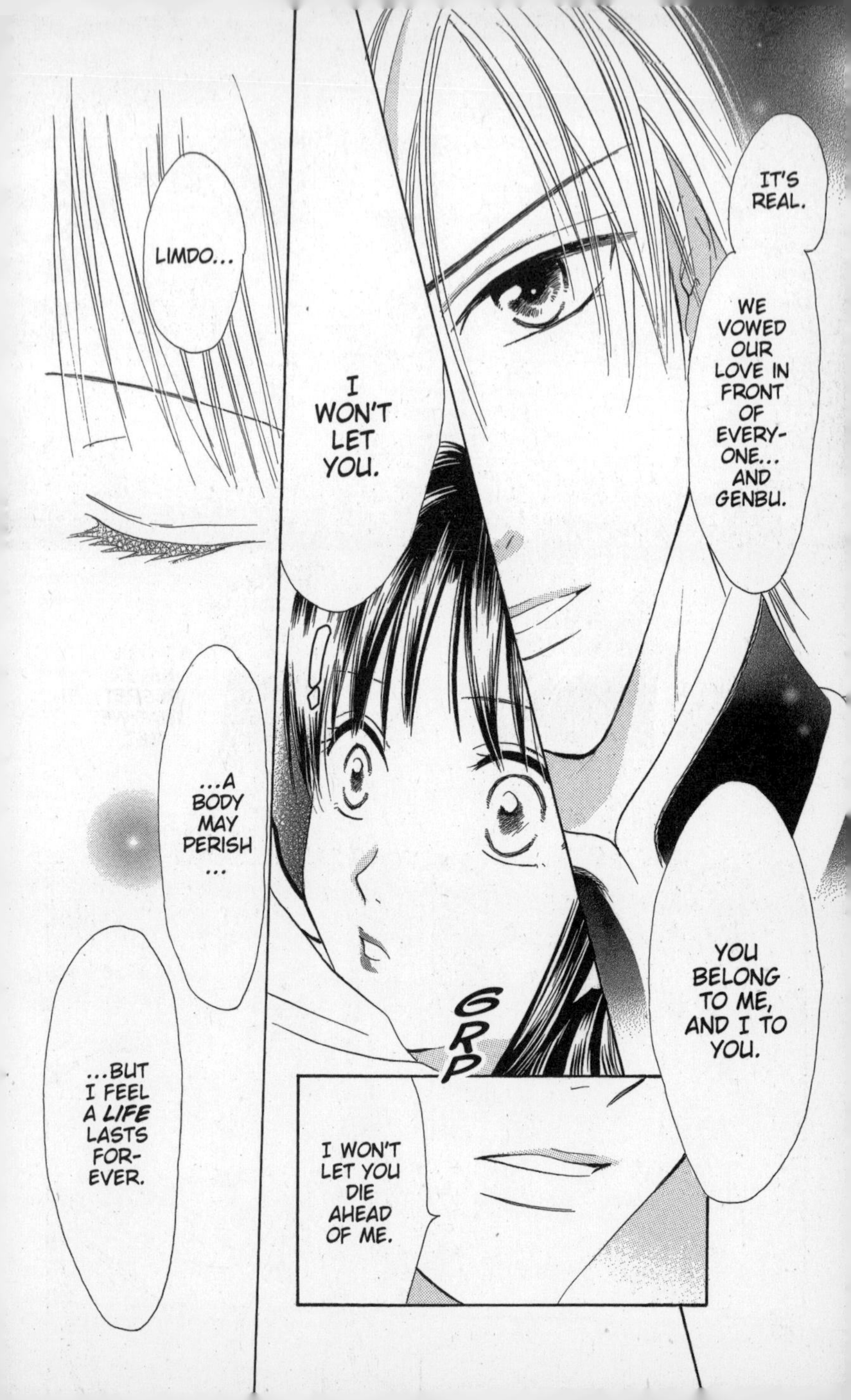
IT'S REAL.
WE VOWED OUR LOVE IN FRONT OF EVERY-ONE... AND GENBU.
I WON'T LET YOU.
YOU BELONG TO ME, AND I TO YOU.
GRP
I WON'T LET YOU DIE AHEAD OF ME.
LIMDO...
...A BODY MAY PERISH...
...BUT I FEEL A *LIFE* LASTS FOR-EVER.

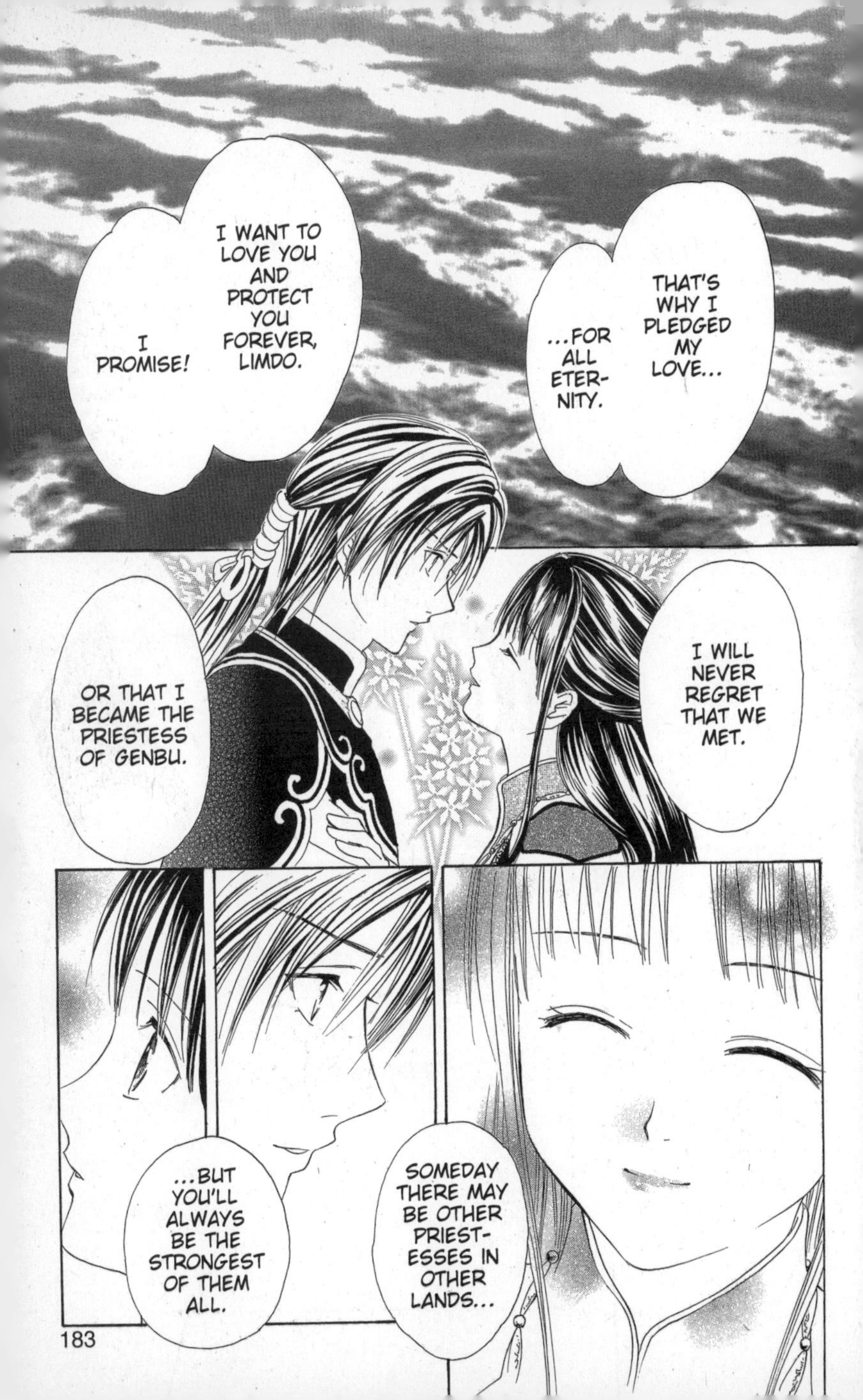
THAT'S WHY I PLEDGED MY LOVE...
...FOR ALL ETERNITY.
I WANT TO LOVE YOU AND PROTECT YOU FOREVER, LIMDO.
I PROMISE!
I WILL NEVER REGRET THAT WE MET.
OR THAT I BECAME THE PRIESTESS OF GENBU.
SOMEDAY THERE MAY BE OTHER PRIESTESSES IN OTHER LANDS...
...BUT YOU'LL ALWAYS BE THE STRONGEST OF THEM ALL.

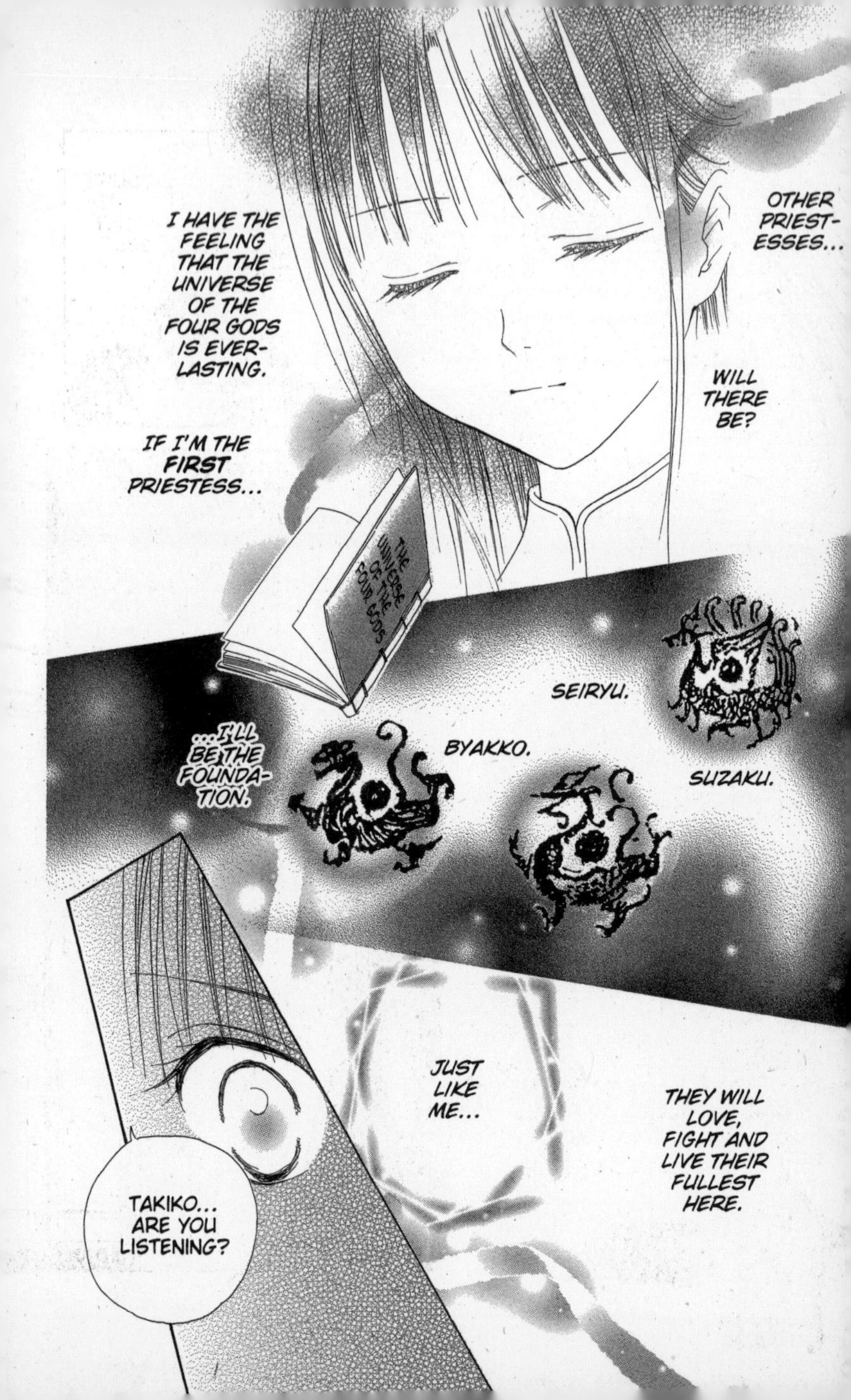
OTHER PRIESTESSES...
WILL THERE BE?
I HAVE THE FEELING THAT THE UNIVERSE OF THE FOUR GODS IS EVERLASTING.
IF I'M THE FIRST PRIESTESS...
THE UNIVERSE OF THE FOUR GODS
SEIRYU.
SUZAKU.
BYAKKO.
...I'LL BE THE FOUNDATION.
THEY WILL LOVE, FIGHT AND LIVE THEIR FULLEST HERE.
JUST LIKE ME...
TAKIKO... ARE YOU LISTENING?

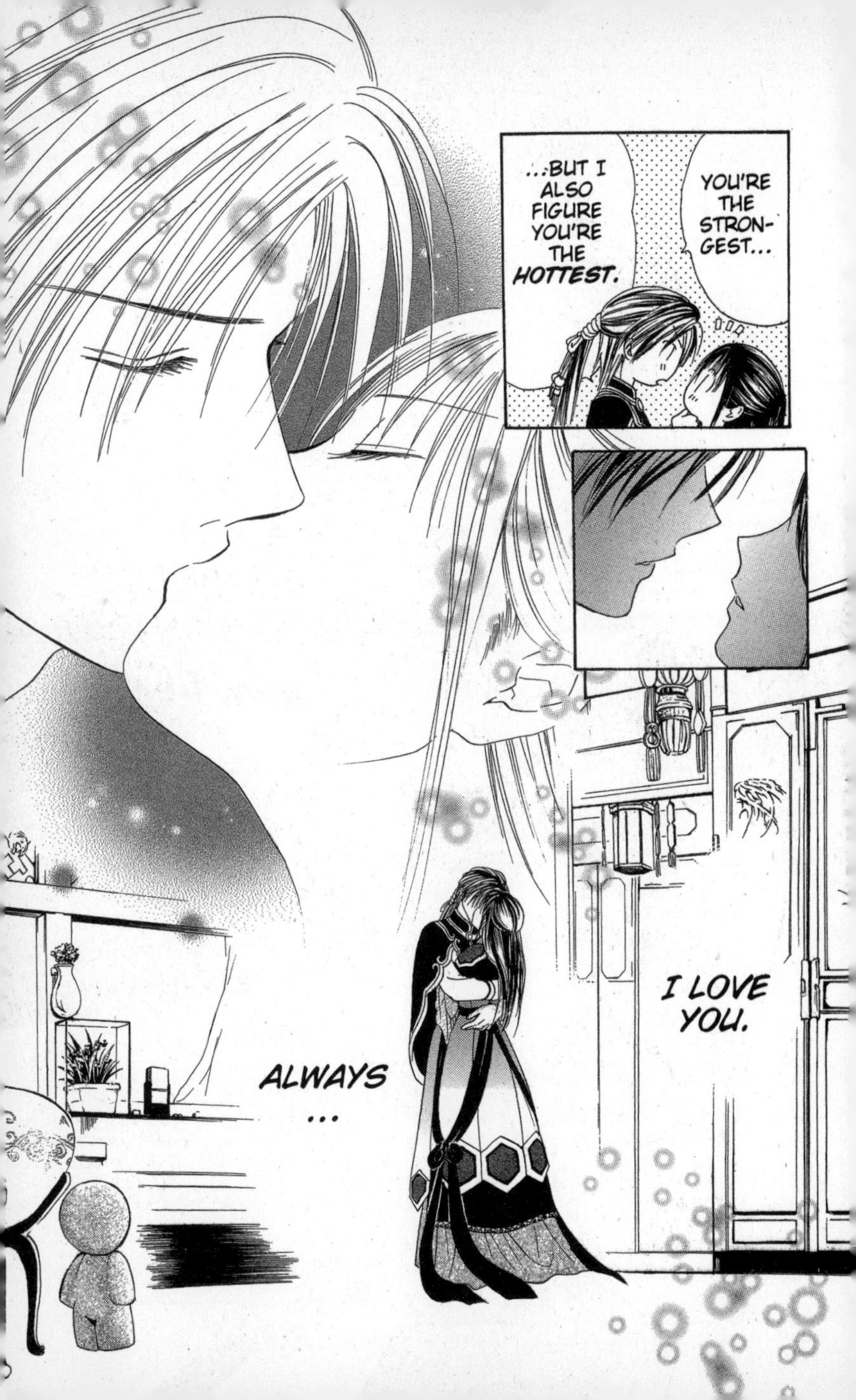
YOU'RE THE STRONGEST...
...BUT I ALSO FIGURE YOU'RE THE HOTTEST.
I LOVE YOU.
ALWAYS ...

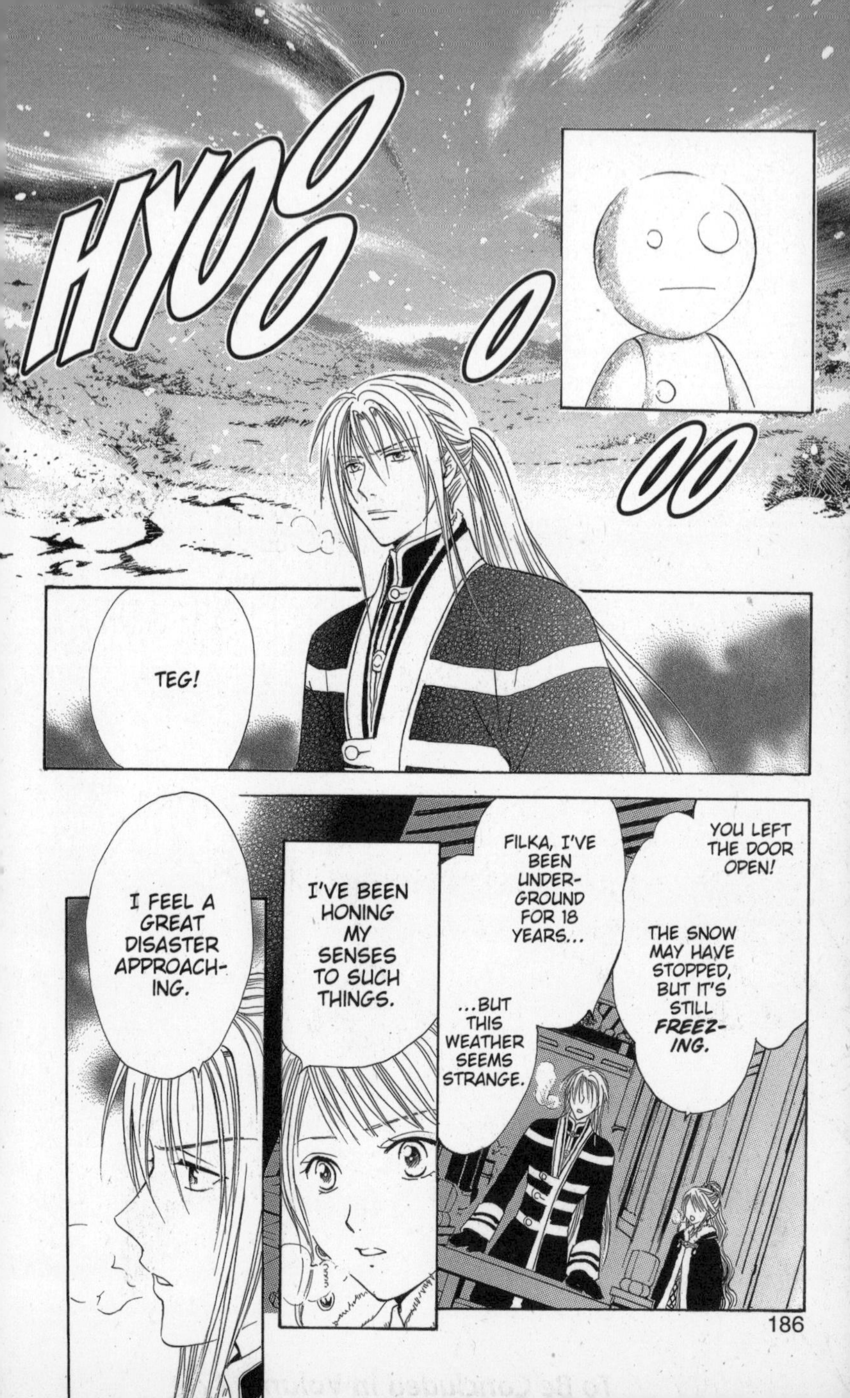
HYOOOOOOOO
TEG!
YOU LEFT THE DOOR OPEN!
THE SNOW MAY HAVE STOPPED, BUT IT'S STILL FREEZING.
FILKA, I'VE BEEN UNDERGROUND FOR 18 YEARS...
...BUT THIS WEATHER SEEMS STRANGE.
I'VE BEEN HONING MY SENSES TO SUCH THINGS.
I FEEL A GREAT DISASTER APPROACHING.

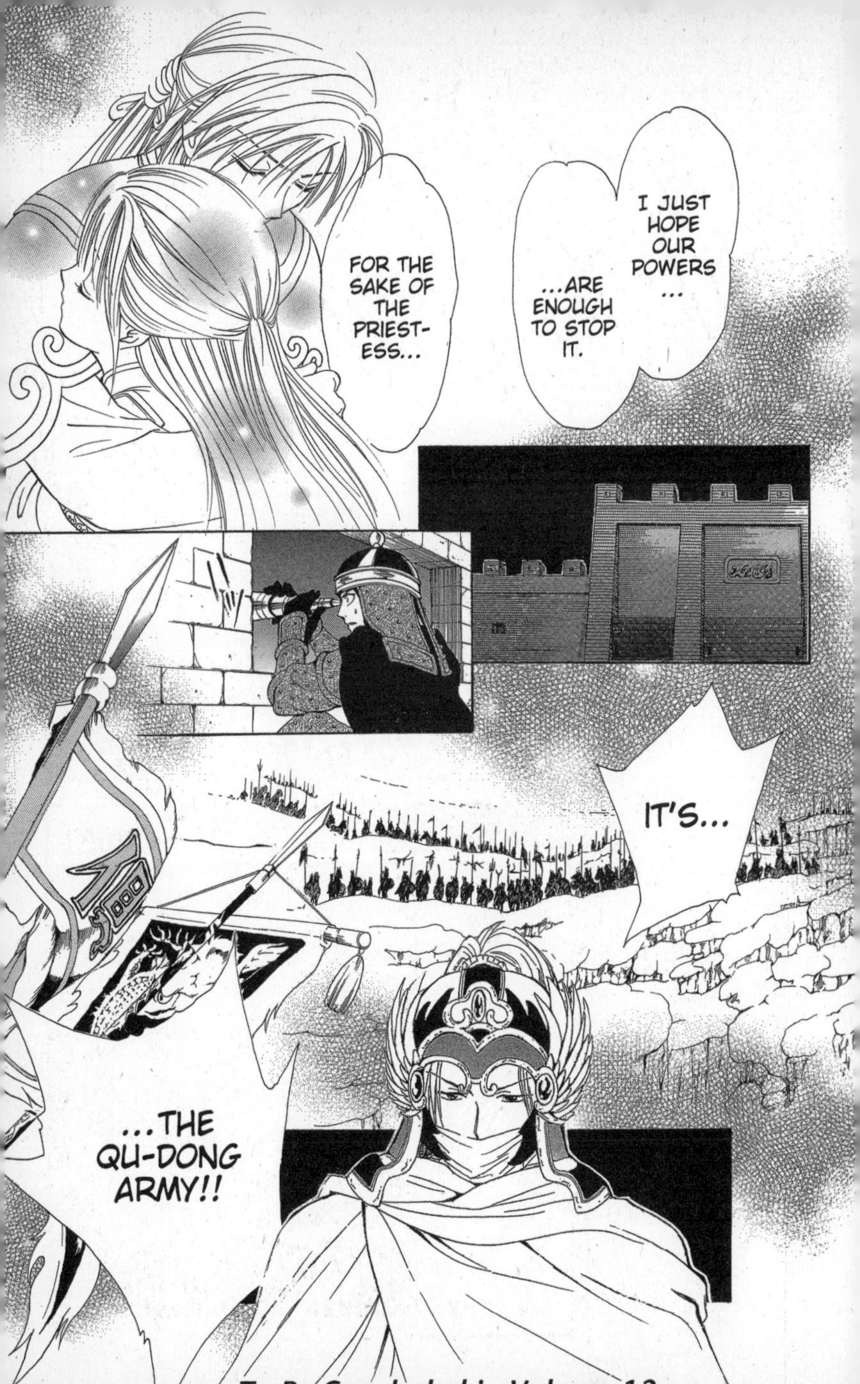
I JUST HOPE OUR POWERS...
...ARE ENOUGH TO STOP IT.
FOR THE SAKE OF THE PRIEST-ESS...
IT'S...
...THE QU-DONG ARMY!!

To Be Concluded in Volume 12

FUSHIGI YÛGI:
GENBU KAIDEN

Yuu Watase was born on March 5 in a town near Osaka, Japan. She was raised there before moving to Tokyo to follow her dream of creating manga. In the decade since her debut short story, *Pajama De Ojama* (An Intrusion in Pajamas), she has produced more than 50 volumes of short stories and continuing series. Her latest work, *Absolute Boyfriend*, appeared in Japan in the anthology magazine *Shôjo Comic*. Watase's other beloved series, *Alice 19th*, *Imadoki!*, and *Ceres: Celestial Legend*, are available in North America in English editions published by VIZ Media.

Fushigi Yûgi:
Genbu Kaiden Vol. 11
Shojo Beat Edition

STORY AND ART BY
YUU WATASE

© 2003 Yuu WATASE/Shogakukan
All rights reserved.
Original Japanese edition "FUSHIGI YUGI GENBUKAIDEN"
published by SHOGAKUKAN, Inc.

Translation/Lillian Olsen
Touch-up Art & Lettering/Rina Mapa
Design/Shawn Carrico
Editor/Shaenon K. Garrity

Printed in Canada

Published by VIZ Media, LLC
P.O. Box 77010
San Francisco, CA 94107

10 9 8 7 6 5 4 3 2 1
First printing, March 2013

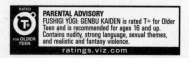

PARENTAL ADVISORY
FUSHIGI YÛGI: GENBU KAIDEN is rated T+ for Older
Teen and is recommended for ages 16 and up.
Contains nudity, strong language, sexual themes,
and realistic and fantasy violence.
ratings.viz.com

www.viz.com

www.shojobeat.com

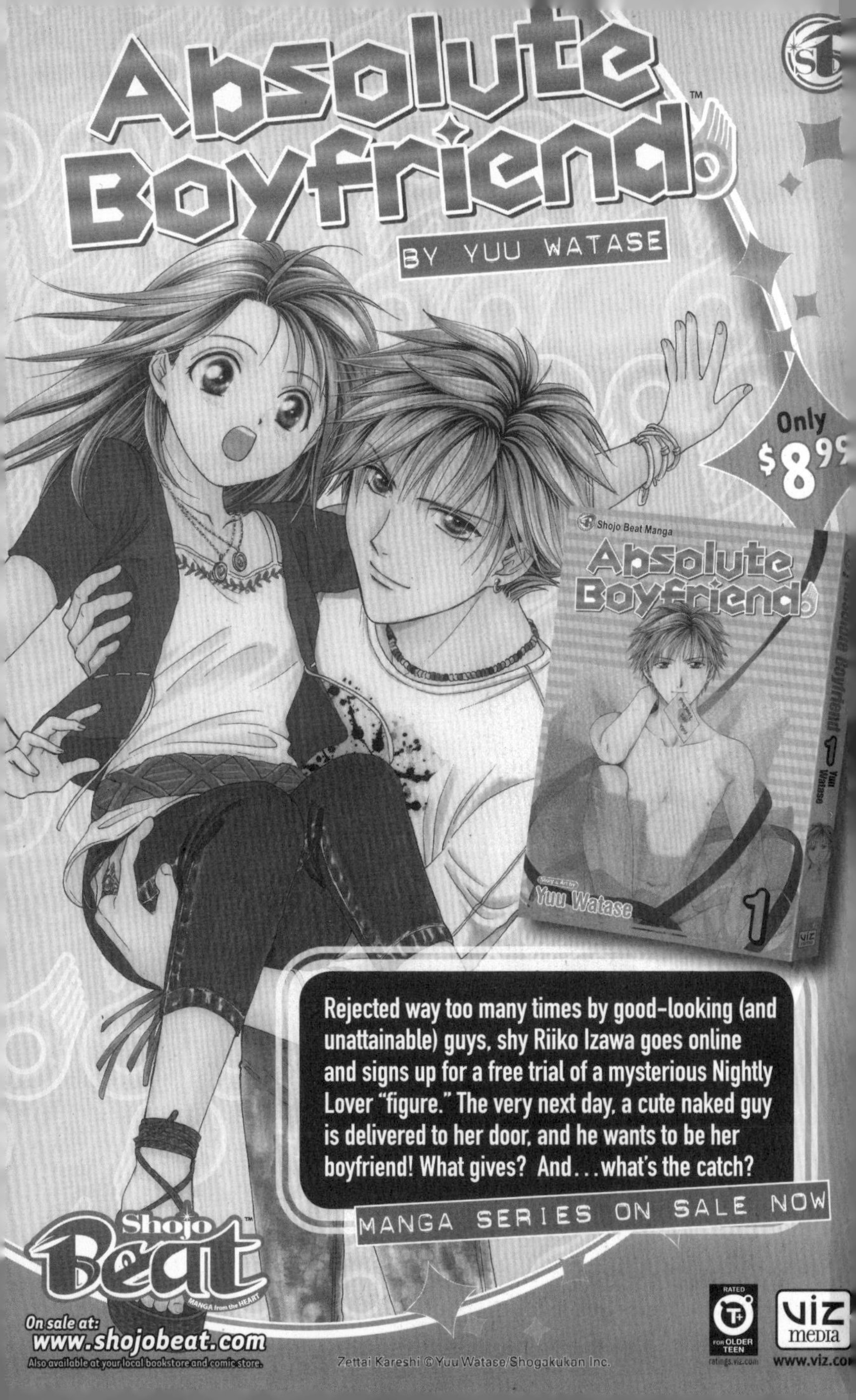
Absolute Boyfriend™
BY YUU WATASE
Only $8.99
Shojo Beat Manga
Absolute Boyfriend
Absolute Boyfriend 1 Yuu Watase
Story & Art by Yuu Watase
1
Rejected way too many times by good-looking (and unattainable) guys, shy Riiko Izawa goes online and signs up for a free trial of a mysterious Nightly Lover "figure." The very next day, a cute naked guy is delivered to her door, and he wants to be her boyfriend! What gives? And...what's the catch?
MANGA SERIES ON SALE NOW
Shojo Beat™
MANGA from the HEART
On sale at:
www.shojobeat.com
Also available at your local bookstore and comic store.
Zettai Kareshi © Yuu Watase/Shogakukan Inc.
RATED T+ FOR OLDER TEEN
ratings.viz.com
viz media
www.viz.com

SURPRISE!

You may be reading the wrong way!

It's true: In keeping with the original Japanese comic format, this book reads from right to left— so action, sound effects, and word balloons are completely reversed. This preserves the orientation of the original artwork—plus, it's fun! Check out the diagram shown here to get the hang of things, and then turn to the other side of the book to get started!

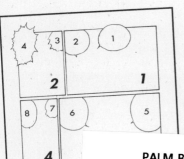